# Transnational Social Work and Social Welfare

The underlying frame of social work is the nation state, and it is from within the state that welfare strategies and social policies are devised and implemented. However, post-colonialism, globalisation, migration and the associated implications for human rights, social justice and social welfare policies contest the idea of a clearly defined space for social work and present new challenges for researchers and practitioners.

*Transnational Social Work and Social Welfare* argues for the increased importance of the transnational perspective in social work theory and practice. The book challenges the idea of the nation state as a given entity and argues that globalisation and an increasing number of people crossing borders must have an impact on the theories and strategies of social work. The international contributors are critical of a restricted focus on a geographically defined space and the impact on work with clients.

With cases covering China, France, Germany, India, Israel, Malaysia, Turkey and the UK, the book highlights the challenges as well as the opportunities this new perspective can open up for theories and strategies in social work. It will be of interest to students, researchers and social workers interested in migration, social care, poverty and cultural competency in health and social care.

**Beatrix Schwarzer** is Senior Lecturer at the Department of Health and Social Work at Frankfurt University of Applied Sciences, Germany.

**Ursula Kämmerer-Rütten** is Senior Lecturer at the Department of Health and Social Work at Frankfurt University of Applied Sciences, Germany.

**Alexandra Schleyer-Lindenmann** is Associate Professor of Psychology at the Science Faculty of Aix-Marseille University, France.

**Yafang Wang** is Assistant Professor at the Department of Social Work, Shanghai University, China.

# Routledge Advances in Social Work

## New titles

**Analysing Social Work Communication**
Discourse in Practice
*Christopher Hall, Kirsi Juhila, Maureen Matarese and Carolus van Nijnatten*

**Feminisms in Social Work Research**
Promise and possibilities for justice-based knowledge
*Stéphanie Wahab, Ben Anderson-Nathe and Christina Gringeri*

**Chronic Illness, Vulnerability and Social Work: Autoimmunity and the Contemporary Disease Experience**
*Liz Walker and Elizabeth Price*

**Social Work in a Global Context**
Issues and Challenges
*George Palattiyil, Dina Sidhva and Mono Chakrabarti*

**Contemporary Feminisms in Social Work Practice**
*Nicole Moulding and Sarah Wendt*

**Domestic Violence Perpetrators**
Evidence-Informed Responses
*John Devaney and Anne Lazenbatt*

**Transnational Social Work and Social Welfare**
Challenges for the Social Work Profession
*Beatrix Schwarzer, Ursula Kämmerer-Rütten, Alexandra Schleyer-Lindenmann and Yafang Wang*

**The Ecosocial Transition of Societies**
The Contribution of Social Work and Social Policy
*Aila-Leena Matthies and Kati Närhi*

## Forthcoming titles

**Responsibilization at the Margins of Welfare Services**
*Kirsi Juhila, Suvi Raitakari and Christopher Hall*

**Homelessness and Social Work**
An Intersectional Approach
*Carole Zufferey*

**Supporting Care Leavers' Educational Transitions**
*Jennifer Driscoll*

# Transnational Social Work and Social Welfare

Challenges for the social work profession

**Edited by Beatrix Schwarzer,
Ursula Kämmerer-Rütten,
Alexandra Schleyer-Lindenmann
and Yafang Wang**

LONDON AND NEW YORK

First published 2016
by Routledge
2 Park Square, Milton Park, Abingdon, Oxon OX14 4RN

and by Routledge
711 Third Avenue, New York, NY 10017

*Routledge is an imprint of the Taylor & Francis Group, an informa business*

© 2016 B. Schwarzer, U. Kämmerer-Rütten, A. Schleyer-Lindenmann and
Y. Wang.

*British Library Cataloguing-in-Publication Data*
A catalogue record for this book is available from the British Library

*Library of Congress Cataloging in Publication Data*
Names: Schwarzer, Beatrix, editor. | Kämmerer-Rütten, Ursula, editor. |
Schleyer-Lindenmann, Alexandra, editor. | Wang, Yafang, editor.
Title: Transnational social work and social welfare : challenges for the
social work profession / edited by Beatrix Schwarzer, Ursula
Kämmerer-Rütten, Alexandra Schleyer-Lindenmann and Yafang Wang.
Other titles: Routledge advances in social work.
Description: Abingdon, Oxon ; New York, NY : Routledge, 2016. | Series:
Routledge advances in social work | Includes bibliographical references
and index.
Identifiers: LCCN 2016008814 | ISBN 9781138912786 (hardback) | ISBN
9781315691794 (ebook)
Subjects: | MESH: Social Work | Social Welfare | Internationality
Classification: LCC HV40 | NLM HV 40 | DDC 361--dc23
LC record available at http://lccn.loc.gov/2016008814

ISBN: 978-1-138-91278-6 (hbk)
ISBN: 978-1-315-69179-4 (ebk)

Typeset in Times New Roman
by Saxon Graphics Ltd, Derby

Printed and bound by CPI Group (UK) Ltd, Croydon, CR0 4YY

# Contents

# Illustrations

## Figure

## Tables

# Contributors

## Editors

**Beatrix Schwarzer** is Senior Lecturer at the Department of Health and Social Work at Frankfurt University of Applied Sciences, Germany. She graduated in Sociology from Goethe University in Frankfurt, Germany. She works in the field of social movements and transnational social work and created and implemented a new Bachelor degree course 'Social Work: transnational' – the first in Germany – in 2012. She teaches widely in the field of inclusion and exclusion, diversity, and international as well as transnational social work. Currently, in her PhD thesis she deals with the institutionalisation of women's movement demands in post-1994 South Africa. Her publications in the field of transnational social work and social movements include: (2014) 'Teilhabe als Grundlage Sozialer Arbeit', as well as 'Diversity als Perspektive für Soziale Arbeit', in B. Bretländer, M. Köttig, T. Kunz, (eds), *Vielfalt und Differenz in der Sozialen Arbeit*, W. Kohlhammer; (2009) 'Discourses on race and gender in South Africa's transition process: A challenging liaison', in C.J. Korieh, P. Okeke-Ihejirika, (eds), *Gendering Global Transformations*, Routledge, 220–36; and (2009) 'Gleichheit oder Gleichgültigkeit? Vom Ende der Regenbogennation', *Femina Politica* 18(2), 2, 74–83 (with Mageza-Barthel, R.).

**Ursula Kämmerer-Rütten**, PhD, is Senior Lecturer at the Department of Health and Social Work at Frankfurt University of Applied Sciences, Germany. She is a graduate of the University of Stirling (UK) where she completed her PhD on 'Outcomes in Community Mental Health Care' as a comparative analysis of social policy foundations and support options in different countries (Germany and the UK). Her academic career and professional experiences include community-based case work and social inclusion, and her teaching focus is on social work in health care with clients threatened by precarious living conditions and social exclusion. She has published on national and international social work. Her recent publications include: (2014) 'Vielfalt im Alter', in B. Bretländer, M. Köttig, T. Kunz, (eds), *Vielfalt und Differenz in der Sozialen Arbeit*, W. Kohlhammer; (2011) 'International education and the cross-cultural classroom: Learning and teaching in international settings', in *Interprofessional and International Learning Experiences in Social and Health Care Higher*

*Education*, Lahti University of Applied Sciences, Lahti, Finland; (2011) 'Ethnozentrisch oder multikulturell? Perspektiven für die interkulturelle Öffnung sozialer Dienste und Versorgungsinstitutionen für ältere MigrantInnen', in *Migration und Soziale Arbeit*, ISS Frankfurt; (2009) 'Biografiearbeit und ihre ethische Handlungsdimension: Kritische Bestandsaufnahme und Perspektiven für ein ethisch legitimiertes professionelles Handeln', *Neue Praxis*.

**Alexandra Schleyer-Lindenmann**, PhD, has studied psychology in Germany (JLU Giessen) and France (Université de Provence), where she completed her PhD. She is Associate Professor of Psychology at the Science Faculty of Aix-Marseille University. Currently she is assistant director of ESPACE lab (CNRS 7300) and director of the European Diploma of Social Sciences (DEUSS) proposed to students of social work. Her research integrates the intercultural and environmental perspective in developmental psychology with research topics such as environmentally-friendly attitudes and behaviours at different ages of life, developmental tasks and moral development. Her main publications in the field of social work are: (2013) 'L'immigration en France et en Allemagne: différences, convergences et une même interrogation pour le travail social' (with Th. Neuer-Miebach), in Ph. Hirliet, J.L. Meyer, Y. Molina and B. Muller, (eds), *Travail Social sans Frontières: Innovation et Adaptation*. Rennes: Presses de l'Ecole des Hautes Etudes en Santé Publique, 45–61; (2011) *Soziale Arbeit im Dialog. Hochschulpartnerschaft Frankfurt – Marseille. Le travail social en dialogue – le partenariat des établissements d'enseignement supérieur de Francfort-sur-le-Main et de Marseille* (co-ed. Th. Neuer-Miebach), Frankfurt: Fachhochschulverlag.

**Yafang Wang**, PhD, is Assistant Professor at the Department of Social Work, Shanghai University since 2010. She studied educational sciences first in Beijing Normal University, China, and then in Bielefeld University, Germany where she completed her PhD in 2009 on 'New Educational Chances for the Disadvantaged through Reconstruction of Online Social Capital – An Empirical Research into Informal Learning of Migrant Youth in Online Socio-cultural Networks'. She has taught Social Work Theories and Ethics of Social Work and has also been supervisor for social work students in placement. Her major research interests revolve around professionalisation and indigenisation of social work, social work and education, education inequality in migrant children, and social work with children of rural workers in China. Her recent main publications in English include: (2014) 'Educational Inequality of Rural Workers' Children in China: From Visible Exclusion to Invisible Discrimination', in Hunner-Kreise and Bohne, (eds), *Childhood, Youth and Migration – Connecting global and local perspectives*, Springer (forthcoming); 'Social Work in China – Historical development and current challenges for professionalisation', *Social Work and Society*; (2011) 'New Educational Chances for the Disadvantaged Migrant Youth through Reconstruction of Social Capital in Online Informal Learning', in Arbeitskreis 'Jugendhilfe im Wandel', (ed.), *Jugendhilfeforschung*, VS-Verlag, Wiesbaden.

## Contributors (Alphabetical order by surname)

**Kartini Aboo Talib**, Dr, is an Associate Professor in policy analysis and Deputy Director at the Institute of Ethnic Studies, Universiti Kebangsaan Malaysia. She was appointed as a Country Consultant for Malaysia to the United Nations Entity for Gender Equality and the Empowerment of Women (2014), a grantee for Sumitomo Foundation Japan (2011), and a Fulbright scholar to Northeastern University, Boston Massachusetts (2000–2005). Her research focus includes civil society, gender, comparative politics, and consumerism. She has published several chapters in books and articles on various issues pertaining to policy including dispute resolutions and consumer rights, labour law and legal immigrants, gender and policy, managing consensus in a plural society, non-profits and policy implementation, election and good governance, and environmental policy and sustainability. Her book *Policy Implementation and People Processing Organisations* was published in 2014.

**Arvind Kumar Agrawal**, PhD, is currently First Vice Chancellor of Mahatma Gandhi Central University, Motihari, Bihar, India. He was Professor and Dean of the School of Fine Arts and Art Education and Controller of Examinations at the Central University of Himachal Pradesh. He finished his MA, MPhil. at JNU, and completed his PhD in Germany. He was former Professor and Head of the Department of Sociology and former Director of the Centre for Study of Social Exclusion and Inclusive Policy at University of Rajasthan, Jaipur (India). He has been elected as Vice-President (for 2014–2018) of the Research Committee on Sociology of Law of the International Sociological Association and has been visiting professor in many European universities. His major research focuses cover Social Theory, Research Methodology and Globalisation and Sociology of Law. He has published five books and many research articles in reputed academic journals.

**Abha Bhaiya** is one of the founding members of the feminist organisation Jagori, set up in 1983 in Delhi. She has been active in women's movements in India and in the neighbouring south Asian countries for nearly 40 years. She has been working on a range of issues including women's social, political and economic rights; the status of single women; women's right to health, bodily integrity and well-being; sex and sexualities; against militarisation, fundamentalisms; on food securities and livelihoods, organic agriculture and the increasing erosion of civil rights of the poorest. She is known as a feminist trainer with extensive experience in conducting feminist training for multiple constituencies and in many different countries. In 2002 she set up a feminist retreat, TARA, in one of the villages of the lower Himalayas and also implemented a feminist community programme, now spread over nearly 150 villages. She is a member of some significant regional and transnational platforms and organisations and also the India OBR national coordinator.

**Adrian Braithwaite** is a Practice Educator and Registered Social Worker. He has a background in statutory children and families' social work and experience working with children's disability services. Previously he had been a tenancy support worker for young people who required assistance to develop skills of independent living. He has also spent time working with asylum seekers and refugees within a hostel setting. He is currently working at the University of Hull with social work students and undertaking research into the student experience of supervision in the development of social work practice. His major focus includes children and families, social work and law, providing teaching and learning for students with early intervention strategies and developing professional skills such as assessment across a range of social work support needs, a systemic approach encompassing diversity, multi-agency partnerships and a holistic approach with supporting families.

**Sema Buz**, PhD, is Associate Professor and lectures at undergraduate, master and PhD programmes at the Faculty of Economics and Administrative Sciences, Department of Social Work, Hacettepe University, Turkey. Her major focuses in research are on asylum-refugee-migrant issues, LGBTI, old age, poverty, feminist social work, and social work ethics. Her recent publications include: (2012) (with O. Cankurtaran Ontas and B. Hatiboglu), 'Opinions of social work students from Turkey on social justice', *International Social Work*, 56(6); (2013) (with O. Cankurtaran Ontas and B. Hatiboglu), 'Youth and political participation: case in Turkey', *European Journal of Social Work*, 16(2).

**Charlotte L. Clarke** is Professor and Head of Health in Social Science at the University of Edinburgh. She is a Registered Nurse, who started working in the university sector in the 1990s at Northumbria University as a Lecturer and then as Professor and Associate Dean (Research) for the last eight years. She then moved to the University of Edinburgh as Head of School in 2011. Her major research focuses are on older people and dementia, risk and resilience theory. She is the author of more than 65 peer-reviewed papers and six books and more than 20 book chapters. Her recent publications include: (2014) (with S. Visram and M. White) 'Making and maintaining lifestyle changes with the support of a lay health advisor: longitudinal qualitative study of health trainer services in England', *PLoS ONE*, 9(5); (2015) (with N.A.S. Rickard) 'The involvement of older people in their rehabilitation: generating a substantive Grounded Theory', *International Journal of Therapy and Rehabilitation*, 22(8), 361–9.

**Sarah Cresswell** completed her social work degree in 1989 and became a Practice Educator in 2006, joining the University of Hull in 2010. She worked as a Practice Educator at FASU at the University of Hull where she assessed social work students. Her current role is as an Independent Reviewing Officer at Doncaster Children's Services Trust where she chairs reviews for looked-after children and ensures that their needs are met. Her major professional focus is on transnational social work and child protection.

**Filiz Demiröz**, PhD., is Assistant Professor at the Department of Social Work, Administrative and Social Sciences Faculty of Hacettepe University, Turkey. She is a HAMER-Founding Member and HUGO Board Member. Her major research focuses are migration, social work theories, disaster and trauma, family counselling. Her main publications include: (1989) 'The Difficulties of Remigrant Families', 9th ISFW European Seminar, Bildiri, Basel, Switzerland; (1998) 'Schwierigkeiten bei der Remigration und Lösungsvorschläge' *Chancen und Risiken von Migration*, Lambertus; (2000) 'Yurtdışına Göç Sürecinin Aile Üzerindeki Etkileri Prof. Dr. Vedia Emiroğlu'na Armağan', ed. G. Erkan and V. Işıkhan, 194–204, *Hacettepe Üniversitesi Sosyal Hizmetler Yüksekokulu Yayını*, No 6, 194–204, Ankara; (2003) 'Die Rückkehr und die damit verbundenen Schwierigkeiten', Türkische Migrantinnen im Ausland – Probleme und Lösungsansätze, Internationales Symposium, eds N. Alkan, N. Küçükkarac, T. Temiz and E. Hermann, Ankara, 167–77; (2007) 'Das Thema Migration im deutsch–türkischen Fachkräfteaustausch – aus türkischer Sicht', Qualität zeigt Wirkung-Entwicklungen und Perspektiven. Forum Jugendarbeit International. IJAB. Deutschland.

**Nathalie Durand-Le Zallic**, is a social work trainer at the Institut Méditerranéen de Formation et de Recherche en Travail Social (IMF, Mediterranean Institute for Training and Research in Social Work), Marseille, since 2006. She completed her Master in Business and Social Administration, specialising in social politics and local development. She has worked as a social worker in child welfare for 20 years (Association 'Sauvegarde 13' in Marseille). Her major professional interests focus on social policies; protection and rights of the child; writing professional reports in child protection; social work and professional secrecy.

**Caroline Humphrey**, Dr, is Senior Lecturer in Social Work at the University of Hull. She is a registered social worker and specialised in child and family social work in statutory settings in England prior to embarking upon an academic career. She teaches modules in Child and Family Social Work, Child Protection and Court Work and Practice Skills Development. Her current research interests revolve around culture, religion and spirituality. Her major publications include: (2011) *Becoming a Social Worker: A Guide for Students*, London: Sage; (2015) 'Evil, Child Abuse and the Caring Professions', *Journal of Religion and Health*, 54(5), 1660–71; (2015) 'Grand Narratives of Spirituality: Some Critical Reflections', *Journal for the Study of Spirituality*, 5(1), 20–32.

**Lena Inowlocki**, Dr, is Professor and Managing Director of the Institute for Migration Studies and Intercultural Communication (IMiK) at the Department of Health and Social Work, Frankfurt University of Applied Sciences. She is also Professor (extraordinary) at the Department of Social Sciences, Goethe-University Frankfurt/Main. Her major research focuses are qualitative-interpretive research on transmission and change through generations in migrant families; gender, adolescence, and transformation of tradition, religion and ethnicity; European 'identity work'; inclusion and interculturality in institutions of psychosocial care. Her main publications include: (2014) (with co-eds U. Apitzsch, D. Bertaux, C. Delcroix) 'Thematic issue on "Socialization, family, and gender in the context of migration'", *ZQF* 14. Jg., Heft 1–2; (2013) 'Collective trajectory and generational work in families of Jewish Displaced Persons: Epistemological processes in the research situation', in M.L. Seeberg, I. Levin, and C. Lenz, (eds), *Holocaust as active memory: the past in the present.* Series Memory studies: 20th and 21st century philosophy, methodology and ontology, Vol. 1, Farnham: Ashgate, 29–43.

**Richard Isralowitz**, Dr, is Professor and Director of the Regional Alcohol and Drug Abuse Research Center, Spitzer Dept. of Social Work, Ben Gurion University. He received the US-National Institute on Drug Abuse Award for 'Contributions to Scientific Diplomacy through Outstanding Efforts in International Collaborative Research on Drug Abuse and Addiction'. He was also awarded Distinguished International Scientist by US NIDA. He worked as Fulbright Fellow at National University of Singapore. In addition, he is advisor for Social Research and Program Development in the Middle East and Africa, Israel Ministry of Foreign Affairs – International Cooperation. His research mainly focuses on patterns and problems of substance abuse and drug policy. He has published over 100 scientific articles, 12 books, and 13 chapters in edited books, as well as 16 major scientific reports focused on prevention of health and social problems among high risk populations.

**Nathalie Jami** worked as a social worker specialising in addictions for 12 years. Since 2000, she has been working as a trainer of social workers, and since 2002 as training manager at the Institut Méditerranéen de Formation et de Recherche en Travail Social (IMF, Mediterranean Institute for Training and Research in Social Work), Marseille, France. In 1988 she completed her Diploma as Assistant de Service Social at the IRTS (Regional School of Social Work) Montrouge. In 2002 she achieved her Licence (Bachelor) in Educational Sciences at the University of Provence – Aix-Marseille. In 2014 she completed her State Diploma of Social Engineering at the Collège Coopératif in Aix-en-Provence. Her main research focus is on collective social work. Her main publications include: (2014) 'L'impact des European Credits Transfer System (ECTS) dans la formation' (with J. Victor-Baptiste-Grebert) in *Revue française de service social, De la formation à la recherche en travail social, Défis et perspectives*, n. 252, Jan.; (2014) 'Mémoire DEIS: Les solidarités à l'épreuve de l'Intervention Sociale d'Intérêt Collectif; Quels enjeux pour les postures professionnelles des Assistants de Service Social?'.

**Diqing Jiang** is a visiting research fellow of the School of Sociology and Political Science at Shanghai University. After his BA and MA degrees in history which he gained in China, he further studied at the political science department at Marquette University (USA) with a Master's in international relations and later studied at Brown University. He shifted to work at Cato Institute from 2006 to 2011 with a research focus on China's political economy. In 2011 he started studying at Washington University, concentrating on social development and social policy, and China's social and economic development. His main publications include: (2015) *Poverty, State and Paradox of Tocqueville Paradox: ideas of Tocqueville's social policy*, Xuehai, Issue 1 (in Chinese); (2014) 'The challenge to Citizen Empire', *Journal of Wenhui Book Review*, August (in Chinese); (2013) 'Why social policy is a discipline?' *Journal of Wenhui Book Review*, August (in Chinese).

**Shewli Kumar**, PhD, is Associate Professor at Tata Institute of Social Sciences, India. She completed her MPhil and PhD in Social Work from Delhi University, India, and began her career with an NGO, Prerana, working with young girls in rural areas of North India. From 1999 to 2005, she worked as Assistant Professor at the Department of Social Work, University of Delhi. Her major research focuses are women, development and gender; children's rights; social policy; group work. She has published articles on adolescence, gender and reproductive rights; Dalit and excluded women, children's rights; policy analysis.

**Muriel Mellon-Mustafa** completed her studies and training as a social worker at Frankfurt University of Applied Sciences (Germany). Since 2007, she has been working as social worker in a reception centre for asylum seekers in Marseille (France). She is an undergraduate of Law at the University Paris 1 Panthéon Sorbonne, and currently a master's student in International and European Law at the Law Faculty of Grenoble University.

**Merav Moshe Grodofsky**, Dr, is Chair of the School of Social Work of Sapir College, and Founder as well as Academic Director of the Rights-based Community Practice Center Network. He is a specialist in teaching, practice, writing and research on human rights advocacy, community organising, and the combination of the two as a method to promote people-to-people relationships and peace-building among disadvantaged and multicultural groups within societies and between societies in conflict. His major research interests revolve around rights-based community practice, social work and human rights, and service user involvement in social work education. The following are his selected publications: (2012) 'Community-based human rights advocacy practice and peace education', *International Social Work*, 55(5), 740–53; (2007) 'The contribution of law and social work to interdisciplinary community development and peace building in the Middle East', *Journal of Community Practice*, 15(1/2), 45–65; (2001) 'Peacebuilding: A conceptual framework', *International Journal of Social Welfare*, 10, 14–26.

**Yochay Nadan**, Dr, is Lecturer and holds a tenure-track position at the Paul Baerwald School of Social Work and Social Welfare, the Hebrew University of Jerusalem. His research areas include diversity and multiculturalism; culturally competent and context-informed social work practice and education; cultural and contextual aspects of child maltreatment; multicultural family therapy; narrative therapy; psychotherapy research. Selected publications include: (2013) (with A. Ben-Ari) 'What can we learn from rethinking "multiculturalism" in social work education?' *Social Work Education*, 32(8), 1089–102; (2014) 'Rethinking "Cultural Competence" in international social work', *International*

*Social Work*, Advanced online publication; (2014) (with E. Segev) 'Facing reality: Context-oriented reflection in social work education', *British Journal of Social Work*, Advanced online publication; (2015) (with J. Spilsbury and J. Korbin) 'Culture and context in understanding child maltreatment: Contributions of intersectionality and neighborhood-based research', *Child Abuse & Neglect*, 41, 40–48; (2015) (with G. Weinberg-Kurnik and A. Ben-Ari) 'Bringing context and power relations to the fore: Intergroup dialogue as a tool in social work education', *British Journal of Social Work*, 45(1), 260–77.

**Therese Neuer-Miebach**, Dr. rer. Pol., is Professor at the Department of Social Work and Health, and also teaches Civil Engineering and Geomatics at the Faculty of Architecture, Frankfurt University of Applied Sciences. She is the Head of Department of International Affairs and Ethics in a Federal Association for Mentally Handicapped People and a member of different ethics committees on national and international levels. The areas of her research activities are community and agglomeration development; urban space, social structure and housing; local social policies; 'social city' / politique de la ville and participation; urban sociology. Some selected publications are: (2010) (with AG Sozialraum) *Sozialraumuntersuchung Wohnsiedlung Riederwald – Empirische Untersuchung im Auftrag des Diakonischen Werks Frankfurt des Evangelischen Regionalverbandes Frankfurt*, Frankfurt; (2011) (with A. Schleyer-Lindenmann) *Soziale Arbeit im Dialog – Le travail social en dialogue*, Frankfurt; (2013) (with A. Schleyer-Lindenmann) 'Immigration en France et en Allemagne. Différences, convergences et une même interrogation pour le travail social', in P. Hirlet, J.L. Meyer, Y. Molina, B. Muller, (eds), *Travail Social sans frontières*, Presses de l'EHESP, Rouen, 45–61.

**Dagmar Oberlies**, Dr, is Professor of Law at Frankfurt University of Applied Sciences. She worked as a researcher at the Hamburg Institute for Social Research from 1984 to 1989 and as a legal practitioner from 1984 to 1992. From 1991 to 1995, she was Head of Department at the Ministry of Women, Employment, Health and Social Services in Saarland. From 1995 to 1996, she worked as research assistant for the Social Democratic parliamentary working group on legal policy. Between 2002 and 2005, she was team leader for the German Development Cooperation. In 2006 and 2014, she was guest professor at the International Islamic University and the National University of Malaysia respectively. Her major research and teaching focuses include anti-discrimination law, refugee and migration law, criminal law and criminology. Her publications include: (2015) 'Soziale Arbeit als Menschenrechtsprofession', *Sozial Extra*, 39(2), 6–9; (2015) 'Recht im Kontext von Exklusion und Inklusion', in B. Bretländer, M. Köttig and T. Kunz, (eds), *Vielfalt und Differenz in der Sozialen Arbeit*, Kohlhammer Verlag, Stuttgart, 48–59; (2014) 'Frauenkriminalität als Paradoxe Anwendung des Strafrechts', in K.H. Schäfer and H. Bunde, (eds), *Ökumenische Faktoren in der Straffälligenhilfe*, Lambertus, Freiburg im Breisgau, 117–125; (2013) *Strafrecht und Kriminologie für die Soziale Arbeit*, Kohlhammer Verlag, Stuttgart.

**Shanmin Peng** completed his PhD in 2005 at Shanghai Normal University and is currently Professor at the Department of Social Work, School of Sociology and Political Sciences, Shanghai University. He is Director of China Association of Sociology. His major research interests revolve around social work administration, community study and social policy. His main publications include: (2014) 'NPO and Social Education Problem of Migrant Children – Based on the Case Study of Shanghai', *Journal of Social Sciences*, 2; (2011) 'Social Work and the Construction of Public Life', *Study and Practice*, 7; (2011) 'An Analysis of the Career Identity of Social Work Trade Association: A Case Study of Pudong New District', *Fujian Tribune*, 12; (2010) 'Seal-cutting Art Group: An Indigenous Innovation of Social Work of Drug Treatment', *Fujian Tribune*, 7; (2010) *Exploration of Social Work Indigenization – Based on Local Practices in Shanghai*, Hefei University of Technology Press.

**Yves Pillant** completed his Bachelor in Educational Sciences in 2000 and achieved the Certificate of Abilities as Manager for Social Services in 2004. He is now a PhD candidate in political philosophy on the theme: Is a policy of vulnerability thinkable? at the Mediterranean Institute for Training and Research in Social Work (IMF), and teaches social engineering. He is manager for the development of social work's formations towards professionals in the establishments and services of the social action field. His publications include: (2014) 'Inclusion, word games or new paradigm for the social action?' *Ergologia* 12; (2014) 'Sexuality is not a need. Emotional and sexual life of adults in residential shelters', *Le Sociographe*, 47; (2013) 'From a society of integration to an inclusive society', *Revue française de service social – ANAS* (French social services magazine).

**Asutosh Pradhan**, Dr, is Associate Professor and Head of Department of Social Work, School of Social Sciences at Central University of Himachal Pradesh, India. He is a leading social work educator in India with 24 years' post-graduate teaching experience and three years' consultancy work in the NGO/Development Sector particularly in a World Bank funded Resettlement and Rehabilitation Project titled 'Facilitation of Community Participation in Implementation of Rehabilitation Action Plans & Indigenous People's Development Plans' in the Coal Mines of Odisha. He has been teaching Research Methodology, and Social Policy and Social Development. His major research interests are in the field of social capital, micro-credit, resettlement and rehabilitation, domestic violence, indigenous peoples and social exclusion and social inclusion. He has published 20 articles on social capital and micro-credit, social work advocacy, ethics, spirituality, development, and one co-authored book titled *Redress Mechanisms for Women Victims of Domestic Violence*.

**Rashila Ramli** is Principal Fellow, Professor of Political Science and Director at the Institute of Malaysian and International Studies (IKMAS), Universiti Kebangsaan Malaysia. Her areas of specialisation are Political Development, Gender and Politics, and Human Security. Her current research is on the governance of the South China Sea and its implication on ASEAN, and promoting social inclusion through public policies. Two selected publications are: (2015) (with Sity Daud and Zarina Othman) *Human security in Archipelagic Southeast Asia*; (2011) (with Nor Azizan Idris and Zarina Othman) 'Social Constructivism and Malaysia's International Relations', *Akademika* 8(1), 39–51. Her professional engagement includes, among others, President of the Malaysian Social Science Association (PSSM); member of the Council of Security Cooperation in Asia Pacific (CSCAP), Malaysia; regional council member of the Asia Pacific Forum for Women, Law and Development (APWLD); and Asst. Sec-General of the National Council for Women's Organizations (NCWO), Malaysia.

**Irit Regev**, Dr, is a lecturer in the School of Social Work at Sapir College. She received her PhD from the Hebrew University of Jerusalem. She established and manages the 'Tzmatim Institute' – Consultation for the Aging Population and their Families. She is engaged in gerontological research on the following subjects: the effects on the elderly of exposure to prolonged stress and threat; the effects of retirement on the individual and the influence and efficacy of retirement preparation programmes; life stories and perceptions of life and self among older adults in Israel. Her main publications include: (2010) 'Retirement preparation programs and counseling – snapshot and reflections on the future', *Gerontology*, 37(2–3), 155–68; (2015) (with O. Nuttman-Shwartz and R. Dekel) 'Continuous exposure to life threats among different age groups in different types of communities', *Psychological Trauma: Theory, Research, Practice, and Policy*, 7(3), 269–76; (submitted for publication) (with O. Nuttman-Shwartz) 'The impact of living in a continuous traumatic reality on elderly persons residing in urban and rural communities.'

**Alexander Reznik**, Dr, is currently Senior Research Associate at the Regional Alcohol and Drug Abuse Research Center, Spitzer Dept. of Social Work, Ben Gurion University. He has served as lecturer and researcher at the Military Naval Academy of Far Eastern Federal University, and as Chairman at the Department of Psychology of Maritime State University in Vladivostok, Russia. He has also worked as Consultant and Group Counsellor at the Israel Anti-Drug Authority. His major focus in research includes patterns and problems of substance abuse; immigration, acculturation and drug use. He is the author of more than 60 scientific articles; five books; eight chapters in edited books; and four major scientific reports focused on the prevention of health and social problems among high risk populations.

**Nathalie Segura** is Assistant Director of the Mediterranean Institute for Training and Research in Social Work (IMF), Marseille, France. She studied Sociology at Toulouse University and achieved additional qualifications in Human Resources, Quality Analysis and Financial Decision-Making. She has worked as a research assistant at the CIREJ Lab Toulouse and at the Paris Higher School of Social Sciences (EHESS Paris). She completed her CAFDES Diploma (Qualification for the position as director of an institute or service of social intervention) and has occupied positions as assistant director in several organisations in the health and social sector. She teaches demographics, methodology in sociology, urban sociology, action-research, evaluation of public policies, care and social sector.

**Sohini Sengupta** has a PhD in Anthropology from SOAS, University of London. She joined the Centre for Community Organization and Development Practice, School of Social Work of the Tata Institute of Social Sciences as an Assistant Professor in 2012. Prior to her academic career, she has worked in the development sector in rural India and as a research fellow with the World Commission on Dams – the secretariat's Social Impacts Team, based in Cape Town, South Africa. Her areas of research interest are indigenous people, land rights, rural livelihoods, gender and work, poverty and social protection and food security. She teaches courses on Social Policy, Gender and Livelihoods and Ethnography for MA Social Work students. She has a major publication forthcoming: 'Wronged by Development? The impasse in Development – Human Rights Debate', *Journal of The National Human Rights Commission*, India.

**Ute Straub**, Dr, has been Tenured Professor for Humanities and Social Pedagogy since 1997 at Frankfurt University of Applied Sciences. She is the International Coordinator and Head of the International Committee of the Department, and a member of the International Board of the University. She also works as Head of the International Social Work Division of the German Association for Social Work. In addition to academic areas, she has practised professionally in the fields of social-pedagogical care of mentally and physically challenged young people, gender-oriented work with boys/girls with migrant backgrounds, domestic violence (shelter for mistreated women and their children), media pedagogy etc. Her research areas focus on family support (family welfare, family care, family education), international and comparative social work, history of education and social work, PR in social work /public image of social work, gender issues: working with male and female service users, domestic violence, gender-oriented perspectives on youth and family care, community development and organisation. Her publications include: (2016) '"All my relations" – indigene Ansätze und Relationalität in der Sozialen Arbeit', in F. Früchtel, M. Strassner and C. Schwarzloos, (eds), *Relationale Sozialarbeit – versammelnde, vernetzende und kooperative Hilfeformen*, Weinheim, Beltz-Juventa, 54–74; (2015) 'Machtungleichgewichte – Konflikte in der Internationalen Sozialen Arbeit. Die neue Globale Definition und indigene Soziale Arbeit', in S. Stövesand and D. Röh, (eds), *Konflikte – theoretische und praktische Herausforderungen für die Soziale Arbeit*, Opladen, Berlin &Toronto, Verlag Barbara Budrich, 58–68; (2014) '"Whose voice is being heard?" - Die Diskussion um die neue Definition für Soziale Arbeit von IASSW und IFSW', in *FORUM sozial* 2(14), 29–30; (2012) '"Kreise schließen"- Indigenisierte Soziale Arbeit auf dem Weg in den Mainstream', in G. Thiele, (ed.), *Gesellschaftlicher Wandel – wohin? Innovative Entwicklungen in den Sozialwissenschaften*, Berlin, Frankfurt am Main: Peter Lang, 47–63.

**Uğur Tekin**, PhD, is Professor and Head of the Social Work Department, Faculty of Health Sciences, İstanbul Aydın University. He completed his PhD at Köln University, Germany. Between 2000 and 2010, he was Academician at Köln University, Klagenfurt University and the University of Applied Sciences in Düsseldorf. Since 2011, he has worked as Academician Prof. Dr. at the Faculty of Education and Faculty of Health Sciences, İstanbul Aydın University. The areas of his research interests cover social work, migration, youth sociology and criminal sociology. Selected publications include: (2003) 'Wie sich Ethnisierungs- und Kriminalisierungsprozesse in Biographien von allochthonen Jugendlichen verknüpfen. Eine sozialkonstruktivistische Analyse'; (2011) (with B. Pusch) *Migration und Türkei: Neue Migrationsbewegungen am Rande der Europäischen Union*, Ergon Verlag; (2011) 'University-community partnership in working with street children: accounts given by students', *Maltepe University Journal*, 134ff; (2013) 'Effects of the Erasmus Programme on Turkish Universities and University Students', *Trakya University Journal of Social Science*, 15(1), 109–22; (2012), 'The Social Aspect in the Juvenile Justice System', in International Justice for Children Symposium, (eds), Opening Speeches and Plenary Sessions, 21–4. Available online at www.unicef.org.tr/files/bilgimerkezi/doc/Openning%20Speeches_eng.pdf, [Accessed 10 January 2016].

**Irmgard Vogt**, PhD, is Professor and Senior Researcher of the Institute of Addiction Research Frankfurt, University of Applied Sciences Frankfurt am Main, Germany. She was Full Professor at the Department of Health and Social Work of UAS Frankfurt from 1992 to 2009, and has been Adjoint Professor since 1983 at the Department of Sociology of Goethe-University Frankfurt. Her major research focuses are mental health, addiction research and gender, addiction policies and health psychology. Some selected publications are: (2015) (with J. Fritz and N. Kuplewatzky) *Frauen, Sucht und Gewalt: Chancen und Risiken bei der Suche nach Hilfen und Veränderungen*, gFFZ Online-Publikation; (2012) (with M. Schmid and M. Schu) *Motivational Case Management*, Heidelberg, Medhochzwei-Verlag; (2011) *Auch Süchtige altern*, Frankfurt, Fachhochschulverlag; (1989) (with S. Scheerer) *Drogen und Drogenpolitik*, Frankfurt, Campus.

**John Watson** is Lecturer in Social Work and Disabled Students Advisor at the University of Hull. His research focuses on substance misuse policy and interventions, and communication and counselling skills. His main publications include: (2014) 'Alcohol and other drug treatment', in B. Teater, (ed.) *Contemporary Social Work Practice: A Handbook for Students*, Maidenhead: Open University Press; (2012) 'The good, the bad and the vague: Assessing emerging Conservative drug policy', *Critical Social Policy*; (2011) 'Resistance is Futile? Exploring the potential of motivational interviewing', *Journal of Social Work Practice*, 25(4), 465–79; (forthcoming) (with N. Stanley, B. Fell, P. Miller, and G. Thomson) 'Men's Talk: Men's Understandings of Violence Against Women and Motivations for Change', *Violence Against Women*; (2009) (with N. Stanley, B. Fell, P. Miller and G. Thomson) *Men's Talk:*

*Research to inform Hull's social marketing initiative on domestic violence*, Preston: University of Central Lancashire.

**Xiaoxiao Xie** is a PhD candidate at the Department of Asian Studies of the University of Adelaide, Australia. Before starting his PhD in Adelaide in 2011, he studied history at Shanghai University. His research interests revolve around the New Left, globalisation theory, sociology (archaeology) of knowledge, social work theory, and Shanghai studies. Selected publications include: (2015) 'Roland Robertson's Theory of Globalization' (in Chinese) in *Global Studies Review* Volume Two, ChangGang Guo, (ed.), Commercial Press.

**Ziqian Xu** is a MSW student at the Department of Social Work of Shanghai University. Her research interest is focused on health care social work. She is co-author (with F. Yang and K.F. Li) of the following publication: 'A Qualitative Insight into the Psychosocial Adjustment to Cancer in Chinese Culture', North American Chinese Sociologists Association Annual Conference. Chicago, USA. August, 2015.

**Fang Yang**, Dr, is Assistant Professor at the Department of Social Work of Shanghai University. Her research interests focus on health care social work, social gerontology, health psychology. Her main publications include: (2015) (with J.E. Ramsay, O.C. Schultheiss, and J.S. Pang) 'Implicit achievement motivation moderates the effect of motive-relevant challenge on salivary cortisol', *Motivation and Emotion*, 39(3), 321–34; (2015) (with C.T. Salmon, J.S. Pang, and W.J.Y. Cheng) 'Media exposure and smoking intention in adolescents: a moderated mediation analysis from a cultivation perspective', *Journal of Health Psychology*, 20(2), 188–97; (2014) (with K.A. Tan and W.J.Y. Cheng) 'The effects of connectedness on health-promoting and health-compromising behaviors in adolescents: evidence from a statewide survey', *Journal of Primary Prevention*, 35(1), 33–46; (2013) (with W.J.Y. Cheng, R.M.H. Ho, and K. Pooh) 'Psychosocial correlates of cigarette smoking among Asian American and Pacific Islander adolescents', *Addictive Behaviors*, 38(4), 1890–3.

**Ute Zillig** completed her Diploma in Social Sciences and Social Work and is currently working at Frauen-Notruf e.V. Göttingen, a women's counselling centre on sexual and domestic violence as well as at the Frankfurt University of Applied Sciences. In both positions she offers trauma-informed counselling for women and children (intimate partner violence and sexual abuse) and gives lectures and training on trauma-informed social work and counselling. Her research interests are focused on consequences of gender-based violence, trauma-related counselling/social work, and transgenerational consequences of traumata.

# Preface

*Ursula Kämmerer-Rütten, Alexandra Schleyer-Lindenmann, Beatrix Schwarzer and Yafang Wang*

The idea for this book evolved from an International Summer School Programme at Frankfurt University of Applied Sciences, where social work professionals and academics from different countries worked together on themes relating to 'Human Rights and Social Justice'. As soon as we started working together we saw that we shared professional interests in relation to common social problems. Furthermore, we observed that transnational contexts constitute a rising matter of concern in many countries and that each country proposed its own ways of coping with it. We took the opportunity to start a dialogue about theoretical approaches and strategies for practice. Using case study examples as starting points we worked on the potential needs of social workers:

- shared competencies, for example (inter)cultural awareness;
- professionalisation or continuous training to cope with national and international social challenges;
- social policies and legislation in a rapidly changing world.

We saw that a growing number of people lead 'transnational lives', i.e. lives that transcend national boundaries and that these individuals or families – usually labelled as migrants, refugees, asylum-seekers – are often traumatised, exploited and vulnerable and in need of psycho-social support. Also their competencies, such as language skills and social networks across national borders, are often ignored by social workers as a resource for potential empowerment.

We also saw that there are often tensions between social workers and their own employers, which may be the State itself or often state-supported institutions. In some countries, the welfare state has entered a period of re-organisation and economisation by rolling back its boundaries and thus, social workers may find themselves trapped in narrow legal and financial frameworks influencing their working conditions as well as the range of support available to people in need. In other countries, the welfare state is not (yet) developed but statutory control is powerful and influences social work practice substantially. In all cases, the role of social work professionals is strongly affected and needs to be critically assessed as well as strengthened. Therefore, we strongly believe that it is important for social workers all over the world to engage in professional networking and dialogue across countries and furthermore, to participate in professional associations, in order to be heard and to exercise power and influence, not only in the best interest of their clients but also to promote the process of professionalisation.

We saw that the relationship between social workers and the people seeking advice is strongly influenced by national frameworks that affect professional social work. This may become evident through the conflicting priorities of help and control (the double mandate) and the numerous aspects that shape the relationship between professionals and the recipients of support, such as professional education/qualification, social support policies or legal claims.

The discourse emerging from our summer schools prompted our decision to collect and share professional experiences and perspectives and write a book on transnational topics in social work practice.

'Transnational Social Work' (TSW) has gained increasing importance in social work theory and practice in recent years. Although the term transnationalism can be traced back to the beginning of the twentieth century, the debate surrounding transnationalism as a (positively connected) concept has gained more recognition through the influence of global developments such as migration (Hytten and Bettez 2011; Ife 2012).

Midgley (2001) was one of the first scholars to talk about transnational social work, highlighting the importance of globalisation and regionalism for social work practice. Transnational issues in relation to social work practice were taken further by other scholars, including Nalini Junko Negi and Rich Furman (Furman *et al.* 2010) who explored psychosocial, economic, environmental and political aspects that affect vulnerable individuals/groups and recommended the incorporation of transnational social work into the curriculum of social workers. Gray and Hetherington (2013) in particular took environmental issues as the starting point for transnational analyses and examined the impact of aspects such as climate change, natural disasters, sustainability or environmental justice on social work practice.

The underlying – and often not revealed – frame of social work is the nation state. Social policy is mainly based on political structures and decisions and played out in institutions/organisations in a designed geographical environment. The nation is often seen as a container (Pries 2011; Reutlinger 2011; Herz and Olivier 2013) – there is a defined inside and outside. Inside this container, welfare strategies and social policies are taking place. Outside the container there are other containers interacting (as mainly covered by international social work). Globalisation and migration increasingly challenge this idea of a clearly defined space for social work (Giebeler 2002; Faist 2011; Soysal 2011; Faist 2014), and new developments are raising questions about identification, identity, social networks and social pressure (e.g. remittances). The book focuses therefore mainly on two developments:

- Individuals and groups who regularly cross the borders of the nation state (physically or virtually). These crossings influence their life and their social networks as well as strategies for survival and decision making (e.g. refugees).

- Ideologies and challenges such as poverty, equity, environment, and human rights travelling across national borders and influencing social policies, social work practices and strategies.

Transnational social work challenges the idea of the nation state as a given entity and argues that globalisation and the new media, as well as an increasing number of people crossing borders, must inevitably have an impact on the theories and strategies of social work (Furman *et al.* 2008; Dahinden 2011). Transnational social work indeed criticises social work for its restricted focus on a geographically defined space (Kniffki 2011; Lightman 2012). This restriction influences work with clients including not recognising competencies such as language knowledge and survival strategies as well as social networks outside the nation state (Leiprecht and Vogel 2008).

However, what constitutes TSW needs further discussion and a deepening not only of its theoretical base but also of its practical outcomes based on the exchange of ideas and practices. We are currently witnessing that the nature of the nation state is rapidly changing and people's lives are less bound to traditional structures and institutions – instead they are more and more controlled by global movements and processes emerging from economic, technological, cultural and/or religious influences. This – we assert – requires a (professional) dialogue across boundaries and across countries and one of the aims of this book is to contribute to this dialogue.

Social work is increasingly being labelled as a 'human rights profession' (Foucault 1977; Hunt 2007; Staub-Bernasconi 2007) and we trust that a continuing transnational dialogue is a valuable contribution to the further recognition of human rights as a fundamentally transnational issue affecting and also addressing social work as a human rights profession.

Theoretical and practical knowledge is needed in order to reflect on the potential and the limitations of social work in general and of transnational social work in particular. Transnational social work practices – as part of social work in general – are embedded in the possibilities as well as the restrictions of national contexts, since these contexts function as the framework for professional interventions in social work practice.

In order to provide important theoretical components on TSW as well as practical examples from different countries, this book is structured in three parts:

- Theoretical Perspectives
- Country Profiles
- Case Studies.

The profiles and case studies survey examples from eight countries. A brief outline of all three parts is given below, while more detail is provided at the beginning of each section.

*Part I* comprises chapters which characterise and frame transnational social work from different *theoretical perspectives* including: first, an approach to define transnational social work for the present context; second, an overview of international professional activities, structures and dynamics and the impact of indigenous theories; third, a comparison between influential Western theories and some indigenous Indian approaches; and fourth, a focus on social work as a Human Rights profession based on a critical discussion of the concept of Human Rights itself.

*Part II* includes *country profiles* of all countries included in this book: China, France, Germany, Great Britain, India, Israel, Malaysia, and Turkey. This selection is determined by the Frankfurt Summer School Programme and its participating countries. The country profiles provide basic information on the respective national welfare systems as well as on the current and evolving role of professional social work. The country profiles aim to offer a better understanding of the opportunities that social work professionals encounter in their everyday work, but also the challenges they face. Each country profile can also be used to obtain a basic understanding of the case studies as well as the comments provided in Part III.

*Part III* is composed of eight *case studies* concerning transnational social work embedded in a national context as well as two comments from other national contexts in relation to each case study. The case studies take the reader 'into the field' of social work in the respective national setting, by analysing specific situations or cases and highlighting national social work practice. Each chapter concentrates on a specific transnational 'case' and the involvement of social work professionals. To encourage the transnational dialogue, these case studies are taken as a starting point by colleagues from other countries for commentary and to answer the following question:

How would social work in the national context of the respective commentator deal with this specific case?

It is hoped that this book, with its multilevel theoretical and applied approach, offers a useful contribution to the development of the emerging field of transnational social work. This book provides information and reflections on transnational social work for students and professionals of social work, but also for readers from other disciplines, e.g. politics, sociology, psychology, law. Particularly, through the present book, we hope to

- raise awareness of relevant issues in social work theory and practice from a transnational perspective and develop sensitivity for a transnational approach in social work;
- provide practice-oriented case study materials from different national/cultural backgrounds;
- highlight similarities and differences in dealing with specific cases and trigger questions about the situation in one's own country and the professional field;
- stimulate discussions on further development of transnational social work both in theory and in practice;
- foster a dialogue approach across nation states.

We argue that the dialogue principle across nations and cultures – especially reflected in our approach to include case studies and comments – may be a fruitful way to foster transparency, equality and mutual understanding.

We recognise that we are living in a post-colonial global society and that there is an increasing need to enforce and strengthen the development of transnational standards of citizenship and rights – and this also applies to professional involvement and transnational expertise for social work professionals worldwide.

This is what this book tries to accomplish, mainly as an 'Eastern–Western Dialogue', in the form of contributions from Asia and Europe. That we are missing the perspectives and experiences of countries from the African, Australian and American continents is a great regret for us. However, we fully expect that the dialogue will continue, and grow to embrace more countries and other continents.

Frankfurt a. Main/Marseille/Shanghai, February 2016
The Editors

## References

Dahinden, J., 2011. 'Wer entwickelt einen transnationalen Habitus? Ungleiche Transnationalisierungsprozesse als Ausdruck ungleicher Ressourcenverteilung', in C. Reutlinger, J. Kniffki, and N. Baghdadi, eds, *Die soziale Welt quer denken. Transnationalisierung und ihre Folgen für die soziale Arbeit.* Berlin: Frank & Timme, 83–107.

Faist, T., 2011. 'Transnationalism. Migrant Incorporation beyond Methodological Nationalism', in Heinrich Böll Stiftung, ed., *Transnationalismus & Migration. Dossier*, 25–33.

Faist, T., 2014. '"We are all Transnationals now". The Relevance of Transnationality for Understanding Social Inequalities', *SFB 882 Working Paper Series* (25), 1–25 [Accessed 14 April 2014].

Foucault, M., 1977. *Discipline and punish. The birth of the prison.* London, New York: Penguin Books.

Furman, R., Negi, N.J., Schatz, M.C.S., Jones, S., 2008. 'Transnational Social Work. Using a wraparound model', *Global Networks* 8(4): 496–503.

Furman, R., Negi, N.J., and Salvador, R., 2010. 'An Introduction to Transnational Social Work', in N.J. Negi and R. Furman, eds, *Transnational Social Work Practice.* New York: Columbia University Press, 3–19.

Giebeler, C., 2002. '"Global Social Work – Interkulturelle Soziale Arbeit". Globale und interkulturelle Kompetenz in der Sozialarbeitswissenschaft', *ZEP: Zeitschrift für internationale Bildungsforschung und Entwicklungspädagogik* 25(2): 27–30.

Gray, M. and Hetherington, T., 2013. 'Indigenization, indigenous social work and decolonization: Mapping the theoretical terrain', in M. Gray, J. Coates, M. Yellow Bird, T. Hetherington, eds, *Decolonizing social work.* Burlington: Ashgate Pub. Company (Contemporary social work studies), 25–41.

Herz, A., and Olivier, C., 2013. 'Das Transmigrantische der Sozialen Arbeit. Thematischer Aufriss einer spannungsreichen Suchbewegung', in A. Herz and C. Olivier, eds, *Transmigration und Soziale Arbeit. Ein öffnender Blick auf Alltagswelten.* Baltmannsweiler: Schneider Hohengehren, 1–18.

Hunt, L.A., 2007. *Inventing human rights. A history.* Princeton, N.J: Recording for the Blind & Dyslexic.

Hytten, K., and Bettez, S.C., 2011. *Understanding Education for Social Justice* [online]. Available from: www.stjohns.edu/sites/default/files/documents/adminoffices/asl-understanding-education-social-justice.pdf [Accessed 1 February 2016].

Ife, J., 2012. *Human Rights and Social Work.* Cambridge University Press Textbooks.

Kniffki, J., 2011. 'Lokale Folgewirkungen transnationaler Prozesse', in C. Reutlinger, J. Kniffki, and N. Baghdadi, eds, *Die soziale Welt quer denken. Transnationalisierung und ihre Folgen für die soziale Arbeit.* Berlin: Frank & Timme, 63–80.

Leiprecht, R., and Vogel, D., 2008. 'Transkulturalität und Transnationalität als Herausforderung für die Gestaltung Sozialer Arbeit und sozialer Dienste vor Ort', in H.G. Homfeldt, W. Schröer, and C. Schweppe, eds, *Soziale Arbeit und Transnationalität. Herausforderungen eines spannungsreichen Bezugs.* Weinheim, München: Juventa-Verl, 25–44.

Lightman, E., 2012. 'Transnational Social Policy and Migration', in A.S. Chambon, W. Schröer, and C. Schweppe, eds, *Transnational Social Support.* New York: Routledge, 13–29.

Midgley, J., 2001. 'Issues in International Social Work. Resolving Critical Debates in the Profession', *Journal of Social Work* 1(1): 21–35 [Accessed 14 April 2014].

Pries, L., 2011. 'Transnationalisierung der sozialen Welt als Herausforderung und Chance', in C. Reutlinger, J. Kniffki, and N. Baghdadi, eds, *Die soziale Welt quer denken. Transnationalisierung und ihre Folgen für die soziale Arbeit.* Berlin: Frank & Timme, 17–36.

Reutlinger, C., 2011. 'Transnationale Sozialräume. Zur (neuen) Bedeutung von Ort und Raum in der Sozialen Arbeit', in C. Reutlinger, J. Kniffki, and N. Baghdadi, eds, *Die soziale Welt quer denken. Transnationalisierung und ihre Folgen für die soziale Arbeit.* Berlin: Frank & Timme, 37–62.

Soysal, Y.N., 2011. 'Postnational Citizenship. Rights and Obligations of Individuality', in Heinrich Böll Stiftung, ed., *Transnationalismus & Migration. Dossier*, 73–7.

Staub-Bernasconi, S., 2007. 'Soziale Arbeit: Dienstleistung oder Menschenrechtsprofession? Zum Selbstverständnis Sozialer Arbeit in Deutschland mit einem Seitenblick auf die internationale Diskussionslandschaft', in A. Lob-Hüdepohl and W. Lesch, eds, *Ethik Sozialer Arbeit. Ein Handbuch.* Paderborn: Schöningh; UTB, 20–54.

# Acknowledgements

This truly transnational project was created, developed, nurtured, and edited in a continuous dialogue starting in 2013 and being made public today. It would not be successful without the opportunities for personal meetings which opened the space for academic arguments and exchange, cultural (mis)understandings and intercultural communication, as well as debates about different knowledge and approaches. Therefore, we would like to thank the German Academic Exchange Service (DAAD) and the European ERASMUS+ Programme for their funding to provide such spaces during the Summer Programmes.

As editors, we wish to express our deepest gratitude to all the people who have collaborated in the process of developing this book.

First, we wish to thank our chapter authors from around the world, who have been willing to contribute with their experience, expertise and knowledge. We thank them especially for their patience as they responded to our repeated, and numerous editorial comments, questions and suggestions, and appreciate their understanding of the deadlines and limitations.

In addition, we would like to thank a number of people for their specific contribution which made publication possible: Dagmar Oberlies for the initial idea of the book and Rachel Wareham for language editing.

We also thank Frankfurt University of Applied Sciences for their financial support and the team at Taylor and Francis for welcoming our concept and encouraging us to write this book. Their support was invaluable and most appreciated.

Finally, our gratitude goes to everyone in our professional and personal networks who supported and encouraged us tirelessly along the journey to realise this project.

Frankfurt a. Main/Marseille/Shanghai, February 2016
The Editors

# A note on terminology and comparisons

*Ursula Kämmerer-Rütten, Alexandra Schleyer-Lindenmann, Beatrix Schwarzer and Yafang Wang*

Editing a book on transnational social work including authors from various countries is a challenge in many ways – terminology, alone, is a very tricky matter.

This already starts with social work. In this book we adhere to the terms 'social work' and 'social workers', but these terms can have different meanings in different countries, making comparisons difficult. However, whilst this variability makes formal comparisons problematic, it is useful as an aid to reflection and can offer insights into different ways of understanding and constructing the social work task, and social work professions (Meeuwisse and Swärd 2007: 491). Professional social work in one country may have different historical, political and educational foundations compared to another country, but we have asked our authors to provide this information so that the foundations and frameworks become as transparent as possible. Comparison may also appear difficult concerning professional autonomy: while in some countries social workers represent the authorities and the political system more directly and are perhaps less independent, in others social workers appear to be more autonomous concerning their professional interventions as well as their participation in policy development and decision-making. However, according to our dialogue principle we suggest abstaining from simple comparisons and categorisations and instead encourage mutual understanding in the light of diverse and distinct national and professional characteristics.

Another important issue is the terminology we use concerning the recipients of social work. What do we call the people seeking help and/or advice? We do not want to ask our authors to use a standardised term to describe the relationship between those who assess and commission services and those who are the recipients of these services. Therefore, throughout the book a variety of terms appear, and while many authors talk about clients or service users, others refer to people in need or in need of support. We are aware that different labels conjure up differing identities and suggest differing relationships and differing power dynamics – as has been pointed out by McLaughlin (2009) – but the terminology used is the professional and political choice of each individual author emerging from their particular national and professional contexts.

Globalisation is a complex idea and the authors in this book refer to it in many contexts: as a global discourse concerning human rights policies and social justice, as an economic strategy (free trade, open market), as a compression of time and place (fast mobility of individuals/news/goods) etc. In many articles globalisation refers to something awkward, something difficult to influence, something people are exposed to. However, for our purpose, we step back from negative connotations and instead perceive globalisation as the emergence of a global awareness respecting diversity but uniting people by this shared feeling and identity (Ahmadi 2003; van Ewijk 2009: 11).

## References

Ahmadi, N., 2003. 'Globalisation of consciousness and new challenges for international social work', *International Journal of Social Welfare* 12: 14–23. Available from: http://ehs.siu.edu/socialwork/_common/documents/articles/ahmadi.pdf [Accessed 16 May 2016].

McLaughlin, H., 2009. 'Editor's Choice: What's in a name: "Client", "Patient", "Customer", "Consumer", "Expert by Experience", "Service User" – What's next?' *British Journal of Social Work* 39(6): 1101–17.

Meeuwisse, A., and Swärd, Hans, 2007. 'Cross-national comparisons of social work – a question of initial assumptions and levels of analysis', *European Journal of Social Work* 10(4): 481–96.

van Ewijk, H., 2009. 'Citizenship-based social work', *International Social Work* 52(2): 167–79.

# Abbreviations

| | |
|---|---|
| AFRUCA | Africans Unite against Child Abuse |
| AIDS | Acquired Immune Deficiency Syndrome |
| AMHP | Approved Mental Health Professionals |
| ANESEM | Agence nationale de l'évaluation et de la qualité d'accueil des établissements et services sociaux et médico-sociaux |
| ARKH | Asylum Seekers & Refugees of Kingston upon Hull |
| ASSWI | Association of Schools of Social Work in India |
| ASYE | Assessed and Supported Year in Employment |
| BA | Bachelor of Arts |
| BASW | British Association of Social Workers |
| BCE | Before the Common Era (Equivalent to BC, Before Christ) |
| BME | Black and Minority Ethnic People |
| CADA | Centre d'accueil pour les demandeurs d'asile – Reception centre for asylum seekers |
| CAMHS | Child and Adolescent Mental Health Service |
| CBO | Community Based Organisation |
| CBS | Central Bureau of Statistics |
| CEAS | Common European Asylum System |
| CEDAW | Convention on the Elimination of Discrimination against Women |
| CESEDA | Code de l'entrée et du séjour des étrangers et du droit d'asile / code concerning the entry and stay of foreigners and asylum rights |
| CNDA | Cour nationale du droit d'asile / National court for the right to asylum |
| CPA | Central Plan Assistance |
| CRC | Convention on the Rights of the Child |
| CRPD | Convention on the Rights of Persons with Disabilities |
| CV | Curriculum Vitae |
| DBH | Fachverband für soziale Arbeit, Strafrecht und Kriminalpolitik |
| DBSH | Deutscher Berufsverband für soziale Arbeit und Heilberufe |
| DGSA | Deutsche Gesellschaft für soziale Arbeit |

| | |
|---|---|
| DMW | Domestic Migrant Workers |
| DoH | Department of Health |
| DREES | Direction de la recherche, des études, de l'évaluation et des statistiques |
| e.V. | eingetragener Verein (= registered association) |
| ECTS | European Credit Transfer System |
| EU | European Union |
| FNARS | Fédération nationale des associations d'accueil et de réinsertion sociale |
| GDP | Gross Domestic Product |
| GOI | Government of India |
| HAT | Heroin Assisted Therapy |
| HCPC | Health and Care Professions Council |
| HIV | Human Immunodeficiency Virus |
| HRLN | Human Rights and Law Network |
| HUDA | Hébergement d'urgence dédié aux demandeurs d'asile / emergency accommodation for asylum seekers |
| Hukou | Household Registration System |
| IASSW | International Association of Schools of Social Work |
| ICERD | International Convention on the Elimination of All Forms of Racial Discrimination |
| ICMR | Indian Council of Medical Research |
| ICPS | Interpersonal Cognitive Problem Solving |
| ICRPD | International Convention on the Rights of Persons with Disabilities |
| ICSW | International Council of Social Welfare |
| ICU | Intensive Care Units |
| IEP | Institute of Economics and Peace |
| IFSW | International Federation of Social Workers |
| ILO | International Labour Organisation |
| INSEE | Institut national de la statistique et des études économiques |
| IOM | International Organization for Migration |
| ISA | Informationssystem Studienwahl und Arbeitsmarkt |
| ISW | International Social Work |
| IT | Information Technology |
| ITC | Israel Trauma Coalition |
| KPSS | Kamu Personel Secme Sinavi |
| LGBT | Lesbian, Gay, Bisexual and Transgender |
| LOI | Letter of Intent |
| MAA | Malaysian Association of Almoners |
| MAMSW | Malaysian Association of Medical Social Workers |
| MASW | Malaysian Association of Social Workers |
| MDG | Millenium Development Goals |
| MIND | Mental health charity organisation |
| MMT | Methadone Maintenance Therapy |

| | |
|---|---|
| MoU | Memorandum of Understanding |
| NABARD | National Bank for Agriculture and Rural Development |
| NGO | Non-Governmental Organization |
| OBC | Other Backward Classes |
| OECD | Organisation for Economic Co-operation and Development |
| OFII | Office Français d'immigration et d'intégration / French office for immigration and integration |
| OFPRA | Office Français de protections des réfugiés et apatrides / French office for refugees and stateless persons |
| OHCHR | Office of the High Commissioner for Human Rights |
| ONPES | Observatoire National de la Pauvreté et de l'exclusion sociale |
| PCF | Professional Capabilities Framework |
| PTSD | Post-Traumatic Stress Disorder |
| REM | Réseau européen des migrations |
| RHA | Regional Health Agencies |
| RMB | Renminbi (Chinese Currency) |
| SC | Scheduled Castes |
| SHCEK | Sosyal Hizmetler Kocuk Ezirgeme Kurumu (Social Services and Child Protection Agency) |
| SHUD | Sosyal Hizmet Uzmanları Dernegi (Turkish Association of Social Workers) |
| SSW | School Social Workers |
| ST | Scheduled Tribes |
| SWE | Social Work Education |
| TCSW | The College of Social Work |
| TEPAV | Turkiye Ekonomi Politikaları Arastirma Vakfi |
| TIP | Trafficking in Persons |
| TISS | Tata Institute of Social Sciences |
| TSW | Transnational Social Work |
| TUIK | Türkiye Istatistic Kurumu (Turkish Statistical Institute) |
| UDHR | Universal Declaration of Human Rights |
| UGC | University Grants Commission |
| UK | United Kingdom |
| UN | United Nations |
| UN Convention | United Nations Convention |
| UNHCR | United Nations High Commission for Refugees |
| UNICEF | United Nations Children's Fund |
| UNODC | United Nations Office on Drugs and Crime |
| USA | United States of America |
| USD | US Dollar |
| WAO | Womens Aid Organisation |
| WHO | World Health Organization |
| YOK | Yüksekögretim Kurulu (Council for Higher Education) |

# Part I

# Theoretical Perspectives

*Ursula Kämmerer-Rütten, Alexandra Schleyer-Lindenmann, Beatrix Schwarzer and Yafang Wang*

## Introduction

Part I of this book concentrates on theoretical discourses concerning professional social work in international and transnational contexts. While international developments and dialogue regarding professional social work have largely been confined to academic exchanges, worldwide social work practice is based on, and often confronted primarily with, local, regional and national developments. Only more recently are professionals becoming involved in transnational issues as they deal with problems caused by global inter-dependencies, international conflicts and transnational movements/migrations.

Since its birth in the last third of the nineteenth century social work has become a global profession practised in more than 144 countries (IASSW 2012). Its spread and development have been accompanied by a drive to attain professional status (Weiss-Gal and Welbourne 2008) and international activities and engagement have led to an ever growing professional community networking globally and crossing boundaries and areas of practice.

In 2003 Ahmadi observed that:

> International migration makes poverty, political and religious oppressions, and the lack of civil rights in one society the concern of other societies. Woman trafficking and sex tourism make the sexual exploitation of women and children in one part of the world the moral, legal and public health concern of other parts. Low wages, harsh work conditions and the exploitation of an underage work force in one country affect national employment policies and labour markets in other countries.
>
> (Ahmadi 2003: 15)

These examples offer striking proof that the transnational perspective is becoming more and more integral to social work professions both in theory and practice. It is therefore important to address issues of human rights and social justice from a transnational perspective and provide insight into specific areas of transnational social work to foster shared understanding and collective responsibility.

Against a background of globalisation, rising social problems can originate from one nation or from a set of nations, but have regional and continental effects. In 2015, the movement of people inside and across national borders reached its highest level since the beginning of records on this issue (UNHCR). This has led to the need to reformulate national social policies and practice as well as representing a further challenge to social work strategies. In addition this has led to the emergence of Transnational Social Work (TSW) as a new concept which gained recognition in the field of social work around the turn of the twenty-first century.

Levitt and Glick Schiller define transnational processes as follows: 'The term transnationalism or transnational processes emphasize [sic] the ongoing interconnecting or flow of people, ideas, objects or capital across border [sic] of nation-states' (Levitt and Glick Schiller 2004: 5).

But is crossing a border a necessary condition to label a social issue transnational and are all cross-border movements automatically a concern for social work?

Beatrix Schwarzer stipulates that transnational exchanges of people, ideas and goods are not always related to social work. Not all migrants are potential clients and not all transnational political decisions are suitable for support by social work as a human rights profession. The transnational perspective, for Schwarzer, is not restricted to the social work fields directly confronted with migrants or intercultural exchange but rather, challenges social work as a discipline and profession as such. Social work is primarily based on unmarked national identity and stereotypes, which can function as an underlying force in the construction of 'Otherness'.

The terms 'international social work' and 'transnational social work' are often confused. However, they do not share the same meaning and origin. International social work has a longer history – emerging initially in the global north – and serves as a foundation for exchange between social workers from different countries. In her chapter, Ute Straub starts by giving an account of international professional activities and relevant networks and organisations and their objectives. She then widens the picture of largely Western-based concepts produced by the global north and questions the 'Westernness' by confronting it with indigenous approaches from the global south.

The integration of Western and indigenous approaches is also highlighted by Arvind Agrawal's contribution. He reviews theoretical developments in social work by focusing on Western theoretical approaches and contrasting them with Indian philosophy. After recalling relevant classical approaches including social capital theory, empowerment theory as well as the capability approach, the author reflects upon classical Indian theories such as Jainism, the Bishnois Sect's philosophy and Gandhian ideas, and he argues the need for an integrated theoretical paradigm for transnational social work.

Finally, Dagmar Oberlies considers transnational social work within the framework of social work as a human rights profession. She points out that human rights are embedded in global political processes. This formulation of human rights is challenged by religious, regional, ideological and ethical perspectives. At the same time human rights function as a global ethical framework for social work. This leads to tensions mirrored in contrasts such as individualism versus collectivism-based approaches or rights-based versus culturally sensitive perspectives.

# References

Ahmadi, N., 2003. 'Globalisation of consciousness and new challenges for international social work', *International Journal of Social Welfare* 12: 14–23. Available from: http://ehs.siu.edu/socialwork/_common/documents/articles/ahmadi.pdf [Accessed 15 April 2016].

IASSW, 2012. *Directory of Social Work Schools/Programs* [online]. International Association of Schools of Social Work. Available from: www.iassw-aiets.org/uploads/file/20121025_IASSW-Directory-October-2012.pdf [Accessed 14 December 2015].

Levitt, P., and Glick Schiller, N., 2004. 'Conceptualizing Simultaneity. A Transnational Social Field Perspective on Society', *International Migration Review* 38(145): 595–629.

UNHCR. *The refugee story in data and statistics* [online]. UN Refugee Agency. Available from: www.unhcr.org/pages/49c3646c4d6.html [Accessed 10 January 2016].

Weiss-Gal, I., and Welbourne, P., 2008. 'The professionalisation of social work. A cross-national exploration', *International Journal of Social Welfare* 17(4): 281–90.

# 1 Transnational social work

## An introduction

*Beatrix Schwarzer*

'The world is getting smaller' is a phrase most people agree on. Virtual social networks offer the possibility of being a part of events happening thousands of miles away from where they take place. The so-called Arab Spring is just one example. Knowledge can travel fast and information can be accessed through the Internet in no time. Literally more and more people cross national borders – often more than once – to live elsewhere. Reasons can be manifold, such as holidays, seeking work or refuge, moving closer to family members or friends, experiencing a different part of the world by voluntary work or studying, to mention but a few. The duration of the stay is variable, from merely a couple of days to an entire lifetime. Often national borders are crossed multiple times, and migration can no longer be seen as a one-off process of simply leaving a country and spending the rest of one's life in another (Lightman 2012). However, out of these many diverse crossings, only a few are of concern to social work theory and practice.

Generally speaking, social work focuses on groups of people whose 'global basic needs' (Gil 2012: 20) are neglected or who are facing structural inequalities. Social work is connected to local and national structures such as law and social security on the one hand and is also responsible for individual people on the other.

> The social work profession promotes social change, problem solving in human relationships and the empowerment and liberation of people to enhance well-being. Utilising theories of human behaviour and social systems, social work intervenes at the points where people interact with their environments. Principles of human rights and social justice are fundamental to social work.
>
> (IFSW 2012).

Transnational social work (TSW) shares this basic foundation with social work in general but can also be understood as a critical perspective pointing to unseen, unmarked and unnoticed boundaries of Social Work (Levitt and Glick Schiller 2004; Lightman 2012). It is related to crossing and transcending national borders and is influenced by the diversity of migration and refugee processes. In this chapter, I will take a critical view on three issues TSW is concerned with: (1) the boundaries embedded in social work through the often unnoticed relation to the nation state; (2) the part social work plays in questions of cultural norms and belonging; and (3) pointing to unmarked ground. Finally, the difficulties resulting from the wide variety of fields of social work will be explored – from supporting individual well-being to structural (in-)equalities. All these share a concern with the impact global and international developments have in social work.

TSW can open the spectrum of theoretical thinking in social work by taking into account the context of hybrid formations of different national and cultural backgrounds when working with individuals. Hybrid formations in the present context are:

- The diverse cultural influences impacting on everyday life, such as questions of belonging and identity of the individual or group;
- The play of different cultures in forming specific social networks, including belonging to certain communities with similar life challenges;
- The tensions with social and cultural norms that can result in social isolation for individuals which might reduce possibilities for social participation and political involvement as well as difficulties claiming rights;
- The special needs of clients which might not be recognised and therefore taken seriously by social workers; clients not infrequently find support only outside the profession, like family, community or social networks, including those outside the nation state they live in.

Taking plural local connections seriously also means to focus on social, political and economic structures in and around social work. Generally speaking, TSW demands complex knowledge of thinking and working in the field. Social work practices as well as theoretical thinking have to be related to global processes and developments, whilst at the same time being embedded in local structures and contexts.

## Critical perspectives on the nation state as a container

Social work struggles with the complexity of a wide spectrum of responsibilities ranging from individual needs to struggles against structural inequalities. Questions arise, such as: What are the boundaries of social work and what are its main aims and targets? Which boundaries should social work accept, and which need to be challenged? Should social work position itself in political debates or should it be neutral?

*On the international level*, developments such as globalisation influence social interdependencies all around the world (Lyons and Huegler 2012; Faist 2011). International associations for social work (e.g. IASSW/ISSW/ICSW) have increasingly addressed important issues such as post-colonialism and globalisation over the last decades. These associations have highlighted that principles of human rights, social justice, collective responsibility and respect for diversities are global fundamentals basic to social work (Gray *et al.* 2010; Midgley 2001, 2010).

The complex *relationship between the international and the national level* is the focus of the Human Rights debate (Soysal 2011). Human Rights build the framework for international social work, and therefore social work is often called 'the Human Rights profession' (Staub-Bernasconi 2012) and theories, strategies and practices are judged to these exacting standards. Conflicts arise when the global importance of human rights and social rights clash with restrictions such as supporting only people with a certain national citizenship. These conflicts are at play in everyday social work practice, they define the spectrum of issues that social work is concerned with, the finances of organisations and the access to basic rights like safety, housing, education and food (Gil 2012).

*On the national level*, the nation state is often seen as a container (Herz and Olivier 2013; Furman et al. 2008) – there is a defined inside and outside. Inside this container, welfare strategies and social policies are taking place and a common history is being constructed. Outside the container there are other containers. Human rights are meant to cut through this division but questions remain as to how that should be played out in everyday practices at a certain place in the world. This problem also arises in the education of social workers; social work professional education focuses mainly on the national context – often without naming these boundaries of knowledge and the resulting implications. This has been critiqued from different angles such as: (1) the rooting of human rights in a certain western thinking (see Oberlies, Chapter 4); (2) the implicit European and North American influences on the discipline; (3) the ignorance of indigenous approaches and theories (see Agrawal, Chapter 3); and (4) the ongoing demand to decolonise social work (Gray *et al.* 2013).

The container model suggests that the borders are solid and fixed and therefore are able to protect the inside.[1] Globalisation, migration, world trade, environmental changes, and wars not only cross these borders, but show the problems that arise when we think of them as fixed and impermeable. On the one hand there are manifold influences from economics and world trade, where borders are flexible or have little if no meaning at all. On the other hand, for refugees and migrants the borders, while contested, still seem as solid and meaningful as ever. This is especially true for borders around economically strong regions such as Europe and North America.

## Critical perspective on cultural norms and belonging

The container model also mirrors the idea of a national culture with implicit ideas about who belongs to that culture and who does not. TSW looks for answers to tackle the container concept as well as the effects this unmarked foundation has. It challenges the notion of 'who belongs' and focuses on the construction 'who does not belong' (Teater 2014: 78).

There are people who appear to 'belong' and fit well into the national container with its culture and traditions. But there are also people who do not belong. For example, people who are crossing a border to live elsewhere may be seen (and treated) differently from those who are not crossing. From the perspective of people who 'belong' to one national container, people who cross borders are often seen as 'sitting between chairs'. This notion of an in-between is rooted in an idea of two separate cultures uninfluenced by each other. People who migrate can be seen as inhabiting a (conflicting) space which does not properly belong to either of these cultures.

Questions of right and wrong – covering all areas of life, such as behaviour, language, clothing, food etc. – are deeply embedded in societies. They result in norms – mostly seen as normality – and also in differences – mostly seen as deviations. Processes of 'othering' are taking place (Holliday *et al.* 2004: 21ff), where the 'other' is different from the so-called 'us'. This difference is embedded in power structures and stigmatisations. The 'other' seems to have all the negative characteristics and the 'us' does not include negative connotative features into their self-perception. Usually the divide goes along binary terms such as modern–traditional, emancipated–backwards, civilised–not civilised. The process of 'othering' always simultaneously exposes the construction of powerful, unmarked norms. The differences function like a mirror, with the 'us' projecting negative characteristics on to the 'other'. The result of this process is a positive reflection of the self for people in the position of power (Holliday *et al.* 2004: 30ff). But it also keeps the power hierarchies intact.

On a structural level, social work is often at the forefront of dealing with processes of 'othering'. Migrants and refugees as well as their descendants are seen as culturally different, even when they themselves do not claim that difference. This idea can often be found in social work concepts of intercultural competence and communication (Samovar *et al.* 2006). Social work therefore actively constructs (or acknowledges) this difference, often labelled as 'ethnic' or 'cultural'. This is a basic part of the thinking of transnationalism as Nina Glick Schiller, Linda Basch and Cristina Szanton-Blanc showed in their groundbreaking article in 1992. 'The hegemonic context imposes a discipline on newcomers who develop self-identifications, if not broader collective action, in accordance with categories and related behaviors that are not of their own making' (Glick Schiller *et al.* 1992: 14).

There are, however, two sides to the coin. On the one side, social workers acknowledge differences in the experiences of their clients and tackle inequalities that migrants and refugees face. On the other hand, social workers also mainly still hold to the idea of a national culture where migrants are in between two cultures (Adelson 2001). Social work is embedded, it influences and actively participates in disciplining and judging the notion and behaviours of the 'others', confronting them with unmarked judgments – of the rights and wrongs of cultural norms. The experience of migration is taken as a fundamental difference dividing people into two groups – those with, and those without it. This seems to play a role in the practices of social workers – even when not put forward explicitly by the clients.

TSW sees that migration and cross-border (family and friendship) networks are important, and should be taken into account in social work practice, but it also claims that cross-border experience cannot be taken as a general explanation for individual attitudes. TSW criticises the notion of an in-between space between two or more distinguishable national cultures. It challenges the underlying – often stereotypical – thinking that there are people who belong and that there are fundamentally different people like migrants and refugees. TSW acknowledges differences in experiences and knowledge and even points to them as resources (e.g. language skills), whilst criticising the power hierarchies embedded in this separation. TSW thereby has a critical perspective on norms, and challenges the inequalities associated with them.

> People live in and create a new social and cultural space which calls for a new awareness of who they are, a new consciousness, and new identities. However, both the actors and analyst still look around them with visions shaped by the political boundaries of nation-states.
>
> (Glick Schiller *et al.* 1992: 14)

Being embedded in cross-border social networks and/or being socialised in different national contexts also affects identity (Holliday *et al.* 2004: 6ff; Römhild 2004). Multiple influences continuously (re)form national culture(s) into something new and hybrid. Migrants, refugees and also descendants of migrants are affected by and affect cultural norms. They find their own symbiosis of local, regional and national identities (Römhild 2004) which may be labelled differently from – and not as part of – the national cultures they live in.

Social workers need to acknowledge that people with multiple cultural influences are not by themselves problematic or challenging, but come to regard these experiences and knowledge as resources, e.g. language skills, cross-border social networks and cultural competences. Accelerated through technology like social networks, mobile phones and affordable long-distance communication, the ties between families and friends all over the world can deepen. These ties have to be taken into account as a resource for social work practices (Duscha and Witte 2013). But migration also often brings special challenges – these cross-national ties can signify serious commitments, e.g. financial contributions and support to family members (IOM 2010; Furman *et al.* 2010).

### Critical perspective on pointing to unmarked foundations of social work

Like social work, TSW is interwoven into the nation state (Midgley 2001: 4). The difference between social work and TSW is the reflecting on these foundations and the potential in crossing, rather than accepting, boundaries. It is not the place where someone lives that defines their entitlement to receive (professional or social) support; the decisive criterion is citizenship (or at least a legal status in the country where someone is living) and this defines who has access and who does not (Owen 2011). As an example: social workers who work with refugees are caught between commitment to the client and the restriction of social services mainly reserved for citizens. Support is connected to legal status and provided by social work organisations. Access to jobs, food, education and accommodation is given through social workers and they have to act via the relevant national law (Hayes 2005: 185).

TSW indeed criticises social work for its restricted focus on a geographically defined space (Lightman 2012; Kniffki 2011). This restriction influences the work with clients, including not recognising competences like language knowledge, survival strategies and social networks outside the nation state (Leiprecht and Vogel 2008).

TSW questions the restriction concerning the idea of a defined 'inside' and 'outside' (for example, social workers' focus on citizens) by bringing into the spotlight topics such as inequality, poverty or demands for global justice as a reality connected to everyone's everyday life. Global capitalism and trade as well as violent conflicts, both within and across nation states, influence the further consolidation of existing national and global hierarchies such as those between the global north and south, between poverty and wealth, between legal citizens and people without a legal status – and thus affect society at large.

TSW takes up the challenge to add a cross-national dimension. This creates the space to look at the following:

* Similar challenges in different contexts – what can we learn from each other?
* Local aspects of globalisation – how are global developments connected to local practices?
* Equality – what are the opportunities of a transnational perspective?

TSW points to the possibilities for social work theorists and practitioners to *learn from experience and thinking in other national contexts*. This exchange needs to start in someone's own context by knowing and critically reflecting on norms and national framing as well as in other contexts. Taking this into account opens the possibilities for transferring or translating strategies and knowledge as well as seeing the limits of this. Translation means a process of hearing, understanding and reflecting the possibility of applying knowledge to a new context. TSW sees itself as simultaneously embedded in local and national contexts whilst focusing on migration practices crossing them. Exchanges across borders create a social space, characterised by academic and practical knowledge grounded in context and reformulated at the same time (Bartley *et al.* 2012). Social work practices are diverse and learning through international exchange is important. TSW therefore focuses on the specific resources and needs of people who are not usually included in social work structures. It raises questions such as what prevents people from seeking help from social workers? It also challenges social work in a general way by pointing to the lines within which social work strategies and solutions are commonly framed.

TSW supports the necessary *relationships between the local and the global*. Local changes and challenges are connected to global politics and economics. Processes of migration and refuge are caused by these changes. Social work practitioners are confronted with new clients, different cultural norms and experiences and challenges in positioning themselves in conflicts resulting from these global developments (Ahmadi 2003). Unspoken norms surface, such as what is right and what is wrong and for whom; what if the rights of individuals conflict with the cultural rights of groups? Questions like this are asked and maybe even answered daily by social workers.

TSW as a critical perspective of social work also commits to *equality and equal rights*. Social work as a Human Rights profession is deeply committed to a wider ethical framework (Bisman and Bohannon 2014). In addition to national-focused social work TSW makes the claim for positioning itself in a global context. It states that topics like women's rights, racism and poverty cannot be approached on the local level only. All of these inequalities are acted out between people on the local level but need to be tackled on a structural level. Poverty can only be addressed when trade structures and global economies are changed. Gender equality can only be reached by talking about power hierarchies and construction of femininities and masculinities. TSW needs to take political standpoints in these debates and needs to get involved in political processes from the local to the global level (Gray and Fook 2004).

## Conclusion

TSW can function as a critical perspective claiming sensitivity for boundaries and pointing to neglected needs and resources. The nation state is an important frame that enables social work as well as restricting it – it can both provide welfare and access to social work organisations but also exclude those without legal status in the country they reside in. Claims for social welfare are always combined with questions relating to the boundaries of 'inside' and 'outside'. Social work practices are often limited to providing support to citizens only or, at least, to those people with legal status. Having a particular citizenship therefore frames social work to a great extent.

TSW itself has limits. Its main concern is the crossing of borders (physically as well as virtually). This raises the question as to the difference from intra-national migration. Why not take intra-national migration into account when thinking about transnational social work? The common focus of both types of migration could be access to rights. Citizenship rights are only valuable if they can be claimed as 'rights to have rights' (Arendt 1951).

TSW as a critical perspective enlarges the picture from the needs of people excluded to the mechanisms of exclusion itself. How is normality constructed to give way to exclusion? How do mechanisms of 'othering' stabilise exclusion? TSW challenges norms and normality by pointing to the role global developments play in everybody's lives every day. It also supports the view that crossing borders and having plural local connections are resources to draw on. This is true for clients but also for social workers. Facing the challenges of movement might enable a sensitive knowledge for the questions TSW is most concerned with.

## Note

1   The 'inside' of a nation is itself diverse and framed by various power hierarchies. Social work acknowledges this diversity in different concepts such as social justice (Austin 2014), diversity (Appiah 2010) and intersectionality (Pease 2014).

## References

Adelson, L.A., 2001. 'Against Between. A Manifesto', in S. Hassan and I. Dadi, eds, *Unpacking Europe. Towards a critical reading.* Rotterdam: Museum Boijmans Van Beuningen, 19–36.

Ahmadi, N., 2003. 'Globalisation of consciousness and new challenges for international social work', *International Journal of Social Welfare* (12): 14–23. Available from: http://ehs.siu.edu/socialwork/_common/documents/articles/ahmadi.pdf [accessed 18 April 2016].

Appiah, K.A., 2010. *The honor code. How moral revolutions happen.* 1st ed. New York: W.W. Norton.

Arendt, H., 1951. *The origins of totalitarianism.* 1st ed. New York: Harcourt Brace.

Austin, M.J., ed., 2014. *Social Justice and Social Work. Rediscovering a Core Value of the Profession.* Los Angeles, London, New Delhi: SAGE.

Bartley, A., Beddoe, L., Fouché, C. and Harington, P., 2012. 'Transnational Social Workers. Making the Profession a Transnational Professional Space', *International Journal of Population Research* 1: 1–11.

Bisman, C., and Bohannon, A., 2014. *Social Work. Value-Guided Practice for a Global Society.* New York: Columbia University Press.

Duscha, A., and Witte, M.D., 2013. 'Erziehungshilfe und Transnationalisierung. Eine Einführung', *Sozialmagazin* 38(9–10): 6–13.

Faist, T., 2011. 'Transnationalism. Migrant Incorporation beyond Methodological Nationalism', in Heinrich Böll Stiftung, ed., *Transnationalismus & Migration. Dossier,* 25–33.

Furman, R., Negi, N.J., Schatz, M.C.S. and Jones, S., 2008. 'Transnational Social Work. Using a wraparound model', *Global Networks* 8(4): 496–503.

Furman, R., Negi, N.J., and Salvador, R., 2010. 'An Introduction to Transnational Social Work', in N.J. Negi and R. Furman, eds, *Transnational Social Work Practice.* New York: Columbia University Press, 3–19.

Gil, D.G., 2012. 'Social Work, Social Policy, and Welfarism', in M. Gray, J. Midgley, and S.A. Webb, eds, *The Sage Handbook of Social Work.* London, Thousand Oaks, New Delhi, Singapore: SAGE, 19–32.

Glick Schiller, N., Basch, L., and Szanton-Blanc, C., 1992. 'Transnationalism: A New Analytic Framework for Understanding Migration', *Annals of the New York Academy of Sciences* (645): 1–24.

Gray, M. and Hetherington, T., 2013. 'Indigenization, indigenous social work and decolonization: mapping the theoretical terrain', in M. Gray, J. Coates, M. Yellow Bird and T. Hetherington, eds, *Decolonizing social work.* Burlington: Ashgate Pub. Company (Contemporary social work studies), 25–41.

Gray, M., Coates, J., and Hetherington, T., 2010. 'Hearing Indigenous and Local Voices in Mainstream Social Work', in M. Gray, J. Coates, and M. Yellow Bird, eds, *Indigenous social work around the world. Towards culturally relevant education and practice.* Farnham, England, and Burlington, VT: Ashgate, 257–69.

Gray, M., and Fook, J., 2004. 'The Quest for a Universal Social Work: Some Issues and Implications', *Social Work Education* 23(5): 625–44.

Hayes, D., 2005. 'Social Work with Asylum Seekers and Others Subject to Immigration Control', in R. Adams *et al.*, eds, *Social work futures. Crossing boundaries, transforming practice.* Basingstoke, Hampshire: Houndmills; and New York: Palgrave Macmillan, 182–94.

Herz, A., and Olivier, C., 2013. 'Das Transmigrantische der Sozialen Arbeit. Thematischer Aufriss einer spannungsreichen Suchbewegung', in A. Herz and C. Olivier, eds, *Transmigration und Soziale Arbeit. Ein öffnender Blick auf Alltagswelten.* Baltmannsweiler: Schneider Hohengehren, 1–18.

Holliday, A., Kullman, J., and Hyde, M., 2004. *Intercultural communication. An advanced resource book.* London, New York: Routledge.

IASSW, and IFSW, 2004. *Global Standards for the Education and Training of the Social Work Profession* [online]. IASSW; IFSW. Available from: http://cdn.ifsw.org/assets/ifsw_65044-3.pdf [Accessed 26 February 2012].

IFSW, 2012. *Global Standards* [online]. International Federation of Social Workers. Available from: http://ifsw.org/policies/global-standards/ [Accessed 10 March 2014].

IOM, 2010. *Gender, Migration and Remittances* [online]. International Organization for Migration. Available from: www.iom.int/sites/default/files/about-iom/Gender-migration-remittances-infosheet.pdf, updated on 27/08/2010 [Accessed 18 August 2014].

Kniffki, J., 2011. 'Lokale Folgewirkungen transnationaler Prozesse', in C. Reutlinger, J. Kniffki, and N. Baghdadi, eds, *Die soziale Welt quer denken. Transnationalisierung und ihre Folgen für die soziale Arbeit.* Berlin: Frank & Timme, 63–80.

Leiprecht, R., and Vogel, D., 2008. 'Transkulturalität und Transnationalität als Herausforderung für die Gestaltung Sozialer Arbeit und sozialer Dienste vor Ort', in H.G. Homfeldt, W. Schröer, and C. Schweppe, eds, *Soziale Arbeit und Transnationalität. Herausforderungen eines spannungsreichen Bezugs.* Weinheim, München: Juventa, 25–44.

Levitt, P., and Glick Schiller, N., 2004. 'Conceptualizing Simultaneity. A Transnational Social Field Perspective on Society', *International Migration Review* 38(145): 595–629.

Lightman, E., 2012. 'Transnational Social Policy and Migration', in A.S. Chambon, W. Schröer, and C. Schweppe, eds, *Transnational Social Support.* New York: Routledge, 13–29.

Lyons, K., and Huegler, N., 2012. 'Migration and Refugees', in L.M. Healy and R.J. Link, eds, *Handbook of International Social Work. Human rights, development, and the global profession.* New York: Oxford University Press, 220–25.

Midgley, J., 2001. 'Issues in International Social Work. Resolving Critical Debates in the Profession', *Journal of Social Work* 1(1): 21–35.

Midgley, J., 2010. 'Promoting Reciprocal International Social Work Exchanges. Professional Imperialism Revisited', in M. Gray, J. Coates, and M. Yellow Bird, eds, *Indigenous social work around the world. Towards culturally relevant education and practice.* Farnham, England, and Burlington, VT: Ashgate, 31–45.

Owen, D., 2011. *Transnational Citizenship and Rights of Political Participation* [online]. Available from: publikationen.ub.uni-frankfurt.de/files/22387/Transnational_Citizenship.pdf [Accessed 15 July 2012].

Pease, B., 2014. 'Transforming Privileged Subjectivities. Toward a Pedagogy of the Oppressor', in M. Pallotta-Chiarolli and B. Pease, eds, *The Politics of Recognition and Social Justice. Transforming Subjectivities and New Forms of Resistance.* New York: Routledge, 159–72.

Römhild, R., 2004. 'Global Heimat Germany. Migration and the Transnationalization of the Nation-State', *Transit* 1(1): 1–8. Available online at www.escholarship.org/uc/item/57z2470p.pdf [Accessed 14 April 2014].

Samovar, L.A., Porter, R.E., and McDaniel, E.R., eds, 2006. *Intercultural Communication. A Reader.* 11th ed. Belmont, CA: Thomson/Wadsworth.

Soysal, Y.N., 2011. 'Postnational Citizenship. Rights and Obligations of Individuality', in Heinrich Böll Stiftung, ed. *Transnationalismus & Migration. Dossier,* 73–7.

Staub-Bernasconi, S., 2012. 'Social Work as Theory and Practice', in L.M. Healy and R.J. Link, eds, *Handbook of International Social Work. Human rights, development, and the global profession.* New York: Oxford University Press, 30–36.

Teater, B., 2014. *An introduction to applying social work theories and methods.* 2nd ed. Maidenhead: McGraw-Hill Education; Open University Press.

# 2 International social work – an overview

*Ute Straub*

Why should students, teachers and social workers concern themselves with international perspectives in their work? Is social work, on the basis of the varying legal situations, not limited to a certain location (Gray and Webb 2008)? Can there be such a person as an 'international social worker'? Further critical questions are: isn't there enough to be done at the local level; isn't the idea of being globally effective perhaps part of the (often disappointed) fantasy of omnipotence that afflicts 'do-gooders', who imagine they can save the world, or does it have something to do with professional vanity – with wanting to polish up one's own image, so as to be able to compete with others on the international stage (Webb 2003)?

On the other hand, global interdependence leads to the situation where significant new areas of international responsibilities are opening up, so that the tasks and the working environment of social work are changing:

- Jointly acquired knowledge and exchanges about field projects, teaching and research, as well as a global professional literacy strengthen the professional profile regarding the commitment to contribute to solving global social problems (Healy 2014: 378).
- Worldwide social upheavals and disturbances, as a result of climate change and migration as well as the growing number of refugees, change the focus and aims of local social work and demand competencies in new fields of practice, such as disaster relief and management (Mathbor and Bourassa 2012; Dominelli 2014), social development (Midgley 1995; Homfeldt and Reutlinger 2009) and ecology-oriented approaches (Alston and Besthorn 2012).
- Neoliberalism as a constantly expanding political guideline makes it necessary to defend the profession as a politically independent entity (Ferguson 2015; Abramowitz 2012).
- Global governance as a political form of globalisation, which also includes non-governmental organisations, has become an important dimension of international social work (Bähr *et al.* 2014: 15)
- Social problems have a growing mutual impact, both in industrial and in developing countries. Furthermore, innovations in practice with certain target groups that have been developed in the global south are also relevant for the north, e.g. families or victims/offenders (Straub 2012: 47ff).

- The self-definition of social work as a human rights profession (Staub-Bernasconi 2008; IASSW 2015) demands the extension of activities beyond national borders.
- Through the formation of international umbrella organisations and various global initiatives, most recently the Global Agenda for Social Work and Social Development (see below), the profession now is globally present.

This chapter aims to give an overview of international perspectives in social work. The focus will be on the following questions: What formal structures are there in international social work? What issues are being discussed?

## Definition

As far as a definition of International Social Work (ISW) is concerned, it is repeatedly emphasised that a binding definition does not exist: it is 'a slippery phrase with various meanings' (Dominelli 2012: 42). Healy (2001) and Cox and Pawar (2006) have to be thanked for the current, most-frequently cited listing of the dimensions of international social work. These are as follows:

- Internationally related domestic practice and advocacy, because as a consequence of globalisation, it is no longer possible to work on the local level without an international perspective.
- Professional exchange has become inevitable as a result of global interdependence. It is necessary, however, to create or expand corresponding structures in order to be able to exchange information at different levels (teaching, research, and practice).
- International practice[1] assumes that social work has the task and the competence to actively disseminate professional values, targets and methods.
- International policy development and advocacy describes the political dimension of social work, without which it would be impossible to achieve the goal of implementing greater social justice.
- Promoting social work around the world as an integrated international profession (Cox and Pawar 2006: 20, 25ff) implies that the diversity of the profession is taken into account, which can be very different depending on local conditions, and also includes the integration of the themes of human rights, globalisation, ecology and social development (Cox and Pawar 2006: 19, 37ff).
- In addition, Healy (2014: 369ff) mentions three different directions in which ISW is developing: first, as a movement that campaigns for the spread of universal standards for practice and training; second, as a form of specific practice; and third, as a (professional-) political activity which strives to be involved in global political developments.

## International organisations

The three big umbrella organisations,[2] the International Association of Schools of Social Work (IASSW), the International Federation of Social Workers (IFSW) and the International Council of Social Welfare (ICSW) form the umbrella for social work on the global level and cooperate closely with regional associations in Africa, Asia/Pacific, Europe, Latin America/Caribbean, and North America. All of them trace their origins to the First International Conference of Social Work that took place in Paris in 1928 (Healy 2008; Kruse 2009; Lyons and Lawrence 2009: 108ff). Women played a very important role in national women's movements and associations and, above all, in the International Council of Women (ICW). These were partly the same women who joined the women's and peace movements and were responsible for the development of social work as a women's profession (Kniephoff-Knebel 2006; Kruse 2009).

Although worldwide exchange was interrupted by the Second World War, it was possible to revive the international dimension of social work and the commitment to human rights and social justice (Cox and Pawar 2006: 55ff; Hall 2013; Healy and Hall 2009). This article concentrates on a part of each of the umbrella organisations; IASSW is used as an example of the historical ups and downs of the international collaboration; the commitment to human rights is shown through the example of IFSW; and for the ICSW, its development as a representational body of NGOs, especially from the global south, is highlighted.

## *IASSW*

Its members are universities that offer Social Work as a course of study, but also individuals (teachers) can become members. Various European schools of social work met in Berlin in 1929 to launch the 'International Committee of Social Work' (Kniephoff-Knebel and Seibel 2008). The founding members were from 46 schools from 11 countries. They agreed that the goal should be: 'to bring about an exchange of opinion and experience between schools of social work and to deal with all problems of international co-operation of these schools' (Healy 2008: 2).

There were great conflicts on the issues of religious ties versus neutrality, and nationalistic-militaristic trends versus pacifism. The German schools played an inglorious role: in 1936 they demanded the resignation of Alice Salomon, a Jew, as President of the International Committee and withdrew from the IASSW when they were unable to get their way. The first post-war conference took place in Paris in 1959. In the following years, the organisation, which thus far had been limited to the global north, began to open itself to the global south. For the first time, world conferences were held outside Europe and North America (Healy and Hall 2009: 251) and with the coming of new members from previously colonised, now independent, African and Asian countries, the community grew. The 1980s brought, on the one hand, initial contact with Eastern European countries and the Soviet Union and, on the other hand, a renewed split; there were disagreements on how to deal with the issue of apartheid, and regarding the role of the South African Association of Social Workers (Healy and Hall 2009: 254), leading to the temporary resignation of the Scandinavian schools. In 2004, after 76 years, the first non-northern President, Abye Tasse from Ethiopia, was chosen.

## *IFSW*

Originally founded in 1932 and called 'The International Permanent Secretariat of Social Workers', the organisation was renamed 'The International Federation of Social Workers' at the World Conference in Munich in 1956. Its members are the professional associations of social workers worldwide, but only one organisation per country is allowed to become a member (if necessary, in a coordinated coalition). From the very beginning, the subject of ethics was of particular importance, and in 1957, work on compiling the ethical principles of social work was begun (Healy and Hall 2009: 245). Since the 1980s, the focus of the IFSW has been on human rights: externally, by engaging in public relations, and internally, by promoting among its professional members an awareness of their own human rights legacy. A human rights commission works actively as an advocate for those social workers who are persecuted or arrested because of their politically oriented engagement. In addition, the IFSW has published two policy documents: 'Social Work and Human Rights' (1994) and 'Social Work and Children's Rights' (2002) (Hall 2013). Policy statements regarding human rights topics are published regularly, most recently on 'Reproductive Tourism' (cross-border reproductive services) and 'Elderly and Old People' (IFSW).

## *ICSW*

Currently, a growing number of more than 80 non-governmental organisations (NGOs) in the area of social services and social development from 70 countries are represented by national committees in the ICSW (ICSW; Healy and Hall 2009: 245). Originally called the 'International Conference of Social Work', in 1966 the organisation was renamed the 'International Council on Social Welfare'. This was done in order to show that members and their activities were not limited to professional social work; rather that they cooperate in an inter-disciplinary manner, and that through the NGOs, non-professional and para-professional social activists could also be included. The preparation for and participation in the UN Summit for Social Development in Copenhagen in 1995 showed the importance of the strong link between Promoting Social Welfare and the Development Movement.

### *Joint activities*

All three organisations have a consultative status with the UN and cooperate with various UN organisations: the World Health Organization (WHO), the office of the United Nations High Commissioner for Refugees (UNHCR) and the Office of the High Commissioner for Human Rights (OHCHR). Of great importance for the exchange regarding practice, teaching and policy-oriented issues are: (a) international conferences;[3] (b) jointly issued professional journals;[4] and (c) basic policy papers.

The most important joint policy papers are 'Ethics in Social Work, Statement of Principles' and 'Global Standards for Social Work Education and Training of the Social Work Profession', both of which were published in 2004. In 2010 it was decided to revise them every ten years. Discussions about conflicts have entered the professional debate in the context of globalisation and post-colonialism (Gray *et al.* 2010; Midgley 2010; Rehklau and Lutz 2009). Thus, new categories such as 'social cohesion' and 'social development' are incorporated. Similarly, 'indigenous knowledge' has been recognised as an essential part of social work (Straub 2014). In the past, the worldwide standardisation of (ethical) norms and professional standards had been paramount, in order to create a common basis for all the disparate members and to make their voices heard regarding the concerns of social work on the political level. Now, however, the focus of attention is increasingly directed at diversity within the globally active profession itself.

The 'Global Standards for the Education and Training of the Social Work Profession' (IASSW) describe the guidelines and goals for schools/universities, for the curriculum, internships, the teaching staff and students as well as for the administration and management of educational institutions. The latest joint effort is the ten-year project 'Global Agenda for Social Work and Social Development' (IFSW), which was publicly launched in 2010. It is supposed to monitor the activities of social workers, teachers and practitioners in the area of social work and development and make it more visible in the political arena, thus strengthening its influence. In addition, the content of the Global Agenda complies with the UN's Millenium Development Goals (MDG) and the Post-2015 Development Agenda. The monitoring and checking instrument draws on information from members about successful approaches in practice and in teaching.

## Critical discussion of internationalisation

Although there is no doubt that international organisations have contributed a great deal to the spread, professionalisation and acceptance of social work, their work has long been oriented towards the social work of the global north. It seems that the organisations represent less than half the nations of the world (Cox and Pawar 2006: 18). This not only raises the question of how representative they are but shows as well that social work as a profession still is either not very widespread, fails to meet the standards adequately or that the organisations may not be accepted as representative.

Though slowly, but with increasing openness toward diversity in their own ranks, global organisations are beginning to open up to the voices of the global south (Straub 2012).

### *Colonisation/professional imperialism*

In the colonial period, national or church social organisations took over the function of supporting the colonial powers in spreading their stance and attitudes rather than contributing to local development (Cox and Pawar 2006: 3ff). Modernisation theories of the 1950s (Coates *et al.* 2006: 10ff), based on the idea that only through adaptation to northern standards would it be possible to join the modern and 'civilised' world, were reflected in a brutal way in the 'welfare treatments' of, for example, Canada's First Nations (Bruyere 2010) and Australia's aborigines (Fejo-King 2014). Even after most of the colonies had become 'independent', the perception 'West is Best' continued (and continues), prevailed and was shared by many of the local political elites (Cox and Pawar 2006: 5; Midgley 2010: 31ff). This shows effects that continue to be felt even today, such as a lack of appreciation of, or even disrespect for, local and indigenous values and lifestyles (for a list of the first critics of traditional social work see Osei-Hwedie and Rankopo 2007: 19).

In the 1980s, Midgley coined the term 'professional imperialism' to describe the colonial as well as the current post-colonial export of northern (education and training) concepts of social work to countries of the global south. Thirty years later, he concluded that not much had changed, especially in regard to standards of training, teaching content, accreditation requirements for courses of study and the resulting hegemony of northern approaches over the southern education market (Cox and Pawar 2006: 6; Midgley 2010). Tamburro argues that the phase of colonisation has by no means ended (Tamburro 2013: 4) and demands the 'de-colonisation' of social work.

The continually recurring debate about universalism versus cultural relativity (for the genesis of the debate about universal or differentiated social work see Bar-On 2003: 27; Healy 2007) reflects the increasingly critical attitude in the global south towards northern social work. Can action-theoretical approaches that were developed in a de-traditionalised and individualising society and in the context of an urban environment, industrialisation and 'social question' in the global north be transferred to developing societies? To what extent are traditional/ local approaches considered? These and related questions have not been answered conclusively and continue to be discussed at national and international gatherings.

A further critical objection concerns the possibilities for participation: those who are in a position to take part in the discussion about professional development on the global stage are usually the academically educated and privileged and not grassroots social workers. Financial problems and the lack of internationally recognised training and language barriers prevent the majority of social workers – even in the IFSW member countries – from participating (Haug 2005). All this presents new challenges to the efforts made so far to find internationally accepted definitions and standards for the profession and its training.

### Social work of the south

One expression of the resistance to 'professional imperialism' is the social work of the south, which sets different priorities in both theory and practice. This can be seen in the priority of (socio-politically oriented) approaches like social development instead of individual help (inherent in the system).

Established individualising casework and clinical social work are substituted by educational and community work and organisation which builds awareness, strengthens the community and opposes repression (Pawar and Cox 2009: 25ff;

Rehklau and Lutz 2009: 40; Midgley 2010). These approaches are often clearly politically oriented and, in contrast to the neoliberal tendencies of the north, they call for an active role in bringing about socio-political changes, above all in the fight against poverty, landlessness and lack of education. Therefore: (a) radicalisation is a characteristic of social work of the south. Further characteristics are: (b) authentication, which means the focus is placed on local knowledge resources and processes; and (c) reconceptualisation – the orientation of social work practice toward the existing socio-political situations and efforts to change them (Osei-Hwedie and Rankopo 2007: 20; Rehklau and Lutz 2009: 43ff).

An essential part of the social work of the south is the indigenous approach or the 'indigenisation' of social work (Gray *et al.* 2010). In the debate about the mutual influencing of northern and southern approaches (Osei-Hwedie and Rankopo 2007: 20; Rehklau and Lutz 2009: 43ff), Barise describes indigenisation as a mainly 'bottom-up' process that develops approaches rooted in the local context but also adjusts mainstream social work to it (Barise 2005).[5]

## Conclusion

Internationalism has been an essential characteristic of social work since its beginnings as a profession. This is true in spite of the fact that this dimension was lost during the Second World War and could only be regained in the post-war years (Pfaffenberger 1994). International contact and exchange have contributed greatly to professionalisation and to making the profession and its contribution to civil society and social justice more visible all over the world. Activities are currently continuing on this point through the Global Agenda, and, at the same time, cooperation with the UN is being strengthened and made more effective so as to take advantage of synergy effects (IASSW 2015). Critical voices from the global south and indigenous groups have ensured that local and cultural/ethnic characteristics as well as norms and values of the profession, long considered to be laws, have been called into question. Furthermore, the post-colonial legacy has been the subject of (self-)critical discussion in international professional debates. One challenge is the establishment of areas of practice in which social work can bring in its inter-disciplinary competencies and highly flexible intervention possibilities, as, for instance, in the management of natural disasters and flows of refugees (Cox and Pawar 2006: 356ff). A central future field of activity will be (local) social development, which has to become a part of training, practice and research as a must, if the profession wishes to be internationally qualified and not surrender these tasks to other disciplines (Patel 2009).

Another topic of international social work in this context will be the question about varying training levels (social assistant, social worker, senior social worker), so that it will be possible to establish social work in order to meet local requirements and needs (Cox and Pawar 2006: 361ff).

The chief challenge of the coming years, however, will be to counter neoliberal developments including marketisation, consumerisation, and managerialisation – a tendency that threatens social work in its original function as the advocate for social justice in many countries. Social work is (once again) in danger of becoming instrumentalised to carry out policies oriented towards discrimination and exclusion. It is necessary to maintain and strengthen its political independence. This autonomy is not to be viewed as a privilege, rather as the necessary degree of freedom for its commitment to alternative social policies, and bringing about social change for the common good (Ferguson 2015). This will depend greatly on the extent to which global influence is gained through international umbrella organisations and their networks. However, this in turn presupposes that the nature and content of the proposed advocacy is accepted equally in the global north and south.

## Notes

1  This is also valid for transnational social work. For definition and differentiation see Schwarzer, Chapter 1.
2  This chapter only refers to the big three umbrella organisations; their regional associations, which are of course international organisations as well, and other international profession-oriented federations like the International Consortium for Social Development are not taken into account.
3  E.g. World Conference 2014 in Melbourne, Australia, as well as the next one to be held in Seoul, South Korea in 2016.
4  Journals *International Social Work* and *Social Dialogue*, a monthly newsletter 'Global Cooperation'.
5  A chronological list of the definitions of indigenisation, see Gray and Coates (2010: 26ff).

## References

Abramowitz, M., 2012. 'Theorising the neoliberal welfare state for social work', in M. Gray, J.O. Midgley, and S.A. Webb, eds, *Sage handbook of social work*. Thousand Oaks, Calif.: Sage, 33–50.
Alston, M., and Besthorn, F.H., 2012. 'Environment and sustainability', in K.H. Lyons *et al.*, eds, *Sage handbook of international social work*. London: SAGE Publications, 56–69.
Bähr, C., *et al.*, 2014. 'Weltatlas Soziale Arbeit. Jenseits aller Vermessungen', in C. Bähr, *et al.*, eds, *Weltatlas Soziale Arbeit. Jenseits aller Vermessungen*. Weinheim, Basel: Beltz Juventa, 9–30.
Barise, A., 2005. 'Social work with Muslims. Insights from the teachings of Islam', *Critical Social Work* 6(2). Available from: www1.uwindsor.ca/criticalsocialwork/social-work-with-muslims-insights-from-the-teachings-of-islam [Accessed 13 May 2016].
Bar-On, A., 2003. 'Indigenous practice. Some informed guesses – self-evident but impossible', *Social Work/ Maatskaplijke Werk* 39(1): 26–40.
Bruyere, G., 2010. 'Picking up, what is left by the trail. The emerging spirit of aboriginal education in Canada', in M. Gray, J. Coates, and M. Yellowbird, eds, *Indigenous social work around the world. Towards culturally relevant education and practice*. Farnham: Ashgate, 231–44.
Coates, J., Gray, M., and Hetherington, T., 2006. 'An "ecospiritual" perspective. Finally, a place for indigenous approaches', *British Journal of Social Work* 36(3): 381–99.
Cox, D.R., and Pawar, M.S., 2006. *International social work. Issues, strategies, and programs*. Thousand Oaks, Calif.: Sage.

Dominelli, L., 2012. 'Globalisation and indigenization. Reconciling the irreconcilable in social work?' in K.H. Lyons *et al.*, eds, *Sage handbook of international social work.* London: SAGE Publications, 39–55.

Dominelli, L., 2014. 'Learning from our past. Climate change and disaster interventions in practice', in C. Noble, H. Strauss, and B. Littlechild, eds, *Global social work. Crossing borders, blurring boundaries.* Sydney: Sydney University Press, 341–51.

Fejo-King, C., 2014. 'Indigenism and Australian social work', in C. Noble, H. Strauss, and B. Littlechild, eds, *Global social work. Crossing borders, blurring boundaries.* Sydney: Sydney University Press, 55–68.

Ferguson, I., 2015. *Hope over fear*, with assistance from Bicocca-University, Milano (Social Work Education in Europe). Available online at www.eassw.org/userfiles/file/eassw-programma-finale-20150529.pdf, updated on 6/29/2015, [Accessed 10 January 2016].

Gray, M., and Coates, J., 2010. 'From "Indigenization" to Cultural Relevance', in M. Gray, J. Coates, and M. Yellowbird, eds, *Indigenous social work around the world. Towards culturally relevant education and practice.* Farnham: Ashgate, 13–30.

Gray, M., and Webb, S.A., 2008. 'The myth of global social work. Double standards and the local-global divide', *Journal of Progressive Human Services* 19(1): 61–6.

Gray, M., Yellowbird, M., and Coates, J., 2010. 'Towards an understanding of indigenous social work', in M. Gray, J. Coates, and M. Yellowbird, eds, *Indigenous social work around the world. Towards culturally relevant education and practice.* Farnham: Ashgate, 49–58.

Hall, N., 2013. 'International Federation of Social Workers (IFSW)', *Encyclopedia of Social Work.* Available online at http://socialwork.oxfordre.com/view/10.1093/acrefore/9780199975839.001.0001/acrefore-9780199975839-e-202 [Accessed 31 July 2015].

Haug, E., 2005. 'Critical reflections on the emerging discourse of international social work', *International Social Work* 48(2): 126–35.

Healy, L.M., 2001. *International social work. Professional action in an interdependent world.* 2nd ed. New York: Oxford University Press.

Healy, L.M., 2007. 'Universalism and cultural relativism in social work ethics', *International Social Work* 20(1): 11–26.

Healy, L.M., 2008. 'Introduction. A brief journey through the 80 year history of the international association of schools of social work', *Social Work and Society* 6(1): 1–13.

Healy, L.M., 2014. 'Global education for social work. Old debates and future directions for international social work', in C. Noble, H. Strauss, and B. Littlechild, eds, *Global social work. Crossing borders, blurring boundaries.* Sydney: Sydney University Press, 369–80.

Healy, L.M., and Hall, N., 2009. 'Internationale Organisationen der Sozialen Arbeit', in L. Wagner and R. Lutz, eds, *Internationale Perspektiven Sozialer Arbeit.* Wiesbaden: VS-Verlag, 243–60.

Homfeldt, H.G., and Reutlinger, C., eds, 2009. *Soziale Arbeit und Soziale Entwicklung.* Baltmannsweiler: Schneider Verlag Hohengehren.

IASSW [online]. International Association of Schools of Social Work. Available from: www.iassw-aiets.org/ [Accessed 25 November 2015].

IASSW. *Global Standards for Social Work Education and Training* [online]. International Association of Schools of Social Work. Available from: www.iassw-aiets.org/global-standards-for-social-work-education-and-training [Accessed 25 November 2015].

IASSW, 2015. *IASSW mission within the UN* [online]. International Association of Schools of Social Work. Available from: www.iassw-aiets.org/uploads/file/20140929_IASSW%20mission%20with%20the%20UN.pdf [Accessed 31 July 2015].

ICSW [online]. International Council on Social Welfare. Available from: www.icsw.org/ [Accessed 25 November 2015].

ICSW, Members list [online]. International Council on Social Welfare. Available from: www.icsw.org/index.php/members/members-list [Accessed 25 November 2015].

IFSW [online]. International Federation of Social Workers. Available from: http://ifsw. org/ [Accessed 25 November 2015].

IFSW. *Global Agenda for Social Work and Social Development* [online]. International Federation of Social Workers. Available from: http://ifsw.org/the-global-agenda-observatory/ [Accessed 25 November 2015].

IFSW. *Policies* [online]. International Federation of Social Workers. Available from: http://ifsw.org/policies/ [Accessed 25 November 2015].

International Consortium for Social Development [online]. Available from: www. socialdevelopment.net/ [Accessed 20 November 2015].

Kniephoff-Knebel, A., 2006. *Internationalisierung in der sozialen Arbeit. Eine verlorene Dimension der weiblich geprägten Berufs- und Ideengeschichte*. Schwalbach/Ts.: Wochenschau-Verlag.

Kniephoff-Knebel, A., and Seibel, F.W., 2008. 'Establishing international cooperation in social work education. The first decade of the "International Committee of Schools for Social Work"', (ICSSW). *International Social Work* (51, November 2008), 790–812.

Kruse, E., 2009. 'Zur Geschichte der internationalen Dimension in der Sozialen Arbeit', in L. Wagner and R. Lutz, eds, *Internationale Perspektiven Sozialer Arbeit*. Wiesbaden: VS-Verlag, 15–32.

Lyons, K., and Lawrence, S., 2009. 'Social work as an international profession. Origins, organisations and networks', in S. Lawrence *et al.*, eds, *Introducing International Social Work*. Exeter: Learning Matters Ltd., 108–20.

Mathbor, G.M., and Bourassa, J., 2012. 'Disaster management and humanitarian action', in K.H. Lyons *et al.*, eds, *Sage handbook of international social work*. London: SAGE Publications, 294–310.

Midgley, J.O., 1995. *Social development. The developmental perspective in social welfare*. London: Sage.

Midgley, J.O., 2010. 'Promoting reciprocal international social work exchanges. Professional imperialism revisited', in M. Gray, J. Coates, and M. Yellowbird, eds, *Indigenous social work around the world. Towards culturally relevant education and practice*. Farnham: Ashgate, 31–45.

Osei-Hwedie, K., and Rankopo, M., 2007. 'The socio-cultural basis of indigenising social work in Southern Africa', in C. Rehklau and R. Lutz, eds, *Sozialarbeit des Südens*. Oldenburg: Paulo Freire Verlag, 19–30.

Patel, L., 2009. 'Developmental social work in South Africa. Lessons from the south', in H.G. Homfeldt and C. Reutlinger, eds, *Soziale Arbeit und Soziale Entwicklung*. Baltmannsweiler: Schneider Verlag Hohengehren, 47–67.

Pawar, M., and Cox, D.R., 2009. 'The importance of social development for the internationalization of social work', in H.G. Homfeldt and C. Reutlinger, eds. *Soziale Arbeit und Soziale Entwicklung*. Baltmannsweiler: Schneider Verlag Hohengehren, 25–46.

Pfaffenberger, H., 1994. 'Zeitgeschichtliche Abläufe und Entwicklungen der internationalen Dimension der deutschen Sozialpädagogik/Sozialarbeit', in F. Hamburger, ed., *Innovation durch Grenzüberschreitung*. Rheinfelden, Berlin: Schäuble Verlag, 7–19.

Rehklau, C., and Lutz, R., 2009. 'Partnerschaft oder Kolonialisation?' in L. Wagner and R. Lutz, eds, *Internationale Perspektiven Sozialer Arbeit*. Wiesbaden: VS-Verlag, 33–53.

Staub-Bernasconi, S., 2008. 'Menschenrechte in ihrer Relevanz für die Theorie und Praxis Sozialer Arbeit. Was haben Menschenrechte überhaupt in der Sozialen Arbeit zu suchen?' *Widersprüche, Bielefeld: KleineVerlag* (107): 9–32.

Straub, U., 2012. 'Sharing circles. Family group conferences in the context of indigenized social work', in R. Clarijs and T. Malmberg, eds, *The quiet revolution. Aggrandizing people power by family group conferences.* Amsterdam: SWP Publishing, 43–53.

Straub, U., 2014. 'Whose voice is being heard? Die Diskussion um die neue Definition für Soziale Arbeit von IASSW und ISSW', *FORUM sozial* 2(14): 29–30.

Tamburro, A., 2013. 'Including decolonization in social work education and practice', *Journal of Indigenous Social Development* 3(1): 1–16.

Webb, S.A., 2003. 'Local orders and global chaos in social work', *European Journal of Social Work* 6(2): 191–204.

# 3   Towards an integrated theoretical framework for transnational social work

*Arvind Kumar Agrawal*

The emerging inter-related world necessitates a social work perspective which has to deal with global issues that are neither localised nor nation-specific but rather have a transnational character such as: increased incidences of communal strife; civil war; cross-border conflicts; terrorism; problems of refugees; violence against women; hunger; AIDS; environmental degradation etc. 'Unless we can offer an alternative to the struggle between Jihad and McWorld, the epoch on whose threshold we stand – post-communist, post-industrial, post-national, yet sectarian, fearful, and bigoted – is likely also to be post-democratic' (Barber 2004). The fast-paced powerful juggernaut of globalisation is commonly viewed as a Western evil-incarnated ideology out to annihilate non-Western culture, resisted by traditional cultural protagonists leading to cultural strife. Besides contributing to paranoid, parochial recidivist tribalism as seen in Bosnia, Rwanda, Ossetia and Iraq, it seems to drag humanity into new miseries where mostly the weaker sections, minorities, women and children suffer.

A theoretical framework for transnational social work has to be based on an integrated approach with inputs from all over the world that have in the past provided evidence of sustainable solutions to problems and issues faced. Edward Said highlights the circulation of ideas and travelling theory in his essay *The World, the Text and the Critic*. He welcomes travelling theories because they can unblock intellectual and cultural formations, however, he cautions against ideas turning into dogma (Said 1984). The grim reality of a world full of strife and problems highlights an urgent need to look for an alternative framework for transnational social work.

Referring to the circulation of ideas, Amartya Sen observes:

> The misdiagnosis that globalisation of ideas and practices has to be resisted because it entails dreaded Westernisation has played quite a regressive part in the colonial and postcolonial world. This assumption incites parochial tendencies and undermines the possibility of objectivity in science and knowledge. It is not only counterproductive in itself; given the global interactions throughout history, it can also cause non-western societies to shoot themselves in the foot – even in their precious cultural foot.
>
> (Sen 2004: 17)

In fact, for thousands of years there has been a history of ideas travelling worldwide – Amartya Sen argues that in AD 1000 paper, printing press, the crossbow, gunpowder, the iron-chain suspension bridge, the kite, the magnetic compass, the wheel barrow, the rotary fan all travelled from China to the wider world. Similarly, he talks of astronomy, mathematics, including the decimal system and zero, travelling from India to Europe via the Arab world, thus laying the foundation for the modern scientific revolution. He further establishes how these ideas on mathematics came back to India later on from Europe through 'Western' education (Sen 2004: 16).

In view of threatening cultural intolerance, communal hatred and religious fanaticism, Hans Kueng proposes 'a global ethic as a foundation of global society' (Kueng 2004: 44). Defining the global ethic he says: 'Every human being must be treated humanely; and what you wish done to yourself, do to others' (Kueng 2004: 47). Hans Kueng suggests that the global ethic requires the development of basic values of respect for life, freedom, justice, mutual respect, readiness to help, and integrity. He concludes by quoting the UN Commission Report on Global Governance 1995 (Commission Our Global Neighborhood 1995) on the civil ethic that 'all people share a responsibility to:

- Contribute to common good;
- Consider the impact of their actions on the security and welfare of others;
- Promote equity, including gender equity;
- Protect the interests of future generations by pursuing sustainable development and safeguarding the global commons;
- Preserve humanity's cultural and intellectual heritage;
- Be active participants in governance; and
- Work to eliminate corruption.' (Commission Our Global Neighborhood 1995: 49)

In line with Kueng's ideas, transnational social work could look for a theoretical approach based on the following three elements:

1 Peaceful co-existence with nature and treating other fellow human beings with dignity and compassion;
2 Social justice and sustainable development through a collective and synergetic effort to alleviate poverty and misery; and
3 Value pluralism and non-violence that would save humanity from cultural extremism including religious extremism.

In common with most social science disciplines, social work grew in the social milieu of the Western hemisphere, in consonance with the evolving religious,[1] cultural,[2] political[3] and economic[4] ethics with the backdrop of industrial and urban growth. However, unlike other social sciences, social work, a somewhat nascent discipline, rather than working on the epistemology of the discipline, concentrated more on developing strategies and methods in the shape of case work, group work and community organisation as well as the delivery of services in a professional manner. This chapter is an attempt to look at some of the theories, namely Social Capital and Social Network Analysis (Robert Putnam), Empowerment Approach (Naila Kabeer) and Justice and Capability Approach (Amartya Sen and Martha Nussbaum) in contrast to indigenous approaches from India, namely Jainism; the Bishnoi Sect's philosophy and practices; Gandhian ideas, the Sarvodaya movement and Integral Humanism of Pandit Deen Dayal Upadhyaya that could be integrated in an epistemologically justifiable manner (sharing the aforementioned three elements) to beget an integrated theoretical framework for transnational social work.

## Social capital and social network analysis

Robert Putnam (2000) brought the concepts of community, social capital and social networking to centre stage of the fast emerging multi-ethnic global society. For him the connections among individuals – social networks and norms of reciprocity and trust emanating from them – constitute social capital. Social capital helps members of densely networked communities to pursue their shared goals. He gave two more concepts: *bonding* – networks between members of similar culture sharing communities – and *bridging* – networks between members of dissimilar culture sharing communities. Whilst bonding can potentially lead to in-group and out-group formations (if one uses the terminology used by W.G. Sumner, in his book *Folkways*), social cohesion can achieve intercultural community bridging in a multi-ethnic society. It is vital for harmonious democracy with diversity. Thus, this approach could contribute to a peaceful co-existence between human beings and value (cultural) pluralism by community based social work in and between communities. In terms of Said's travelling theory, this approach has travelled far and wide, for instance, with an empirical study carried out by a Chinese immigrant scholar in New Zealand.

## Empowerment approach

Julian Rappaport points out that 'by empowerment I mean our aim should be to enhance the possibilities for people to control their own lives' (Wu 2011: 205). Rappaport's concept of empowerment, 'conveys both a psychological sense of personal control or influence and a concern with actual social influence, political power and legal rights' (Wu 2011: 121). According to Nina Wallerstein (1992), empowerment is a social-action process that promotes participation of people, organisations, and communities towards the goals of increased individual and community control, political efficacy, improved quality of community life, and social justice.

Naila Kabeer defines empowerment as a process of change by which individuals or communities with little or no power gain the power and ability to make life choices that affect their lives (Kabeer 1999: 435ff). This notion of empowerment is inescapably bound up with the condition of disempowerment and refers to the processes by which those who have been denied the ability to make choices acquire such ability. Disempowerment may be understood as (political/legal/ social) restrictions on participation in processes of decision making and the expression or enforcement of one's own interests. It is precisely in this context where the social work profession is challenged to support the empowerment of people through political reflection and the exertion of influence on the one hand – and strengthening individuals in order to speak up for themselves on the other hand. This notion of empowerment could contribute to a collective and synergetic effort to alleviate poverty and misery. We could say that this idea of empowerment already exists in Mahatma Gandhi's approach: Gandhi sought to empower the weak in India as part of his struggle against colonial powers and against a highly oppressive and discriminatory traditional feudal system. Gandhi sought to empower the poor, oppressed castes, untouchables, minorities and women through non-violent means and *Sarvodaya* ('welfare' or 'rise of all', implying the welfare of the individual is inherently contained in the welfare of all). He was inspired by John Ruskin's book *Unto the Last* in calling for *Sarvodaya*. He picked up the essence of non-violence and humanism from Jainism, Leo Tolstoy's book *The Kingdom of God is within You* and the Bible. This is a very clear example of travelling theories (Said 1984), from one place to another – and back. Gandhi's concept of *Sarvodaya* focused on village industries, communal harmony, abolition of untouchability, village sanitation, basic education, prohibition, environmental preservation (Gandhi said, 'Nature has enough to meet human need but not for human greed'), welfare of tribal communities, women's welfare, labour welfare etc. It advocated the Spartan life, and making village communities self-reliant, self-sufficient and free so that they would stand up for their own rights.

Gandhi propounded the concept of 'trusteeship' for the industrial sector. This envisages industrialists as trustees of wealth-generating industries with profits voluntarily shared with the poor, a precursor perhaps to the twenty-first century's concept of corporate social responsibility. Gandhi advocated the awakening of consciousness of people for voluntary help to reduce inequalities, completely in line with the three elements as a common basis for social work suggested above.

In social work one of the key methods of empowerment is through advocacy, seen as public and professional support concerning the recommendation of a particular cause or policy, with the aim to influence decisions within political, bureaucratic and economic institutions and systems. However, Kabeer (1999) clarifies that those who stand to gain most from such advocacy carry very little clout compared to those people who set the agendas in major policy-making institutions. Thus empowerment is about change, choice and power, but its scope and relevance will be determined by the context, i.e., by the socio-cultural and political conditions that affect people's options. Furthermore, for empowerment to come into being there are three dimensions of power that need to be realised: resources, agency and achievements. *Resources* – economic, human and social – are necessary preconditions; *agency* refers to people's capacity to define their own life-choices and to pursue their own goals; and *achievements* are assessed in terms of the outcomes and the constraints in achieving the desired goals or ends (Kabeer 1999: 435). Gandhi used his tools of non-violent resistance and advocacy to persuade oppressive racist regimes in South Africa and India to amend policies and laws in favour of discriminated, oppressed and poor people. Gandhi led the great struggle for freedom based on non-violent, peaceful and passive resistance through empowerment, mass awakening and mass participation to achieve independence for India from British colonial power.

## Justice and capability approach

Amartya Sen (1992) proposes an approach concerned with human capabilities and freedom. Often poverty is understood as capability deprivation; one could be deprived because of ignorance, state repression, lack of resources or traditional cultural constraints such as caste-related oppressive barriers. Sen differentiates between commodities, human functioning/capability and utility (e.g. happiness). By capability he means that people are able to attain goals and achieve something for themselves. Often freedom is defined in a rather narrow and negative way, i.e. the absence of any kind of coercion. However, it does not always include effective or substantive freedom in the sense of participation and shared decision making. For instance, there is no law to prevent a poor student pursuing higher studies in an expensive elite university but if he/she cannot afford it then he/she does not have substantive freedom. Another example refers to people with disabilities or mental health problems, who were long denied personal autonomy and independent living until social movements for Independent Living in the USA and UK gained influence in order to change restrictive policies and attitudes in the 1970s.

Hence, Sen believes that a key measure of human well-being is that a person's real quality of life is linked to their degree of substantive freedom. He believes that opulence of income or commodities in a nation or utility in terms of happiness and/or desire fulfilment does not lead to human well-being or deprivation amelioration; instead a more direct approach is required that focuses on human functioning(s) and the capability to achieve valuable functioning(s) that would lead to deprivation amelioration.

This theory recognises human heterogeneity and diversity, group disparities (such as gender, race, class or age) and different cultural and human specificities in terms of values and aspirations. However, Robert Sugden raises the question as to 'how far Sen's framework is operational' (Sugden 1993: 1953) and notes that there is a great deal of disagreement about the nature of a good life (Sugden 1993: 1952f). Nussbaum (1988: 176) criticises Sen for not providing a coherent list of important capabilities. Charles Beitz (1986: 282ff) criticises Sen for making the general agreement on inter-personal comparison of well-being about the valuation of capabilities. Sen is nevertheless optimistic about achieving agreement about evaluations (Sen 1985: 53ff). This discussion could contribute to value pluralism as advocated before.

In this context, Pandit Deen Dayal Upadhyaya (1965) provides a model of 'Integral Humanism' quite like Gandhi's *Sarvodaya*. Upadhyaya speaks of appropriate technology as opposed to arbitrary mechanisation, advocates sustainable consumption and sets out principles of corporate ethics and social responsibility. This is in line with sustainable development and a peaceful co-existence with nature. This also goes well with the concept of substantive freedom advocated by Sen. Subramanian Swamy (2010) writes:

> Integral Humanism recognized that in a democratic market economy an individual has technical freedom of choice but the system without safeguards fails to accommodate the varying capabilities and endowments of a human being. Since the concept of survival of the fittest prevails in such a system, therefore some individuals achieve great personal advancement while others get trampled on or disabled in the ensuing rat race. We need to build a safety net into our policy for the underprivileged or disabled while simultaneously rewarding the meritorious or gifted. Otherwise, the politically empowered poor in a democracy who are in a majority will clash with the economically empowered rich who are the minority, thereby causing instability and upheaval in a market system.
>
> (Swamy 2006: 82)

Going beyond Sen, Nussbaum (2000) develops the capability approach further into a more explicit political theory of universal justice and rights. While she agrees with Sen that quality of life cannot be appropriately measured by Gross National Product, she differs from Sen in arguing that substantive freedom alone can lead to human well-being (Nussbaum 2000: 70ff). She defines human capability as the capability to function well and provides a definitive list of 'central human capabilities' as (Ibid.: 72ff): (i) Life (defined as 'being able to live to the end of a human life of normal length') (Ibid.: 78); (ii) Bodily health; (iii) Bodily integrity; (iv) Senses, imagination and thought; (v) Emotions; (vi) Practical reason; (vii) Affiliation; (viii) Other species; (ix) Play; and (x) Political and material control over one's environment. She further adds that this list 'isolates those human capabilities that can be of central importance in any human life, whatever else the person pursues or chooses' (Ibid.: 74). She also claims that the list represents 'years of cross cultural discussion' (Ibid.: 76). This list is 'based on the commonness of myths and stories from many times and places' that reveal 'what it is to be human rather than something else' (Nussbaum 1990: 217). Nussbaum further points out that the items in her list are 'core ideas' that constitute good human life with dignity. For Nussbaum, 'dignified free being [is] who shapes his or her own life in co-operation and reciprocity with others', rather than being passively shaped or pushed by the world in the manner of 'flock' or 'herd' animal (Nussbaum 2000: 72). She also clarifies unambiguously that the various capabilities do not form any hierarchy (Ibid.: 81). Rejecting cultural relativism, Nussbaum argues that the capability approach accommodates cultural diversity in many ways and that the list is a product of reflection across cultures and across time, therefore it is open and subject to constant revision (Ibid.: 77). This list is capable of 'multiple realisability' in different ways and in different cultures.

Human well-being requires that people enjoy certain basic capabilities to do and be what they want to be in any culture or society. For Nussbaum, it is common for all humanity and not confined to any cultural/nation specific situation (Nussbaum and Cohen 1996: 7). As such, it could also be a helpful approach in line with our three basic elements. In this context, the above approach can be augmented with ideas of cognitive pluralism (*anekandtavada*) or scepticism enshrined in the philosophy of Jainism, enunciating a relativism that shuns all kinds of dogmas, absolutism and respects all possible points of views (Agrawal 2004: 223ff). This cognitive pluralism believes that every proposition is true only up to a certain extent as illustrated by the 2,500-year-old Jain legend of the seven blind men and the elephant (Wallace 1969). At the philosophical and intellectual levels this doctrine promotes *ahimsa* or non-violence of thoughts and ideas, and compassion.

Thus the combined approach of Sen, Nussbaum, Upadhyaya and the cognitive pluralism within Jainism (*anekandtavada*) can provide a fundamental political substratum to be ingrained in all constitutional guarantees, human rights laws and development policy of any society.

Coming back to Said's 'travelling theory', Jainism indeed influenced many thinkers and social reformers (Long 2009) directly or indirectly, such as Gandhi, the Dalai Lama, Martin Luther King, Nelson Mandela, Cesar Chavez and Thich Nhat Hanh who have followed the path of non-violence in order to influence social change positively.

In fact, one of the earliest known precursors of environmental movements in an effective non-violent manner came from India through Bishnoi religious philosophy and history. Bishnoi religious principles require the community to adhere to eco-friendly and sustainable practices such as protecting trees and animals; being simple, truthful, tolerant pacifists; and forbidding adultery, addiction and intoxication of any kind. The commitment of the Bishnoi to environmental preservation made history. In 1730, a local king needed wood for construction of a new fortress. Therefore, his soldiers went to nearby villages to cut down Khejri trees (*Prosopis cineraria*) that grow under harsh arid conditions and provide shade, fodder and fruit. Local Bishnoi community members hugged the trees and offered themselves to be killed before any axe harmed the trees. Consequently, on 9 September 1730, 363 lives were lost in saving trees. As a consequence, the local king had to rescind his orders and make environmental conservation a state policy. This incident inspired the 'Chipko (Hug) Movement' in post-independent India in the Uttarakhand region in 1977 led by Chandi Prasad Bhatt and Sundar Lal Bahuguna. It has inspired theorists of eco-feminism including Vandana Shiva (Shiva 2009) and Chandra Mohanty (Mohanty 2003).

## Towards an integrated theoretical paradigm for transnational social work: conclusion

In the wake of present day global issues, an integrated approach of ideas from all over the world (in terms of Said's 'travelling theory') with pacifist principles is needed for a theoretical framework to beget practical strategies and methods in transnational social work. The basic tenets of this integrated theoretical framework should comprise the values of peaceful co-existence and value pluralism, human rights, individual liberties, free trade, liberal democratic governance along with preservation of environment, *Sarvodaya*, non-violence (*ahimsa*), truthfulness, trusteeship and cognitive pluralism (*anekandtavada*).

After delineating these elements the next major requirement is to devise strategies for transnational social work practitioners according to the following stages:

1   Social work focuses on problem solving and aims at helping individuals, within their own environment, to solve their problems using different methods such as social casework, social group work or community organisation. In the first stage, for this integrated theoretical framework to succeed, social work professionals have to be sensitised to develop strong personal conviction and commitment concerning the principles of empowerment, justice and capability.

2   In stage two, committed social work professionals develop an attitude to strengthen the social consciousness of communities and the self-help capabilities of individuals with a missionary zeal and fierce commitment.

3   In stage three, communities and individuals should be empowered, leading to community determination (as exemplified by the Bishnoi Community in preserving the environment or to some an extent as demonstrated by volunteers of the Grameen Bank in Bangladesh).

4   The final stage would involve raising up the collective power of the people as a whole that would break the status quo and create an ethos for a system that is in the interest of all as witnessed in the non-violent struggle against colonialism led by Gandhi. This would aim for a transparent, accountable, democratically decentralised, free society based on human dignity and human rights. Such a set-up may be supported by competent social workers who contribute to the empowerment of people in order to fight discrimination, exploitation and oppression.

To some sceptics, this may appear to be utopia but there is enough empirical evidence from the last century wherein positive social reformation took place through non-violent, peaceful and passive resistance brought about by collective will, awakening people's consciousness and collective determination. Examples are as follows:

*   End of oppressive British colonialism in India under the charismatic leadership of Gandhi;
*   End of racial discrimination in 1960 in the USA, brought on by the efforts of Martin Luther King;
*   End of apartheid in South Africa under the charismatic leadership of Nelson Mandela;
*   Successful continuity of environmental movements of the Bishnoi (1730) and Chipko (Hug) movement (1977); and
*   Pursuance of vegetarianism as well as non-use of intoxicants by the Bishnoi.

Hence, this integrated theoretical framework for transnational social work, too, can succeed if applied sincerely in its true spirit.

## Notes

1 Evolution of Protestant Ethics (Calvinist ethics) favouring growth of industrial capitalism as captured by Max Weber in his classical work *The Protestant Ethic and the Spirit of Capitalism* (1996).
2 The cultural ethics after the French Revolution that took over all of Europe.
3 Evolution of the Nation State after the Westphalian Treaty and the historic document of Magna Carta, besides the evolution of modern bureaucracy as analysed by Max Weber (1996).
4 Evolution and growth of capitalism and industrialisation over feudalism in Europe.

## References

Agrawal, A., 2004. *Max Weber and modern sociological theories*. Jaipur: Rawat Publications.

Barber, B., 2004. 'Jihad vs. McWorld', in F.J. Lechner and J. Boli, eds, *The Globalization Reader*. Oxford: Blackwell Publishing, 32–40.

Beitz, C.R., 1986. 'Amartya Sen's resources, values and development', *Economics and Philosophy* 2(2): 282–91.

Commission Our Global Neighborhood, 1995. *Our global neighborhood. The report of the Commission on Global Governance*. Oxford, New York: Oxford University Press.

Deen Dayal Upadhyaya, Pt., 1965. Speech delivered on 'Integral Humanism' in Bombay on April 22–25 1965 by Pt. Deendayal Upadhyaya in the form of four lectures. Available online at http://deendayalupadhyay.org/speeches.html [Accessed 10 January 2016].

Kabeer, N., 1999. 'Resources, agency, achievements. Reflections on the measurement of women's empowerment', *Development and Change* 30(3): 435.

Kueng, H., 2004. 'A global ethic as a foundation of global society', in F.J. Lechner and J. Boli, eds, *The Globalization Reader*. Oxford: Blackwell Publishing, 44–50.

Long, J.D., 2009. *Jainism. An introduction*. London: I.B. Tauris.

Mohanty, C.T., 2003. *Feminism without borders. Decolonizing theory, practicing solidarity*. Durham, London: Duke University Press.

Nussbaum, M.C., 1988. *Nature, function and capability. Aristotle on political distribution*. Oxford: Oxford University Press.

Nussbaum, M.C., 1990. 'Aristotelian Social Democracy', in R.B. Douglass, G.M. Mara, and H.S. Richardson, eds, *Liberalism and the good*. New York: Routledge, 207–22.

Nussbaum, M.C., 2000. *Women and human development. The capability approach*. Cambridge: Cambridge University Press.

Nussbaum, M.C., and Cohen, J., 1996. *For love of country. Debating the limits of patriotism*. Boston: Beacon Press.

Putnam, R., 2000. *Bowling alone. The collapse and revival of American community*. New York: Simon and Schuster.

Said, E., 1984. *The world, the text and the critic*. Harvard: Harvard University Press.

Sen, A.K., 1985. *Commodities and Capabilities*. Oxford: Elsevier.

Sen, A.K., 1992. *Inequality reexamined*. Oxford: Oxford University Press.

Sen, A.K., 2004. 'How to judge globalism', in F.J. Lechner and J. Boli, eds, *The Globalization Reader*. Oxford: Blackwell Publishing, 17.

Shiva, V. *Empowering Women* [online]. Available from: https://likeawhisper.files.wordpress.com/2009/03/empoweringwomen.pdf [Accessed 30 June 2015].

Sugden, R., 1993. 'Welfare, resources and capabilities. A review of inequality reexamined by Amartya Sen', *Journal of Economic Literature* (31): 1952–3.

Swamy, S., 2006. *Hindus under siege. The way out*. New Delhi: Har-anand Publications.

Wallace, W.L., 1969. *Sociological theory. An introduction*. London: Heinemann.

Wallerstein, N., 1992. 'Powerlessness, empowerment and health. Implications for health promotion programs', *American Journal of Health Promotion* 6(3): 197–205.

Weber, M., 1996. *The Protestant ethic and the spirit of capitalism*. Los Angeles, Calif.: Roxbury Pub. Co.

Wu, B., 2011. *Whose culture has capital? Class, culture, migration and mothering*. Bern: Peter Lang AG, International Academic Publishers.

# 4 Social work as a human rights profession?

*Dagmar Oberlies*

Social work is often characterised as a 'human rights profession' (UN 1994). In its Ethical Principles, the International Federation of Social Workers (IFSW) describes social work as 'based on respect for the inherent worth and dignity of all people, and the rights that follow from this. Social Workers should uphold and defend each person's physical, psychological, emotional and spiritual integrity and well-being' (IFSW 2012b). Moreover, the Federation makes repeated reference to human rights in its global educational standards and requires educational institutions to educate students regarding the basic questions of human rights and international human rights instruments (IFSW 2012b, Subsection 8.8).

Human rights appear as something general, as something 'you cannot not want', and therefore face persistent criticism from postcolonial theory for their paradoxes and limitations (Spivak 1991: 235), and also from a humanistic perspective regarding their use in justifying international interventionism (Chandler 2006). However, the stance that human rights offer a non/anti-neoliberal idea (Staub-Bernasconi 2007) is, at best, unhistorical (Joas 2006) and socially romantic, and at worst misleading, since the freedom to act and contract is one of the oldest human rights (Weber 1976; Joas 2006). Therefore, human rights might better be viewed as a hybrid construct, which provides arguments on many sides but no clear orientation.

## Derivation of human rights

There is no unanimity on the question of exactly when or where the recognition of human rights began: while many start with antiquity (e.g. the Cyrus Cylinder, about 600 BC), lawyers might point to the (hard-won) Magna Carta of 1215, which prohibited arbitrary arrests. Still others see its intellectual origins in the Enlightenment or in the revolutionary and independence movements of the late eighteenth century. Contrary to these Euro-centric interpretations, Sen refers to early roots in Asia (Sen 2004).

There is also no uniform opinion on how religious values (altruism etc.) have influenced the intellectual history of human rights. Often enough, human rights had to be enforced against religious institutions (Joas 2013: 40). However, protestant dissenters who fled to America to escape religious persecution had an important influence on the formulation of the Declaration of Independence (Joas 2006, 2013: 40). This is evident even today in how differently western and Islamic countries understand freedom of belief – as the right to change one's belief (western), and the right to profess one's belief without interference (see Article 10 of the Cairo Declaration on Human Rights in Islam). But still, the fact that human rights principles of the late eighteenth century have survived (with only the 'right to resist', originally also considered a 'human right', falling by the wayside), and are a worldwide reference point, shows their 'weight' as an idea – and as an emancipation project: just think of the abolition of slavery or of female suffrage.

The modern history of human rights begins with the atrocities of Nazi Germany, whose crimes against humanity effectively unified nations in the formulation of basic values and standards. Today all 193 recognised countries of the world are members of the United Nations and accept its founding Charter, including the obligation to protect human rights (Art. 1 No. 3). Since the founding of the United Nations, the instruments for the protection of human rights have been continually refined: if the right to civil and political freedom was the initial rallying point (first generation), economic and social rights were subsequently formulated (second generation), and supplemented by a third generation of collective rights, including rights for ethnic and cultural minorities.

Table 2.1 lists the UN conventions and protocols since 1969 and their ratification by the countries included in this book.

Currently, there are efforts to develop human rights with respect to sexual orientation and gender identity: a Resolution to this effect by the UN General Assembly has been signed by 95 (western) countries; whereas 54 – predominantly Islamic countries – have expressly rejected this Resolution.

### The theory of human rights

Human rights are consensus builders – including through their formulation. In his theory of human rights, Sen (2004: 339) describes human rights as values that are widely supported regardless of how repressive the system is and that they would find broader acceptance if they could be discussed openly.

#### Human rights as a claim for respect

In the light of traditional (philosophical) understanding, human rights are 'natural' (inherent), i.e. pre-state rights, which can be claimed not only vis-à-vis governments but vis-à-vis all people. Every person has a right to be respected by others and is obliged to respect others. Therefore, human rights have been called 'moral rights' or 'ethical demands' (Sen 2004). They demand the same moral respect for and from all people – regardless of their national origin, gender, sexual orientation or ethnic, cultural or religious backgrounds (Benhabib 2007: 7). Therefore, human rights should apply equally to all individuals, i.e. they should be universal and egalitarian, and should not exclude anyone anywhere.

Table 4.1 Human rights instruments (UN)

| Human Rights Instrument | Abb. | Date into force | China | France | Germany | India | Israel | Malaysia | Morocco | Turkey | UK |
|---|---|---|---|---|---|---|---|---|---|---|---|
| International Convention on the Elimination of All Forms of Racial Discrimination | ICERD | 1969 | 1981* | 1971* | 1969* | 1968* | 1979* | NA | 1970* | 2002* | 1969* |
| International Covenant on Civil and Political Rights | ICCPR | 1976 | NA | 1984* | 1973* | 1979* | 1991* | NA | 1979 | 2006* | NA |
| Optional Protocol to the International Covenant on Civil and Political Rights | ICCPR-OP1 | 1976 | NA | 2008* | 1993* | NA | NA | NA | NA | 2011 | 2003 |
| International Covenant on Economic, Social and Cultural Rights | ICESCR | 1976 | 2001* | 1980* | 1973 | 1979* | 1991 | NA | 1979 | 2003* | 1976* |
| Convention on the Elimination of All Forms of Discrimination against Women | CEDAW | 1981 | 1980* | 2007* | 1985* | 1993* | 1991 | 1995* | 1993* | 2006 | 1999 |
| Convention against Torture and Other Cruel, Inhuman or Degrading Treatment or Punishment | CAT | 1987 | 1988* | 1980* | 1990 | (1997) | 1991 | NA | 1993 | 2003* | 1976* |
| Convention on the Rights of the Child | CRC | 1990 | 1992* | 1990* | 1992 | 1992* | 1991 | 1995* | 1993 | NA | NA |
| Second Optional Protocol to the International Covenant on Civil and Political Rights, aiming at the abolition of the death penalty | ICCPR-OP2 | 1991 | NA | 2015 | 1992 | NA | NA | NA | NA | 1995 | 1991* |
| Optional Protocol to the Convention on the Elimination of All Forms of Discrimination against Women | CEDAW-OP2 | 2000 | NA | 2003 | 2002 | NA | NA | NA | NA | 2002* | 2009* |

| Convention | Abbrev. | | | | | | | | | |
|---|---|---|---|---|---|---|---|---|---|---|
| Optional Protocol to the Convention on the Rights of the Child on the involvement of children in armed conflict | OP-CRC-AC | 2002 | 2008* | 1983* | 2004* | 2005* | 2005 | 2012* | 2002* | 1985 | 1986* |
| Optional Protocol to the Convention on the Rights of the Child on the sale of children, child prostitution and child pornography | OP-CRC-SC | 2002 | 2002 | 2000 | 2009 | 2005 | 2008 | 2012* | 2001 | 2002 | 2004 |
| International Convention on the Protection of the Rights of All Migrant Workers and Members of their Families | ICRMW | 2003 | NA | 2008* | NA | NA | NA | NA | 1993* | NA | NA |
| Optional Protocol to the Convention against Torture and Other Cruel, Inhuman or Degrading Treatment or Punishment | OP-CAT | 2006 | NA | (2014) | 2008 | NA | NA | NA | 2014 | (2012*) | NA |
| Convention on the Rights of Persons with Disabilities | ICRPD | 2008 | 2008 | 1986* | 2009 | 2007 | 2012* | 2010* | 2009 | 1988 | 1988* |
| Optional Protocol to the Convention on the Rights of Persons with Disabilities | ICRPD | 2008 | NA | 2010 | 2009 | NA | NA | NA | 2009 | 2015* | 2009* |
| International Convention for the Protection of all Persons from Enforced Disappearance | ICPPED | 2010 | NA | 2010* | 2009* | (2007) | NA | NA | 2013* | 2009 | 2009* |
| Optional Protocol to the International Covenant on Economic, Social and Cultural Rights | OP-ICESCR | 2013 | NA | 2003* | NA | NA | NA | NA | NA | 2004* | 2003* |
| Optional Protocol to the Convention on the Rights of the Child | | ongoing | NA | NA | 2013* | NA | NA | NA | (2012) | 2004* | NA |

Notes: (Signature, no ratification)
*Declarations/Reservations
NA = No Action

Two questions arise when this stance is taken as a starting point: the question of the enforceability of moral rights (Sen 2004; Benhabib 2007) and the additional question of who is obliged to grant these moral 'rights' (Nussbaum 2003: 37). This approach assumes that everyone knows what 'respect for human dignity' and 'the right to its recognition' mean. It does not define concepts but takes their 'natural' meaning for granted. However, this matter has been disputed over the centuries. Current questions are: Is there an 'entitlement to respect' (Appiah 2010) or does 'recognition' have to be earned (Internet Encyclopedia of Philosophy)?

### Human rights as a postulate of equality

The U.S. Declaration of Independence (1776) asserted the equality of all 'men' to be 'self-evident'. Nevertheless, women (and slaves) were excluded from the category of 'men with rights' (Hunt 2007: 148). The distinction between civil rights, which presuppose 'membership', and human rights, which belong to all people, also highlights this problem (Hunt 2007: 184). Even today, conventions against racial discrimination contain permissions to treat 'foreigners' differently (Arts. 1, par 2 of ICERD and 3, par 2 of Directive 2000/78/EC). So, what does 'equality' mean in the face of obvious differences?

### Human rights as a commitment to (social) justice

The concept of equality is closely linked to the question of social justice (Nussbaum 2003). Again, the definition of 'just' is subject to a (difficult) theoretical debate. There appears to be no dispute that opportunities must be equally distributed within a society (distributive justice). However, the extent to which wealth may be 'redistributed' is subject to controversial discussion (re-distributive justice) since there is also something 'unjust' about taking things away from people. Rawls (1999) focuses on the question of fairness: he argues that social inequality is only justified if it is advantageous to all. By contrast, Sen (2004, 2005, 2009) and Nussbaum (2003) wish everybody to receive as much as is needed to create lives with the greatest possible opportunities (capabilities). Human Rights are then 'entitlements to capabilities' (Sen 2005). Perceptions of social justice reveal a three-tier concept: (1) equal opportunities and/or rights, including equal access to resources; (2) fairness for and acceptance of everyone, embracing or tolerating differences among diverse groups, and acting ethically towards other people regardless of group membership; and (3) promoting justice and combating injustice and unfair treatment, especially for oppressed or disadvantaged groups. This implies that social justice means, 'actively working or doing something to promote social justice ... such as working to empower people from diverse groups, or doing something about injustices' (Torres-Harding et al. 2014: 59). However, putting the idea into practice is yet another challenge that social work has to face (Hytten and Bettez 2011).

*Human rights as rights of the individual*

However, the history of human rights is best described as a process, 'in which every single human being has increasingly, and with ever-increasing motivational and sensitising effects, been viewed as sacred, and this understanding has been institutionalised in law' (Joas 2013: 5). As Pinker puts it, human rights are a humanitarian revolution in the rise of empathy and the regard for human life (Pinker 2011: 175). Nevertheless, even if one places the individual at the centre, it is not easy to derive decision-making processes for social work, e.g.

- While it is easy to agree that there is no such thing (and should not be) as euthanasia, meaning 'life not worth living', abortion law in some countries such as Germany 'allow(ed)' an abortion if there was a danger that the child might be disabled (§ 218a, par 4 of the German Criminal Code [StGB]).
- While there is an agreement on the principle of 'inclusion' of children with disabilities in mainstream institutions, the German Federal Constitutional Court had to decide a case where the admission of children with brittle bone disease to an (integrative) Kindergarten could physically endanger them (BVerfG 1 BvR 91/61).
- While the 'right of persons with disabilities to freely and responsibly decide on the number of their children' (Art. 23, par 1) is unquestioned, it might result – in practice – in children with developmental disorders because their main contact is with their mentally challenged parents.

Moreover, the very idea of the individual endowed with (sacrosanct) rights is seen critically from a global perspective: e.g. the African Human Rights Charter emphasises obligations of the individual toward family, society, the state, and other communities, including the 'international community' (Art. 27), alongside rights and freedoms.

### Summarising

The concept of 'human rights' is anything but 'crystal clear' (Nussbaum 2003: 37). Its acceptability is purchased at the price of leaving underlying questions unanswered: what does human dignity mean exactly and when is it violated? How can we conceptualise 'equality' in a World of Inequality (Sennett 2002)? Do we all mean the same by 'freedom of belief' (see Art 18 ICCPR vs. Art 10 of the Cairo Declaration on Human Rights in Islam)? Why is marriage entitled to special protection (Art. 16 UDHR) – but not people who live alone?

A human rights orientation should not be understood as a timeless 'morality', but describes a process of continuous debate among competing interests and social relationships. However, unlike national law, the discussion lacks an arena within which the process of universalisation can be organised:

- On an international level, there is no elected parliament which could conduct a public debate (with a claim to representation).

- There are no adversarial proceedings in which various points of view can be argued on an international level.
- The arena of science has human rights specialists, but they do not reflect all parts of the world, especially not a balanced ratio.

The question remains: who defines human rights once we leave the moral high ground to look at the world from the grass roots?

## Human rights in practice

### Human rights as a government guarantee

Shortly after the adoption of the Universal Declaration of Human Rights, Hannah Arendt pointed out that not all people have the right to have rights, but 'only ... citizens of the most prosperous and civilized countries' (Arendt 1951: 275). The authors of the Universal Declaration of Human Rights wanted to protect these (moral) rights for all through the rule of law (Preamble). Therefore, human rights documents place obligations on signatory states (see Art. 2 of ICERD/CEDAW/CRC and Art. 4 of the ICRPD).

International human rights are commitments made by various states: they place no obligations on any state that does not place them on itself. Even after ratification, each state itself decides how to implement the obligations it has assumed into national law. 'Development aid' is often used as leverage to convince countries to implement human rights (see Art. 32 CRPD). Reports must be made at regular intervals, on the progress in implementing rights. Inappropriate implementation is denounced in 'recommendations' made by the competent UN Commission. Increasingly, human rights are being included in national constitutions – although being idealised as being supranational (Luhmann 1995: 233). Violations of law can be punished and social rights can be demanded this way. Social services are expected to support and protect such aggrieved parties. This system is, however, not without problems, since it is often the governments themselves that disregard human rights – as in the time of Hannah Arendt.

### Human rights as the everyday business of professionals

Sen sees 'a radical contrast between an arrangement-focused concept of justice and a realization-focused understanding: the latter must, for example, concentrate on the actual behaviour of people, rather than presuming compliance by all with ideal behaviour' (Sen 2009: 7). Therefore, in his considerations, he speaks of an 'imperfect' obligation (Sen 2004: 321), i.e. an obligation of an unspecified degree upon every person to advocate a right of mutual respect at all times and places.

### Professional ethics

The idea of human rights has been codified into specific ethical principles for social work professionals (IFSW 2012b). These principles place an obligation on social workers to oppose discrimination, recognise diversity, allocate resources equitably, object to unjust practices, and work against social exclusion and for an inclusive society. Ife has identified some issues with respect to the practice of social work: language, the labelling and handling of clients, supervision and training, structures, modes of operation, and boundaries as well as personnel selection (Ife 2012: 256).

The question remains: who decides on the choice of means – the 'affected parties' or the 'experts'? Social workers have largely seen themselves as the 'protectors' of human rights. This is surprising since encroachments on human autonomy, i.e. potential violations of human rights, are inherent in social work (Sennett 2002: 215). This ambivalence necessitates a focus on:

- Professional self-concept, particularly one's personal attitude toward clients;
- (Constant and institutionalised) evaluation of one's own actions and their – intended and unintended – effects; and
- Openness of structures and the 'inclusiveness' of institutions, both with respect to social work practitioners and their clients.

Concluding, three central mandates can be identified:

- Protection of individuals against violations of their 'rights' (freedom, needs);
- Opposition to systematic 'rights violations' and the denial of opportunities;
- Education in human rights and guarantees of institutional precautions.

### Organised advocacy and the mainstreaming of human rights

In all 'organized advocacy' (Sen 2004: 343) a central role is played by the media and lobbying groups, collecting information, contributing to the debate, launching campaigns and undertaking supportive projects. They publicise the human rights implications of decisions and expose violations of rights: human rights, says Luhmann (1995: 234), are recognised in their infringement.

A form of human rights orientation is the 'rights-based approach' and the request for 'mainstreaming' human rights. Human rights become the central focus of development and implementation of programmes and projects. However, a problem arises when social movements set a (human rights) agenda, which makes it difficult for individuals and organisations outside of the mainstream to be heard, and to obtain funding (Kennedy 2004). At times, the question may be raised whether the human rights discourse itself is a part of hegemonic (dominant) cultures.

### Education and standards

The Global Standards for the Education of the Social Work Profession (IFSW 2012a) can serve as an example of this. A comparison with the German Social Work qualifications framework clarifies the differences between human-rights-oriented and service-oriented approaches.

The Global Standards favour 'a critical understanding of how socio-structural inadequacies, discrimination, oppression, and social, political and economic injustices impact human functioning and development at all levels, including the global' (IFSW 2012b) rights-based approach. They require the 'ability to deal with the complexities, subtleties, multi-dimensional, ethical, legal and dialogical aspects of power' (Ibid.), and aim at 'reflecting cultural and ethnic diversity, and gender analysis' (Ibid.), allowing people to form relationships, and treating all persons with respect and dignity.

In contrast, the German Social Work qualifications framework 5.1 focuses on: knowledge, description, analysis and evaluation, planning and conceptualisation, organisation, argumentation and problem solving – and therefore can be seen as a service-oriented approach.

### The exercising of rights

What conditions must exist so people can exercise their rights? What does it mean for the affected parties when advocacy and empowerment are components of an approach? How can clients of social interventions, 'subalterns', speak and be heard (Spivak et al. 2008)? Persons living without papers, who work, might not be able to exercise their rights under the employment relationship not – as students often assume – because they have no such rights but because they fear legal consequences resulting from their residence status. This example shows that we can fail to empower people if we encourage someone to exercise his or her rights. At the same time, social work has to answer questions such as to what extent can the profession grant rights to its own clients: do they really have the right to make an autonomous decision (Sennett 2002: 215)?

### In summary

The formulation of Educational Standards or Qualification Frameworks does not relieve individual social workers and the profession as such from answering – for itself and for others – what constitutes the professional core. At the centre of this discussion is the tension between managing realities and changing them. The characterisation of social work as a 'human rights profession' appears to offer such self-positioning and self-description. After all, the International Federation of Social Workers (IFSW), the International Association of Schools of Social Work (IASSW), and more than 80 professional associations worldwide have adopted these principles and standards. However, how they shape the self-image of the profession primarily depends on how they are implemented in practice.

## The connection between human rights and social work

### Social justice

The history of social work is closely linked to so-called social questions: impoverishment, hunger, existential insecurity, urbanisation, migration. Today these matters are again (or still) global questions. In the past, social work included organising social aspects against the prevailing conditions. Debate over 'professionalisation' seems to have replaced the debate over social goals and conditions. The question is whether and, if so, how, the discourse on human rights can refocus the debate. Human rights, as individual rights to freedom, tempt one to push the plight of individuals to the forefront. Having said this, such rights can only be understood in a global context and implemented from a 'person-in-environment' perspective.

### Individuals as the focus of social work

Social environments embody 'resources' and 'repression' at the same time. Traditions, religious practices, or even group pressures are often the starting point for – if not the cause of – human rights violations. This necessitates a discussion of how social work makes individuals the focus of its work. Sennett charges that 'organized welfare services' (Sennett 2002: 215) do not accept that their clients are capable of determining the conditions of their dependency: only those who accord the weak their autonomy leave them their dignity, writes Sennett (2002: 317). Following a definition by the German Federal Constitutional Court, clients should not become 'objects' of social work. This presents social workers with the difficult task of addressing their clients and not their afflictions (Khan and Miles 2011), in other words, making dealing with needs of the individual – and not the social structure causing these needs – the focus of any action. As Kennedy (2004) points out, it is important that social work takes people's aspirations for emancipation seriously.

### Protection of minorities

Fear of the 'tyranny of the majority' (Tocqueville *et al.* 2010: 410) is very real for social minorities. The human rights discourse could demonstrate its greatest strengths here: by claiming equal respect for all people, despite – or even because of – their differences. Social work is not a natural ally here. Not without reason does Foucault (1977: 304) include 'teacher–judge' and 'social worker–judge' as part of the 'normalizing power' that measures, evaluates, diagnoses, and differentiates the normal from the abnormal. Sennett's question as to how much autonomy, i.e. deviation, among its subjects is tolerated by social work is also relevant here (Sennett 2002). Only if social work honestly appreciates the stubbornness, the deviation, and the otherness of its clients (and not so much the colourful bouquet of diversities) can it support minorities in their 'right' to deviate from the norm.

## Outlook: inclusion of a global perspective

In his history of violence, Pinker considers the Declaration of Human Rights to be a 'signal event': 'Each component', he writes, 'of the war-friendly mind set – nationalism, territorial ambition, an international culture of honor, popular acceptance of war, and indifference to its human costs – went out of fashion in developing countries' (Pinker 2011: 257). In turn, social human rights have significantly improved the economic situation in poorer countries in the last 30 years; halved the number of people living on less than one USD per day; improved school enrolments; reduced mother and child mortality rates; and increased access to safe drinking water (UN *News on MDG*). Recent history speaks for itself – despite all criticism of the details. However, the 'international community' has failed in at least two major areas:

1   Women: only two of the 130 so-called developing countries have equal participation of girls in primary education. Violence against women continues to be the greatest criterion for exclusion. It might take 150 years for women to receive worldwide equal pay for equal work.
2   Trade and the environment: trade barriers have not been dismantled; customs imposed by rich countries on imports from poor countries continue. $CO_2$ emissions have increased by 46 per cent worldwide since 1990 (UN *Goal 7*).

It is of some concern that the societal commitment of students of social work has had a tendency to decrease and idealistic motives are seldom seen. The reason may be that social workers feel more effective when working with (indigent) individuals than with respect to social conditions or within the global context.

## References

Appiah, K.A., 2010. *The honor code. How moral revolutions happen.* 1st ed. New York: W.W. Norton.

Arendt, H., 1951. *The origins of totalitarianism.* 1st ed. New York: Harcourt Brace.

Benhabib, S., 2007. 'Another Universalism. On the Unity and Diversity of Human Rights', *Proceedings and Addresses of the American Philosophical Association* 81(2): 7–32. Available from: www.yale.edu/polisci/sbenhabib/papers/On%20the%20Unity%20 and%20Diversity%20of%20Human%20Rights.pdf [Accessed 1 February 2016].

Chandler, D., 2006. *From Kosovo to Kabul and beyond. Human rights and international intervention.* London, Ann Arbor, MI: Pluto.

Foucault, M., 1977. *Discipline and punish. The birth of the prison.* London, New York: Penguin Books.

Hunt, L.A., 2007. *Inventing human rights. A history.* Princeton, N.J: Recording for the Blind & Dyslexic.

Hytten, K., and Bettez, S.C., 2011. *Understanding Education for Social Justice* [online]. Available from: www.stjohns.edu/sites/default/files/documents/adminoffices/asl-understanding-education-social-justice.pdf [Accessed 1 February 2016].

Ife, J., 2012. *Human Rights and Social Work.* Cambridge University Press Textbooks.

IFSW, 2012a. *Global Standards* [online]. International Federation of Social Workers. Available from: http://ifsw.org/policies/global-standards/ [Accessed 10 March 2014].

IFSW, 2012b. *Statement of Ethical Principles* [online]. International Federation of Social Workers. Available from: http://ifsw.org/policies/statement-of-ethical-principles [Accessed 30 June 2014].

Internet Encyclopedia of Philosophy. *Social and Political Recognition* [online]. Available from: www.iep.utm.edu/recog_sp/ [Accessed 20 November 2015].

Joas, H., 2006. 'Max Weber and the Origin of Human Rights. A Study on Cultural Innovation' (IIIS Discussion Paper, 145). Available online at www.tcd.ie/iiis/documents/discussion/pdfs/iiisdp145.pdf [Accessed 12 August 2015].

Joas, H., 2013. *The sacredness of the person. A new genealogy of human rights*. Washington, DC: Georgetown Univ. Press.

Kennedy, D., 2004. *The dark sides of virtue. Reassessing international humanitarianism*. Princeton, N.J: Princeton University Press.

Khan, A., and Miles, D., 2011. '"Talk to me, not my illness". Relevance of human rights and social justice in child and adolescent mental health intervention', in P. Jones, ed., *Eco-social justice. Issues, challenges and ways forward*. Kerala, Australia, Bangalore: De Paul Institute of Science and Technology; James Cook University; Books for Change, 307–26.

Luhmann, N., 1995. 'Das Paradox der Menschenrechte und drei Formen seiner Entfaltung', in N. Luhmann, ed., *Soziologische Aufklärung*. Opladen, Köln: Westdt. Verl., 229–36.

Nussbaum, M.C., 2003. 'Capabilities as Fundamental Entitlements. Sen and Social Justice', *Feminist Economics* 9(2–3): 33–59.

Pinker, S., 2011. *The better angels of our nature. Why violence has declined*. New York: Viking.

Rawls, J., 1999. *A theory of justice*. Cambridge, Mass: Belknap Press of Harvard University Press.

Sen, A., 2004. 'Elements of a Theory of Human Rights', *Philosophy & Public Affairs* 32(4): 315–56. Available from: www.mit.edu/~shaslang/mprg/asenETHR.pdf. [Accessed 18 April 2016].

Sen, A., 2005. 'Human Rights and Capabilities', *Journal of Human Development* 6(2): 151–66. Available from: www.unicef.org/socialpolicy/files/Human_Rights_and_Capabilities.pdf [Accessed 1 February 2016].

Sen, A., 2009. *The idea of justice*. Cambridge, Mass: Belknap Press of Harvard University Press.

Sennett, R., 2002. *Respect in a world of inequality*. 1st ed. New York: Penguin Books.

Spivak, G.C., 1991. 'Neocolonialism and the Secret Agent of Knowledge. An interview with Robert J.C. Young', *Oxford Literary Review* 13(1): 220–51. Available from: www.robertjcyoung.com/Spivakneocolonialism.pdf [Accessed 1 February 2016].

Spivak, G.C., Steyerl, H., Joskowicz, A. and Nowotny, S., 2008. *Can the subaltern speak? Postkolonialität und subalterne Artikulation*. Wien: Turia + Kant.

Staub-Bernasconi, S., 2007. 'Soziale Arbeit: Dienstleistung oder Menschenrechtsprofession? Zum Selbstverständnis Sozialer Arbeit in Deutschland mit einem Seitenblick auf die internationale Diskussionslandschaft', in A. Lob-Hüdepohl and W. Lesch, eds, *Ethik Sozialer Arbeit. Ein Handbuch*. Paderborn: Schöningh; UTB, 20–54.

Tocqueville, A.d., Heffner, R.D., and Gregorian, V., 2010. *Democracy in America*. Signet.

Torres-Harding, S.R., Steele, C., Schulz, E., Taha, F., and Pico, C., 2014. 'Student perceptions of social justice and social justice activities', *Education, Citizenship and Social Justice* 9(1): 55–66. Available from: http://esj.sagepub.com/content/early/2014/02/05/1746197914520655.full.pdf [Accessed 1 February 2016].

UN, *Goal 7: Ensure Environmental Sustainability* [online]. Available from: www.un.org/millenniumgoals/environ.shtml [Accessed 20 November 2015].

UN, *News on Millennium Development Goals* [online]. Available from: www.un.org/millenniumgoals/ [Accessed 20 November 2015].

UN, *Ratification of 18 International Human Rights Treaties* [online]. Available from: http://indicators.ohchr.org/ [Accessed 20 August 2015].

UN, 1994. *Human Rights and Social Work* [online]. Available from: http://cdn.ifsw.org/assets/ifsw_24626-7.pdf [Accessed 20 September 2013].

Weber, M., 1976. *Wirtschaft und Gesellschaft*. Tübingen: J.C.B. Mohr.

# Part II

# Country profiles

*Ursula Kämmerer-Rütten, Alexandra Schleyer-Lindenmann, Beatrix Schwarzer and Yafang Wang*

## Introduction

During the past decades, interest in transnationalism as a concept and in transnational social work as a disciplinary approach has intensified. The following part of the book presents country profiles of all the countries included in the case studies presented in Part III of this book, because we think that on global and transnational issues the 'local' answer can reflect a very practical way of (social) intervention. 'Local', however, must be understood in a wider context – nowadays as much shaped by global implications (globalisation) as by local or national frameworks. These frameworks are influenced by a number of aspects such as specific historical, legal, political, social and cultural implications. That is why we asked for a 'national' description – laid out in the following country profiles – of statutory, social and professional foundations concerning the countries presented in this book. The country profiles all follow the same structure, providing basic information on national data and statistics, historical background, legislation and policy as well as current debates and major challenges in relation to professional social work concerning education, policy and practice.

The country profiles aim to provide an overview on national particulars and developments relevant to an understanding of the emergence and the role of professional social work within its wider framework of national social policy. We are aware that within the restricted scope of a book it is not possible to provide a more detailed account on these issues. Therefore, the authors were asked to outline selective aspects, initiatives, reforms and debates concerning national policy foundations and professional social work to illustrate national characteristics and allow a deeper understanding of the case studies presented in Part III of the book.

Part II thus includes country profiles of China, France, Germany, Great Britain, India, Israel, Malaysia, and Turkey. The selection of countries (and authors) is based on the academic exchange during the international summer schools held in Frankfurt in 2013 and 2014. A number of criteria are relevant to explain the limited selection of countries: first, it is not explicitly intended to work along continental structures (Asia and Europe), because we argue that countries such as China and Malaysia should not simply be summarised or categorised as 'typically' Asian. Second, the aim is to avoid simple classifications and provide exemplary but more in-depth knowledge on a smaller number of individual countries. Third, the number of countries should also be manageable and thus limited.

Historically, social work as a profession grew mainly out of the development of social welfare policies and programmes in Judeo-Christian and Muslim countries (Leighninger 2008) which may be seen as a common link between the majority of countries included in this book. The major aim is to foster the transnational transfer of social work policies, practices and ideas. We consider the respective national frameworks – i.e. historical contexts, welfare state context and social work training and education – as important background knowledge in understanding the development of social work in each country.

Principally, the countries presented show individual national approaches concerning transnational issues in social work practice and particular ways in dealing with cultural, linguistic, political, socioeconomic and professional barriers. To a great extent these countries share similar problems and common social challenges in the twenty-first century but they also show differences concerning policy foundations and potential solutions for (trans-)national social questions.

It is difficult to compare the countries by using specific criteria which could be applied to all of them and which have influenced welfare state development as well as professional social work and social service provision. Some countries feature a strong secular orientation (China, France, Germany, Great Britain) while in other countries politics and social service provision is shaped by more or less fundamental religious influences (India, Israel, Malaysia and increasingly also Turkey).

In terms of economic developments, China, India and Malaysia may be seen as countries still in the process of growing industrialisation and on their way to developing a welfare state, while countries such as France, Germany and Great Britain are considered as post-welfare states influenced by strong neo-liberal policies and growing privatisation of the social sector.

While some of the countries presented are characterised by a rather strong national ethnic and cultural heterogeneity, such as China, India or Turkey, European countries as well as Israel (still) show a rather homogeneous surface often with a common 'national identity' (e.g. white and Christian in Germany, Jewish in Israel or Citoyenneté in France), despite specific national particulars concerning an evident ethnic heterogeneity resulting from the post-colonial heritage (Great Britain, France).

Most of the European countries presented here share a growing demand for cooperation in matters of immigration and asylum which have become even more important since the influx of millions of refugees from Africa, the Middle East and parts of Asia during 2015. Its significance for political and professional intervention and intermediation has recently expanded rapidly and is presently seen as one of the major challenges for politicians, professionals and the wider society. However, countries outside of Europe have been facing migration processes for decades – often as sending and receiving countries at the same time. Israel, in fact, is a country built on immigration.

In every country social policy and the provision of social work is fundamentally influenced by economic developments as well as by cultural values and religious convictions. The availability of professional social work as well as social work education largely depends on political ideologies and decisions shaped over time within respective national frameworks. While social work is also usually restricted to the national context we are currently witnessing increasing transnational activities and links across many fields of social work.

## Reference

Leighninger, L., 2008. 'The history of social work and social welfare', in B.W. White, ed., *Comprehensive Handbook of Social Work and Social Welfare. The Profession of Social Work.* Hoboken, N.J: John Wiley & Sons, 1–24.

# 5 Social welfare and the development of professional social work in China

*Xiaoxiao Xie and Yafang Wang*

The idea of social work was first introduced into China by western Christian missionaries in the late nineteenth century, and in the 1910s a few elite Chinese universities started offering courses on social work. Over the next few decades, social work experienced a lukewarm growth, before being brought to an abrupt end when the People's Republic of China (PRC) was established in 1949. It was not until the late 1980s that the Chinese government again approved the education and practices of social work. The present chapter will first review the history of Chinese social work since its inception, followed by a discussion of the welfare system in China. We then attempt to explain the systematic integration of social work into the existing Chinese welfare structure and its subsequent influence upon social work development in China. We conclude by pointing out the potential contribution of this country profile to a broad understanding of transnational social work as an emerging professional field committed to achieving greater social justice.

## The early development of social work in China and its revival since the late 1980s

Shortly after the gate of the 'Middle Kingdom' was forced open to the world following the Opium Wars, social work, along with many other 'Western knowledges' was introduced into China. In 1914, the Shanghai College, a higher education institution founded by Christian missionaries, started teaching social work as a mandatory course in its newly established sociology department (Colloqium on Social Work in China in the 21st Century *et al.* 2004). Other universities in China quickly followed this lead, and social work education began to experience a moderate growth in the next few decades. The outbreak of the Second Sino-Japanese War in 1937, and the ensuing Chinese Civil War greatly hindered the development of social work in China. After the Chinese Communist Party (CCP) took over state power in 1949, social work as both an academic discipline and profession was abolished (Xia and Guo 2002: 254ff; Yip 2007: 93ff).

The legitimate status of social work in China was restored after the country experienced rising social unrest and instability as a result of the transition to a socialist market economy in the 1980s (Brandt and Rawski 2008; Vogel 2011; Sun 2003; Wang 2001: 57ff). The first sign of rehabilitation appeared in 1988 when the Ministry of Civil Affairs (MCA) approved the establishment of a BA Social Work programme, first at Beijing University then at three other universities. Henceforth, the growth of Chinese social work was rather rapid (Xiong and Wang 2007: 560ff; Yuen-Tsang and Wang 2002).

At the policy level, social work was recognised as a legitimate profession first by the Shanghai Municipal government in March 2003, followed by the formal approval of the MCA in June the next year. In July 2006, the MCA and the Ministry of Personnel decreed the 'regulations for social work qualifications'.[1] Social work development in China received another major boost in October the same year, when Chinese President Hu Jintao announced the 'Decisions for Crucial Issues Regarding the Political Vision of Building a Harmonious Socialist Society' at the 6th plenary session of the 16th Central Committee of the Chinese Communist Party.

To achieve such an ambitious plan, it was decided that a large and strong social work team should be developed in China; in 2010, the first Master of Social Work (MSW) programmes were launched at a few pre-selected elite universities such as Beijing University and Shanghai University and within the next few years the numbers of university social work programmes mushroomed. It is reported that by 2014, 298 BA degree programmes and 61 MSW programmes were established at different higher education institutions (Yeung 2013; Wang *et al.* 2014). Along with this rapid expansion of social work education in China, we are also witnessing a growing emphasis on specialisation. Nowadays, Chinese social workers are trained to tackle a wide range of issues including care of the elderly, children and youth, schools, children of migrant workers, hospitals, mental health, disability, drug addiction etc. (Colloqium on Social Work in China in the 21st Century *et al.* 2004; Suet-Lin *et al.* 2010; Guo 2011; Wong and Li 2012; Wu *et al.* 2012; Dai 2013; Sim *et al.* 2013). It is also worth mentioning that in recent times, more scholars are concerned with, and are intensively debating, the future direction (indigenisation and professionalisation) of the profession (Yunong and Xiong 2008; Gray 2010; Gray and Coates 2010; Yunong and Xiong 2012).

## A brief introduction to the Chinese 'welfare system'[2]

To illustrate the Chinese welfare system as a basic political framework for the development of social work in China, we will first summarise the achievements and limitations of this system established in the early 1950s, before moving on to consider its current shape.

Shortly after the PRC was founded, a basic welfare system compatible with its avowed socialist planned economy was created. Despite being highly stratified and narrowed, this welfare system was nonetheless capable of meeting four essential social needs. There was, first of all, a governmental aid programme targeting those who suffered from poverty, natural disaster etc. Second, a primitive social insurance system was set up in 1951 to cover the city, though not rural residents who belonged to a work unit. Third, an elementary welfare structure was designed to support those who otherwise could not survive either because of loss of family, lack of resources or inability to work. Finally, Mao's China also took responsibility for the well-being of a few retired war veterans.

There are three distinct features of this old Chinese welfare system: first, it was under full control and continuously regulated by the CCP; second, there was a particular paternalistic aspect to the system (Leung and Nann 1995: 159); third, there was a structurally determined inequality in terms of welfare provision between urban and rural residents. It should be noted that the household registration system/'Hukou' (户口制度) which created this urban/rural division in the first place remains largely intact today.[3]

The old Chinese welfare system of Mao's era started crumbling towards the end of the 1970s. In a new historical context of 'reform and opening up', the Chinese government began to delegate some of its welfare duties to other social or semi-governmental agencies. Nevertheless, this process of restructuring the Chinese welfare system to 'welfare pluralism' is always under the close and incessant supervision of the CCP, and retains rather than discards a few key institutional arrangements and rules of the past. For the moment, we shall highlight four distinctive characteristics of the current Chinese welfare system.

First, the internal governing structure of the Chinese government is still highly centralised despite a recent call for building up 'small government, big society' (Wang 2014). Second, whereas the third sector has continued to grow since 1978, it has not yet acquired a de facto autonomy. Third, it is also noted that the CCP has been gradually adopting a few neo-liberal types of governing strategies (Wang 2012). For example, there is a clear tendency towards increasing marketisation and privatisation of state-provided welfare benefits (public housing, education and medical insurance), which unfortunately has not succeeded in significantly reducing, but rather sometimes increasing, existing social inequalities (Sun and Guo 2013). Finally, although in recent years the central government has become more attuned to the welfare inequality between the city and rural residents caused by the Hukou system, the decision to have it abolished completely has not yet been made.

## The structurally determined dilemma faced by Chinese social work

Based on the above outline of the Chinese welfare system, the remaining part of this chapter will map out the existing structure of welfare agencies/providers before addressing one among many potential challenges faced by future Chinese social work.

In urban areas, welfare providers normally consist of public agencies, mass organisations, work units, street committees/residence committees (RCs), and NGOs. Within the first category of the above-mentioned welfare providers, i.e. public agencies, the main institutions charged for appropriating and delivering welfare benefits include the Ministry of Social Security, the MCA and a few other relevant governmental departments at different administrative levels. In regard to the traditional mass organisations, e.g. Chinese Women's Federation, China Disabled Persons' Federation, and the Communist Youth League, while in theory they are not official governmental agencies, in reality, all of them are supervised by the CCP government and act as a 'second government' or semi-public agencies, and thus are also responsible for distributing certain welfare benefits (Wang 2014).

In addition to the mass organisations just mentioned, RCs are also considered a semi-public agency (Wang 2014); a remnant of the socialist past, RCs were established by the Chinese government in the 1950s as a semi-governmental apparatus deployed at the local and community levels. One of the main duties of RCs is to provide basic welfare benefits to residents living in a particular community or neighbourhood. In the past, typical members of an RC consisted of a few 'old or middle-aged aunts'. Despite the fact of having received little if no formal professional social work training, these semi-official state employees are very efficient in terms of both addressing various issues in the community (e.g. mediating in interpersonal conflicts, caring for the unemployed and the old, etc.) and implementing the tasks assigned by the state (keeping social order, doing propaganda work for the CCP etc., Yan and Gao 2007; Lee and Zhang 2013; Tomba 2014). Nevertheless, in more recent years, we have observed that social workers have been increasingly recruited into existing RCs. It is hoped that in doing so, the community level of governance can be improved. One of the consequences of this development, however, is the potential conflict between the institutional position that RCs occupied in the single party structure and the avowed principle of professional social work. Social workers newly recruited to RCs may find it hard to adjust to such a working environment, because the main duties assigned to them are administrative rather than service-oriented.

Another paradoxical aspect of the Chinese welfare provision structure is the growing importance occupied by the newly emerging 'semi-governmental' NGOs. Established either directly by the government itself or by former public servants, this type of 'semi-governmental' Chinese NGO is entrusted by the government with distributing welfare benefits on its behalf. The relegation of certain welfare responsibilities traditionally reserved by the State is confirmed in a new social policy issued in 2010. What is crucial here is that this particular type of NGO with a strong governmental connection gained an upper hand, when competing for a few already limited opportunities with those without close links to government. It is also worth noting that, more recently, the Chinese government has started referring to both the 'semi-governmental' Chinese NGOs and the aforementioned mass organisations as 'social-hub organisations'. Yet, as Wang contends, what this new title really implies is not that the above-mentioned two types of organisation serve as a 'bridge between government and NGOs' but rather a new model of managing the emerging social organisations in China (Wang 2014).

With regard to those few NGOs striving for high levels of autonomy, it is very unlikely that they will be prosperous in the foreseeable future, largely because of the lack of resources and insufficient institutional support. To a large extent, their survival depends on how well they liaise with different levels of government. It is in this sense that they can be defined as semi-autonomous agencies.

To better explain the current structure of welfare providers in urban China, two illustrative charts are offered below:

*Table 5.1* Basic structure of welfare providers in China's urban areas

| | |
|---|---|
| Ministries of social security, of civil affairs, and governmental welfare departments at various vertical administration levels | Public agencies |
| Hub social organisations, e.g. mass organisations, and semi-public NGOs | Semi-public agencies |
| Street committees or resident committees | Semi-public agencies |
| NGOs | Semi-free agencies |

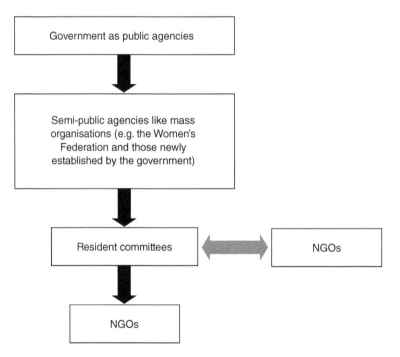

*Figure 5.1* Relationships between NGOs and public/semi-public agencies in providing welfare benefits

Table 5.1 and Figure 5.1 show that NGOs in China normally lie at the bottom of the administrative hierarchy of welfare provision and often have the same status, or even lower, as RCs.

Because most Chinese social workers are employed either by semi-autonomous NGOs or semi-public agencies, both of which, as argued above, are well incorporated into the existing governmental structure of welfare provision, their professional identities have been inevitably compromised by the raison d'être of the Chinese State. In other words, social workers in China often work as de facto government employees whose dual duties include, on the one hand, delivering basic welfare benefits, and on the other, helping to maintain social stability and building a 'harmonious society' (Zhang 2009). This 'instrumentalisation' of social work in China (Chen 2010) also determines that the capacities of Chinese social workers to provide client-centred services and campaign for social justice are rather limited. The challenge faced by Chinese social workers then is how to work within the single party state structure without completely losing their professional identification.

## Concluding remarks

This chapter first reviewed the historical and more recent development of Chinese social work, before turning attention to the welfare system in China. We identified five different types of welfare providers in the country, and considered how the institutional design has shaped and would still influence the professional identity of Chinese social workers. Our argument is that one of the major challenges facing future social work development in China is how to cope with a structurally determined tendency of de-professionalisation. From a transnational perspective, we suggest that the dilemmas faced by Chinese social work indicate the importance of understanding the paradoxical relationship between a commitment of social work to addressing issues related to social injustice/inequality and each country's unique socio-political structure and historical tradition.[4]

## Notes

1 There are three types of social workers according to this regulation: assistant social worker, junior and senior social worker.
2 Please note that we placed the quotation marks around the words 'welfare system'. We used quotation marks here in order to suggest that this term 'welfare system' has acquired a different meaning in the Chinese context; we attempt to explain this difference later in this section.
3 The case study 'Education Inequality of Migrant Children and School Social Work Interventions', Chapter 13 in this book, describes this problem in more detail.
4 A good example is the incapability of social workers to solve problems, especially inequalities such as those faced by rural migrant children. This is discussed in more detail in the case study of China (see Chapter 13).

## References

Brandt, L., and Rawski, T.G., 2008. *China's great economic transformation*. Cambridge, New York: Cambridge University Press.
Chen, T., 2010. Chonggou Shehui Gongzuo Zhuanye de Shiming. *Zhongguo Shehui Gongzuo Yanjiu* (8), 132–74.

Colloqium on Social Work in China in the 21st Century, *et al.*, 2004. *Social work in China. A snapshot of critical issues and emerging ideas: Proceedings of the international colloquium in Beijing 2000*. Toronto: Faculty of Social Work, University of Toronto.

Dai, H., 2013. 'Care for whom. Diverse institutional orientations of non-governmental elder homes in contemporary China', *British Journal of Social Work* 44(7): 1914–33.

Gray, M., 2010. 'Indigenization in a globalizing world. A response to Yunong and Xiong (2008)', *International Social Work* 53(1): 115–27.

Gray, M., and Coates, J., 2010. '"Indigenization" and knowledge development. Extending the debate', *International Social Work* 53(5): 613–27.

Guo, J., 2011. 'Family and parent correlates of educational achievement. Migrant children in China', *Asian Social Work and Policy Review* 5(2): 123–37.

Lee, C.K., and Zhang, Y., 2013. 'The power of instability. Unraveling the microfoundations of bargained authoritarianism in China', *American Journal of Sociology* 118(6): 1475–508.

Leung, J.C.B., and Nann, R.C., 1995. *Authority and benevolence. Social welfare in China*. Hong Kong, New York: Chinese University Press, St. Martin's Press.

Sim, T., *et al.*, 2013. Rising to the occasion. Disaster social work in China. *International Social Work* 56(4): 544–62.

Suet-Lin, H., Shui Lai, N., and Kwok Kin, F., 2010. 'Functions of social work supervision in Shenzhen. Insights from the cross-border supervision model', *International Social Work* 53(3): 366–78.

Sun, L., 2003. *Duan Lie: 20 Shiji 90 Niandai Yilai de Zhonguo Shehui*. Beijing: Shehui Kexue Wenxian Chubanshe.

Sun, W., and Guo, Y., 2013. *Unequal China. The political economy and cultural politics of inequality*. New York: Routledge.

Tomba, L., 2014. *The government next door. Neighborhood politics in urban China*. New York: Cornell University Press.

Vogel, E.F., 2011. *Deng Xiaoping and the transformation of China*.

Wang, S., 2001. *Shilun Woguo Shehui Gongzuo de Bentuhua*. Shejiang Xuekan.

Wang, S., 2012. 'Zhongguo Shehui Fuli de Neijuanhua ji Fazhan. Zhongguo Shichanghua Zhuanxing zhong Shehui Fuli Zhidu de Bianqian', *Zhongguo Shehui Gongzuo Yanjiu* (8): 1–38.

Wang, S., Ruanzeng, Y., and Shi, B., 2014. *Zhongguo Shehui Gongzuo Jiaoyu de Fazhan*. Beijing: Beijing Daxue Chubanshe.

Wang, Y., 2014. 'Social work in China. Historical development and current challenges for professionalization', *Social Work and Society International Online Journal*. Available from: www.socmag.net/?p=1280 [Accessed 25 January 2016].

Wong, F.K.D., and Li, J.C.M., 2012. 'Cultural influence on Shanghai Chinese people's help-seeking for mental health problems. Implications for social work practice', *British Journal of Social Work* 44(4): 868–85.

Wu, Q., Tsang, B., and Ming, H., 2012. 'Social capital, family support, resilience and educational outcomes of Chinese migrant children', *British Journal of Social Work* 44(3): 636–56.

Xia, X., and Guo, J., 2002. 'Historical development and characteristics of social work in today's China', *International Journal of Social Welfare* 11(3): 254–62.

Xiong, Y., and Wang, S., 2007. 'Development of social work education in China in the context of new policy initiatives. Issues and challenges', *Social Work Education* 26(6): 560–72.

Yan, M.C., and Gao, J.G., 2007. 'Social engineering of community building. Examination of policy process and characteristics of community construction in China', *Community Development Journal* 42(2): 222–36.

Yeung, W.-J.J., 2013. 'Higher education expansion and social stratification in China', *Chinese Sociological Review* 45(4): 54–80.

Yip, K.-S., 2007. 'Tensions and dilemmas of social work education in China', *International Social Work* 50(1): 93–105.

Yuen-Tsang, A.W.K., and Wang, S., 2002. 'Tensions confronting the development of social work education in China. Challenges and opportunities', *International Social Work* 45(3): 375–88.

Yunong, H., and Xiong, Z., 2008. 'A reflection on the indigenization discourse in social work', *International Social Work* 51(5): 611–22.

Yunong, H., and Xiong, Z., 2012. 'Further discussion of indigenization in social work. A response to Gray and Coates', *International Social Work* 55(1): 40–52.

Zhang, W., 2009. *Soziale Arbeit in China. Einführung in die Rahmenbedingungen, die Struktur und den Stand* [online]. Available from: www.igfh.de/cms/sites/default/files/Soziale%20Arbeit%20in%20China_Anlage.pdf [Accessed 10 January 2016].

# 6 Social action[1] in France

## Issues and development

*Nathalie Jami, Yves Pillant and Nathalie Segura*

### General presentation of France

France is one of the main actors of the European Union. It is the third largest European economic power behind Germany and the United Kingdom. On 1 January 2015, the number of inhabitants was estimated at 64.2 million inside the French metropolitan area. France is therefore the second most populous country in the European Union behind Germany. It is the largest country of the European Union and because of its history, has many links with the African, American and Oceanic continents.

France enjoys the highest demographic growth in Europe: the fertility rate is 2.01 children per woman which represents 828,000 births in France in 2010 with 54.8 per cent outside marriage. The life expectancy at birth is 84.2 years for women and 78.4 years for men (all statistics from INSEE 2014).

The administration of the French territory, traditionally centrally managed (from Paris), has been profoundly modified by the decentralisation laws of 1982 and 1983. Since then, the state has shared a part of its powers, mainly economic, cultural, and social, at different administrative levels: 13 regions, 101 departments and 36,778 municipalities.

The French social security system, created in 1945, is based on the distribution principle. It is funded by employer and employee contributions. This funding is mainly based on insurance paid by the labour force, managed equally by all the social partners represented by workers' unions and managerial organisations. Especially in times of crisis, these systems and institutions focus on the minimising of social risks and protection of individuals from life hazards, just as an insurance system would (Castel 1995). The total social security budget represents one-fifth of the GDP (Sécurité Sociale 2014). The budget deficit has become chronic and is part of the French national debt.

Concerning social issues, there are two main challenges: increased poverty and an aging population. Indeed, 8.7 million people live below the poverty line and the phenomenon of 'the working poor' is increasing (ONPES). The aging of the French population is an important demographic issue; in 2060, one-third of the French population will be over 60 years old (INSEE 2010).

## Historical evolution of social action

In 1945, out of the rubble of World War II, France reconstructed its national social security system into three branches (sickness insurance/workplace accident/professional illness; family; old age) and funding based on the working society's contributions.

During the 'thirty glorious years' or 'glorious thirties', the period of economic growth between 1945 and 1974, the initiative of social action was mainly private, with non-profit associations developing institutional answers to meet the needs of target populations.

However, the complexities of the social issues outstripped these schemes during the same period. Little by little, France lost the dynamics of a society of 'objective solidarity' based on a working society, where economic and social progress are linked. This mutation led to a social security funding shortage, as it could no longer be supported by the labour force. Instead of the institutional support of social needs, social projects, which must be negotiated between institutions and interest groups, became the norm. Also during this time, ideological debates took place about the role of the state in social action and ways to think of social work within an individual or a group perspective.

During the 1980s, instability and poverty increased, and as an answer to people's needs, the Minimum Income was created in 1988 by law.[2] The implementation of this minimum income affected the shift from an abstract distribution logic to an empowerment and participation logic (see also below). During this period France faced social problems such as massive unemployment (especially for young people and women), difficult life in suburbs, and discrimination issues. Policy was based on positive discrimination, which consisted in giving more to those who have less, in order to catch up. The 1998 law against exclusion[3] reaffirms universal access to rights for everyone, based on common law's social service. The same is true for Dalo's law[4] which takes this universal-access-to-housing logic so far as giving citizens an enforceable right in terms of housing.

Social action was modernised through the 2002 law.[5] A major notion in this law is 'social cohesion', a concept that implies strong engagement by civil society regarding social vulnerabilities (Donzelot 1994). The person affected by social action is then no longer 'just' a beneficiary of a public charity but becomes a subject with rights and plays a role in his/her own care.

The logic of the law of 2002 was extended by the law of 2005.[6] This proposes that society as a whole has to adjust to people's disabilities and has to develop its accessibility. The evaluation of the needs of each disabled person takes into account his/her aspirations as expressed in his/her 'life project'. They have a right to compensation in order to reduce the gap between the possibilities offered to each citizen and the limits imposed by his/her disability, and to increase his/her participation. In a similar vein, the reform of childhood protection (law of 2007[7]) confirms support for parenthood and the strengthening of parental skills.

Therefore, within fifteen years, important reforms and laws have changed the French social landscape. European and international policy guidelines such as the

UN Convention on the Rights of Persons with Disabilities have contributed to these changes.

## The institutional actors of the social action

### *State, social security and civil society*

The French social system has been built around three entities: state, social security and civil society, with an important differentiation between the social and health care sectors. Driven by the NGO (non-governmental, non-profit) sector, the management of specific issues, such as disability or old age, has crossed a divide and now a hybrid sector, combining medical care and social support, has emerged (the medico-social sector). Civil society's development of appropriate answers to the population's needs has thereby led to very specific initiatives which have generated new structures.

Government, local authorities and social security organisations are the principal financers of social services and their implementation is entrusted to non-profit associations as well as social and health care institutions. Thus, the field of social work is mainly funded by the state and based on global, sector-based, local or even cross-cutting policies.

### *The* Département *– the local territorial authority, leader of social action*

With the first social action legislations of 1982 and 1986, the expertise of social action was redistributed, along the subsidiarity principle, amongst the General Councils (elected organism of the *Département*) considered to be the most relevant local actor for setting up this policy. The General Councils implement local solidarity in sectors such as personal independence benefits for the elderly, childhood protection, and housing for dependent and disabled adults. The territorial approach has become a foundation of social action in order to fulfil the population's needs. Its principal aim is to bring the beneficiary closer to the management of social needs and to the funding of social action.[8]

On top of the decentralisation laws' projected aims, the government's own decentralisation has resulted in a split between the medico-social sector, which is managed by Regional Health Agencies (RHA, see below) and those social services which are integrated into the Regional Office of Youth, Sports and Social Cohesion.

However, for the future, an important territorial reform is being planned, and General Councils could disappear by 2020. Observers, for example the *Cour des Comptes* (Court of Auditors),[9] agree that the aim of controlling costs requires – above all – better coordination between the government, territorial authorities and social security organisations.

### *Persistence of state government and new public management*

The requirements of cost rationalisation and balanced spending explain the constant presence of the state, despite successive waves of decentralisation.

A recent example is a law called 'Hospital, Patients, Health, Territory'.[10] Based on this law, the RHA (Regional Health Agencies), created in 2010, have responsibility to manage health policy at the regional level. RHAs have taken over the former decentralised services and report directly to the government. Their purpose is to make health establishments more effective, meaning to give every user (*usager*) access to quality care, and to introduce and develop preventative health care. This regional management shows that the state regained control over the healthcare system with the main aim of reducing costs.

Through the RHAs, the Government also regained control over 'the constant evaluation of every social group member's needs and expectations' (Legifrance. gouv.fr) according to article L116-1 of the Families and Social Action Code. For a long time, social action relied on associative initiatives (mostly NGOs); it was civil society which expressed its needs. From now on, a downward logic is imposed, and the RHAs, which elaborate the Regional Health Plan, define the needs through data collection and fix the necessary actions through the interdepartmental programme concerned with personal independence and disabilities.

Within the new public management system, the general view of public policy is to pursue the control of public spending. In the social and medico-social fields, this objective is entrusted to agencies, which are financed by the Government, and launch projects generating competition between the various actors in the field. At the establishment level, new sharing tools, such as contracts formalising objectives and means, as well as organisations in social and medico-social cooperation, have been set up to meet the demands of reducing costs. The rise of this new logic has considerably weakened the autonomy of the social and medico-social institutions.

## Social workers

### Development of the profession

In France, social work is composed of various complementary professions (e.g. social assistant, specialised educators), which were developed throughout the twentieth century. These professions have been established by a continuous adaptation to social issues (social exclusion, elderly dependency, disability, and childhood protection) but also according to changing perceptions of the interaction between the individual and society.

In 2011, in mainland France, there were 1.2 million social workers, working full- or part-time (DREES 2011); 40 per cent of them work for individual employers, as nursery assistants, in home childcare or home support. The remaining 60 per cent work in various fields. With 383,000 social workers, the elderly dependency care field is the main area of social workers' employment in addition to individual employers. This is followed by the disability field (123,000 workers), early childhood care (55,000 workers) and work with individuals in social distress (51,000 workers) (DREES 2011).

The social work profession is currently attested by 14 diplomas, from level V (Professional Studies Certificate or Professional Competence Certificate) to levels

I and II (master's degree)[11] according to the definition of social work described in the article L 451-1 of the Families and Social Action Code (Legifrance.gouv.fr). To these can be added qualified workers such as nursery assistants who do not have access to a diploma; however, they do need approval from the General Council and must have undertaken specific studies.

Notably, the labelling of social action and intervention has changed; social action, carried out by 'social workers' (*travailleurs sociaux*), has developed and diversified to such an extent that now a multiplicity of 'other social workers' (*intervenants sociaux*) has appeared, having less professional training. These workers assume various functions with poorly defined tasks which are mainly related to social mediation.

### Social work education in France

Since decentralisation, professional training in social work has been entrusted to the regions. However, the diplomas are nationally recognised and thus the state controls the curricula. Social work education is not handled by universities. Historically, this field has been developed by private initiatives such as non-profit associations, who have volunteered to provide professional education to their employees or future employees.

Nowadays, initial and continuous training for social workers is divided between several governmental departments and several associative, university-based and public educational institutions. In general, the training combines theoretical lectures and professional training (placements). The social and medico-social establishments or services are considered as 'qualifying sites' and contribute, just as any training institution, towards transferring the skills necessary to graduate. The creation and successive reforms of diplomas have brought along with them an individualisation of the programmes that helps to transfer skills from one level to another. International partnerships are encouraged in order to exchange theoretical and practical knowledge or to discover specific social issues. At present, the educational sector is trying to harmonise programmes according to the European Credits System (ECTS) in order to ease the legibility and mobility of students and social workers.

Finally a revision project (UNAFORIS) is under consideration in order to simplify the social work education system and to improve coordination and complementarity between the education system's components in order to respond to social workers' needs in the field. A link between social work diplomas and university curricula is also planned.

## Principles of professional intervention

Social work history has been based on an 'assistant logic' (Castel 1995) and a conception of the individual as the beneficiary of social services still persists. However, since 2000, a new dynamic with a revision of the job definition, the introduction of a regulatory framework, and an evolution in favour of the user's individual rights, can be noticed. Social work is not there any more 'to do good', but to consider the choices of each person to steer his/her own life. The notion of 'accompanying' emerges, replacing the notion of 'taking in charge', which did not sufficiently take the person into account. Of course, this approach, i.e. asking the individual to be participative, active and dynamic, also includes the risk of neglecting the fact that some conditions are necessary for a person to be able to take charge of him/herself (Castel 2011). Yet, there is a strong will to consider the individual as a true actor by offering him/her a form of contract regarding the actions developed with him/her ('Active Solidarity Income',[12] 'residence contract'[13]) in a mutually defined project dynamic. The key word is 'participation' which becomes a principle (confirmed by the laws of 2002-2 and 2005-102) as well as a means (by participating the person learns how to participate) and a societal purpose.

The empowerment approach represents the process whereby individuals or groups considered as being excluded or at risk of exclusion learn the necessary skills to increase their power to act and a real capacity to decide how to manage their life. The term 'empowerment', 'almost untranslatable in French, describes a frequent practice of supporting a person who will gradually gain social skills/competences that will allow this person to defend his/her own interests' (Velche 2010: 200). But the concept of empowerment reaches beyond the capacity of acting individually; it is a strategic approach that aims to support the individual's and the community's efforts to develop or regain their capacity of autonomous action. This approach is still not widely considered in France, especially due to the low recognition of community work as an approach in social work (Donzelot *et al.* 2003).

Nevertheless, this approach is receiving growing acknowledgement, e.g. in health care, where HIV patients now directly control and influence the decisions that may affect their treatment and lives; or through official support[14] and financing of mutual self-help groups for people with mental health issues.

Altogether, there is a discernible transition from considering the user as a passive recipient of benefits to an active participant, who not only voices his/her needs but is an agent of his/her development. In order to truly reach this aim, institutions and professionals are obliged by law to use a project-based method and evaluate their work.[15] For a long time, actions have been justified by the right intentions. The current decade has made a 'pragmatic change' with a new logic aiming at goal achievement and evaluation of results for the users.

The professional developments in France promote (new) ethical standards and critical positions regarding exclusion, discrimination and segregation. Social inclusion as well as empowerment and participatory practices confirm the political dimension of social action.

## Notes

1 Social action encompasses social policies, their financing, and the social work implemented or supported by the state or non-profit organisations.
2 Law n° 88-1088 of 1 December 1988 concerning the Minimum Income.
3 Law n° 98-657 of 29 July 1998 against exclusion.
4 DALO: Law n° 2007-290 of 5 March 2007 institutes the right to housing as an enforceable right and includes different measures in favour of social cohesion.

5  Law n° 2002-2 of 2 January 2002, modernising social and medico-social action.
6  Law n° 2005-102 of 11 February 2005 for equal rights and opportunities, participation and citizenship for people with disabilities.
7  Law n° 2007-293 of 5 March 2007 regarding childhood protection.
8  For further reading see Baguenard (2004).
9  Founded in 1807, it is an independent public institution which audits public spending and informs citizens about it; see Cour des comptes (online).
10  For a detailed presentation of this law see www.sante.gouv.fr/IMG/pdf/vademecum_loi_HPST.pdf
11  Breakdown from the lowest level to master's degree level:
    – Diploma of medico-psychologic assistant (AMP)
    – Diploma of social life assistant (AVS)
    – Diploma of familial assistant (AF)
    – Diploma of familial and social intervention engineer (TISF)
    – Diploma of educative monitor (ME)
    – Diploma of social service assistant (ASS)
    – Diploma of specialised educator (ES)
    – Diploma of early childhood educator (EJE)
    – Diploma of specialised technical educator (ETS)
    – Diploma of social and familial economy adviser (CESF)
    – Diploma of familial mediator (MF)
    – Certificate of abilities for management functions and manager of a social interventions unit (CAFERUIS)
    – Certificate of abilities for management functions of an institution or a social interventions service (CAFDES)
    – Diploma of social engineering (DEIS)
12  The Active Solidarity Income assures individuals, without resources or with low resources, a minimum income which varies according to the household's composition.
13  This requires institutions or services to sign a contract with the resident individual specifying the given benefits.
14  Circulaire n° 2005-418 29 August 2005 regarding mutual help groups.
15  Law n° 2002-2 of 2 January 2002, articles 7–13 and 22.

## References

Baguenard, J., 2004. *La décentralisation*. 7th ed. Paris: PUF.
Castel, R., 1995. *Les métamorphoses de la question sociale. Une chronique du salariat*. Paris: Fayard.
Castel, R., 2011. 'Les ambiguïtés de la promotion de l'individu', in Collectif and P. Rosanvallon, eds, *Refaire société*. Paris: Seuil; la République des idées, 13–25.
Cour des comptes [online]. Available from: www.ccomptes.fr/ [Accessed 20 June 2015].
Donzelot, J., 1994. *L'invention du social. Essai sur le déclin des passions politiques*. Paris: Éditions du Seuil.
Donzelot, J., Mével, C., and Wyvekens, A., 2003. *Faire société. La politique de la ville aux Etats-Unis et en France*. Paris: Éditions du Seuil.
DREES, 2011. *1,2 million de travailleurs sociaux en 2011* [online]. Direction de la recherche, des études, de l'évaluation et des statistiques. Available from: http://drees.social-sante.gouv.fr/IMG/pdf/er893.pdf [Accessed 20 June 2015].
INSEE, 2010. *Projections de population à l'horizon 2060. Un tiers de la population âgé de plus de 60 ans* [online]. Institut National de la Statistique et des Etudes Economiques. Available from: www.insee.fr/fr/ffc/ipweb/ip1320/ip1320.pdf [Accessed 20 June 2015].

INSEE, 2014. *France, portrait social - Insee Références* [online]. Institut National de la Statistique et des Etudes Economiques. Available from: www.insee.fr/fr/publications-et-services/sommaire.asp?ref_id=FPORSOC14 [Accessed 20 June 2015].

*La loi HPST à l'hôpital* [online]. Available from: http://social-sante.gouv.fr/IMG/pdf/vademecum_loi_HPST.pdf [Accessed 20 June 2015].

Legifrance.gouv.fr. *Code de l'action sociale et des familles* [online]. Available from: www.legifrance.gouv.fr/affichCode.do?cidTexte=LEGITEXT000006074069 [Accessed 20 June 2015].

ONPES. *Rapport 2013-2014. Les effets d'une crise économique de longue durée* [online]. Observatoire national de la pauvreté et de l'exclusion sociale. Available from: www.onpes.gouv.fr/IMG/pdf/Fiche_synthese.pdf [Accessed 20 June 2015].

Sécurité Sociale, 2014. *Evolution de la part des dépenses de protection sociale (hors transferts entre régimes) dans le produit intérieur brut* [online]. Available from: www.securite-sociale.fr/Evolution-de-la-part-des-depenses-de-protection-sociale-hors-transferts-entre-regimes-dans-le?type=pro [Accessed 30 September 2015].

UNAFORIS. *Ré-architecture des formations* [online]. Available from: www.unaforis.eu/dossiers-thematiques/re-architecture-des-formations [Accessed 20 June 2015].

Velche, D., 2010. 'La diversité du travail protégé et assisté en Europe et son avenir', *Les cahiers de l'Actif* (404–5): 197–231.

# 7 Social policy and social work in Germany

*Ursula Kämmerer-Rütten*

Germany has about 81 million inhabitants (Statistisches Bundesamt 2015). It is the largest country in the European Union (EU) in terms of population. Germany likes to present itself as a modern, cosmopolitan country with a society shaped by a plurality of lifestyles and ethno-cultural diversity. Indeed, German society has become more diverse, more flexible and perhaps even more tolerant in recent decades, and yet the challenge to combat social exclusion and work against the discrimination of minorities is still a political as well a professional task and a major challenge for civil society.

The socio-economic change over the past few years – accelerated through the consequences of the worldwide economic and financial crisis – has led to the emergence of new social risks and greater diversification in Germany as well as in many Western societies.

'New poverty' and precarious living conditions are rising in Germany accelerated by a growing low-wage sector and insecure working conditions. This change is accompanied by the withdrawing of the welfare state and the reduction of public expenditure, which is influencing the provision of social services and the living conditions of many citizens directly, but more vulnerable people – e.g. people with disabilities, unemployed people, young families and single mothers, (ethnic) minorities or elderly people – are most severely affected (Uhlendorff *et al.* 2013; Schilling and Klus 2015).

This country profile, first of all, looks into the changing pattern of the German welfare state, which is still providing a comprehensive – albeit receding – foundation for social care and support, before, second, the significance of professional social work is considered.

## The welfare state context[1]

The roots of the present German system of social security date back to the last century when social reforms (enactment of sickness, accident, old age insurance) introduced by Bismarck at the end of the nineteenth century took place.

German health care funding relies on compulsory insurance contributions (sickness insurance scheme, long-term care insurance)[2] that workers and employers are obliged to make to designated health funds, which in turn pay the treatment costs of their members, while social care is mainly funded by state subsidies (taxes).

The German sickness insurance scheme maintains a sharp division between the state of acute ill-health and long-term care needs. Non-clinical health and social care/personal social services, such as supported accommodation or residential care, are usually not covered by the sickness insurance scheme but by a locally administered means-tested social assistance scheme.

The German welfare system rests on the traditionally strong idea of subsidiarity including the administrative structure that a body of welfare organisations is responsible for the provision of health and social care (based on state subsidies). In Germany, public authorities will only be involved in the production of services when the abilities and resources of the family, the community and organisations to serve their members have been fully exhausted. It is a complex system, which influences not only the provision of care and support but also how caring responsibilities are perceived in public.

## The role of the non-profit sector and the principle of subsidiarity in Germany

Pursuing the principle of subsidiarity, Germany is the prime example of a non-profit organisation approach to service production. Non-profit or welfare organisations are responsible for an important share of health care and social services and they depend heavily on public subsidies. Based on the long tradition of the 'subsidiary' role of the state, the role of intermediary organisations as providers of social services and health care became legally approved.

Today in Germany the institutions of voluntary welfare work[3] are organised in six large bodies, the so-called Central Associations (*Spitzenverbände*) serving also as 'umbrella' organisations (Bieker and Floerecke 2011). In 2012 German Welfare Associations ran more than 105,000 units providing health care and social services for people with special needs – e.g. children/youth and families, people with disabilities, elderly people etc. – employing almost 1,700,000 staff (BAGFW 2014: 7). The important role of the non-statutory sector has to be seen in the context of subsidiarity, the principle which applies not only to the responsibilities of families for their members but also to the relationship between statutory and voluntary bodies. Conditional priority is given to voluntary non-profit organisations which wish to provide such social help, and public social assistance bodies are obliged to support the voluntary welfare organisations (Jarré 1991: 212ff; Bieker and Floerecke 2011).

Among the six major associations providing personal social services in Germany (Wienand 2007; Bieker and Floerecke 2011) those of the two churches (the Catholic Deutscher Caritasverband and the Protestant Diakonisches Werk der Evangelischen Kirche in Deutschland) play a traditionally influential role.[4] They share the major part as provider of social services among voluntary agencies (Bieker and Floerecke 2011: 29), which has certain ideological consequences such as a corporate policy concerning service provision and staff selection.

However, although these considerations may often be more formal than ideological, they are oppressive retaining elements of control and repression, at least concerning the selection of staff. Major conceptual differences, for example, between a day care centre for mental health patients or drug users run by the churches or non-religious agencies are usually not apparent in an everyday working context.

German welfare associations still play a dominant role in health and social care however, increasingly applying structures similar to private enterprises in order to survive mounting competitive pressure, while private/profit-oriented providers are also entering the social and health care market in greater numbers, a process critically observed by different stakeholders (Wohlfahrt 2011: 92ff).

## Economisation and privatisation

The German welfare state has come under increasing attack during the last two decades and is experiencing considerable reform pressure. This has to do with the ideological onslaught of neoliberalism and increasing global competition, but also with the challenges arising from demographic change (aging societies), social change (erosion of traditional family structures) and rising public debt. To ease what was considered to be an increasingly unsustainable financial burden and a constraint on competitiveness, contraction of social safety nets in combination with labour market reforms and regressive tax reforms substantially yields inequality in Germany as in many European or Western societies (OECD 2008; Grabka and Kuhn 2012).

Today, issues such as globalisation, demographic pressures, individualisation, unemployment, greater social diversity and fiscal scarcity (Leibfried and Mau 2008) raise the question as to whether the welfare state is indeed sustainable. Increasingly, we witness that economisation and privatisation have a negative impact on the provision of social and health care services in terms of expenditure cuts and austerity policies, which are affecting citizens in need of care, but also social workers as part of the caring professions.

## Current issues in social work

### Social work education

Historically, the development of professional social work in Germany was influenced by strong Anglo-Saxon initiatives going into the twentieth century. Well-educated middle-class women in particular had strong political and social visions of equal rights and individual freedom (first-wave feminism, women's suffrage) and demanded participation: among them were popular activists and social reformers such as Mary Richmond and Jane Addams (winner of the Nobel Peace Prize in 1931) and their German colleague, Alice Salomon, who founded the first German college for social work in the 1920s in Berlin. Ever since, there has been a strong drive towards professionalisation in German social work. This has led – over the decades – to higher academic qualifications, further diversification and a strong emphasis on professional standards based on scientific methods, theory development and research as well as a professional code of ethics (Schilling and Zeller 2012).

Education and training for social workers is regulated in Germany. The regulatory bodies are usually the responsible ministries on a federal level. From the 1970s until the turn of this century the academic education was split into two different academic tracks indicating a relatively strong divide: social pedagogy or social work. Today, both tracks are combined under the heading of social work and to qualify and work as a professional social worker you need at least three years' principal academic education leading to a bachelor's degree in Social Work. The BA is the condition for state recognition, while licensing procedures through state recognition are in force in some regions but not nationwide. In addition to the bachelor's degree it is possible to go on for a master's degree[5] and specialise in particular areas of professional interest. The title of social worker is protected and in many areas of social work practice only qualified social workers will be accepted.

In 2004 the number of qualified social workers/social pedagogues centred around 160,000, but numbers have risen remarkably within ten years ranging around 283,000 in 2013 (Bundesagentur für Arbeit 2015). Some sources even estimate a number of more than 300,000 social workers/social pedagogues/counsellors in Germany including professionals who have other relevant and/or additional qualifications, of which 72 per cent are female. The rate of part-time employees (50 per cent) is remarkably high, made up mainly of women, who often shoulder part-time work and family responsibilities at the same time (ISA; DBH 2012).

There are two major professional associations for social work in Germany: the DBSH (Deutscher Berufsverband für Soziale Arbeit und Heilberufe) and the DGSA (Deutsche Gesellschaft für Soziale Arbeit). While the DBSH – member of the IFSW – primarily addresses social work practitioners, providing practical advice such as professional standards and a code of ethics, the DGSA has a strong focus on educational issues and research concerning theory development to strengthen the scientific basis for social work practice.

### Social work practice

In Germany, qualified professionals work in many fields of social work practice and with different client groups, such as:

- children, youth and families
- health care/patients (mental health care, hospitals, rehabilitation centers, etc.)
- elderly care
- people with disabilities
- criminal offenders
- substance/drug abusers
- refugees, migrants.

The national social legislation (Sozialgesetzbücher I-XII) provides the foundation for the provision of social services in Germany, and the availability of qualified social work is broadly grounded in respective national laws – e.g. in relation to child protection – and further accomplished by federal laws and directives.

Social workers address issues which have a profound effect on people's lives such as illness, poverty, violence, abuse and neglect, and provide multi-level interventions drawn from an eclectic knowledge base. Contemporary aims of social work education and practice in Germany are to empower clients, enable social participation and combat social exclusion (Sheppard 2006; Schilling and Zeller 2012).

While the German welfare state provides shelter and protection from severe threat (hunger, neglect) and social support to those in need, this does not mean that full social participation is always possible for people threatened by social exclusion. The reasons for this are twofold: first, neoliberalism and economic pressure have led to increasing cuts in public expenditure affecting the provision of personal social services in many ways and, second, discrimination (e.g. against race, sex, gender, religion, disability) and prejudice concerning 'otherness' (Bauman 1991: 8) are still influential and often affect the living conditions of social work clients.[6] At the time of writing it seems particularly worrying that social and racial exclusion and discriminatory attitudes are prevalent among the German population and displayed more openly, e.g. in relation to the current admission of refugees arriving in Germany in increasing numbers.

Nevertheless, there are areas of social work practice, e.g. working with drug users, where Germany exhibits a deliberately progressive and liberal approach in relation to social support.

Social workers in Germany have to assume a wide range of professional roles ranging from professional care and case management to advocacy and 'reflexive modernization' (Beck *et al.* 1994). Therefore, practices of assessment, management and the resolution of individualised 'problems' are one part of the professional profile, but beyond rather 'technical' interventions and the simple notion of 'problem solving' there should be knowledge about the influence of power, attitudes and (cultural) values.

Social work professionals in Germany often carry high responsibilities, for example, between the conflicting priorities of care and control. This situation is commonly known as the double mandate and social workers may sometimes find themselves 'trapped' between the mandate given by the state/agency (control) and the mandate given by the client (care). This becomes evident if agencies cut budgets and the support for families and children is reduced or even cancelled and/or high caseloads are difficult – if not impossible – to handle. In some fields of practice, for example child protection under the child protection act (Bundeskinderschutzgesetz), social workers are increasingly under pressure to fulfil their responsibility in the light of their heavy caseloads (DBSH 2014).

A third mandate (Staub-Bernasconi 2007: 198ff) is scientifically and ethically based and includes both a theoretical basis for interventions, methods and policies and a professional code of ethics with a focus on human rights and social justice. The third mandate emphasises the modification or refusal of illegitimate claims and mandates from society, social agencies and clients and may be seen as a base for the critical questioning of local, national/constitutional and international laws (Wronka and Staub-Bernasconi 2012: 81).

## Challenges and perspectives

The challenges for professional social workers are manifold, covering issues that will affect our societies deeply. Most pressing for the German welfare state and the 'social' professions are:

- demographic change and changing family structures
- global migration and internationalisation of social problems
- poverty and social exclusion
- modern technologies and the change of employment patterns in a post-industrialised world.

One of the major challenges for German society is certainly the demographic development: a low birth rate, an increasing life expectancy and an aging society. For more than 30 years now Germany has been witnessing fewer births: with slight fluctuations, since 1975 the number of newborn infants has been approximately 1.3 children per woman. This means that for 35 years the generation of children has been smaller than that of their parents. High rates of immigration to Germany prevented the overall population from shrinking accordingly. At the same time, as in other wealthy nations, life expectancy has risen continuously, and is now 77 years for men and 82 years for women with rising tendency (Statistisches Bundesamt 2015).

Germany is an immigration country. Only very recently has this notion become official governmental policy, although the country experienced some waves of immigration after the 1950s and the size of the population with a foreign background continued to grow, comprising around 16 million immigrants in 2011 (Hoßmann and Karsch 2011). However, social work professionals have been involved in working with immigrants for decades now, and successful professional efforts for social integration have been made, especially in cities and metropolitan regions. Nevertheless, there is still a considerable demand for (better) integration, which is currently further fuelled by the exodus of refugees from Africa and the Middle East among which we find high numbers of children/unaccompanied minors. For economically and politically stable Western countries such as Germany it should be manageable to provide food, shelter and acceptable living circumstances for refugees, but it seems more difficult to provide a framework for social acceptance among the general population. This is evident by increasing public activities (demonstrations, even violence) against migrants and refugees in Germany. Therefore, we are currently witnessing a strong demand for political response but also for continuing professional intervention to foster integration and social participation.

The Federal Government's latest report on poverty and wealth states that one in four Germans counts as poor or has to be protected from poverty through state subsidies. The EU defines those households as 'poor' that have less than 60 per cent of median income at their disposal (Lelkes and Gasior 2011). Especially at risk of poverty are children and single mothers, migrants and – increasingly – elderly people.

Although unemployment in Germany is currently officially not considered as a problem, because labour market reforms have created more (low-paid) jobs, the number of citizens with insecure working conditions and low-paid jobs is rising. That means increasing numbers of people and families are living on state subsidies although they are working full-time.

The German welfare state is under pressure, as has been shown above, but it is worthwhile utilising professional interest and power to keep its original interventionist sense: i.e. to handle tensions, help provide social security, social justice and to improve opportunities for disadvantaged groups and prevent social exclusion.

## Notes

1 Further reading: Wienand (2007: 20ff).
2 Long-term care insurance was implemented in 1995 in order to meet the rising demand of care in an aging population; since then it has undergone many reforms due to rising expenditure and more cost-effective service patterns.
3 Here the term 'voluntary' for German welfare organisations refers to non-governmental, non-profit making associations, which operate as *freie Träger* oder *private Vereine*. They are nowadays highly professional services and also may or may not draw on the work of volunteers.
4 Traditionally, Christian churches and their services can rely on special protection by the German state guaranteed by law.
5 Bachelor's and master's programmes have been implemented in Germany according to what is commonly known as the 'Bologna Process', facilitating European convergence in higher education institutions in the European Higher Education Area (EHEA).
6 In 2006 Germany transposed European Anti-Discrimination Directives into national law (General Equal Treatment Act) – eventually after many years of political campaigning. This needs to be regarded as a successful European policy outcome highlighting the importance of transnational cooperation concerning the exchange of ideas and policies (Chopin and Germaine 2014).

## References

BAGFW, 2014. *Die freie Wohlfahrtspflege. Von Menschen für Menschen* [online]. Bundesarbeitsgemeinschaft der freien Wohlfahrtspflege. Available from: www.bagfw. de/uploads/media/BAGFW_Imagbrosch_Webversion.pdf [Accessed 4 October 2015].
Bauman, Z., 1991. *Modernity and ambivalence*. Ithaca, N.Y.: Cornell University Press.
Beck, U., Giddens, A., and Lash, S., eds, 1994. *Reflexive modernization. Politics, tradition and aesthetics in the modern social order*. Stanford: University Press.
Bieker, R., and Floerecke, P., 2011. *Träger, Arbeitsfelder und Zielgruppen der Sozialen Arbeit*. Stuttgart: Kohlhammer.
Bundesagentur für Arbeit, 2015. *Gute Bildung - gute Chancen. Der Arbeitsmarkt für Akademikerinnen und Akademiker* [online]. Available from: http://statistik.arbeitsagentur. de/Statischer-Content/Arbeitsmarktberichte/Akademiker/generische-Publikationen/ Broschuere-Akademiker-2014.pdf [Accessed 10 January 2015].

Chopin, I., and Germaine, C., 2014. *Developing Anti-Discrimination Law in Europe. The 28 EU Member States, the Former Yugoslav Republic of Macedonia, Iceland, Liechtenstein, Norway and Turkey compared* [online]. European Commission. Available from: www.equalitylaw. eu/index.php?option=com_edocman&task=document.download&id=1328&Itemid=295 [Accessed 13 January 2016].

DBH, 2012. *Sozialarbeiter sehen sich als Experten für das Soziale* [online]. Fachverband für Soziale Arbeit, Strafrecht und Kriminalpolitik. Available from: www.dbh-online.de/ themen.php?id=417 [Accessed 10 January 2016].

DBSH, 2014. *Pressemitteilung. Kinderschutz - die Sau wird durchs Dorf getrieben* [online]. Deutscher Berufsverband für Soziale Arbeit e.V. Available from: www.dbsh.de/fileadmin/ downloads/2014-02-17_PM_DBSH_Kinderschutz.pdf [Accessed 16 December 2015].

European Higher Education Area (EHEA). *Bologna Process. European Higher Education Area* [online]. Available from: www.ehea.info/ [Accessed 10 January 2016].

Grabka, M.M., and Kuhn, U., 2012. *The evolution of income inequality in Germany and Switzerland since the turn of the millennium* [online]. Deutsches Institut für Wirtschaftsforschung e.V. (DIW). Available from: www.diw.de/documents/publikationen/ 73/diw_01.c.407154.de/diw_sp0464.pdf [Accessed 16 December 2015].

Hoßmann, I., and Karsch, M., 2011. *Germany's integration policy* [online]. Berlin-Institut für Bevölkerung und Entwicklung. Available from: www.berlin-institut.org/en/online-handbookdemography/population-policy/germanys-integration-policy.html [Accessed 3 September 2015].

ISA. *Sozialwesen. Sozialarbeit und Sozialpädagogik* [online]. Informationssystem Studienwahl & Arbeitsmarkt. Available from: www.uni-due.de/isa/fg_sozial_gesund/sozialwesen/ sozialwesen_am_frm.htm [Accessed 10 January 2016].

Jarré, D., 1991. 'Subsidiarity in social services provision in Germany', *Social Policy & Administration* 25(3): 211–17.

Leibfried, S., and Mau, S., eds, 2008. *Varieties and transformations*. Cheltenham: Elgar.

Lelkes, O., and Gasior, K., 2011. *Income Poverty in the EU. Situation in 2007 and Trends* [online]. Available from: www.euro.centre.org/data/1295444473_73292.pdf [Accessed 10 January 2016].

OECD, 2008. *Growing unequal? Income distribution and poverty in OECD countries*. Paris: Organisation for Economic Co-operation and Development Publ.

*Racial Discrimination in Germany* [online]. Available from: http://tbinternet.ohchr.org/ Treaties/CERD/Shared%20Documents/DEU/INT_CERD_NGO_DEU_19968_E.pdf [Accessed 10 January 2016].

Schilling, J., and Klus, S., 2015. *Soziale Arbeit. Geschichte, Theorie, Profession.* 6th ed. München, Basel: Ernst Reinhardt Verlag.

Schilling, J., and Zeller, S., 2012. *Soziale Arbeit. Geschichte, Theorie, Profession.* 5th ed. München, Basel: E. Reinhardt.

Sheppard, M., 2006. *Social work and social exclusion. The idea of practice*. Aldershot: Ashgate.

Statistisches Bundesamt, 2015. *Kurz erläutert. Bevölkerungsentwicklung* [online]. Statistisches Bundesamt. Available from: www.destatis.de/DE/ZahlenFakten/ GesellschaftStaat/Bevoelkerung/Bevoelkerung.html [Accessed 19 December 2015].

Staub-Bernasconi, S., 2007. *Soziale Arbeit als Handlungswissenschaft. Systemtheoretische Grundlagen und professionelle Praxis*. Bern, Stuttgart: UTB.

Uhlendorff, U., Euteneuer, M., and Sabla, K.-P., 2013. *Soziale Arbeit mit Familien*. München: Ernst Reinhardt Verlag.

Wienand, M., 2007. *Social system and social work in the Federal Republic of Germany*. 3rd ed. Berlin: Dt. Verein für Öffentl. u. Private Fürsorge.

Wohlfahrt, N., 2011. 'Privatisierung und Ausgliederung auf kommunaler Ebene', in H.-J. Dahme and N. Wohlfahrt, eds, *Handbuch Kommunale Sozialpolitik.* Wiesbaden: VS Verlag für Sozialwissenschaften, 89–101.

Wronka, J., and Staub-Bernasconi, S., 2012. 'Human Rights', in K.H. Lyons *et al.*, eds, *Sage handbook of international social work.* London: SAGE Publications, 70–85.

# 8 Social welfare and social work in Britain[1]

*Caroline Humphrey*

The United Kingdom (UK) comprises four countries – England, Wales, Scotland and Northern Ireland – and the adjective British is applied to citizens and residents across the UK. However, Great Britain refers only to the first three countries, and Britain refers only to England and Wales. Initially I shall sketch out the development of the welfare state in Britain, although some of the material is also pertinent to the wider UK. The focus then shifts to social work in England, since the devolution of central government powers means that professional education and practice harbour significant inter-country variations. Finally, I will survey the contemporary ethnic profile of the UK population and transcultural dilemmas in safeguarding young black and minority ethnic (BME) people. This transports us back to England, particularly its capital city, London, which is home to large BME communities.

## The welfare state in Britain

Britain has one of the oldest welfare states in the world. The Poor Law was formulated in 1601 creating institutions such as orphanages, houses of correction for delinquent youths, workhouses for adults and alms houses for elderly people. During the nineteenth century, this state apparatus was supplemented by the work of charitable organisations wedded to a conservative Christian philanthropy. By the turn of the twentieth century, socialists and feminists were pioneering a more radical community settlement movement, so that when social work became officially recognised as a profession, it bore the imprints of contradictory philosophies (Pierson 2011: 1ff). However, social workers across the political spectrum overlooked the global context of colonialism in which Great Britain had been incubated (Hall 1998), along with the suffering of Irish immigrants (Cemlyn 2008).

The welfare state was reconstructed in the aftermath of the Second World War. Its central pillars then were compulsory education, a National Health Service, social security benefits and the personal social services, with the latter being administered at local government level and delivered by social workers (Clarke *et al.* 2001). During this era of welfare expansion, the government encouraged the migration of workers from Commonwealth countries to compensate for the shortfall of indigenous labour. African, Caribbean and Asian immigrants helped to build the material infrastructure of modern Britain and to serve its welfare organisations, and created distinctive communities in metropolitan areas. They enjoyed citizenship by virtue of being born into former British colonies, but in practice it was a subaltern citizenship – immigrants were appointed to low-status jobs, confined to poor neighbourhoods, and subjected to racism (Laird 2008: 1ff).

The cyclical downturn of the capitalist economy in the 1980s and 1990s generated widespread unemployment, along with a raft of anti-immigration legislation. The UK carried an enormous debt from wars and welfare spending into the twenty-first century, and successive governments have been more or less captivated by a neo-liberal ethos which attempts to decouple welfare from the state (Mishra 1990: 18ff; Alcock 2009). There have been savage cuts to public sector budgets, repeated restructurings of health and social care bureaucracies, and incentives to develop privately funded alternatives to state schools and hospitals. These austerity measures have unfolded during a period of spiralling inequalities, and by 2012–13 it was estimated that more than 14 million people in the UK (23 per cent of the population) were living in poverty after taking account of housing costs (Belfield *et al.* 2014: 5). Most people who access the personal social services as voluntary service users or involuntary clients are poor (Hood and Johnson 2014).

## Social work education in England

The title of social worker is protected so that only those who are qualified and registered as social workers are allowed to appropriate this name. Those who work in social care without a social work qualification are designated as 'social care workers'. Social workers must be educated to degree level, and both undergraduate and postgraduate degrees are available. The British Association of Social Workers (BASW) is an overarching professional body for social workers across the UK, but the regulatory framework for education and practice is unique to each country in the UK, and much of the intellectual scaffolding for social work education in England came from the work of The College of Social Work (TCSW).

The education and career development of social workers in England is currently governed by the Professional Capabilities Framework (PCF). Its nine capability domains cluster around four themes i.e.

- Personal qualities manifested in professional life: demonstrating professionalism in one's entire modus operandi (Domain 1) and eventually professional leadership in a specialist area of practice, education or research (Domain 9);
- Ethico-political principles: adhering to social work ethics and values (Domain 2); recognising diversity and anti-discriminatory principles (Domain 3); and advancing human rights, social justice and economic well-being (Domain 4);
- Intellectual skills: acquiring myriad sets of disciplinary knowledge (Domain 5) and applying them in a critically reflective and analytic manner (Domain 6);
- Practical skills: assessing the needs and risks of service users and carers as the basis for service provision, care planning and legal interventions (Domain 7); and operating effectively in complex organisations and multi-professional networks (Domain 8) (TSCW 2012).

The curriculum reform associated with the PCF ensured that students rehearse practice skills in the university before embarking upon placements, and that service users and carers are valued co-teachers and co-assessors in social work education. However, it may not necessarily enhance inter-cultural working, and there is no inter-cultural capability as such in the PCF. Whilst there are three references to culture in this sense – i.e. race and faith are aspects of diversity; cultural and spiritual factors are components of our knowledge around human development; and adapting communications to take account of cultural differences is a practical skill – there are more references to organisational cultures and learning cultures (TSCW 2012). Arguably the 'unspoken atheism' in English social work has largely deprived us of the foundation for a critical appreciation of the role of religion in peoples' lives (Whiting 2008), notwithstanding recent efforts to bridge the gulf (Furness and Gilligan 2009). Ironically, part of the solution to inter-cultural working is already in our midst insofar as 25 per cent of social work students and practitioners in England belong to a minority ethnic group (Centre for Workforce Intelligence 2012), suggesting that social work educators could tap into this resource for inter-cultural classroom dialogues.

Once graduates have registered as qualified social workers with the Health and Care Professions Council (HCPC), they undertake an Assessed and Supported Year in Employment (ASYE). Subsequent career progression involves the pursuit of one of three pathways, although they are not necessarily mutually exclusive i.e. a social worker can remain in grassroots practice and undertake more specialist training, or climb the ladder into management, or carve out a niche as a professional educator of students and ASYE novices (TSCW 2014).

## Social work practice in England

Local government is responsible for providing statutory services to children and adults as prescribed by law, and has traditionally been the main employer of qualified social workers. However, about 50 per cent of the 87,442 registered social workers in England now work outside of local government – they may be located in education, health or the independent sector (Centre for Workforce Intelligence 2012). The latter encompasses charities, private businesses and self-employed individuals. Major charities providing social work services such as Age UK, Mind and Barnardo's are successful fundraisers, but smaller charities are often dependent upon local government grants; most residential care homes for adults are run as profitable enterprises; and social workers can supply their services to various agencies on an independent basis.

Local government caters to citizens who meet specified eligibility thresholds for statutory services, i.e. people harbouring complex needs, people at risk of serious harm and people who have neither the capacity for self-care nor the support of suitable informal carers. Those who fail to meet such thresholds are re-routed to relevant charities, so smaller charities and their clientele are destined to suffer when eligibility thresholds for statutory services become more stringent whilst local government funding for charities dwindles. Under these circumstances, social workers devote increasing resources to shoring up informal care by relatives and friends (Wilson *et al.* 2011: 428ff). Statutory welfare is brokered on an inter-professional and inter-agency basis on account of the multifaceted nature of needs and risks (Ibid.: 384ff), and The College of Social Work (TSCW 2014) has issued advice on when social workers should occupy the 'lead professional role', charged with co-ordinating the efforts of all relevant professionals.

In child care settings, many roles are reserved for social workers in accordance with primary legislation such as the Children Act 1989, the Adoption and Children Act 2002 and the Children and Families Act 2014 (TSCW 2014). First, it is mandatory for a social worker to be the lead professional when assessing children in need and their families for voluntary services. 'Children in need' includes children with disabilities; children whose welfare may be compromised by their parents' disability, domestic abuse, drug dependency or poverty; and unaccompanied asylum-seeking minors. If the threshold criteria are met, social workers will tailor a support package to the presenting needs. This could include emergency funds, equipment, parenting programmes or alternative accommodation (Wilson *et al.* 2011: 461ff). Children with disabilities and those with special educational needs are entitled to Education Health and Care Plans which can run from birth to 25 years, and parent carers and young carers are also eligible for support (Brammer 2010: 185ff).

Second, social workers assume the lead role in investigating child protection referrals when there are allegations of neglect, emotional maltreatment, physical injuries or sexual abuse (TSCW 2014). They convene child protection conferences and co-ordinate child protection plans, and if they require additional powers they can apply to the family courts under the Children Act 1989 for a range of orders to intervene on a compulsory basis in the life of a child and their family (Brammer 2010: 230ff). When there are parallel criminal proceedings, the police take the lead role in dealing with alleged perpetrators of abuse.

Third, a social worker is appointed to any child who becomes 'looked after' by the local authority, whether on a voluntary basis (i.e. children in need who are accommodated) or a compulsory basis (i.e. children subject to a Care Order) (Brammer 2010: 285ff). Finally, social workers undertake assessments of suitability vis-à-vis adults who are offering a home for a child (Brammer 2010: 309ff).

In adult care settings, there is no legislative mandate for specific roles to be reserved for social workers, so the roles which are typically discharged by social workers may be delegated to other caring professionals or social care workers (TSCW 2014). Three areas of work can be highlighted here. First, social workers are usually the lead professional when assessing the social care needs of elderly and disabled people and determining their eligibility for services under the Care Act 2014. This work typically involves securing a care package to enable people to maintain independent living in the community or to return to the community after a period of hospitalisation.

Second, social workers should act as the lead professional when making enquiries into allegations that adults are being neglected, abused or exploited (TSCW 2014). However, there is the presumption in English law that adults have the right to choose relationships and lifestyles which may be harmful to them. Consequently, social workers can offer advice on practical alternatives to adults who are neglecting themselves or being ill-treated by others, but they cannot resort to legal measures to enforce health and safety except when a service user lacks the mental capacity to make an informed decision on the relevant matter. The Mental Capacity Act 2005 enables social workers to assess the mental capacity of adults and to make decisions which are in the best interests of adults who lack mental capacity. Under these circumstances referrals to other specialists in the civil and criminal justice systems may also be necessary (Brammer 2010: 465ff, 487ff).

Third, social workers act as Approved Mental Health Professionals (AMHPs) under the Mental Health Act 1983. This legislation confers a wide range of powers and duties upon AMHPs when dealing with people suffering mental disorders, i.e. they can receive a mentally disordered person into local authority guardianship and they can undertake advocacy to protect the human rights of people deprived of liberty (Brammer 2010: 428ff; Wilson *et al.* 2011: 595ff).

In a nutshell, it is incumbent upon social workers in the statutory sector to manage the nexus of dilemmas around 'care versus control', 'liberty versus security' and 'rights versus risks'. This means that social work is a risky business, and when our service users or carers are the victims or perpetrators of serious harm, the media typically lambasts the lead professionals and their allies (Stanley and Manthorpe 2004).

## Transcultural dilemmas in the metropolis

The UK's transnational profile can be decoded from the 2011 Census: of the 63 million registered residents in the UK, 87 per cent identify as white British, leaving 13 per cent who trace their origins or that of one or both parents or grandparents to another country (Office for National Statistics 2011).

The increase in the BME population from 8 per cent in the 2001 Census to 13 per cent in the 2011 Census is attributable to the propensity of BME couples to have more children than their white counterparts, rather than any influx of migrants, asylum seekers or refugees (Laird 2008). According to the United Nations (UN 2014), there are fewer asylum seekers in Britain than in many other European countries, with only 23,500 new applications in 2013. Whilst adult asylum seekers can be held in detention centres or dispersed around the country pending the adjudication of their claim, unaccompanied minors are accommodated by the local authority (Brammer 2010: 565ff), and children who may have been trafficked into the UK are dealt with under child protection protocols (HM Government 2011).

The Equality Act 2010 defines race and religion as 'protected characteristics' (along with age, gender, disability and sexual orientation) in order to prohibit negative discrimination (Brammer 2010: 151ff). Nevertheless, research has consistently revealed the under-representation of BME citizens as voluntary service users and the over-representation of African, Caribbean and dual heritage citizens as compulsory clients in the child protection, mental health and criminal justice systems (Graham 2007). BME citizens have established their own support networks, often housed in religious centres such as black churches, mosques and temples (Laird 2008: 64ff, 88ff, 108ff), as well as charities campaigning against racial inequalities in the welfare state (e.g. the AFIYA Trust).

Questions of racial injustice have been superseded in recent years by those of cultural harm (International NGO Council on Violence against Children 2012). The pivotal event was the death of an eight-year-old African girl Victoria Climbié in London in 2000. She had been malnourished and maltreated by her carer who claimed that the girl was 'possessed' by 'evil spirits', and she was due to undergo a deliverance or exorcism ceremony at a black church on the day of her death (Laming 2003: 32ff). Anti-oppressive ethics and politics have not yet countenanced the conundrums wrought by cultural harm, and incommensurable worldviews, but government policy is that when culturally framed beliefs and behaviours cause objective harm to young people then the protection of youth must override respect for cultural diversity (Department for Education and Skills 2007). London has become the umbrella for transcultural work between the safeguarding children authorities, churches of all denominations, black communities and black charities such as the Victoria Climbié Foundation, the Congolese Family Centre and AFRUCA (Africans Unite against Child Abuse). Groups have been convened for African parents and young people respectively so that they can debate their cultural norms, values and beliefs and those of child care professionals (Briggs *et al.* 2011: 35ff, 41ff, 50ff). A key divergence is that the rights of the elders are enshrined in most African cultures, whilst the rights of the child are emblazoned on the child protection apparatus in the UK. AFRUCA has been at the forefront of transcultural education, rolling out training on African cultures for child protection workers and guidance on parenting and child protection for African parents (AFRUCA 2012). This has culminated in the launch of a National Working Group on Child Abuse Linked to Faith or Belief (2012), with a remit extending to mosques and Muslim communities, to other metropolitan areas, and covering multiple forms of cultural harm.

New civil orders and safeguarding policies are in place to prevent other forms of cultural harm such as female genital mutilation and forced marriages, along with criminal offences to punish those who transgress (HM Government 2014b; HM Government 2014a). Tragically, cultural harm may be exacerbated by cultural transitioning (Briggs *et al.* 2011: 32ff). For example, the elders of a family are more likely to maintain cultural traditions around arranged marriages whilst the younger generation is assimilating norms and values from the mainstream culture around autonomy and choice of romantic partner. This ignites intergenerational strife within the family. Formal remedies in the civil and criminal courts can only come into play if the authorities are aware of the problem. Yet it is extraordinarily difficult for a young person from a minority ethnic community to disclose their predicament to social workers as this is tantamount to shaming their elders. It is also disturbing for social workers to deal with such cases since it requires a departure from their professional norms around mediating in family disputes. The policy guidance is to protect the young person by invoking legal measures and removing them to a refuge if necessary whilst refraining from attempts at family mediation (HM Government 2014b). Charities such as Karma Nirvana have emerged from BME communities to campaign against forced marriages and to support victims and survivors, paving the way for more transcultural safeguarding initiatives.

## Conclusion

The United Kingdom is arguably a misnomer for a deeply divided queendom. There are economic divisions between a wealthy elite and an increasingly impoverished working class and unemployed underclass. Under these circumstances, policies of welfare retrenchment are likely to generate more social problems and safeguarding failures. There are also cultural differences within and between majority and minority ethnic communities. Given that inequality, diversity and population growth are positively correlated with social conflict, we are likely to witness more prejudice against asylum seekers and less compassionate understanding for cultural harms which manifest in some BME communities. Finally, there are institutional segregations within the social work profession, so that social workers in England, Wales, Scotland and Northern Ireland are educated and organised quite differently.

## Note

1 Acknowledgements: Dave Marsland and Liz Price provided guidance on social work with adults in England.

## References

AFRUCA, 2012. *Manual on child protection for African parents in the UK. A step-by-step guide to help prevent abuse towards children* [online]. Foundation for the Protection of the Rights of Vulnerable Children. Available from: www.baspcan.org.uk/files/Afruca%20Final%20Parents%20manual%202012.PDF [Accessed 3 November 2015].

Alcock, P., 2009. 'The United Kingdom. Constructing a third way?' in P. Alcock and G. Craig, eds, *International social policy. Welfare regimes in the developed world.* Basingstoke, Hampshire: Palgrave Macmillan, 109–29.

Belfield, C., Cribb, J., Hood, A., and Joyce, R., 2014. *Living standards, poverty and inequality in the UK* [online]. The Institute for Fiscal Studies. Available from: www.ifs. org.uk/uploads/publications/comms/r96.pdf [Accessed 21 May 2015].

Brammer, A., 2010. *Social work law.* 3rd ed. Harlow, England, New York: Pearson Longman.

Briggs, S., Whittaker, A., Linford, H., Bryan, A., Ryan, E. and Ludick, D., 2011. *Safeguarding children's rights. Exploring issues of witchcraft and spirit possession in London's African communities.* London: Tavistock, Portman. Available online at www.trustforlondon.org.uk/wp-content/uploads/2013/11/Safeguarding-final-report.pdf [Accessed 3 November 2015].

Cemlyn, S., 2008. 'Human rights and gypsies and travellers. An exploration of the application of human rights perspective to social work with a minority community in Britain', *British Journal of Social Work* 38(1): 153–73.

Centre for Workforce Intelligence, 2012. *The future social worker workforce. An analysis of risks and opportunities* [online]. Centre for Workforce Intelligence. Available from: www.cfwi.org.uk/publications/social-workers-workforce-risks-and-opportunities-2012/@@ publication-detail [Accessed 7 January 2015].

Clarke, J., Langan, M., and Williams, F., 2001. 'The construction of the British welfare state 1945-1975', in A. Cochrane, J. Clarke, and S. Gewirtz, eds, *Comparing welfare states. Britain in international context.* London: SAGE Publications, 29–69.

Department for Education and Skills, 2007. *Safeguarding children from abuse linked to a belief in spirit possession* [online]. Her Majesty's Stationery Office (HMSO). Available from: http://webarchive.nationalarchives.gov.uk/20130401151715/http://www.education.gov.uk/publications/eOrderingDownload/DFES-00465-2007.pdf [Accessed 10 January 2016].

Furness, S., and Gilligan, P., 2009. *Religion, belief and social work. Making a difference.* Bristol: Policy Press.

Graham, M., 2007. *Black issues in social work and social care.* Bristol: Policy Press.

Hall, C., 1998. 'A family for nation and empire', in G. Lewis, ed., *Forming nation, framing welfare.* London, New York: Routledge in association with the Open University, 10–47.

HM Government, 2011. *Safeguarding children who may have been trafficked* [online]. Available from: www.gov.uk/government/uploads/system/uploads/attachment_data/file/177033/DFE-00084-2011.pdf [Accessed 20 April 2016].

HM Government, 2014a. *Multi-agency practice guidelines. Female genital mutilation* [online]. Available from: www.gov.uk/government/uploads/system/uploads/attachment_data/file/380125/MultiAgencyPracticeGuidelinesNov14.pdf [Accessed 10 January 2016].

HM Government, 2014b. *Multi-agency practice guidelines. Handling cases of forced marriage* [online]. Available from: www.gov.uk/government/uploads/system/uploads/attachment_data/file/322307/HMG_MULTI_AGENCY_PRACTICE_GUIDELINES_v1_180614_FINAL.pdf [Accessed 10 January 2016].

Hood, A., and Johnson, P., 2014. *What is welfare spending?* [online]. Available from: www.ifs.org.uk/publications/7424 [Accessed 21 May 2015].

International NGO Council on Violence against Children, 2012. *Violating Children's Rights. Harmful practices based on tradition, culture, religion or superstition* [online]. United Nations. Available from: http://srsg.violenceagainstchildren.org/sites/default/files/documents/docs/InCo_Report_15Oct.pdf [Accessed 10 January 2016].

Laird, S.E., 2008. *Anti-oppressive social work. A guide for developing cultural competence.* London: SAGE Publications.

Laming, H., 2003. *The Victoria Climbié inquiry report. Cm 5730.* London: The Stationery Office.

Mishra, R., 1990. *The welfare state in capitalist society. Policies of retrenchment and maintenance in Europe, North America and Australia.* Hemel Hempstead: Harvester Wheatsheaf.

National Working Group on Child Abuse Linked to Faith or Belief, 2012. *National action plan to tackle child abuse linked to faith or belief* [online]. Available from: www.gov.uk/government/uploads/system/uploads/attachment_data/file/175437/Action_Plan_-_Abuse_linked_to_Faith_or_Belief.pdf [Accessed 21 May 2015].

Office for National Statistics, 2011. *Census 2011* [online]. Available from: www.ons.gov.uk/ons/publications/index.html [Accessed 7 January 2015].

Pierson, J., 2011. *Understanding Social Work. History and Context.* Maidenhead: McGraw-Hill.

Stanley, N., and Manthorpe, J., 2004. 'The inquiry as Janus', in N. Stanley and J. Manthorpe, eds, *The age of inquiry. Learning and blaming in health and social care.* London, New York: Routledge, 1–16.

TSCW, 2012. *The professional capabilities framework* [online]. The College of Social Work. Available from: www.basw.co.uk/pcf/ [Accessed 10 January 2016].

TSCW, 2014. *Roles and functions of social workers in England. Advice note* [online]. The College of Social Work. Available from: http://cdn.basw.co.uk/upload/basw_115640-9. pdf [Accessed 10 January 2016].

UN, 2014. *The facts. Asylum in the UK* [online]. United Nations. Available from: www. unhcr.org.uk/about-us/the-uk-and-asylum.html [Accessed 21 May 2015].

Whiting, R., 2008. 'No room for religion or spirituality or cooking tips. Exploring practical atheism as an unspoken consensus in the development of social work values in England', *Ethics and Social Welfare* 2(1): 67–83.

Wilson, K., Ruch, G., Lymbery, M. and Cooper, A., 2011. *Social work. An introduction to contemporary practice*. 2nd ed. Harlow: Pearson/Longman.

# 9 Evolution of professional social work in India and transnational issues faced

*Arvind Kumar Agrawal and Asutosh Pradhan*

India is an emerging economy and promises high growth rates, even against the backdrop of global economic recession. However, with a population of 1.2 billion it is faced with numerous problems of poverty. With a Human Development Index of 0.547 it occupies the 135th position worldwide, which proves the point that its scarce resources have to be invested heavily in social welfare.

Other major problems faced at present are large-scale inequality; unemployment; costly health services and inadequate public health care; lack of quality universal education, particularly in rural areas; corruption and inefficient governance; low female literacy; street children and child labour; malnutrition, high maternal and infant mortality; domestic violence; increased incidence of rape; lack of social development infrastructure in rural and tribal areas; environmental pollution; barrier-free access for the disabled population etc. To compound all this, liberalisation and privatisation have led to a lurking fear of reduced welfare spending which may affect ordinary people.

## Evolution of social welfare in India

Notions of welfare are rooted in the ancient values of dana[1] and punya[2]. Kautilya's Arthsastra (fourth century BCE) specifies the role of the state and citizens which includes help, social services and social development (Jha 1999). During the eighteenth century, India witnessed a drastic change in its polity under colonial rule. The spread of modern values and missionary work, including in the fields of health and education, were significant developments. Social reform movements during this period saw the enactment of social legislation. Colonial rule, however, became the main reason for marginalisation and acute poverty. Leaders of the freedom struggle also pioneered social development projects which continued in independent India (Singh 1996).

Post-independence, India declared itself a Welfare State and enshrined in its constitution various strands of social welfare, justice and human rights. The socially and economically backward, such as the Scheduled Castes (SC), Scheduled Tribes (ST), Minorities, Other Backward Classes (OBC), poor, and women in particular, were targeted for development. This also included the disabled, elderly, children, juvenile and adult offenders, refugees, the mentally challenged etc. (Goel 2010). Other prominent legislation and programmes were developed in relation to social security, social assistance and social insurance for the poor and disadvantaged; environmental protection laws related to land, water, forest, pollution, sanitation, slum improvement, displacement, resettlement and rehabilitation etc.

These welfare programmes and services were developed and carried out after independence by the Department of Social Security, in 1964 upgraded into the full-fledged Ministry of Social Welfare, further renamed in 1988 the Ministry of Social Justice and Empowerment. This evolution in nomenclature is evidence of the changing paradigm of social welfare in India. Power to the people was enshrined through the 73rd and 74th Constitutional Amendments in relation to local self-governance, ensuring adequate representation of SC, ST and women in various local bodies and the enactment of the Right to Information Act 2005. Since 2010 various state governments too have started enacting laws related to citizens' rights to public services.

Professional social workers made valuable contributions to this evolution in a way that had a lasting impact on social welfare systems in India – from a *service-reformist-ameliorative mode* to a *developmental-empowerment-rights-based mode*. The purpose over the years was to usher in planned change in multiple sectors. In the last two decades, the goal of the government has been to bring about inclusive growth and development so that the marginalised and vulnerable get a fair and just chance to benefit from the policies and programmes launched by the government (Desai 2002).

## Prevailing social welfare systems in India

India has a federal structure of governance, with powers shared by the central government and the states. Various welfare schemes are implemented by state governments independently or with part funding from the central government, termed 'Central Plan Assistance' (CPA). For example, CPA for 'Social Security and Welfare' covers debt relief for farmers; pension schemes for the unorganised sector titled Swavalamban (self-help) Scheme; the Social Security Fund under Aam Aadmi Bima Yojana (insurance for the common citizens); and grant-in-aid to the National Bank for Agriculture and Rural Development (NABARD) to finance Women's Self Help Groups, to name just a few. These and other similar programmes are implemented by various ministries and departments of the central and state governments. If it were not for issues of governance, ineffective service delivery and corruption, these welfare programmes could have definitely contributed to the amelioration of the disadvantaged.

Provision of Social Assistance is currently by way of cash transfer or conditional cash/in-kind transfers under food-for-work or employment guarantee under the Mahatma Gandhi National Rural Employment Guarantee Act of 2005 or subsidies for construction of houses in rural areas, scholarships for SC and STs; in-kind transfers under child welfare programmes including Midday Meals in schools; disaster relief or relief to victims of domestic violence; assistance to the elderly in the form of shelter, day care services, pension-, or food security; health assistance, and disability programmes.

To improve governance the Government of India (GOI) has embarked on efforts for large-scale financial inclusion by providing banking access to all families in the country. This aims to prevent corruption and reduce large scale pilfering of welfare funds. A paradigm shift is taking place since cash transfers to the beneficiary's bank account have been initiated for various welfare schemes.

The number of beneficiaries targeted through most of the flagship social welfare programmes is quite large and this requires the involvement of professionals in service delivery. A positive outcome of this has been that in recent years the government is recruiting social work professionals as Consultants or Project/ Programme Coordinators for effective implementation of these programmes. However, the recognition of social workers in terms of salary and working conditions is inadequate. The lack of any active national professional body or association of social work or a National Council for Social Work similar to that of the International Association of Schools of Social Work (IASSW) or International Council on Social Welfare (ICSW) has deprived the social work profession in India of much deserved status and recognition within the country that could influence the government to identify and reserve positions in various sectors of welfare and social policy for professional social workers for more effective service delivery.

## Social work profession and social work education

In the pre-independence era, the Nagpada Neighbourhood House (1926) was established in Bombay by Dr Clifford Manshardt on the lines of the Settlement House, USA, which set in motion the early years of professionalisation of social work in India (Bose 1987). Its basic objective was to work in the context of social problems in slums. Professional Social Work Education (SWE) in the form of a diploma course in Social Service Administration began in 1936 at the Sir Dorabji Tata Graduate School of Social Work, Bombay, later renamed the Tata Institute of Social Sciences (TISS). The 1950s and 1960s saw a number of schools of social work established in different parts of the country, mostly by Christian Missionaries. Initially diploma courses were offered, but within two to five years master's programmes with specialisations were started while undergraduate programmes began 30 years later in 1971. At present there are more than 500 schools of social work in India.

Due academic recognition of social work came when the University Grants Commission (UGC) instituted the 1st and 2nd Review Committee for social work education in 1960 and 1975 respectively. The mandate was to develop structured social work curricula for social work education and evolving mechanisms for the promotion and maintenance of standards of education, training, research and practice. In 2001 the UGC Model Curriculum for Social Work Education was developed (UGC 2011), the aim being the indigenisation of SWE and provision of flexibility in choices of courses that suited local needs (Thomas 2010). In 1961 the Association of Schools of Social Work in India (ASSWI) was established and stressed improvement of social work training including standardisation of pedagogical aspects. After the ASSWI became defunct, the Indian Association of Social Work Education (IASWE) was established in 2014.

Currently most schools of social work offer a generic programme, having moved away from specialisations. Concerns that SWE in India adopted a Western model (Nagpaul 1993) continue to haunt even today, mostly because of a lack of indigenous literature and non-existence of evidence-based research on social work practice. Contextualising SWE to the Indian situation during the 1940s and even now continues to be a huge concern. Some of the most striking areas of focus of social work intervention could have been in effecting structural changes, especially to benefit the dalits[3] or SCs, STs and large sections of the poor. There is an emerging view that specialisation in dalit and tribal social work, rural development, social development, advocacy work and policy advocacy etc. would make the profession more ethnically tuned to the Indian setting. There are also emerging concerns and challenges that social work needs to address, which – as outlined below – have transnational moorings.

## Contextualising transnational social work (TSW) in India: key issues faced

It would be pertinent to understand the effects of globalisation and global forces in the Indian context and the transnational character of social issues faced. Issues that need to be addressed under TSW include: the economic impact of globalisation in production processes leading to large-scale displacement or retrenchment of labour and a rise in unemployment (Sen and Dasgupta 2009); labour unrest that is a result of mechanisation and modernisation (Agarwala *et al.* 2004); farmer suicide caused by crop failure and resulting indebtedness; increased urbanisation leading to intra-country migration and the problem of slums; and privatisation of the health sector making health services out-of-reach of the poor (Peters 2002; Iyer 2005). Social impacts of modernisation and globalisation are believed to be in the form of the nuclearisation of families including an increase in single family norms and empty nest phenomena due to increased emigration. Modern and liberal thinking has led to an increase in inter-caste marriages inviting the ire of Khap Panchayats[4]; and promiscuous relationships affected by loosening of traditional forms of social control. Global feminist movements (Mitra 2011) have led to the enactment of The Protection of Women from Domestic Violence Act, 2005, while the influence of international civil society has led to environmental and human rights movements.

Liberalisation policies have attracted huge investments from multi-national companies. However, such investments have not resulted in the overall development of the local or indigenous peoples. Mining of mineral resources has caused large-scale displacement and suffering to tribal peoples (Mathur 2013). Modern and mechanised operations and relaxation of labour laws have not increased job opportunities but contributed instead to pollution and increased health hazards. Globalisation has thus increased the misery of the local and indigenous peoples and the government has failed to serve its citizens as a welfare state as enshrined in the Indian Constitution and in protecting their right to life and a dignified living (Aerthayil 2008). Other key transnational issues faced are:

## *Migration*

Out-Migration has increased in recent years, mostly from the states of Kerala, Punjab, Rajasthan, Andhra Pradesh and Karnataka, leading to a range of issues and problems such as exploitative and abusive employers; unhygienic and inhumane work and living conditions; duping of potential migrants by cheats; abuse of brides in the case of transnational marriages. In the case of Punjab in particular, parents of girls often want a transnational marriage alliance so that their loved one would have a bright future which in many cases has turned out to be a disastrous assumption. Cases of desertion, divorce, abuse, illicit relationships and extra-marital affairs often crop-up later (Hawley 2013; Mishra 2015).

## *Infiltration and refugee problems*

Infiltration from across the border from Bangladesh, Sri Lanka, Pakistan, Myanmar, and Tibet has created national security and law and order issues and refugee problems (Muni and Baral 1996; Chirantan 2009). Border states including Assam, Nagaland, Tripura and West Bengal, which have a common and porous boundary with Bangladesh, are faced with a demographic crisis (Sinha 1998). Local resentment and opposition has resulted in violent attacks on migrants and has led to a humanitarian crisis. Such large-scale violence has led to frequent breakdowns in peace in the region caused by persistent conflict, leading to human deaths and destruction of houses.

## *Surrogacy*

Transnational surrogacy is fast catching on in India (Qadeer and John 2009). The absence of a strict regulatory regime to deal with transnational surrogacy may put surrogate mothers at risk, including in situations like the death of the surrogate mother, birth deformities in the new-born child prompting desertion by biological parents, or disputes over fees for surrogacy. Legislation currently only exists in draft form, known as 'The Assisted Reproductive Technologies (Regulation) Bill 2010' (ICSW 2010). 'Non-medical evaluation' of surrogate and biological parents by trained social workers would help 'determine the party's suitability to parent' by considering not only '[t]he ability and disposition of the person being evaluated to give a child love, affection and guidance,' but also '[t]he ability of the person to adjust to and assume the inherent risks of the contract' (Rao 2003: 29).

## *Inter-country adoption*

Inter-country adoption is another area where professional social workers can play a key role in the appropriate screening, selection and monitoring of adoptive parents (Bhargava 2005). There have been instances in the past where adoption was undertaken as pretext to having someone who would act as a domestic help at home. Sexual abuse of such children has also been reported in inter-country adoption. Hence, international law concerning the transnational adoption of children has developed in response to breaches of human rights, such as child trafficking (Pfund 1994; Graff 2010). Screening and verification of potential adoptive parents could possibly be better managed through intergovernmental and transborder NGO networks working in the field of adoption.

### Clinical trials

Another burning issue that calls for advocacy action and policy intervention is the problem of the illegal practice of surreptitious clinical trials (Dave 2009) conducted by private hospitals and multi-national pharmaceutical companies (Sandhya 2009). Frequently the subjects of such clinical trials are poor and illiterate people who are not aware of their rights nor of the risk of adverse effects of such trials. In the event of death, disability or any other adverse health impact on the subjects, they often fail to receive adequate compensation and justice.

## Summary

To sum up, it is expected that some of the transnational issues highlighted in the Indian context would initiate further reflection and research in this grey area of social work practice. They call for an understanding of global factors impinging on social and welfare systems at the micro (e.g. individual, family, community), meso (e.g. larger community, panchayat or district) and macro (in terms of policy or programme) levels. Transnational social work practice would necessarily require skills in policy advocacy, cross-cultural competencies, general advocacy work, human rights practice etc. This may even prompt a course correction in social work education and training in India to ensure the coverage of emerging transnational issues and challenges.

## Notes

1  Denotes religious giving or charity.
2  Attainment of *Moksha* or salvation of the spirit through the pious practice of religious giving.
3  The term dalit, meaning 'oppressed' in South Asia, is the self-chosen political name of castes which are classed as 'untouchable' in Hindu caste society. It implies a condition of being underprivileged and deprived of basic rights and refers to people who are suppressed on account of their lowly birth (Michael 2007).
4  *Khap Panchayat* or 'Caste Council' is a traditional patriarchal institution that consists of selected members of the representing villages who often hail from upper and dominant caste groups. Lately they have emerged as quasi-judicial bodies that pronounce harsh punishments based on age-old customs and traditions, often bordering on regressive measures to modern problems.

## References

Aerthayil, M., 2008. *Impact of globalisation on tribals. In the context of Kerala*. Jaipur: Rawat Publications.

Agarwala, R., Kumar, N., and Riboud, M., eds, 2004. *Reforms, labour markets, and social security in India. International conference in New Delhi on 1 - 3 November 1999 on social security policy*. New Delhi: Oxford Univ. Press.

Bhargava, V., 2005. *Adoption in India. Policies and experiences*. New Delhi, Thousand Oaks, Calif.: SAGE Publications.

Bose, A.B., 1987. 'Development of social welfare services', in GOI, ed., *Encyclopedia of social work in India. Volume I.* New Delhi: Government of India, 203–15.

Chirantan, K., 2009. 'Migration and refugee issue between India and Bangladesh', *Scholar's Voice: A New Way of Thinking* 1(1): 64–82.

Dave, H., 2009. *Multinational research company shuts unit at Rajkot hospital* [online]. Available from: http://archive.indianexpress.com/news/%20multinational-research-company-shuts-unit-at-rajkot-hospital/454517/ [Accessed 15 July 2015].

Desai, M., 2002. *Ideologies and social work. Historical and contemporary analyses*. Jaipur: Rawat Publications.

Goel, S.L., 2010. *Social welfare administration*. New Delhi: Deep & Deep Publications.

Graff, E.J., 2010. *The baby business* [online]. Available from: http://democracyjournal.org/magazine/17/the-baby-business/ [Accessed 17 September 2015].

Hawley, M., 2013. *Sikh Diaspora. Theory, Agency, and Experience*. Leiden: BRILL.

ICSW, 2010. *The assisted reproductive technologies (regulation) bill* [online]. International Council on Social Welfare. Available from: http://icmr.nic.in/guide/ART%20 REGULATION%20Draft%20Bill1.pdf [Accessed 10 January 2016].

Iyer, A., 2005. *Ill and impoverished. The medical poverty trap* [online]. Infochange Agenda. Available from: http://infochangeindia.org/agenda/access-denied/ill-and-impoverished-the-medical-poverty-trap.html [Accessed 16 May 2016].

Jha, V.N., 1999. *Kautilya's arthashastra and social welfare*. Delhi: Sahitya Academy.

Mathur, H.M., 2013. *Displacement and resettlement in India. The human cost of development*. London: Routledge.

Michael, S.M., 2007. *Dalits in modern India: Vision and values*. Los Angeles: Sage Publications.

Mishra, R., 2015. 'Vulnerability of Women in International Marriage Migration', in S. Irudaya Rajan, ed., *Gender and migration.* New Delhi: Routledge, 73–9.

Mitra, N., 2011. 'Domestic violence research. Expanding understandings but limited perspective', *Feminist Review* e62–e78.

Muni, S.D., and Baral, L.R., 1996. *Refugees and regional security in South Asia*. Delhi: Konark Publishers.

Nagpaul, H., 1993. 'Analysis of social work teaching material in India. The need for indigenous foundations', *International Social Work* 36(3): 207–20.

Peters, D.H., 2002. *Better health systems for India's poor. Findings, analysis, and options*. Washington, D.C: World Bank.

Pfund, P.H., 1994. 'Inter-country Adoption. The 1993 Hague Convention: Its purpose, implementation and promise', *Family Law Quarterly* 28(1): 53–75.

Qadeer, I., and John, M.E., 2009. 'The business and ethics of surrogacy', *Economic & Political Weekly* 44(2): 10–12.

Rao, R., 2003. 'Surrogacy Law in the United States. The Outcome of Ambivalence', in R. Cook, S. Day Sclater, and F. Kaganas, eds, *Surrogate motherhood. International perspectives.* Oxford: Hart Publishing, 23–34.

Sandhya, S., 2009. 'The clinical trials scenario in India', *Economic & Political Weekly* 44(35): 29–33.

Sen, S., and Dasgupta, B., 2009. *Unfreedom and waged work. Labour in India's manufacturing industry*. New Delhi, Thousand Oaks, Calif.: SAGE Publications India.

Singh, M., 1996. *Social policy and administration in India*. New Delhi: M D Publications.

Sinha, S.K., 1998. *Report on illegal migration into Assam. Submitted to the president of India* [online]. Available from: www.satp.org/satporgtp/countries/india/states/assam/documents/papers/illegal_migration_in_assam.htm [Accessed 10 January 2016].

Thomas, G., 2010. *Origin and development of social work*. Delhi: IGNOU.

UGC, 2011. *UGC model curriculum. Social work education* [online]. University Grants Commission. Available from: http://docplayer.net/5901659-Ugc-model-curriculum-sociology.html [Accessed 10 January 2016].

# 10 The development of social welfare services and the social work profession in Israel

*Merav Moshe Grodofsky*

Israel is a young state. It was formally recognised by the United Nations Partition Plan in 1948; however, the history of the country can be traced back to over three thousand years ago, to the time of the forefathers, Abraham, Isaac and Jacob.

The foundations of the social work profession and the social welfare services were laid in the early twentieth century, prior to the establishment of the modern-day state. In 1931, under the rule of the British Mandate, the Va'ad Haleumi, the independent governing institution of the Jewish settlement, established the first social work department (Gal and Weiss 2000; Spiro 2012).

Different models have influenced the development of the social service system and the social work profession in Israel. The British Beveridge social insurance model with its emphasis on social assistance for the poor, was crucial for the formation of the initial social welfare institutions and structures and ultimately for the development of the welfare state. The social work profession on the other hand evolved under the influence of German and American social work models (Gal and Weiss 2000; Doron 2004).

## Israel and Israeli society

### Population

Data released by the Israeli Census Bureau in 2013 reported that Israel's population has exceeded 8 million. Three-quarters of the population are reported to be Jewish; approximately 20 per cent Arab, and approximately 4 per cent other religions including Arab Christians (Zeiger 2013). There is a clear Jewish majority and Arab minority.

Israel is a country of immigrants. Since its establishment, the country has seen an influx of immigrants from Europe, North Africa and – more recently – from the former Soviet Union, Ethiopia and Western countries including the United States, Canada and France. It has been defined as a 'divided society' characterised by 'deep schisms running through the social fabric … with each group having distinct cultural, religious and political identities' (Desivilya and Yassour-Borochowitz 2010: 38). Divisions within the Jewish majority can be found between religious and secular communities, Ashkenazi (European) and Mizrahi (Asian-African) communities, new immigrants and veteran communities as well as along political lines (Moshe Grodofsky and Yudelevich 2012).

Alongside the Palestinian or Arab-Israeli minority, there are apparent divisions among community subgroups, including Muslims, Christians, Druze and Bedouin. Schisms within Israeli society are compounded by the ongoing, more than 100-year-old, conflict between Israel and its Arab neighbours and more than five wars fought since the establishment of the state.

### *Political system*

Israel's political system is based upon a parliamentary democracy. The President of Israel, an apolitical ceremonial figurehead, is the head of the state. The Prime Minister of Israel is the head of the government. The prime minister appoints a Cabinet. The Parliament, known as the Knesset, has 120 members elected for a four-year term. In the 2015 elections, ten different political parties secured representation in the Knesset.

Israel does not have a Constitution but in 1992 the Knesset enacted two Basic Laws that address basic individual rights: they are Freedom of Occupation, and Human Dignity and Liberty. There is ongoing debate in Israel surrounding the nature of Israel's democracy, in that the state defines itself as both Jewish and democratic. Religion continues to play a major role in public affairs, including matters of marriage and divorce. Religion in public affairs has served to alienate non-religious Jewish citizens while simultaneously ignoring and often undermining the interests of Israel's Arab minority.

## The Israeli social welfare system

Israeli social welfare services developed over three distinct periods; according to Doron (2004) the development of the system was influenced by the leadership of each period. The first period (1940s until early 1960s) laid the foundations for the social service system and – particularly between 1948 and 1951 – the emerging country absorbed 700,000 new immigrants, among them Holocaust survivors and entire communities from North Africa, Yemen and Iraq (Spiro *et al.* 1998; Stypinska 2007). With few resources and growing populations in need of basic services, social welfare institutions were in great demand.

Three basic principles influenced social service growth: the recognition of the family as the primary unit of social service assistance, the recognition of local services funded by the state as the primary provider of assistance and the recognition of social workers as the professionals mandated to provide social services (Spiro *et al.* 1998; Gal and Weiss 2000; Spiro 2001).

Professional development of the social service system during the initial post-state period was directed primarily by women influenced by social work pioneers in pre-state Israel, among them Dr Henrietta Szold and Sidi Vronsky, a colleague of the well-known German social work educator Alice Salomon. In its initial stages, the social welfare system adopted the predominant Zionist ethos of the time – that it was the responsibility of the Jewish State to absorb waves of immigration (Doron 2004) and to ensure that the collective look after individuals and families in need. During this period social services included both financial and material assistance as well as professional support and care. According to Doron (2004) the system was highly hierarchical and centralised and driven by the values and the ethics of those women who served as its leaders. In 1958 legislation formalised the operation of the local social service system.

### The Israeli social welfare system – second phase of development

Changes in Israeli politics between the 1960s and the 1980s influenced the second stage of the development of the social service system. Professionals who advanced the system in its initial stages were replaced by male non-professionals aligned with the National Religious political party. Leaders of this period spearheaded the development of the legal basis for the social welfare system, including policy to delineate criteria for the allocation of benefits and entitlements and institutionalisation of the professional social work role. Laws and regulations set forth in 1958 formalised and institutionalised the mandate and operations of the local welfare offices and clarified professional roles (Doron 2004; Gal and Weiss 2000).

It was during the first half of the 1970s that the Israeli welfare state experienced rapid growth. Gal and Weiss (2000) attribute this to the country's military victory in the Six Day War of 1967 and the economic growth that followed. The country experienced additional waves of immigration from the West and the Soviet Union. Simultaneously, poverty, growing social gaps and civil unrest were challenges of the time.

These developments led to new social welfare programmes and an increase in welfare expenditure per annum between 1970 and 1975 (Cnaan 1998). During this period, financial and material assistance provided together with psychosocial support during the first phase of social welfare service development were separated and eventually, during the 1980s, financial and material assistance was moved from the welfare system to the National Insurance Institute (Gal and Weiss 2000).

### The Israeli social welfare system – third phase of development

During the 1980s and the 1990s, The Ministry of Welfare was in part controlled by Israel's two major political parties, Likud and Avodah, yet also fell under the leadership of ultra-Orthodox sectoral political parties including Tami, Agudat Yisrael and Shas. Not only did the leadership lack an understanding of social welfare, but as Doron (2004) notes, they encountered an ideological rift between particular and universal orientations: the ultra-Orthodox parties envisioned the role of social welfare through a religious lens where values of charity and assistance to one's own were dominant, as opposed to services that ensure basic social rights as a matter of universal citizenship.

Doron (2004) notes that these parties chose to cope with the ideological conflict through the transfer of resources to newly emerging non-governmental organisations that shared the values of the ruling ultra-Orthodox party. In effect this advanced the privatisation of Israeli social services at the same time that the government was encouraging the private provision of education and health services. Gal and Weiss (2000) suggest that the trend to privatise social, educational and health services, severe cuts in welfare expenditure and changes in universal programmes were influenced in part by worldwide economic stagnation, an economic crisis in Israel enhanced by the 1973 Yom Kippur War and a shift to conservative and economic thought.

## The development of the social work profession in Israel

During the 1950s the social work profession functioned without formal legislation but since the establishment of the state the profession has undergone a gradual process of professionalisation (Doron *et al.* 2008). Social work professionalisation has been the product of a number of processes, among them professional training (including academic recognition of the profession), the expansion of professional research, knowledge and expertise, the promotion of professional methodologies and fields of intervention, the establishment of the professional association and the professional code of ethics, and the advancement of legislation delineating the mandate of the profession (Doron 2004; Doron *et al.* 2008; Spiro 2012; Spiro *et al.* 1998; Gal and Weiss 2000). According to Doron, Rosner and Karpel, 'in legislative terms social work has developed to the point where over 60 different laws and hundreds of regulations assign a wide range of roles and responsibilities to social workers' (Doron *et al.* 2008: 4).

The first social work training programme opened in Jerusalem in 1934. Prior to the establishment of the state and until 1948, 150 social workers completed their professional training (Spiro 2012). In 1958 the profession gained recognition as an academic field. The first undergraduate programme in social work education was established at the Paul Baerwald School of Social Work, at the Hebrew University in Jerusalem. The Israeli social welfare system was highly dependent upon aid from Jewish organisations in North America to advance the profession. These organisations sent professionals to Israel and simultaneously secured scholarships for Israelis to attend academic programmes in social work in North America (Spiro *et al.* 1998).

Casework and the distribution of financial assistance to the neediest populations in the country characterised the professional social work role during the 1950s. The majority of social workers were employed by local welfare offices with only a minority working in psychiatric hospitals, in schools, within the probation system and special services for immigrants and finally in community work. Moreover, social workers rarely engaged in policy or social change work. Similar to North American social work, the profession in Israel did not identify social change work as an integral part of the professional mandate (Gal and Weiss 2000).

During the 1970s social justice principles were at the forefront of the social work profession. Social workers trained in community organising were instrumental during the protests staged by immigrants from North African countries to combat the discrimination and prejudice that they had experienced since the establishment of the state. Concurrently, social workers went on strike to force the Jerusalem municipality to fund needy clients when state funds ran out. Finally, social workers provided recommendations to the Prime Minister's Committee on Children and Youth in Need and as Gal and Weiss (2000) note, were successful in influencing the social welfare policy and legislation of the following decade.

### *The Israeli Association of Social Workers*

The Israeli Association of Social Workers was established in 1937 and has been an influential body in the development of the social work profession in Israel. The association is active in the development of social services, the advancement of professional competencies and status, the promotion of job security and social lobbying (Spiro 2012). Spiro (Spiro 2012) suggests that the greatest success of the association was the creation of a monopoly for the professional mandate ensuring that no other professions can engage in areas defined within this mandate. In 1996, after years of political lobbying, The Israeli Association of Social Workers succeeded in the passage of The Social Workers Act 1996.

### *The Social Workers Act 1996*

The Social Workers Act 1996 has two goals. The first is to ensure that social workers heed the principle of professionalism and have appropriate qualifications to function as social workers. According to the law, practising social workers must hold an academic degree and must be registered for practice in the social work registry (Doron *et al.* 2008). The second goal is to ensure the protection of social work clients and to safeguard the professional status of social workers in society (Doron *et al.* 2008). In light of the challenges that face the profession, not only in Israel but internationally as well, the law provides a safety net for those engaged in the profession.

## Current state of the social work profession in Israel

Over the past two decades the social work profession in Israel has grown in size, and has become both more professional and more diverse. While in the late 1960s there were just over a thousand social workers, by 1997 there were over 10,000 professional social workers in the country (Gal and Weiss 2000: 490). Whereas in the late 1960s the majority of social workers were employed by the local welfare departments, today social workers are employed in health and mental health facilities, senior citizen services, counselling centres, corrections, factories and more (Gal and Weiss 2000). Social workers are also engaging in feminist social work (Peled and Krumer-Nevo 2012) and in multicultural social work (Korin-Langer and Nadan 2012).

Gal and Weiss (2000) discuss two dominant trends: first, a separation between the income-maintenance role and the treatment role of the profession within the social welfare services as the beginning of a predominant trend that identifies the individual as the source of his/her distress. Following this school of thought social work professionals are more inclined to engage in individual work (psychotherapeutic) and group therapy methods with mainstream social work populations.

A second major trend in the profession has been the entry of social work professionals into the market sector. Growing social service privatisation has led to professional employment in non-governmental non-profit and for profit organisations, as well as to a growth in private practice (Gal and Weiss 2000).

Perhaps in response to this and in the aftermath of social work involvement in the social protests of the early 1970s, the profession has seen a gradual yet steady rise in social activism and in activity that targets the environment, institutions and policy as the source for individual distress. The Israeli Association of Social Workers has adopted a more activist role and the code of ethics, revised in 1994, emphasises the professional commitment to social justice principles (Gal and Weiss 2000).

Israeli social workers are gradually becoming more apt to engage in political work through the establishment of social work organisations such as Ossim Shalom – Social Workers for Peace and Social Welfare that recognises the relationship between the ongoing Israeli–Palestinian conflict and welfare expenditure or lack thereof. Social work students have established the organisation, Ossim Shinui – Social Workers for Change. Furthermore, during the 2011 Israeli social protest movement, social work professionals were actively involved in a variety of aspects of the protests (Moshe Grodofsky and Makaros 2016). Certainly there is a sense that a new generation of social workers is making its way into social work education and the profession.

## Problems and challenges for social work development

Looking towards the future, social work in Israel faces a myriad of challenges including those that relate to the on-going political conflict within a volatile Middle East, growing levels of inequality and poverty within society and the phenomena that accompany them, and population changes. All of these have a bearing on transnational social work and the social work profession has become increasingly concerned with its role in political conflict around the world (Ramon *et al.* 2006; Moshe Grodofsky and Yudelevich 2012; Moshe Grodofsky 2007; Moshe Grodofsky 2001). This is, for example, evident in increasing numbers of asylum seekers from Africa making their way to Israel's borders. According to available data, by 2011 more than 20,000 asylum seekers had entered the country (Raijman and Barak-Bianco 2015: 4). Yacobi contends that 'the flow of non-Jewish, non-white migrants into Israel is having a significant impact in the Israeli ethnocratic context' (Yacobi 2009: 48). The question of refugee status challenges Israel's social and political discourse which Yacobi notes is 'caught between its own ethnocratic ideologies and a wider commitment to universal human rights' (Yacobi 2009: 51).

Within this complexity social workers are engaged in human rights and psychosocial work with asylum seekers. Social workers have voiced the dual loyalty conflict that characterised their work – on the one hand the guiding principles of social justice; on the other hand the complexity of working within governmental systems that have not fully recognised the status or rights of asylum seekers.

## References

Cnaan, R., 1998. 'The evolution of Israel's welfare state', in R.R. Friedman, N. Gilbert, and M. M. Sherer, eds, *Modern welfare states.* Brighton: Wheatsheaf.

Desivilya, S.H., and Yassour-Borochowitz, D., 2010. 'Israel's moral judgements of government aggression and violation of human rights. Is democracy under siege?' *Beliefs and Values* 2(1): 38–48.

Doron, A., 2004. 'Individual social services in Israel. Changing leadership and its implications on the system', *Bitachon Sociali* 65: 11–32.

Doron, A., Rosner, Y., and Karpel, M., 2008. 'Law, social work and professionalism. Israeli social workers' attitudes towards the 1996 social work act', *Journal of Social Welfare and Family Law* 30(1): 3–16.

Gal, J., and Weiss, I., 2000. 'Policy practice in social work and social work education in Israel', *Social Work Education: The International Journal* 19(4): 485–99.

Korin-Langer, N., and Nadan, Y., 2012. 'Social work in a diverse, multicultural society', in: M. Hovav, E. Lawental, and J. Katan, eds, *Social work in Israel.* Tel Aviv: Hakibbutz Hameuchad, 506–26.

Moshe Grodofsky, M., 2001. 'Peacebuilding. A conceptual framework', *International Journal of Social Welfare* 10(4): 14–26.

Moshe Grodofsky, M., 2007. 'The contribution of social work and law to interdisciplinary community development and peacebuilding in the Middle East', *Journal of Community Practice Special Issue Interdisciplinary Community Development: International Perspectives* 15(1–2): 45–65.

Moshe Grodofsky, M., and Makaros, A., 2016. 'Social workers' conflict of loyalty in the context of social activism. The case of the 2011 social protests in Israel', *Journal of Policy Practice* 15 (forthcoming).

Moshe Grodofsky, M.M., and Yudelevich, D., 2012. 'Organising across-identity group divisions in the context of acute political conflict. A case study', *British Journal of Social Work* 42(6): 1–14.

Peled, E., and Krumer-Nevo, M., 2012. 'Feminist social work', in M. Hovav, E. Lawental, and J. Katan, eds, *Social work in Israel.* Tel Aviv: Hakibbutz Hameuchad, 479–505.

Raijman, R., and Barak-Bianco, A., 2015. 'Asylum seeker entrepreneurs in Israel', *Economic Sociology The European Electronic Newsletter* 16(2): 4–13. Available from: http://econsoc.mpifg.de/downloads/16_2/raijman_16_2.pdf [Accessed 25 January 2016].

Ramon, S., Campbell, J., Lindsay, J., McCrystal, P. and Baidoun, N., 2006. 'The impact of political conflict on social work. Experiences from Northern Ireland, Israel and Palestine', *British Journal of Social Work* 36: 435–60.

Spiro, S.E., 2001. 'Social work education in Israel. Trends and issues', *Social Work Education: The International Journal* 20(1): 89–99.

Spiro, S., 2012. 'The history of the social work profession', in M. Hovav, E. Lawental, and J. Katan, eds, *Social work in Israel.* Tel Aviv: Hakibbutz Hameuchad, 50–67.

Spiro, S., Sherer, M., Korin-Langer, N. and Weiss, I., 1998. 'The professionalization of Israeli social work', in F.M. Loewenberg, ed., *Meeting the challenges of a changing society. Fifty years of social work in Israel.* Jerusalem: Magnes Press; the Hebrew University, 29–50.

Stypinska, J., 2007. 'Jewish majority and Arab minority in Israel. Demographic struggle', *Polish Sociological Review* 1(157): 105–20.

Yacobi, H., 2009. '"Let me go to the city". African asylum seekers, racialization and the politics of space in Israel', *Journal of Refugee Studies* 24(1): 47–68.

Zeiger, A., 2013. 'Israel at 65. Population tops 8 million' [online]. *The Times of Israel.* Available from: www.timesofisrael.com/israel-at-65-population-tops-8-million/ [Accessed 10 January 2016].

# 11 Social welfare in Malaysia
## Provision and limitation

*Kartini Aboo Talib*

## Politics and government

Malaysia is a federal constitutional monarchy with a parliamentary democracy largely influenced by the British system. The bicameral parliament consists of a House of Representatives and the Senate. One of the unique features of the political system in Malaysia is that the sovereign (Paramount Ruler or Yang di-Pertuan Agong in Malay) is elected every five years by and from the nine hereditary rulers of the nine states of the Malay Peninsula. This division of powers amongst the different organs of government provides a system of checks and balances.

The Malay Peninsula started to become a plural society in the early 1920s with a substantial influx of workers and labourers from Southern China and Southern India. By the end of the 1930s, the Malay Peninsula had evolved into a plural society with the Chinese population reaching 30 per cent and the Indian 14 per cent, respectively (Teo Seong 2010). Today, Malaysia is an ethnically diverse modern society that exhibits ethnic heterogeneity (Marger 2003). After 57 years of independence, Malaysia continues to demonstrate unity amongst its multi-ethnic population and little ethnic confrontation relative to Sri Lanka (Abeyratne 2008; Shamsul 2009). Moreover, the east Malaysia states including Sabah and Sarawak comprise numerous indigenous groups and the record of harmonious ethnic relationships is sound since they joined Malaysia in 1963.

Currently, the population is 30 million and Malaysia is a great example of cultural and religious tolerance. Vernacular schools, ethnic programmes, religious festivals and celebrations are supported by the government. Instead of creating a melting pot, Malaysia has painstakingly weaved a rich cultural mosaic into its multi-ethnic society.[1] The plurality in this multifaceted society is like the colours of the rainbow – separate but not apart (Faruqi 2010: 68). Furthermore, this multi-ethnic society is made more plural and colourful with influxes of immigrants.

## Social work in Malaysia

Social work was introduced in Malaysia by the British Colonial Administration as early as the 1930s, mainly focusing on the problems of migrant workers from India and China. After the Second World War, other social problems became prominent, including issues of expulsion as a result of war, juvenile delinquency and poverty, thus the Department of Social Welfare was established in 1946. This department assists specific target groups and provides, for example, financial aid, probation programmes for juveniles, shelters for women and girls exposed to domestic abuse, residential care for people with disabilities as well as care for elderly people. The British Almoners[2] formed the first professional body for social workers called the Malayan Association of Almoners (MAA) in 1955. In the late 1960s, it was renamed the Malaysian Association of Medical Social Workers (MAMSW). In the early 1970s, medical social workers initiated the inclusion of colleagues from social welfare, prisons and social work education programmes. Consequently, the Malaysian Association of Social Workers (MASW) was formed on 3 March 1973 and registered with the Registrar of Societies on 28 March 1974, while the MAMSW was dissolved on 16 May 1975 (Malaysian Association of Social Workers).

The consequences of the Second World War were a powerful impetus that formalised the creation of social welfare programmes in Malaysia (Rashid 2000: 320). Public health issues were among the foremost concerns in this period considering that Malaysian-born social workers were trained by the British. As a colony, colonial knowledge and understanding determined the category of services created in Malaysia. Additionally, the post-war generation of social workers facilitated their inception of knowledge and experience through government-run medical social work. As a result, other forms of social work services managed independently by the state and taken up by non-governmental (NGOs) and community-based organisations (CBOs) came into being, such as shelters for women victims of violence, homeless people, and refugees. Other areas of social work for different target groups include elderly people, people with disabilities, women, children, youths, abandoned children, people with HIV/Aids, etc. These too are handled by the ministry or non-governmental organisations. NGOs are independent entities with workers and volunteers from many disciplines. The majority of active NGOs in Malaysia are advocacy groups campaigning for women's issues.

Social work in Malaysia is often referred to as social welfare. However, such an interpretation of the role and responsibility of the Social Welfare Department is not in line with most social work departments in advanced countries. The common understanding of social welfare in Malaysia is of a department that assists people with charity and provides care for the elderly, orphanages, or care for victims of natural disasters such as floods.

The social work programmes offered in Malaysia at public and private universities include the BA, MA and PhD. To date, there is no statistical material available on the number of trained professionals working in social care. A social work degree is recognised as equal to other social sciences degrees, and the social work graduates normally end up doing other generalist work. Therefore, Crabtree (2005: 732) notes that social work in Malaysia continues to hold a weak and undefined position in both the civil service hierarchy and public perceptions. Although the popularity of social work programmes and courses offered at the universities across the county is increasing, social work jobs and opportunities are limited. Students who have graduated from these courses struggle to find themselves employed in either the government or private sectors, thus they are likely to be diverted permanently from a social work career.

Some gaps and barriers, including lack of recognition, government inertia towards standardising social work training, and budget cuts in public expenditure, especially in state social welfare, further limit improvements in the social work field in Malaysia. Lack of government recognition and incentives to recognise social work as a profession create difficulties for trained social workers to be accepted as experts in many fields of social work practice. Social work positions are in fact filled with graduates from other disciplines including those from general social sciences or humanities (Crabtree 2005: 733). This trend reduces social work professionals to ordinary generalists.

## Social Welfare Department

Due to the lack of government recognition of social work professionalism, issues regarding social welfare are managed by the Social Welfare Department. This department was established in 1946 and its portfolio has evolved over the years. Shifting and moving the department from one ministry to another was intended to result in a bigger budget, more staff and more importance. The initiative to create a national social policy was necessary to achieve national unity among the multi-ethnic population. The policy was established on 19 August 2003 (The Malaysian Government: online) based on a principle to ensure that every individual, family and community regardless of ethnicity, religion, culture, gender, political affiliation and regions can participate in and contribute to national development and improve the social well-being of citizens. The policy is viewed as social development based on virtue and the improvement of human potential to achieve unity and social stability with the aim to empower the society to become progressive.

The mission of the Social Welfare Department (The Malaysian Government: online) is to care for society and achieving such mission demands the government set a course of action, including providing protection and rehabilitation services, creating a caring society through continuous educational and practical programmes, and improving the well-being of the community through professional welfare and social development services.

This department also allocates financial assistance to target groups who need help to live independently. In line with its principle to assist people, the government created the financial assistance scheme. The aim of this financial assistance scheme is to help low income families with their basic needs, to improve the standard of living and to ensure they can live independently.

The financial assistance service requires certain basic criteria for the target group to be eligible for the service. The eligibility requirements include proof of citizenship and residential address, payslips that meet income eligibility standards, disability criteria, and numbers of dependants in a family. The citizenship requirement automatically denies legal immigrants with dependants any assistance from the government.

# Delivering services

The implementation of welfare assistance in Malaysia is consistent with the Concurrent List[3] between the federal and state government. Registered applicants are assessed to verify their eligibility for assistance. However, the legal regulation for social welfare in Malaysia clearly states that the social welfare department is meant to assist citizens with certain eligibility criteria and automatically denies access as well as eligibility to non-citizens. There is therefore an absence of social welfare services that could help other groups in the community, especially legal immigrant workers who are non-citizens.

Although the 1948 Universal Declaration of Human Rights had considerable influence on the development of social work (Brammer 2010), the existing legal provisions in Malaysia provide less than satisfactory protection of rights, particularly those of immigrant workers. There remains a need to review the law and to find ways for social work practice to be extended. It is vital to view the law as an opportunity to promote best practice and be a support to a real culture of rights by empowering service providers and users.

## *Non-governmental organisations*

The limitation on delivering services to non-citizens does not affect the role and contribution played by non-governmental organisations (NGOs).[4] These non-state actors are becoming more significant around the world and this phenomenon is also visible in Malaysia, especially in the context of assisting people in need. NGOs are private, non-profit, professional organisations that are concerned with public welfare such as philanthropic foundations, religious development agencies, academic think tanks, social welfare institutions, human rights activists concerned with issues such as agricultural development, gender equality, health care, environment, indigenous people and many other areas such as sports, culture, etc. (Clarke 1998: 36).

The increasing emphasis on grassroots and local autonomous initiatives in the development process make the involvement of NGOs profoundly important in delivering and providing social services to communities. Their involvement also represents a dramatic departure from the traditional state-centric system to decentralized forms of democratic government. NGOs' efforts are varied, as are the ways in which they empower beneficiary communities to mobilise themselves and improve their living conditions.

Meanwhile, the issue of migrant domestic worker abuse is increasingly a growing concern in Malaysia. Several severe cases of maid abuse have attracted attention not just regionally but around the world. The Trafficking in Persons (TIP) report of 2009 by the United States of America ranked Malaysia at Tier 3 (worst) for its violation against human rights based on the evidence of abused foreign domestic workers (Ab Wahab 2014). As a result, women's organisations have come forward and offered support, such as shelters and advice, to the victims.

## *Case Studies of social work by women's NGOs*

Women's Aid Organisation (WAO)[5] is the NGO that has assisted and attended cases actively. Since its inception in 1982, WAO has received cases of domestic worker abuse and supported women from many different countries including Malaysia. The International Labour Organization (ILO) Convention 189 clearly recognised domestic work as work, but in many countries, domestic workers are not recognised as workers (Crépeau 2014). As a result, domestic workers are not protected by labour laws. They are vulnerable to abuse because their workplaces are in private households, behind closed doors, out of the public eye, and physically isolated, thus it is difficult for them to take collective action. Most migrant domestic workers are women and they feel very discouraged to seek legal redress for abuse which can take years to settle the case. At the moment, there is no specific law in Malaysia to protect migrant domestic workers from violence and the WAO follows a series of protocols to handle the foreign domestic worker abuse cases including:

- Filing complaints with the police, welfare and labour departments
- Processing applications with the Immigration Department
- Gathering medical reports and other evidence of abuse
- Assisting women in obtaining lawyers and initiating civil and criminal suits
- Lobbying the media for case coverage and advocacy.

WAO is making substantial efforts in promoting advocacy and ways to educate the community on changes of attitude towards migrant domestic workers. WAO also strengthens its strategy by lobbying the press to highlight the agenda of migrant domestic workers' rights, the abuse and violations of human rights that are punishable by law. A comprehensive list of access to an effective remedy for human rights violations is stated in the UN Human Rights Council of Twenty-sixth session (Crépeau 2014: 20f). Furthermore, another NGO that is active in building awareness on issues pertaining to migrant domestic workers is Tenaganita. It launched its campaign kit in 2012 demanding the government to include domestic work in the current national labour laws of both origin and destination countries as well as to introduce a Domestic Workers Act in order to protect the rights of migrant domestic workers.[6]

## Conclusion

Overall, social work in Malaysia has traditionally been concentrated in the field of health care (e.g. hospitals). The line between social work and social welfare is still blurred in Malaysia and most people are likely to view both as similar if not the same. Such perspectives mean that social work still is not recognised as important as other professions. Social workers continue to be viewed as generalists rather than highly qualified professional care givers or agents of social change that can contribute to improving the living conditions of society. The paradigm shift must take place through the education system. A career path as a social worker must be introduced in Malaysia as a way to move society forward so that it can adapt to the challenges and complexities it faces. NGOs such as WAO with a strong history of support work to vulnerable members of society can become part of the advocacy to change perceptions and demand for service improvement.

## Notes

1 A report by the Institute for Economics and Peace (IEP) indicated in the Global Peace Index 2011 ranked Malaysia at 19 among 153 countries that succeeded in maintaining peace and political stability. See details at Institute for Economics and Peace (online).
2 An almoner is a chaplain or church officer who originally was in charge of distributing money to the deserving poor. The 1910–1912 *Every Woman's Encyclopedia* drew attention to the new profession offered for women of culture and education. The almoner was an important figure both for the hospital and for the patient. The almoner profession played an important role of assisting social enquiry with significant influence over how and where people were treated, what support they might receive after leaving hospital and how much they would be asked to pay for the care provision and service. In the 1940s almoner activities were recognised as social work within the wider context of health and welfare programmes (Sackville 1987).
3 Concurrent List is referred to as the third list of shared autonomy between the federal list and state list outlined in the Ninth Schedule of the Constitution of Malaysia 1957. See details at Federation of Malaysia Constitution (online).
4 The total list of NGO applications from January until July 2015 was 5,989. However, the statistic did not provide information on the types of organisation. Thus it is difficult to see the number of NGOs that work in social work services. See details at Jabatan Pendaftaran Pertubuhan Malaysia (JPPM).
5 WAO is a registered society with tax exemption status under the Registrar of Societies. WAO is a member of the Joint Action Group for Gender Equality and an affiliate member of the National Council for Women Organization and the Malaysian AIDS Council. See details at WAO (online).
6 Tenaganita Domestic Workers Campaign Toolkit, 2012. Tenaganita Sdn Bhd: Malaysia.

## References

Ab Wahab, A., 2014. *Malaysian anti-trafficking initiatives and the emerging issues. An overview on refugee perspective:* National University of Malaysia (UKM).

Abeyratne, S., 2008. 'Economic development and political conflict. Comparative study of Sri Lanka and Malaysia', *South Asia Economic Journal* 9(2): 393–417.

Brammer, A., 2010. *Social work law*. 3rd ed. Harlow, England, New York: Pearson Longman.

Clarke, G., 1998. 'Non-governmental organizations (NGOs) and politics in the developing world', *Political Studies* 46(1): 36–52.

Crabtree, S.A., 2005. 'Medical social work in Malaysia. Issues in practice', *International Social Work* 48(6): 732–41.

Crépeau, F., 2014. *Report of the Special Rapporteur on the human rights of migrants* [online]. Human Rights Council. Available from: www.ohchr.org/Documents/Issues/SRMigrants/A.HRC.26.35.pdf [Accessed 11 November 2015].

Faruqi, S.S., 2010. 'The federal constitution and the social contract', in H. Khek Hua *et al.*, eds, *Managing success in unity.* Putrajaya, Malaysia: Dept. of National Unity and Integration, 49–70.

Federation of Malaysia Constitution. *Legislative Lists as in the Ninth Schedule* [online]. Available from: www.sapp.org.my/pdf/legislative_list_A9.pdf [Accessed 11 November 2015].

Institute for Economics & Peace [online]. Available from: http://economicsandpeace.org/ [Accessed 18 June 2015].

Jabatan Pendaftaran Pertubuhan Malaysia (JPPM). *Statistik Pendaftaran Pertubuhan* [online]. Available from: www.ros.gov.my/index.php/my/statistik-perkhidmatan/statistik-pendaftaran [Accessed 22 August 2015].

Malaysian Association of Social Workers. *A Brief History* [online]. Available from: www.masw.org.my/ [Accessed 15 June 2015].

Marger, M.N., 2003. *Race and ethnic relations. American and global perspectives*. 6th ed. Belmont, Calif., London: Wadsworth; Cengage Learning.

Rashid, S., 2000. 'Social work and professionalization: a legacy of ambivalence', in C. Davies, L. Finlay and A. Bullman (eds), *Changing Practice in Health and Social Care*, London: The Open University/Sage Publications, 316–25.

Sackville, A., 1987. *Professional Associations and Social Work. From Almoner to Medical Social Worker 1950-1970* [online]. Available from: www.kcl.ac.uk/sspp/policy-institute/scwru/swhn/2013/Sackville-WP04-From-Almoner-to-Medical-Social-Worker-1950-to-1970.pdf [Accessed 13 July 2015].

Shamsul, A.B., 2009. *Culture and governance in Malaysia's survival as a nation*. Bangi: Universiti Kebangsaan Malaysia (UKM).

Teo Seong, K., 2010. 'Malaysia ethnic relations. The challenges 50 years ahead', in H. Khek Hua *et al*., eds, *Managing success in unity*. Putrajaya, Malaysia: Dept. of National Unity and Integration, 7–22.

The Malaysian Government. *Dasar Sosial Negara (DSN)* [online]. Available from: www.jkm.gov.my/content.php?pagename=dasar_sosial_negara&lang=en [Accessed 13 July 2015].

WAO. *Migrant Domestic Worker Abuse* [online]. Women's Aid Organisation. Available from: www.wao.org.my/Migrant+Domestic+Workers_54_5_1.htm [Accessed 18 June 2015].

# 12 A profile of the Turkish social welfare system and social work

*Sema Buz*

## A short history of social welfare in Turkey

The social welfare system in Turkey derives from the Ottoman Empire and so had a different process from those of Western countries. In western societies, social security systems were established as a result of industrialisation in order to find solutions to the problems of the working class such as poverty and overpopulation in cities. In the Ottoman Empire, on the other hand, the industrialisation process was relatively slow because the Ottoman economy was largely based on artisanship, only a few factories existed and the working class did not emerge, therefore no social security system developed in the empire. Instead what we see was the predominance of charity – which in the Ottoman Empire can be divided into three parts: familial aid, religious aid (*zakat*, alms, *sadaqah*), and various professional institutional aid (guilds, foundations) (Cicek 2010: 52).

From the foundation of the Republic of Turkey until the 1960s – when the modern institutions of social welfare were inaugurated – the main institutions were Darülaceze (the poor house), Türkiye Kızılay Derneği (The Turkish Red Crescent Society), and Çocuk Esirgeme Kurumu (The Child Protection Agency). The Child Protection Agency was a social assistance institution founded in order to protect children who were left parentless because of the war in 1921 (Himaye-i Etfal Cemiyeti Association for Protection of Children; in 1980 the name of the institution was changed to The Social Services and Child Protection Agency).

The 1961 Constitution was a breakthrough and an important framework concerning social work, since it focused on basic rights and liberties and emphasised the concept of a social state and a state of law. A five-year plan for social and economic development was scheduled and put into practice in 1963. Some of the major topics of the plan were: ensuring that social justice was seen as developing parallel to financial development, and including social insurance activities in the redistribution and fair distribution of income. Ten developmental plans have been implemented since 1961, with the present one in operation since 2014.

## The structure of the state and society in Turkey

In 1923 the Ottoman Empire collapsed and the Republic of Turkey was founded. The process of transition from empire to nation state with its attendant modernisation was mostly carried out by a group of elite men under the leadership of Atatürk. The new state was built with a modern understanding and secularism was seen as a very important founding principle. In 2013 Turkey's population reached 76,667,864, with 91.3 per cent of the population living in cities and the ratio of male to female population was 50.2 per cent to 49.8 per cent respectively (TUIK 2014).

Population development in Turkey is expected to transform from a young aged society into an old aged society with a decrease of the population under the age of 15 and an increase in the age groups between 15 and 64 (Bugra 2001; Koç *et al.* 2010). These changes indicate that the elderly population will be an important target group.

In the latest report on 'Youth, Skills and Employment Ability' prepared by the OECD (the Organisation for Economic Cooperation and Development) Turkey ranks first among OECD countries, with 28.7 per cent of the population aged between 15 and 29 years not employed and not continuing their education (OECD July 2015). For 2013 the unemployment rate was 9.7 per cent and the employment rate 45.9 per cent of which 23.6 per cent were employed in agriculture, 19.4 per cent in industry, 7 per cent in construction, and 50 per cent in the service sector (TUIK 2013). The needs of those who do not work and do not have any social security are mainly met through family solidarity instead of formal statutory measures. According to Bugra (2001: 25) family solidarity stands at the heart of the traditional welfare regime in Turkey, lacking formal regulations and rational bureaucratic procedures.

## Legal framework

The following laws can be seen as legal foundations providing social protection for target groups relevant to social work professionals:

The 1982 Constitution is the current legislation and Article 41 of the Constitution states the duty to protect the family, particularly women and children; Article 61 mentions the protection of people with disabilities, older people and children who are in need of protection. Besides the Constitution, the Civil Law (1926) – which was adopted from Switzerland – is an important law in terms of social work. This law provides equality between men and women, secures monogamy, regulates the principle of equality in inheritance matters, and protects women in divorces.

The Law to Protect Family and Prevent Violence against Women (2012) is aimed at the protection of women and other family members who are subjected to violence or who are at risk of violence. However, there are a number of aspects that prevent the full force of this law, e.g. reluctance of public officials to apply the measures of the law for women who are subjected to violence; patriarchal perspectives; men's violations of restraining orders; ineffective punishments; femicides by intimate partners even when the victim is under police protection.

This leads to the paradoxical situation that despite the law violence against women cannot be prevented.

The aim of the Juvenile Protection Law (2005) is to support the well-being of children who are in need of protection, and to provide rehabilitation for them through protective and supportive measures should they participate in crime. But the problems in the institutional, physical, infrastructural, financial, administrative and labour force areas that are related to the realisation of cautionary measures and other actions to be taken by the courts have not yet been solved (Acar 2012: 22).

The Law of Encouraging Social Assistance and Solidarity (1986) claims to provide assistance to citizens and external migrants/asylum seekers who are living in poverty and are in need of help and includes measures to strengthen social justice for a more equal distribution of income, and encourage social solidarity. Although the state claims to minimise its role and to include civil society organisations including those with a philanthropic emphasis, the state has been criticised concerning its involvement in the realm of social help – including the levels of social assistance expenditure and extensive bureaucracy (Dodurka 2014: 4). Social workers also refer to the international conventions (1989 Convention on the Rights of Children etc.) and other legislations (family legislation, legislation for people with disabilities, etc.) depending on the field of work.

## Social service delivery in Turkey

The Ministry of Family and Social Policies is linked to the central government and has provincial directorates in 81 cities in Turkey. The ministry is responsible for various welfare services in the provinces, including support for women victims of violence. In addition to this, there are local administration units, namely special provincial administrations, municipalities and villages. The special provincial administrations have an especially important function in the realm of social assistance; they operate at the local level and have a significant budget for social assistance; they provide social services and conduct activities in order to combat poverty; support social protection for people in need and reinforce social welfare (Cicek 2010: 52).

Social services in Turkey were provided by central administrative institutions for a long time. Although this situation provided many advantages in terms of central planning, there were also problems concerning the sensitivity of the services to local needs. According to a current preparation (Ministry of Family and Social Policy Infrastructure Project about Transfer of Service Institutions to Local Authority) social service provision is defined as a responsibility of the municipalities and the special provincial administrations. In addition to these state institutions, NGOs and private institutions are beginning to be effective in the provision of social welfare services. For example, women's groups (Purple Roof) and LGBT organisations (Kaos GL) provide consultations and counselling to individuals, group work (such as with parents with LGBT children), advocacy, support groups and inputs to various policy-making processes, whereas other types of NGOs predominantly give social assistance, and have philanthrophic motives in aid disbursement.

With the marketisation process in the fields of elderly care and disability, many profit-oriented institutions have also started to operate, and there is an increase in the subcontracting of care and cleaning services in institutions (Şahín Taşğin and Özel 2011). But there is no joint plan or programme between central administration, municipality, NGOs and the private sector. Every institution pursues its centre and services with its facilities and calculations (TEPAV 2010).

The number of non-governmental organisations in Turkey is rather low compared to the population: on average there is only one NGO for every 780 people. In India there is one NGO for every 600 people (Mahapatra 2014); in Germany and France there is one NGO for about every 40 people. The geographic distribution of the NGOs is also important; they are concentrated in urban areas, mainly in the western regions of the country. There is no policy influencing the agenda of 65 per cent of the NGOs but they focus on social services and solidarity activities (İçduygu *et al.* 2011: 18). Mainly the NGOs working for children, women, LGBT and people with disabilities have an agenda of active involvement in policy-making processes. This has increased somewhat since Turkey has taken a prominent role in European-wide work regarding violence against women – the Council of Europe Convention on preventing and combating violence against women and domestic violence (The Istanbul Convention) was opened for signature in May 2011, in Istanbul, Turkey.

Social workers are mainly employed in public institutions; the number of social workers working in the private sector is comparatively small. 'Familialisation' tendencies remain at the forefront of the provision of social welfare services. Care in the family is thus provided by unpaid carers.

## Professional social work in Turkey

The Social Work Department was founded in 1961 – linked to the then Ministry of Health and Social Assistance – under the name of 'The Academy of Social Services', providing a four-year higher education course. An academic curriculum based on international standards was prepared by renowned social work experts.

In 1965 the Academy was accepted as a member of the International Association of Schools of Social Work. In 1967 The School of Social Work and Social Services was founded within Hacettepe University Faculty of Administrative and Social Sciences, Ankara. During the 1960s and 1970s social workers' roles varied, including working in village and slum development as well as in social welfare institutions (Uğuroğlu 2003). Following the military coup d'état of 12 September 1980, the Academy of Social Work and the Department of Social Work of the University of Hacettepe were united as the Council of Higher Education (YOK) promulgated in 1982. In 2006 the Social Work Department joined Hacettepe University Faculty of Economics and Administrative Sciences. The Social Services and Child Protection Agency (SHCEK) was established in 1983. It was an important institution in view of being a governmental organisation employing the largest number of social workers providing services at community and family levels including through its sub-organisations for children, women, and people with disabilities. Although the Social Services and Child Protection Agency was an important step for a centralised social service provision system, independent institutions in the fields of women and people with disabilities remained. In 2011 the Ministry of Family and Social Policies was founded.

Until the 2000s, the Social Work Department at Hacettepe University remained the only institution offering social work education. As a result of the growing demand for social workers the number of social work schools has been increasing. Currently there are 67 social work departments in Turkey but nearly 20 of them have not started student admission yet because of a lack of academic staff (Hacettepe Üniversitesi Sosyal Çalışma ve Sosyal Hizmetler Forumu). However, the new social work departments have partly been founded without professional social work knowledge and thus the quality of education and professional standardisation remains inadequate. This has led to a critical debate concerning the quality of social work education in Turkey and also concerning the lack of competencies of social workers graduating from these recently established programmes. Those who have bachelor's degrees in social work can work in institutions with different target groups (children, families, poor people) without any further accreditation. Social workers mostly work in public institutions (after receiving a valid score in the KPSS exam – a national selection examination conducted by the government for the selection of employees in the public sector). In Turkey there is no exam or accreditation for professional competence or work.

In 1965 The Union of Social Workers was founded and it was transformed into the Association of Social Workers in 1970. After the military coup d'état of 1980 the association was closed, and only re-opened in 1988. In 2002, the Turkish Association of Social Workers (SHUD) became a member of the International Federation of Social Workers (IFSW) and published a manual called 'Ethical Codes for Social Workers' based on international ethical standards for social work (NASW, IFSW), (SHUD, Sosyal Hizmet Uzmanlari Derneği 2003). Social workers now learn these ethical principles during their education, and any cases of ethical violations are discussed in the ethical commission of the Association. The total number of social workers in Turkey is 6,150 and members of SHUD working in public institutions is 2,180 (SHUD, Sosyal Hizmet Uzmanlari Derneği 2015).

## Challenges for social work: central problems

Poverty is a very important social issue: throughout the country 9.5–12.5 per cent of families live below the starvation line, 29–36 per cent live below the poverty line. In Turkey 34 per cent of children under the age of 16 are at risk of relative poverty. According to The Turkish Statistical Institute more than 50 per cent of the single resident households who are aged 65 and over are in the lowest income group (TUIK 2014).

Social expenditures in Turkey are insufficient (Candas *et al.* 2010; Bugra and Adar 2011; UNICEF 2012; Özbek 2002). In 2008, 11.5 per cent of GDP was allocated to social protection expenditure, increasing to 13 per cent in the period 2010–2012; this remained the same for the period 2013–2015. Although this is a very positive development, it is highly insufficient for Turkey. One of the most important deficiencies of the social protection system in Turkey is the lack of a steady citizenship-based income support mechanism funded by the tax revenues (Public Expenditures Monitoring Report 2011: 3). The Turkish Government tries to assign its responsibilities of social policy to voluntary agencies, rather than regulating financial policies to increase public social expenditures. Fundraising activities are also an important part of the current operations of the government in the field of social policy. For example, the Rainbow Project conducted by the Administration of People with Disabilities and the Ministry of Education envisages the rehabilitation of people with disabilities and their integration into the job market. The financial obligations of the project are planned to be covered by charitable contributions (Bugra and Adar 2011).

Gender equality is a major challenge and the 'Global Social Gender Gap Report' of the World Economic Forum ranks Turkey 125th concerning gender equality while recent Turkish figures confirm low employment rates (below 30 per cent), and high illiteracy rates among women (five times more among women than men) (TUIK 2014).

Gender-based violence is also a very important issue. According to recent research, 36 per cent of married women are subjected to violence from their husbands; 10 per cent of women are subjected to physical violence during pregnancy; 38 per cent of women are subjected to physical and/or sexual violence; 12 per cent of married women are subjected to sexual violence. Only 11 per cent of women apply for institutional help (*Domestic Violence Against Women in Turkey* 2014: 9).

Another emerging issue is the current problem of Syrian refugees and asylum-seekers: there are approximately 2 million Syrian refugees in Turkey, accommodated in camps and distributed around cities, yet they predominantly do not have access to social welfare services. There are numerous claims that women and girls who cannot meet basic needs and live under the poverty line are forced into prostitution, subjected to sexual harassment or child marriages in return for money and unofficial marriages as a second or third wife (Mazlumder 2014: 26ff).

## Conclusion – outcomes for social work

Whilst Turkey has maintained its traditional and conservative welfare regime, many changes have been implemented in view of the EU accession process and in view of the articulation of neoliberal policies giving rise to changes in legislation, the social security system and delivery of social services. By force of neoliberal policies, the proportion of disadvantaged and marginalised communities in Turkey has increased (Buz *et al.* 2012; Gürses 2009: 210) and as such, new social work policy needs to emphasise social justice and provide for more social workers. In these circumstances, the responsibility of social work to promote social justice has gained increasing importance (Buz *et al.* 2012).

Turkey's transition to philanthropic policies in the social realm, the acceptance of social assistance and services as important tools to maintain political power, and important fund transfers in the field of social assistance are negative developments with regard to social work. Mainstream social policies in Turkey as well as social welfare services are predominantly reduced to social assistance with limited or small-scale professional expertise. This devalues the profession and reduces social work to a 'technical' dimension.

## References

Acar, H., 2012. *10. Beş Yıllık Kalkınma Planı Çocuk Özel İhtisas Komisyonu Ön Rapor.* Ankara: Türkiye Cumhuriyeti Kalkınma Bakanlığı.

Bugra, A., 2001. 'Ekonomik Kriz karşısında Türkiye'nin Geleneksel Refah Rejimi. Turkey's traditional welfare regime against economic crisis', *Toplum ve Bilim* (89): 22–30.

Bugra, A., and Adar, S., 2011. *Türkiye'nin Kamu Sosyal Koruma Harcamalarının Karşılaştırmalı Bir Analizi. A comparative analysis of Turkey's public social protection expenditures.* İstanbul: Boğaziçi Üniversitesi Sosyal Politika Forumu.

Buz, S., Ontas, C.O., and Hatiboglu, B., 2012. 'Opinions of social work students from Turkey on social justice', *International Social Work* 56(6): 724–42.

Candas, A., *et al.*, 2010. *Türkiye'de Eşitsizlikler: Kalıcı Eşitsizliklere Genel Bir Bakış. Inequalities in Turkey: A general outlook at permanent inequalities.* İstanbul: Boğaziçi Üniversitesi Sosyal Politika Forumu.

Cicek, E., 2010. 'Türkiye'de Belediyelerin Sosyal Hizmet ve Sosyal Yardım Faaliyetleri. Social services and social assistance activities of municipalities in Turkey', *Yerel Siyaset Aylık Bilimsel Siyasi Dergi* 39(4): 49–52.

Dodurka, B.Z., 2014. *Türkiye'de Merkezi Devlet Eliyle Yapılan Sosyal Yardımlar. Çalışma Raporu.* İstanbul: Boğaziçi Üniversitesi Sosyal Politika Forumu.

*Domestic Violence against Women in Turkey,* 2014 [online]. Available from: www.hips. hacettepe.edu.tr/ING_SUMMARY_REPORT_VAW_2014.pdf [Accessed 12 December 2015].

Gürses, D., 2009. 'An analysis of child poverty and social policies in Turkey', *Journal of Developing Societies* 25(2): 209–27.

Hacettepe Üniversitesi Sosyal Çalışma ve Sosyal Hizmetler Forumu. *Tarihçe* [online]. Available from: www.scforum.hacettepe.edu.tr/tarihce.shtml [Accessed 20 December 2015].

İçduygu, A., Meydanoğlu, Z., and Sert, D.Ş., 2011. *Türkiye'de sivil toplum. Uluslararası sivil toplum endeksi projesi Türkiye ülke raporu.* İstanbul: TÜSEV Yayınları.

Koç, İ., *et al.*, 2010. *Türkiye'nin Demografik Dönüşümü. Doğurganlık, Aile Planlaması, Anne-Çocuk Sağlığı ve Beş Yaş Altı Ölümlerdeki Değişimler: 1968-2008. Demographic transformation of Turkey.* Ankara: Hacettepe Üniversitesi Nüfus Etütleri Enstitüsü.

Mahapatra, D., 2014. *India witnessing NGO boom, there is 1 for every 600 people* [online]. Available from: http://timesofindia.indiatimes.com/india/India-witnessing-NGO-boom-there-is-1-for-every-600-people/articleshow/30871406.cms [Accessed 20 December 2015].

Mazlumder, 2014. *Syrian asylum seeker women live outside of camps.* Ankara: Mazlumder Yayını.

OECD, 2015. *OECD Employment Outlook 2015* [online]. Organisation for Economic Co-operation and Development (OECD). Available from: www.oecd.org/turkey/Employment-Outlook-Turkey-EN.pdf [Accessed 12 December 2015].

Özbek, N., 2002. Osmanlı'dan Günümüze Türkiye'de Sosyal Devlet. *Toplum ve Bilim* (92): 7–33.

Public Expenditures Monitoring Report, 2011. *2011 yılı Kamu Harcamaları İzleme Raporu Kamuoyu Duyurusu* [online]. Available from: kahip.org/site_media/docs/basinmektubu2011. doc [Accessed 12 December 2015].

Şahín Taşğin, N., and Özel, H., 2011. 'Transformation of social services in Turkey', *Society and Social Work* 22(2): 175–90.

SHUD, Sosyal Hizmet Uzmanlari Derneği, 2003. *Sosyal Hizmet Mesleginin Etik Ilkeleri ve Sorumlulukları* [online]. Available from: www.shudernegi.org/?pnum=42 [Accessed 12 December 2015].

SHUD, Sosyal Hizmet Uzmanlari Derneği, 2015. *Sosyal Hizmet Mesleginin Etik Ilkeleri ve Sorumlulukları* [online]. Available from: www.shudernegi.org/?pnum=175&pt=T%C3 %BCrkiye%27deki+Sosyal+Hizmet+Uzman%C4%B1+Say%C4%B1lar%C4%B1 [Accessed 27 December 2015].

TEPAV, 2010. *Sosyal Hizmetlerin Sunumunda Kademelenme* [online]. Turkiye Ekonomi Politikaları Arastirma Vakfı. Available from: www.tepav.org.tr/upload/files/1285329379-1.Sosyal_Hizmetlerde_Kademelenme.pdf [Accessed 12 December 2015].

TUIK, 2013. *Turkey in statistics* [online]. Turkish Statistical Institute. Available from: www.amasyaplanlama.gov.tr/ortak_icerik/amasyaplanlama/istatistiklerle%20t%C3% BCrkiye%202013.pdf [Accessed 10 January 2016].

TUIK, 2014. *Women in statistics* [online]. Turkish Statistical Institute. Available from: www. turkstat.gov.tr/PreHaberBultenleri.do?id=18619 [Accessed 10 January 2016].

Uğuroğlu, H., 2003. *Dünden Bugüne Türkiye'de Sosyal Hizmet Mesleği* [online]. Sosyal Hizmet Uzmanlari Derneği. Available from: www.shudernegi.org/?pnum=6&pt=Tarih% C3%A7e [Accessed 10 January 2016].

UNICEF, 2012. *Türkiye'de Çocuk ve Genç Nüfusun Durumunun Analizi* [online]. Available from: http://abdigm.meb.gov.tr/projeler/ois/egitim/033.pdf [Accessed 12 December 2015].

# Part III

# Case Studies

*Ursula Kämmerer-Rütten, Alexandra Schleyer-Lindenmann, Beatrix Schwarzer and Yafang Wang*

## Introduction

Case studies are seen as an excellent way to provide insight into theoretical concepts and their practical implementation with a very specific focus on individual examples to illustrate a wider context. Therefore, Part III of this book presents case studies from all the countries introduced in Part II. The case studies aim to address current transnational issues in their respective national contexts and ways of dealing with problems and challenges through social work interventions.

In general, social work has three fields of action:

- First, social workers work with individuals and groups (families, communities etc.) and do 'case work';
- Second, social workers are concerned with social improvements and the overall well-being of their clientele, especially concerning the most vulnerable groups in societies;
- Third, social workers are encouraged to contribute with professional expertise to the development of (national and global) policies to improve the quality of life in society and campaign for social justice and equality.

Transnational social work shares these three fields of action but points to a lack of recognition concerning special demands resulting from international political and social developments such as migration, flight of refugees, violent conflicts and global hierarchies.

The cases in this section shed light on transnational perspectives of social work along at least one of the two related lines:

1  Individual approach: The case studies present specific life situations of people and illuminate the transnational perspective.
2  Global social justice approach: The case studies start from global demands for social justice and enlighten the effects of global developments on the local level.

In order to enlarge the transnational perspective even further, each case is followed by two comments from authors of other countries portrayed in this book. The aim of this approach is to consider a case from different national perspectives and highlight similarities or differences as well as potentials or restrictions in social work practice. Each case study and the corresponding comments should be read and understood as interconnected entities with the aim to facilitate mutual understanding and transnational thinking. It is not deliberately intended to compare or even criticise countries or ways of dealing with similar issues by way of comment – quite the contrary, the case study and comment approach aims to facilitate the transfer of knowledge of social work practices from one context to another and enhance professional interest and comprehension.

The case studies cover eight subjects for transnational social work:

1 Educational inequalities of migrant children (China)
2 Refugees and asylum seekers (France)
3 Drug abuse (Germany)
4 Rights of migrant children (Great Britain)
5 Gender inequalities and violence against women (India)
6 Aging in war zones (Israel)
7 Poverty and exploitation of migrant workers (Malaysia)
8 Returnees (Turkey).

The eight case studies address three challenges for transnational social work:

• Access to social rights
• Relationship between international rights and citizenship rights
• Belonging and hybrid identities.

## Access to social rights

One major challenge for social work is related to industrialisation and world trade as well as their effects, such as exploitation of workers. The case study from China addresses the educational inequality for children of rural workers in the rural–urban migration process: due to increasing industrialisation and economic booms, farmers move to urban areas to meet the demand for (uneducated) workers, seeking at the same time better income and living conditions. Despite the important contribution of rural migrant workers to (urban) economic development, their rights to social welfare are largely restricted. These constraints can be seen in the outright denial of citizenship rights, e.g. education for children and health care for people who cannot register as urban dwellers. The case study reveals the challenges and the restrictions for social workers advocating for these people and attempting to develop strategies to reduce inequalities, especially for children.

The case study from Great Britain also focuses on children's rights but takes up this issue in the context of a refugee family. Different cultural norms influence attitudes concerning the concept of childhood and the importance of the family. The case study illustrates the difficult dynamics resulting from cultural differences between the family and the social worker. Moreover, this case deals with the complex situation of physical and psychological demands caused by fleeing from the Republic of Congo, distrust of the client towards state institutions and misunderstandings caused by different cultural norms and demands. The juggling of these demands by each family member and by the social workers is only one of the interesting aspects of this case.

The case from France also takes up the issue of refugees, highlighting the complex process of seeking asylum and the challenges for social work practice in this context: the case shows the correlation of global issues played out on the local level in connection to a supra-national legal framework. Social work is faced with the dual mandate of caring for people in need and at the same time being the gatekeeper for legal obligations formulated on European and national levels. As in the British case study, (inter)cultural competences are shown as major requirements for social workers.

The case study from Malaysia addresses aspects already perceptible in the case studies from France and China: the case deals with the question of exploitation linked to the absence of citizen's rights. Based on the example of domestic workers from Indonesia, the case study looks into the denial of international labour rights by the dominant host country. Fixed working hours as well as demands to rest and recover – as laid down by national law – do not apply to non-citizens. Moreover, the exploitation of (female) workers – who constitute the majority of domestic workers in Malaysia – is strongly affected by violence against women. The case shows that professional social work nearly does not exist for non-citizens, who fight for better living and working conditions only with the help of legal advocacy organisations and critical media.

The case study from India also takes up the issue of violence against women and the influence of the media. The case focuses on a gang rape that attracted global media attention. The case study links transnational women's movements and advocacy networks and connects the international level to the local proceedings. It points to the dynamics influencing the demands for justice and revenge and raises questions concerning the ongoing violence against women occurring every day. This case shows that social work cannot restrict itself to case work with clients, but also has a political responsibility to promote social and political change and development concerning the liberation of people (IFSW 2014) and the abolition of gender inequalities on local, national and global levels.

The case study from Germany addresses the global issue of drug addiction and shows strikingly that the possibilities of social work interventions are highly dependent on national concepts, laws and politics. This case study indicates that working against isolation and social stigmatisation are major professional objectives and social work in Germany aims to enable drug users to be part of society. Basic rights like access to housing and employment are significant objectives but so also is lobbying on a community level for public health. Considering the issue of drug abuse as a global phenomenon on the one hand, it is the (national) legal framework that enables or disables social (case) work to a large extent.

The political conflict between Israel and Palestine is the starting point and frame for the case study from Israel. In view of the long-term nature of the violent conflict which affects people in this area, the case study focuses on a common issue of social work: aging populations. The case study shows that the experience of dealing with situations like missile attacks differs from one person to another, even among a rather homogeneous age group. The study points to problems like isolation and trauma and emphasises the impact on elderly people but also the potential of social support.

## Relationship of international rights and citizenship rights

Beside the common issues and local strategies the case studies can be read along the line of the challenging relationship of human rights as a global ethical framework applying to everyone regardless of differences such as gender, ethnicity or nationality, and the protective yet exclusive notion of citizenship rights (linked to national territories).

The underlying theme of the case studies of China, France and Great Britain is freedom of movement clashing with the provision of social rights such as education, housing and health care reserved only for certain (obviously more privileged) groups – citizens, or in the case of much of China, urban citizens.

Similarly, this can be seen in the case of Malaysia, where the 'ILO Declaration on Fundamental Principles and Rights at Work' (ILO 1998) does not impact on the everyday experience of domestic workers who are usually unaware of protections provided by law.

The origin and effects of structural inequalities, like gender inequality, are highly debated at international levels. The Convention and the Beijing Platform for Action (UN Women) formulated in 2000 are examples of international agreements informed by local developments and struggles. At best, activities resulting from these conventions should spread their influence on national and local levels and hold political institutions accountable. The case study from India shows this process by focusing on issues of violence against women conflicting with the demand for bodily integrity. In the framework of political activism it is shown by the case study that the women's movement in India finds itself in the position of fighting against gender inequality and violence but also has to stand up against claims for a death penalty.

Social work as a profession needs to juggle with the often conflictual relation between rights formulated on different levels which are to be acted out in order to realise the objective of social justice in a local context.

## Belonging and hybrid identities

Taking into account that transnational social work is concerned with issues of social justice and human rights *across* national borders, we need to consider that the issue of the individual belonging to a community or a nation state or a culture is something that cannot be left aside. (Subjective) belonging (Bhambra 2015) refers to the fact that our categorical objective memberships (e.g. nationality, gender, professional group) are only some of many dimensions that constitute identity. Relating to the question of identity formation, what significance does membership to communities and/or nation states have for us? What are our subjective feelings of belonging and how does that interact with the local surroundings?

The case study from Turkey provides evidence that migration can have a wide range of consequences, especially on questions of categorical boundaries and feelings of belonging. These consequences not only concern the individual (migrant), but also the communities – this is not only about the 'new' community migrants move into, but also the community the migrants have left. On the one hand, migrants change and challenge national culture by adding new cultural features such as food, music and language. On the other hand, migrants are influenced by the new context they are living in. This influence reaches into identity formation, inter-generational conflicts, feelings of belonging and sometimes being an outsider at the same time, especially if coming back to the country of origin after a long period in a foreign country (returnees).

This question of acculturation processes and their effects on identity and identity strategies also emerges from the Israeli case study. By contrasting rural and urban communities and the conditions of belonging, it can be seen that freedom of decision making, e.g. in moving to a certain place, is an important objective.

It can be seen in most of the case studies presented in this section, that the issue of acculturation and identity continuity/change is of crucial importance to the well-being of people – and even more so, when people live transnational lives.

## References

Bhambra, G.K., 2015. 'Citizens and Others. The Constitution of Citizenship through Exclusion', *Alternatives: Global, Local, Political* 40(2): 102–14.

IFSW, 2014. *Global Definition of Social Work* [online]. 'International Federation of Social Workers'. Available from: http://ifsw.org/get-involved/global-definition-of-social-work/ [Accessed 16 January 2016].

ILO, 1998. *ILO Declaration on Fundamental Principles and Rights at Work* [online]. International Labour Organization. Available from: www.ilo.org/declaration/lang--en/index.htm [Accessed 10 January 2016].

UN Women. *Convention on the Elimination of All Forms of Discrimination against Women* [online]. Available from: www.un.org/womenwatch/daw/cedaw/ [Accessed 10 June 2015].

# 13 Educational inequality of migrant children and school social work interventions

*Diqing Jiang, Shanmin Peng and Yafang Wang*

## Migration and educational inequality of migrant children in China

Globalisation, the rise of the market economy and urbanisation have caused continuous intra-country migration in China, which is different from the transnational migration in most Western countries. Whilst intra-country migration does not cross national borders, it does cross what we call the 'rural–urban boundary', which to a great extent represents a dual structure or social divide in China. Through this example, rural–urban migration in China could broaden our transnational perspectives by redefining 'borders': not only national borders but more essentially structural borders or boundaries.

Since the Chinese government adopted an open-door policy in 1978, the last three decades have witnessed fantastic economic growth. As the world factory in the global capitalist system, China's east coast areas drew huge amounts of cheap labour, giving rise to an unprecedented movement of rural-to-urban internal migration. According to the National Bureau of Statistics (National Bureau of Statistics of China 2009), the number of migrant workers rocketed to 242 million (Chan 2009). It is estimated that over 13 million of the children who accompany their migrant parents are eligible for compulsory education (Ministry of Education of the People's Republic of China 2014).

Such huge numbers of migrant children have posed a serious challenge to China's public education system. Although the Compulsory Education Law claims that all children between six and fifteen years of age are entitled to nine years of compulsory education, most migrant children have been deprived of rights to study in urban public schools due to China's Household Registration System (Hukou). The Hukou system was established in 1955 with the purpose of strictly controlling social mobility (Han 2004). This system still divides Chinese people into two classes – urban residents versus peasants. Local governments have obligations to offer social welfare for residents whose Hukou status is registered in their jurisdiction (Solinger 1999).

During the 1980s, market-oriented reforms undermined the Hukou system. In order to exploit cheap labour for the global market, peasants were allowed to work in cities. The majority of migrant workers are concentrated in labour-intensive, low-skill and low-pay occupations, contributing upwards of 16 per cent of China's

GDP growth (Hamey 2008). In spite of this contribution, they are still denied urban Hukou status and related social benefits (Wang *et al.* 2013).

To make things worse, institutional exclusion has extended to their children. From the beginning of the migration movement, urban public schools generally refused to admit migrant children on the grounds that, according to the Hukou system, the migrants' hometown would be in charge of their compulsory education. As a result, migrants who wanted their children to receive education in urban public schools had to pay a great deal of 'school support fees' for admission. The fees charged by public schools varied from several hundred to thousands of RMB for each student, unaffordable for the majority of migrant families (Duan and Liang 2005). Therefore, most migrant children had and still have to enter sub-standard 'private migrant schools' which are notorious for unqualified teachers, out-of-date curricula, and shortage of teaching equipment.

## Educational policies concerning migrant children and the reproduction of inequality

In January 1995, journalist Jianping Li published a report on the education of migrant children. The description of the dire study environment shocked the public and triggered a heated debate. Faced with public pressure, the Chinese government took measures to improve the education of migrant children. In 1996, China's National Committee of Education, the predecessor of the Ministry of Education, issued Interim Measures of School Education for School-age Children among the Rural Migrant Population. These permitted migrant children to apply to urban schools based on their parents' temporary residency certificate instead of the household registration status (Chen and Feng 2013). In 1998, the committee announced the Interim Measures of School Education for Temporary Migrant Children, which ruled that public primary and secondary schools of host cities should offer the majority of migrant children temporary study, implying the transfer of obligation for the education of migrant children from sending areas to receiving areas. In 2001, the State Council articulated two principles for migrant children's education in The Decision of Reform and Development of Elementary Education: first, the government of host cities has the duty to provide migrant children with compulsory education; second, the public school system of host cities should enrol all migrant children. These two principles remain valid.

The policies yielded fruit: by 2014, around 80 per cent of migrant children entered urban schools to study with local urban children under the same blue sky (OECD 2015: 58). In spite of this accomplishment educational inequality is far from disappearing; the Chinese government still denies migrant children urban status and also denies them access to secondary education in urban public schools. Migrant children still have to return to high schools in their home regions if they want to take part in the national college entrance examinations, which are far more competitive and much harder than those in cities (Wang 2011).[1]

In addition to institutional exclusion, social discrimination has profoundly affected migrant children's development. Living in cities year after year, most of the migrant children have become accustomed to an urban lifestyle and identify themselves with urban children, even though they have no urban Hukou status. However, in public schools, they still experience discrimination. Their urban classmates often look down upon them as rural kids of inferior status, seldom talking or playing with them (Wang 2008). Gradually, most migrant children lose the interest and aspiration to enter higher-level schools, which are crucial to social mobility. Studies have shown that the self-esteem of migrant children is much lower than that of urban children (Zhuang 2011) and their academic performance is below the average level (Zhou and Wu 2008). It has been found that a high percentage of migrant children suffer from serious emotional and behavioural disorders (Xiao and Feng 2008). In some schools, migrant children even form a distinctive group and develop a sub-culture similar to what Willis (1981) described in *Learning to Labor* (Xiong 2010). As a result, when graduating from middle school, many migrant children are generally unable to escape their parents' fate.

In sum, despite the gradually improving educational conditions for migrant children, these efforts have not been enough to eradicate all educational inequalities affecting migrant children. In connection with the Hukou system, they even play a role in reproducing such inequalities.

## School social work interventions for migrant children

Confronted with various emotional and behavioural problems among migrant children as well as their learning difficulties, the Chinese government has required school teachers to render more assistance; school teachers are asked to make home visits and support migrant children and their families. However, it is difficult for teachers to meet such requirements since they are already burdened, by exam-oriented teaching, for example.

Recently, many urban public schools and migrant schools have introduced school social workers (SSWs) to support migrant children. Compared with teachers, SSWs have a broader mission to promote social justice and educational equality rather than narrowly focus on academic performance. Moreover, the SSWs are equipped with a unique professional ecological perspective, which takes each child as an inseparable part of various social systems including families, schools and communities. This perspective enables SSWs to broaden their conceptualisation of students' problems and deliver services at various levels. At the micro level, SSWs make interventions to mitigate children's behavioural problems and enhance parenting skills. At the middle level, SSWs improve the school environment and utilise community resources. At the macro level, SSWs advocate new policies on behalf of child welfare (Dupper 2003).

The following section describes the case of Lequn in Shanghai to illustrate SSWs' achievements and challenges in promoting educational equality for migrant children.

### *The Lequn Project*

By 2010, migrant children accounted for one-third of all school-age children in Shanghai (Lan 2014). Since 1990, Shanghai has been one of the few cities that have opened public schools to migrant children. The city has even extended the scheme from compulsory education to vocational education. A range of learning options are provided for migrant children, for example nursing, computer science, engineering, and cooking skills, so that they can have a chance to obtain a stable job with an adequate salary (Chen 2009). However, the Shanghai government found that some serious problems still prevail among migrant children, including poor academic performance, high drop-out rates, behavioural and mental disorders (Li *et al.* 2010).

In order to cope with these problems, the officials from the Education Department at Pudong District in Shanghai introduced SSWs to schools in 2002. They designed a 'one school, one social worker' programme and invited Lequn Social Work Service Organization to deliver social work services to six schools.

With a fund of half a million renminbi (RMB)[2] from the government, Lequn ran a one-year campaign titled 'Simple School Project'. Each school was assigned a social worker. At first, Lequn's social workers employed the House–Tree–Person Psychological Test[3] and Achenbach Children Behaviour Checklist[4] to evaluate migrant children's mental health. They observed children's behaviours and emotional responses in classrooms, playgrounds and dining rooms. The problems they recorded included withdrawal from groups, difficulty in sleeping or eating, anger, aggression, defiance etc. Then they identified ten students with significant behavioural problems at each school. With an ecological perspective, Lequn workers made home visits, interviewed parents, mapped out a genogram, culturagram[5] and social history, and analysed social factors of misbehaviour. They found that migrant children were exposed significantly to more risks than urban students: many migrant children grew up in single-parent families; parents took two or three jobs at the same time with little time to care for their children; often, physical abuse was used to punish children. In addition, poor housing conditions impaired their health. Altogether, the socialisation of migrant children encountered numerous barriers, including discrimination by urban classmates, lack of pocket money to participate in school events, poor health. Thus, migrant students often show low self-esteem and inadequate communication skills. Given those problems, Lequn workers collaborated with teachers to design various intervention plans. Their projects were based on the Interpersonal Cognitive Problem Solving (ICPS) programme model aimed at teaching migrant children communication and decision-making skills (Greenberg *et al.* 2000). They adopted the following intervention methods to modify behaviours and enhance social competencies of the migrant children.

The Simple School Project achieved remarkable effects. Many children improved their behaviours and study results. With extended funds, in 2006, Lequn launched the 'Sunny Childhood Project', which provided a broad range of services like family therapy, counselling classes for teachers, and chances for community participation.

Since 2008, the Shanghai government has allowed migrant children to attend public vocational schools. Lequn set up career orientation for students at middle

*Table 13.1* Intervention methods for behavioural modification and social competence
enhancement of migrant children

| Methods | Grade | Time | Outcome |
|---|---|---|---|
| Counselling | Elementary and middle school | once a week | reduce stress, anxiety, increase social skills |
| Token reward[1] | Elementary and middle school | eight classes per week | reduce disruptive behaviour |
| Chinese chess | Elementary school | two hours per week | enhance attention and prudence |
| Puppet | Elementary school | two hours per week | improve social skills |
| Finger Painting | Middle school | two hours per week | less aggressive, quieter and more creative |

1 Token reward was used to reduce the frequency of disruptive behaviours like screaming and
whistling in class. Lequn workers set agreements with children: if the disruptive behaviours
decreased, the children would get rewards like cakes and pencils.

schools. Migrant students visited automobile factories, top restaurants in
skyscrapers and famous accounting firms in Shanghai. The clean and comfortable
working environment, modern facilities and high salaries inspired them to
pursue new dreams. Most of them began to study much harder in order to enter
vocational schools.

'I am Shanghainese' was a programme to enhance social integration. Lequn
organised a group of elderly Shanghainese as volunteers to teach migrant children
the Shanghai dialect and history at community centres as an extracurricular
activity. At the end of the programme, Lequn arranged a one-day tour of landmark
buildings or museums in the city.

### The dilemmas faced by Lequn social workers

When they started, Lequn social workers shared the same mission, perspective,
and methods as their counterparts in the Western world. However, as they struggle
to adapt to local situations, their practices differ in the following aspects:

Mission: although the original goal of Lequn's projects was to mobilise the
resources of local education agencies and communities to meet the needs of
students and families, in practice their social workers designed and implemented
projects with the priority of reducing or preventing behavioural problems instead
of improving school and living circumstances, and advancing political advocacy
for equal rights of migrant children.

Power: in spite of the broad range of services they provide, the Chinese SSWs
are regarded as assistants and subordinate to teachers. It is the same with Lequn
social workers – they are seldom invited to participate in the policy-making

process of school or community affairs, and intervention plans cannot be implemented without teachers' permission.

## Conclusion and discussion from a transnational perspective

In comparison to migration stories in many developed countries, the migration inside China and the educational inequality of migrant children are more characteristic of structural inequalities than cultural differences; with the development of China's market economy, Chinese migrant children have been experiencing institutional exclusion, (global) economic exploitation and social discrimination. Due to the still prevalent Hukou system as a fundamental structural divide, migrant children have been confronted with educational inequalities in various forms and face the high risk of becoming a new underclass.

In the last decade, Lequn and some other Chinese non-governmental organisations (NGOs) have conducted school social work services in numerous schools and produced many respectable outcomes. However, the situation is far from favourable for the development of a school social work aiming to promote educational equality for migrant children. In general, social work in China still lacks legitimate status and public recognition. School social work in particular can only be subordinate to the powerful conventional school system which is heavily exam-oriented.

What is even more challenging is that social workers in China have rather limited space to critically activate institutional change and policy reform. As a result, despite the crucial help from Chinese SSWs, migrant children still suffer from significant educational inequalities created by various institutional barriers, especially the stratified Hukou system. Only with and through enabling justice-oriented critical social policies (Otto and Ziegler 2014) can social workers fight effectively against the educational inequality and social exclusion for migrant children. Justice-orientation accurately represents one crucial perspective for transnational social work.

## Notes

1 In China, a college sets a fixed admission quota for each province, often with a higher number of students coming from its home province. Because most good colleges are located in east coast cities, those urban children find it much easier to enter college. For example, compared to Shanghai, Henan province has fewer colleges per capita, therefore an applicant in Henan needs a much higher score than his/her Shanghai counterpart to get into the same college.
2 Half a million RMB is around 83,333 USD.
3 The House–Tree–Person drawing is a test invented by Robert C. Burn to evaluate personality in children. It asks each child to draw a house, a tree, and a person in motion, with a different sheet of paper for each.
4 Achenbach Child Behaviour Checklist refers to a standardised measure in child psychology for evaluating maladaptive behavioural and emotional problems.
5 A culturagram is a tool social workers widely use to make a family assessment that provides a graphical representation of various aspects of an individual and family's culture.

# References

Chan, A., 2009. *Paying the price for economic development. The children of migrant workers in China* [online]. Available from: www.clb.org.hk/sites/default/files/archive/en/share/File/research_reports/Children_of_Migrant_Workers.pdf [Accessed 17 September 2015].

Chen, J., 2009. 'Chengshi zhong Zhixiao Zhaoshou Nongmingong Zinü de Shijian yu Sikao – Jiyu Shanghai Shidian Xuexiao de Diaocha', *Jiaoyu Fazhan Yanjiu* 29(13): 444.

Chen, Y.Y., and Feng, S.Z., 2013. 'Access to public schools and the education of migrant children in China', *China Economic Review* (26): 75–88.

Duan, C., and Liang, H., 2005. 'Guanyu Liudong ertong yiwujiaoyu wenti de diaocha yanjiu', *Renkou yu Jingji* (1): 11–17.

Dupper, D.R., 2003. *School social work. Skills and interventions for effective practice.* Hoboken, N.J.: J. Wiley & Sons.

Greenberg, M.T., Domitrovich, C., and Bumbarger, B., 2000. *Preventing mental disorders in school-age children. A review of the effectiveness of prevention programs.* University Park: Pennsylvania State University.

Hamey, A., 2008. *Migrants are China's 'factories without smoke'* [online]. CNN. Available from: http://edition.cnn.com/2008/WORLD/asiapcf/02/01/china.migrants/index.html [Accessed 17 November 2015].

Han, J., 2004. 'Survey report on the state of compulsory education among migrant children in Beijing', *Chinese Education and Society* 37(5): 29–55.

Lan, P.C., 2014. 'Segmented incorporation. The second generation of rural migrants in Shanghai', *The China Quarterly* (217): 243–65.

Li, L., Li, S., and Chen, Y., 2010. 'Better city, better life, but for whom? The hukou and resident card system and the consequential citizenship stratification in Shanghai', *City, Culture and Society* 1(3): 145–54.

Ministry of Education of the People's Republic of China, 2014. *Educational Statistics in 2013* [online]. Available from: www.moe.edu.cn/publicfiles/business/htmlfiles/moe/s8489/index.html [Accessed 10 January 2016].

National Bureau of Statistics of China, 2009. *China Statistical Yearbook* [online]. Available from: www.stats.gov.cn/tjsj/ndsj/2009/indexeh.htm [Accessed 10 January 2016].

OECD, 2015. *OECD Economic Surveys China* [online]. OECD, Organisation for Economic Co-operation and Development. Available from: www.oecd.org/eco/surveys/China-2015-overview.pdf [Accessed 10 January 2016].

Otto, H.-U., and Ziegler, H., 2014. *Critical social policy and the capability approach.* Opladen: Barbara Budrich.

Solinger, D.J., 1999. *Contesting citizenship in urban China. Peasant migrants, the state, and the logic of the market.* Berkeley: University of California Press.

Wang, H., Guo, F., and Cheng, Z., 2013. 'Discrimination in migrant workers' welfare entitlements and benefits in urban labour market. Findings from a four-city study in China', *Population, Space and Place* 21(2): 124–39.

Wang, H.X., 2011. 'Access to higher education in China. Differences in opportunity', *Frontiers of Education in China* 6(2): 227–47.

Wang, L., 2008. 'The marginality of migrant children in the urban Chinese educational system', *British Journal of Sociology of Education* 29(6): 691–703.

Willis, P.E., 1981. *Learning to labor. How working class kids get working class jobs.* New York: Columbia University Press.

Xiao, K., and Feng, B., 2008. *Psychological problems of migrant children.* Hebei: Hebei Education Publishing House.

Xiong, Y.H., 2010. 'Underclass, school and class reproduction', *Open Times* (1): 94–110.
Zhou, H., and Wu, X., 2008. 'School performance of migrant children and its determinants. A hierarchical linear model analysis', *Demographic Studies* (4): 22–32.
Zhuang, Y., 2011. 'Nongmingong Zinü Chengshi Jiuxue de Zibei Xinli ji Jiaoyu Duice', *Taian Jiaoyu Xueyuan Xuebao Daizong Xuekan* 15(1): 19–21.

# 14 Migrant children and social work interventions in India

## Comment on the Chinese case study from an Indian perspective

*Shewli Kumar*

Globalisation in Asia has impacted on existing lifestyles and development processes in multiple ways: Asian economies have traditionally been agricultural, with almost 60–70 per cent of the population living in rural areas (FAO 2014: VI). In India, existing marginalised groups like the scheduled tribes, scheduled castes, girls, disabled and ethnic minorities are bearing the brunt of the state's inability to ensure rights and undertake affirmative action. International pressure for further opening of the economy to trade, the destruction of many traditional livelihoods, specifically agriculture and artisanal trades, and the inability of the local markets to compete with international imports have all combined to destroy sustainable life and livelihoods. This has contributed to near-continuous migration of families belonging to these social categories. Migration in India has been a regular phenomenon, especially from rural to rural based on seasonal cycles; in 1961 there were about 144 million migrants by place of birth, however by 2001, it was 307 million (GOI 2001). The distribution of migrants by migration streams is generally associated with the degree of economic and social development of sending and destination areas. Population pressure on land, increased opportunities for work, education and marriage, in the case of females, contribute to rural and urban migration. However, the number of migrants taking the rural to rural path is estimated at 53.3 million (GOI 2001). This migration is high because of the requirement for particular kinds of skills and a systemic kinship pattern of migration based on the particular cropping pattern (Nandy 2012; Choudhury 2014).[1]

While in China the Hukou system excludes children from rural areas from education in urban areas, in India there are two kinds of education systems, one of which is provided universally by the government and the second which is funded by private entities (though the land and some infrastructure is provided to such schools by the government at subsidised rates) and which caters to elite and upper-class children. With increasing migration from rural to urban areas, the children of migrant parents are uprooted from their socio-cultural contexts and capital and are forced to adapt to new and alien environments, thus facing a peculiarly difficult kind of vulnerability – left unprotected and bereft of education, health and other such facilities. Migrant children do not have the required documentation (like birth certificates, certificate of completion of a particular class etc.) that ensures admission to services in the destination areas. Besides, the landowners who employ the parents do not encourage them to send their children to school since they are a ready source of cheap labour. The informal relations and lack of appropriate legislation, which would ensure social security, health and education benefits for the parents, serve to create an exploitative web around the children (Smita 2008; Nandy 2012; Kendre 2011). When they move to different places their social networks (grandparents, neighbours and relatives) and communal life are disturbed. The breaking of these networks makes children particularly vulnerable – with both parents employed in hard agricultural labour the children are often left to fend for themselves. Many of them are also employed (Nandy 2012; Ghosh 2014) to work in the fields at low rates providing additional family income. The Child Labour (Prohibition and Regulation) Act 1986 prohibits children below the age of 14 years from such work, however the informal nature of the work as well as lack of implementation mechanisms means children remain vulnerable to these forms of exploitation.

Several studies (Nandy 2012; Ghosh 2014; Smita 2008) have revealed how children work in extremely exploitative conditions, with little or no remuneration. The migration patterns are particularly linked to changes in agricultural practices from food crops to cash crops, including cotton and sugarcane, both of which require intensive labour for cutting and selling. Migration for agriculture takes place several times in a year, because sowing, harvesting, transplantation etc. are all seasonal and all require labour. Similarly, there is frequent migration for industrial and agro-industrial work such as salt-making, brick-making, stone-quarrying, fishing etc. The common thread that research (Ghosh 2014; Smita 2008) shows is that the families largely belong to marginalised groups like the scheduled castes and scheduled tribes, who have either been deprived of their small bits of land in villages or displaced from forests where they traditionally live.

## Educational policies and programmes in India

While in China the focus has been to ensure that migrant children are able to access education in urban areas, including through compulsory education programmes, in India due to strong campaigns on the right to education, the 86th amendment of the Indian constitution was evoked, whereby the right to education (RTE) became a fundamental right. This means that children from any social, cultural and economic background have the right to enrol in a neighbourhood school. Together with the RTE, the Sarva Shiksha Abhiyan (SSA) was launched in 2001. The major goal of the SSA is to ensure that every child is in school and studying well. The emphasis is also on community ownership and involvement of parents in monitoring and managing schools.

However, the SSA (Bhatty 2014; Malik 2015) does not spell out the ways in which it will deal with the specific situation of migrant children and ensure their continuation in schools including in destination areas during migration. The circular migration of their families due to the push and pull factors of work and lack of appropriate documentation for children, alongside discriminatory attitudes of teachers and school authorities, all deter migrant children from continuing their education.

## Interventions by social workers: innovations and models

Unlike China there has been no legal provisioning of social workers within the formal school system in India and hence addressing issues of discrimination, providing outreach and counselling to left-out children is not possible in

*Table 14.1* Social work interventions by NGOs

| Migrant children: issues | Specific problems | Interventions by social work NGOs | Outcomes |
|---|---|---|---|
| Dropping out of Education | Denial of education in sending and destination areas<br><br>Potential and existing child labour | SAVE, MAEGA Trust and Janaarth – Bridge schools to enable children to re-enter education in sending areas, residential schools and institutional settings in case of frequent migration<br><br>Health services and vocational training | Better educational outcomes<br><br>Safety and reintegration into the school system<br><br>Better health outcomes<br><br>Prevention of child labour |
| Child Labour | Trafficked by known adults who are contractors for the employers<br><br>Long working hours, ill health from hazardous conditions, inadequate and unpaid wages<br><br>Addiction to alcohol and other substances | SAVE, MAEGA Trust and Janarth – Children rescued, health and other facilities, shelter, advocacy<br><br>Multi-stakeholder networking and rehabilitation<br><br>Mobilisation of parents into unions for wages and services for children<br><br>Mobilisation of children into child unions<br><br>Advocacy with corporate stakeholders for promotion of child labour-free labels as part of fair trade practices | Better informed children and parents<br><br>Reintegration in regular schools<br><br>Empowerment of parents<br><br>Convergence with state programmes to ensure better livelihoods and incomes of the families |
| Sexual exploitation | Impact on girls specifically, health, trauma, and trafficking | Visthar – Rescue and rehabilitation, anti-oppressive counselling, holistic residential, facilities | Overcoming trauma and supporting recovery<br><br>Good educational and vocational skills<br><br>Move towards independent living |

government schools. Working with migrant children is among the most challenging and difficult arenas for social workers. The social work responses for migrant children have been largely voiced through NGOs like SAVE (Tamil Nadu), MAEGA Trust (Tamil Nadu), Janaarth (Maharashtra) and Visthar (Karnataka). Most of their efforts are located within the local contexts, and patterns of intervention are based on the state of the migrant children and the kind of agricultural and other work practices of the specific region. Table 14.1 captures the range of interventions.

## Conclusion and implications for transnational social work practice

Since migration can be both forced and involuntary, the core issues of safe migration, social protection of children and development opportunities for their families are major challenges that need to be addressed. Social workers can work in the sending areas ensuring appropriate rural livelihoods and programmatic interventions to strengthen incomes for families of such migrant children. This would stem the flow of migration and ensure children go to schools on a regular basis. Further, if migrant families in the destination areas are provided with adequate basic services, social protection benefits and wages, social workers can engage with the families to send their children to school. Anti-discrimination and anti-oppressive approaches by social workers to ensure mainstreaming of migrant children in regular schools and advocacy for inclusion of social workers in school systems needs to be made mandatory in India as in parts of China.

## Note

1 Nandy and Choudhury discuss the example of the State of Maharashtra where sugarcane is a flourishing cash crop with good returns and yet for cutting the cane intensive manual labour is utilised. Due to this demand for labour, the families in Central Maharashtra who belong to poor and backward communities are given loans as advance payment for cane cutting. A local villager known to them hires them on behalf of a sugarcane factory owner in the destination rural area, and gives the wages as a loan. When it is harvest time they migrate to Western Maharashtra (the sugarcane belt) along with children in the age group of 6–14 years.

## References

Bhatty, K., 2014. 'Review of elementary education policy in India. Has it upheld the constitutional objective of equality?' *Economic & Political Weekly* 49(43–4): 100–107.

Choudhury, C., 2014. *A Bitter Harvest* [online]. Available from: https://ruralindiaonline. org/articles/the-sugarcane-cutters-bitter-harvest/ [Accessed 1 January 2016].

FAO, 2014. *The state of world food and agriculture. Innovations in family farming.* Food and Agriculture Organization of the United Nations.

Ghosh, B., 2014. 'Vulnerability, forced migration and trafficking in children and women. A field view from the plantation industry in West Bengal', *Economic & Political Weekly* 49 (26–7): 58–65.

GOI, 2001. *Census of India 2001. Migration* [online]. Government of India. Available from: http://censusindia.gov.in/Census_And_You/migrations.aspx [Accessed 20 December 2015].

Kendre, B., 2011. 'Socio-economic background and seasonal migration of sugarcane harvesting workers', *International Journal of Humanity and Social Sciences* 1(2): 15–21.

MAEGA [online]. MAEGA Trust Organization. Available from: http://maegatrust.org/ [Accessed 10 January 2016].

Malik, B.B., 2015. 'RTE and marginal communities. A perspective from the field', *Economic & Political Weekly* 50(5): 25–7.

Nandy, D., 2012. *Child rights situation analysis. Children of families engaged in sugarcane farming in Maharashtra* [online]. Gokhale Institute of Politics and Economics; Save the Children Publication. Available from: http://resourcecentre.savethechildren.se/sites/default/files/documents/childrights.pdf [Accessed 2 January 2016].

SAVE [online]. *Social Awareness and Voluntary Education*. Available from: www.savengo.org [Accessed 10 January 2016].

Smita, 2008. *Distress seasonal migration and its impact on children's education* [online]. Consortium for Research on Educational Access, Transitions and Equity (CREATE). Available from: http://sro.sussex.ac.uk/1869/1/PTA28.pdf [Accessed 2 January 2016].

## 15 The response to educational inequality between cities and the countryside and school social services

Migration from the countryside to cities and its impacts upon the education system

Comment on the Chinese case study from a Turkish perspective

*Uğur Tekin*

The case study about the educational inequalities of rural migrant children in China raises a global problem, which has also brought challenges for the educational system in Turkey during the last decades, and continues to do so. Starting in 1950 as a result of industrialisation and the changes in economic policy pursued by Turkish governments, movement from the countryside to cities has continued increasingly up until now. In 1950, thirty-five per cent of the population lived in cities, whereas this figure has now reached 80 per cent (TUIK 2015). The decade between 1980 and 1990 was the period when this change was most rapidly witnessed as the time when the Turkish economy integrated within the global economy. In 1983, the population was also disrupted in urban and rural areas with megacities emerging in important economic centres due to rapid migration. Today, 16 million people live in the largest city, Istanbul – immigrants, illegally or semi-legally, built houses close to industrial plants on the city peripheries (TUIK 2015). These houses turned into residential areas lacking infrastructure. A majority of such areas, called '*gecekondu*',[1] were later legalised. Today a considerable portion of Istanbul's population live in areas formed in this way (Tekeli 2009: 129).

This movement of intra-national migration brought about inequalities in children's education both in cities and rural areas, adding new problems to the already existing problems in the Turkish education system. Since 2012, compulsory education has been implemented in three stages, each lasting for four years. That means that there are 12 years in total of compulsory education. During the first two four-year stages, which are defined as elementary education, the first period covers the ages from five to nine years, while the second period covers education in middle schools (nine to thirteen years). Education in the third four-year period, which is named secondary education, could be in the form of formal education or administered by non-formal and distance education institutions.

Severe problems exist with regard to schooling rates in elementary education; about 5 per cent of the elementary school-age population cannot make use of their right to education. Likewise, 20 per cent of the secondary school-age population do not or cannot continue with secondary education. Some of the children enrolled in primary schools quit school before the end of the eight-year period. According to the data of the Turkish Statistical Institute (TUIK 2015), of the over 64 million Turkish citizens over the age of six years, nearly five million are illiterate. This figure corresponds to 7.68 per cent of those who have reached the age of literacy. The share of women in this illiterate population is 79.98 per cent (TUIK 2015).

In addition to the existing problems, rapid urbanisation has been creating new problems in immigrant-sending areas as well as in the *gecekondu* of immigrant-receiving big cities. Education is one of the key institutions building social and cultural capital and therefore a major precondition for opportunities to advance in life. Therefore, the different challenges for education in urban and rural areas will be highlighted below.

## Problems in the education system in the countryside brought about by migration

In immigrant-sending areas, the migration from rural to urban areas causes the shutdown of schools and problems in transportation for pupils due to lower population density. Because of limited opportunities, teachers do not usually prefer to work in immigrant-sending areas. As a result, schools in such areas lack a sufficient number of qualified teachers as well as having high turnover rates. Social and cultural capital is harder to build when parents and members of the family are illiterate or not well educated. In such areas where the main source of economic income is agriculture, the number of children per family is above Turkey's average (TUIK 2015). Children of land-owning families often work in farms and therefore fail to attend school regularly. Landless families have to work as seasonal workers and therefore travel with their children even during the education term. The government has introduced new measures in immigrant-sending areas, two of which are explained below (Doğan 2011: 223f).

### *Regional primary boarding schools*

Regional primary boarding schools have been in use since 1962 to ensure access to elementary education services for the primary school-age population in rural areas lacking schools. All expenses of pupils enrolled in these schools are financed by the government. The number of these schools increased in the 1990s and they have been considerably effective in ensuring schooling in immigrant-sending regions (MEB 2003: 17).

*Mobile elementary education*

Mobile elementary education was first introduced tentatively in five schools in 1989–1990 to primary school-age children living in dispersed settlements with small populations. Pupils are taught in multi-grade classes in order to have access to equal education opportunities. Having proven successful, the programme was quickly expanded, and by 2013–2014 more than 825,000 pupils from nearly 24,000 primary schools were signed in to more than 10,000 central boarding schools (MEB 2015).

## Education problems in city peripheries of the immigrant-receiving cities

One of the structural characteristics of the new settlements appearing on the peripheries of immigrant-receiving cities could be defined as the lack of infrastructure resulting from the fact that settlement was already in place before any infrastructure could be built in these areas. Two problems arise through this process:

1  In such areas, the number of pupils per classroom is above Turkey's average[2] both at elementary and secondary school levels (TUIK 2015: 74f).
2  Although settlement areas rank among the first in Turkey in the number of classrooms built, they fail to meet the residents' needs due to continued immigration. The schools lack the necessary equipment. Most of the teachers employed in such areas apply to be transferred to other schools due to negative working conditions.[3]

In terms of social and cultural capital, families living in these settlements usually bear the characteristics of immigrant-sending regions. Most of the time, all family members have to work whenever jobs are available to support themselves in the new environment. With both parents working, girls in particular have to care for their younger siblings and therefore have less time for school and homework. Among immigrant families, those belonging to minority groups speak a language other than Turkish at home, which creates grave problems for the children at school.

*Psychological Counselling and Guidance (PCG) services*

In response to the above-mentioned problems, the most significant change in Turkey's education system has been the introduction of Psychological Counselling and Guidance (PCG) services since 1961. The system of social services in Turkey, which is quite weak, has only made a breakthrough through the legal arrangements as part of the European Union harmonisation process (Şahin Taşğın and Tekin 2013: 133). Particularly in *gecekondu*, substance use, neglect, abuse and violence in schools are common. That causes psychological health problems that should be dealt with by school psychological counsellors. With the introduction of PCG services at schools, school social services were entirely taken over by school psychological counsellors. School counsellors were appointed to educational institutions to deliver guidance and psychological counselling services and to supplement the efforts of these teachers. Counselling and Research Centres (RAMs) were opened up in order to identify individuals with special education needs and carry out guidance and psychological services for them. There are various aptitude, intelligence, and standard achievement tests to survey pupils, and this in itself can be quite problematic (Melekoglu 2009).

Inspired by the American concept in the 1960s, the system was first systematically introduced in Turkey as a practice of school social services in certain pilot schools in 1970–1971. Initial application of the system was limited to secondary education and, following the recognition of PCG services, was taken over by the top institution of the Turkish National Education System. Undergraduate and graduate education programmes were introduced in Educational Faculties to train staff for school PCG units and Counselling and Research Centres (RAMs). There has been a considerable increase in the number of staff employed in the field. For instance, in 2001–2002, the number of pupils per counsellor was 2,836 in elementary schools and 905 in secondary schools (Akkök and Watts 2004). Yet, even today, the number of school counsellors is still insufficient. By 2013, one school counsellor serves 554 students. Apparently, despite all efforts, PCG services in Turkey are still underdeveloped both in terms of the services offered and organisational strength. Nearly all students graduating from PCG programmes work for public institutions, because private psychological counselling centres are not widespread enough. The existing system of school psychological counselling falls short of meeting the demands both in numbers and quality.

## Conclusion

Significant changes taking place in Turkey's rapid urbanisation have brought about new inequalities in education, particularly between the city and the countryside. New institutional structures and practices have been developed to solve the education problems arising both in immigrant-sending regions and in the *gecekondu* in immigrant-receiving cities. Different school models have been introduced in the countryside, such as Regional Primary Boarding Schools and Mobile Elementary Schools in order to ensure equal education opportunities. School social services were superseded by new systems such as the Psychological Counselling and Guidance (PCG) Services at schools and Counselling Research Centres (RAMs) opening up in various *gecekondu* areas. Emerging in a period when other aspects of social services are still underdeveloped, these systems remain rudimentary and in search of a model specific to Turkey.

## Notes

1 *Gecekondu*: 'built during the night' is a Turkish word, meaning houses which were built illegally in urban areas by people from rural areas (intra-country migrants). These settlements are comparable to slums.
2 Average number of students per classroom in Turkey is 29.
3 The classrooms are overcrowded, which affects the level of instruction.

# References

Akkök, F., and Watts, T.G., 2004. *Meslekî Bilgi, Rehberlik ve Danışmanlık Hizmetleri Türkiye Ülke Raporu.* Ankara: Milli Eğitim Basımevi (MEB).

Doğan, İ., 2011. *Eğitim Sosyolojisi.* Ankara: Nobel Akademik Yayıncılık.

MEB, 2003. *Yatılı İlköğretim Bölge Okulları ve Pansiyonlu İlköğretim Okulları Yönetici Kılavuz Kitabı.* İstanbul: Milli Eğitim Basımevi.

MEB, 2015. *Milli Eğitim İstatistikleri. Örgün Eğitim 2014-2015.* Ankara: Milli Eğitim Bakanlığı.

Melekoglu, M.A., 2009. 'Special education in Turkey', *International Journal of Inclusive Education* 13(3): 287–98.

Şahin Taşğın, N., and Tekin, U., 2013. 'Türkiye'de Sosyal Hizmetin Temel Karakteristikleri ve Güncel Görünümü', in H. Acar, N. Negiz, and E. Akman, eds, *Sosyal Hizmet. Temelleri ve Uygulama Alanları.* Ankara: Maya Akademi, 119–35.

Tekeli, İ., 2009. *Kentsel Arsa, Altyapı ve Kentsel Hizmetler.* İstanbul: Tarih Vakfı Yurt Yayınları.

TUIK, 2015. *Statistics on children 2014* [online]. Turkish Statistical Institute. Available from: www.tuik.gov.tr/IcerikGetir.do?istab_id=269 [Accessed 10 January 2016].

# 16 Refugees and asylum seekers in France

*Muriel Mellon-Mustafa and
Alexandra Schleyer-Lindenmann*

The aim of this chapter is to give an outline of social work with refugees and asylum seekers in France. This is a major transnational societal issue which, sadly, is not only the case at the present time of writing but will be in the future: according to the United Nations High Commissioner for Refugees (UNHCR), displacement is the new challenge for the twenty-first century (UNHCR 2013). In Europe, the three top countries receiving refugees in 2013 were Turkey (609,900 persons), France (232,500 persons) and Germany (187,600 persons) (UNHCR 2014: 13). Persons who flee their country and seek protection from another state through the application of an asylum claim are named asylum seekers: 'individuals who have sought international protection and whose claims for refugee status have not yet been determined' (UNHCR 2014: 39). If they fulfil specific conditions, they can obtain the status of refugee; refugees are defined by the UNHCR as 'individuals recognized under the 1951 Convention relating to the Status of Refugees … ; individuals granted complementary forms of protection … and those enjoying temporary protection' (UNHCR 2014: 39). These legal definitions are important because they set the frame of the social workers' agency with this group.

This chapter first places the question of refugee protection in a European perspective, as French policy in this field is strongly influenced by its European framework. Then the French situation is presented and finally a case study from a CADA (Centre d'Accueil pour les Demandeurs d'Asile – reception centre for asylum seekers) illustrates the challenges for social work in this field.

## European framework

The member states of the European Union have included asylum rights in the Charter of Fundamental Rights of the European Union (OJEC 2000). Since 1999, the European Union has also worked towards the creation of a Common European Asylum System (CEAS) (EU Migration and Home Affairs; EC 2008), starting with the Amsterdam Treaty (1999) followed by the Lisbon Treaty (2007). The aim of the treaties and of the CEAS is twofold: on the one hand, they wish to offer better protection to refugees and asylum seekers through harmonisation and minimum standards in procedures. On the other hand, there is also the will to prevent abuse of the asylum system (EC 2008: 11).

Several directives, notably Directive 2011/95/EU on standards for the qualification of third-country nationals or stateless persons as beneficiaries of international protection, and two directives from June 2013 on norms of reception (Directive 2013/33/EU) and procedures (The European Parliament and of the Council of the European Union 2013), as well as two regulations (Dublin and Eurodac) have been written and are or will be integrated in the signature countries' systems (Lochak 2013). On the whole, the European Union has progressed on the path of a more coherent framework for asylum seekers, but there are still inequalities in reception and treatment between member states (Le Pors 2011). Moreover, as Lochak points out, the common asylum system seems rather more oriented towards 'containment and dissuasion than protection' (Lochak 2013: 2).

## French framework

Over recent years, France has fixed a general code for the reception and integration of all foreigners, the Code de l'Entrée et du Séjour des Etrangers et du Droit d'Asile (code concerning the entry and stay of foreigners and asylum rights, CESEDA),[1] which includes questions concerning asylum rights as well. The right to asylum is structured with reference to three frameworks: the Geneva Convention, European policy and the French Constitution (Le Pors 2011).

In its article 711-1 CESEDA indicates the two principal institutions implied in the asylum-seeking procedure in France: Office Français de Protection des Réfugiés et Apatrides (French Office for Refugees and Stateless Persons) (OFPRA) and Cour Nationale du Droit d'Asile (National Court for the Right to Asylum) (CNDA).

### *Office Français de Protection des Réfugiés et Apatrides (OFPRA) – French Office for Refugees and Stateless Persons*

OFPRA has two missions: it is in charge of the procedure of recognition of refugee status or statelessness quality and it can grant subsidiary protection when the Geneva Convention Criteria cannot be applied (CESEDA, book VII, title II). An asylum seeker will submit his or her claim to OFPRA where it is decided upon by a civil officer, after a hearing of the asylum seeker.

### *Cour Nationale du Droit d'Asile (CNDA) – National Court for the Right to Asylum*

If the asylum application has been refused by OFPRA, the asylum seeker can make an appeal to this court. There is a judge and two assessors who hear the asylum seeker's case.

According to the French ministry of home affairs, in 2014 OFPRA received a total of 64,536 asylum claims or applications for refugee status. OFPRA took decisions in 52,004 cases and attributed asylum 8,738 times (1,924 cases of subsidiary protection included). This is an attribution in 16.80 per cent of the cases, and a rise of 46.2 per cent of positive decisions compared to 2013. For its part, CNDA received 39,115 appeals and took decisions on 37,345 cases, cancelling 5,826 decisions by OFPRA. Thus, the CNDA acceptance rate is 15.60 per cent (Ministère de l'intérieur 2015). For France in 2014 European statistics report an acceptance rate in the first instance of 21.74 per cent which is far behind the average acceptance rate for the European Union which stands at an average of 45.22 per cent positive decisions (Eurostat 2015).

Other important institutions are the Prefecture (representative of the French state) where the asylum seeker must register within 90 days of arrival in France, the asylum platform which is the first welcome desk for the asylum seeker, and the CADA (reception centre for asylum seekers).

The mission of the CADA is to offer reception and provide services such as housing for asylum seekers, administrative, social and medical counselling, to put in place school integration for children, to organise socio-cultural activities for the residents and to manage asylum seekers' departure from the institutional system after the end of the asylum claim procedure (MIOMCTI 2011).

In 2012 there were 269 CADAs in France with a total of 21,410 places (REM 2013). This covered about 33.7 per cent of the need for accommodation for asylum seekers in 2012 (REM 2013). In addition, there are places in the Hébergement d'Urgence dédié aux Demandeurs d'Asile (emergency accommodation for asylum seekers, HUDA). For the reception and direct work with asylum seekers at the asylum platform or in the CADAs many of the employees are social workers. The case study we present is from a CADA in Marseille which houses 70 persons who are followed by a team of three social workers, one psychologist and one language teacher. In line with the current approach in social work (see Jami, Pillant and Segura, Chapter 6) these professionals see their work as a process of accompanying and empowering the clients and not as a mission of controlling or assisting passive receivers of social action.

## Case description

The D family arrived in France in July 2010. They are a family of four: the parents, aged about 50 years, and two sons, aged 17 and 27 years. The family is of Kosovar nationality and of Romani origin. They have fled Kosovo because of the severe discrimination and violence they faced as Romani people. After their arrival in France they submitted their asylum claim and were subsequently interviewed at the OFPRA in January 2011. In March 2011 they were taken in for housing by the CADA. They were accommodated in a three-room flat by the social worker and started to familiarise themselves with their new environment, gathering information through a series of appointments with the social worker, as well as through activities at the CADA (e.g. French lessons). In November 2011 they got a negative answer to their claim from the OFPRA. They had one month to submit their appeal to the CNDA, which they accomplished with the help of a social worker. In January 2012 the father died. The rest of the family was interviewed at the CNDA in March 2012 and obtained refugee status in April 2012.

In the following we take up elements of this case to illustrate some points which seem important to us in the context of professional social work with asylum seekers or refugees: competencies of the social worker, trust, empowerment, and time management.

## *Competencies*

First, juridical and geopolitical literacy. The social worker needs to be familiar not only with common law, but also with asylum law, on the national and European levels. He/she also has to keep informed about the geopolitical and cultural context of the countries the asylum seekers come from. Concerning the D family for example, it is important to know what it means to be a Romani family in Kosovo, as opposed to being Albanian.

Second, the social worker has to develop a high intercultural awareness (Guéguen 2012; Verbunt 2009; Gaitanides 2011), and must be able to analyse the impact of cultural filters (Camilleri 1996) in the interaction with his/her client. For example, when the father of the D family died, it was important to understand and respect the mourning rites of the family. Moreover, one task of the social worker is to assist the asylum seeker to produce a written report of the reasons which have forced the person to flee his/her country (this will be submitted as the asylum claim) and to prepare with the asylum seeker the interview with the civil officer of the OFPRA. The asylum seeker needs to understand that the person who will interview him/her at the OFPRA or the CNDA does not share his/her culture and thus does not have the same mind-set and way of reasoning. Thus, it is not sufficient for the asylum seeker to tell his/her story, but it is necessary to make it understandable by explaining its cultural codes. This work of 'cultural translation' is prepared with the social worker who thus must be alert to cultural codes and have a great deal of cultural knowledge.

## *Trust*

Asylum seekers are people with special needs: having fled from their homes, they arrive, often alone, in a foreign country where they usually do not know the culture or the language. They are weakened or traumatised by what they have experienced in their home country or during their flight (and eventually by their non-welcome in the country in which they seek asylum) (Baubet *et al.* 2004). He or she might not be trusting due to this context and it is necessary to first build a relationship based on mutual confidence where it is clear that the social worker is there to support the asylum seeker (ANESM 2014). This might be more difficult if there are cultural or language barriers. It is necessary to listen, but also to exchange and explain the proposed actions. In the case of the D family, as they had already submitted their claim when arriving in the CADA, the exchanges and the social support took place in a positive environment, with the help of an interpreter and without time pressure. The social worker and the family developed confidence in a trusting relationship little by little.

*Empowerment*

Social work means accompanying, not assisting. The notion of accompanying induces the idea of the active participation of the asylum seeker or refugee in the complete procedure. This empowerment (Bacqué and Biewener 2013) or participatory approach, now standard in France (see Jami, Pillant and Segura, Chapter 6), works so that the person is as autonomous as possible at the end of the supporting process. For example, the D family learnt French through the language courses at the CADA, and the youngest son, although beyond obligatory school age (which is 16 years), attended school.

*Time management*

Another challenge is to manage the waiting process. For example, the D family waited ten months for an answer from OFPRA, after their hearing. As they did not have the right to work (a work permit can be obtained under certain conditions which are difficult to attain), the time can seem long, and waiting for an answer from OFPRA or CNDA is a synonym for uncertainty. Very often asylum seekers have difficulties projecting themselves into the future as they do not know whether they will obtain refugee status and the right to stay, or not. The main task of the social workers is to help them manage this time of waiting through social and cultural activities, as well as information workshops, for example on life in France, aimed at enhancing their independence in everyday life, regardless of the result of the asylum claim (ANESM 2014).

The final mission of the CADA is to manage the asylum seekers' leaving of the CADA at the end of the procedure, both for the people who obtained refugee status as well as for those who did not (after their appeal at the CNDA). It is made clear at the beginning to the asylum seekers that the accommodation provided is only given during the time of the procedure. To accompany the exit of a family who have obtained refugee status is relatively easy for several reasons: the client immediately gets a receipt attesting their international protection, is integrated into common law, can look for a job, etc.

People who do not obtain asylum status have one month to leave the CADA. It is not always possible for the families to respect this delay, having no other solution for accommodation. Some decide to return to their country of origin and ask for 'help for voluntary return' at OFII (Office Français d'immigration et d'intégration – French Office for Immigration and Integration). Others face expulsion or staying illegally, and the role of the social worker is to discuss with the person all the possible options, to inform him/her of their rights and to advise him/her on potential support through organisations other than the CADA (ANESM 2014).

## Transnational perspective/Challenges for the future

From a transnational perspective, taking in and working with refugees will remain a priority worldwide for many years. In Europe, the European Migration Forum which is constituted as a platform for dialogue on migration, asylum and migrant integration met for the first time on 26 and 27 January 2015 (EU Migration and Home Affairs). This is also a challenge for social workers: to accompany asylum seekers and refugees efficiently needs – like many other fields of social work – constant training, learning and reflection during professional life, in order to be up to date concerning the legislation and socio-political situation of the countries the persons come from. This training should be part of the education of social workers, but for the moment it is very marginal in terms of volume of teaching (Carrère and Daadouch 2006). The field of intercultural competencies for social workers has received more attention in recent years (Verbunt 2009; Guélamine 2000) and there are sometimes modules of teaching intercultural competencies in social work schools. Moreover, there is a general awakening to transnational questions of social work, especially in training and cross-border cooperation (Hirliet *et al.* 2013).

Recently a law concerning the reform of asylum rights along the lines of the European Directives 'procedure' and 'protection and reception' has been issued.[2] One aim of the law is to accelerate the procedure at OFPRA. Another major change is the possibility for the applicant to be assisted when interviewed by the OFPRA officer. It is all the more important that this person, possibly a social worker, is well informed on cultural and geopolitical questions concerning the country of origin.

Social workers working in this field should also benefit from exchanges with social workers from other countries, in order to get a better understanding of different situations, to exchange information and 'good practices', and to develop a shared position. Currently such a network is being created starting from a French–Italian initiative in Marseille. A first conference on asylum rights in mediterranean countries took place in Marseille in October 2014 (FNARS 2014) and hopefully others will follow which will allow for a transnational perspective on asylum from the social workers' point of view.

## Notes

1 Code de l'Entrée et du Séjour des Etrangers et du Droit d'Asile (CESEDA) Legifrance. gouv.fr (2016).
2 Law n° 2015-925 of 29 July 2015 concerning the reform of asylum rights Legifrance. gouv.fr (2015).

## References

ANESM, 2014. *Personnalisation de l'accompagnement des demandeurs d'asile accueillis en Cada* [online]. Agence nationale de l'évaluation et de la qualité d'accueil des établissements et services sociaux et médico-sociaux. Available from: www.anesm.sante. gouv.fr/IMG/pdf/ANESM-RBPP_CADA_Mai_2014.pdf [Accessed 18 June 2015].

Bacqué, M.H., and Biewener, C., 2013. *L'empowerment. Une pratique émancipatrice*. Paris: La Découverte.

Baubet, T., Abbal, T., Claudet, J., Le Du, C., Heidenreich, F., Levy, K., Mehallel, S., Rezzoug, D., Sturm, G. and Moro, M.R., 2004. 'Traumas psychiques chez les demandeurs d'asile en France. Des spécificités cliniques et thérapeutiques', *Journal*

*International de Victimologie* 2: 107–13. Available from: www.jidv.com/BAUBET,T-JIDV2004_%202(2).htm [Accessed 26 January 2016].

Camilleri, C., 1996. 'Le champ et les concepts de la psychologie culturelle', in C. Camilleri and G. Vinsonneau, eds, *Psychologie et culture. Concepts et méthodes.* Paris: Armand Colin, 7–80.

Carrère, V., and Daadouch, C., 2006. 'Le droit des étrangers, parent pauvre de la formation', *Plein Droit* (70): 19–22.

EC, 2008. *Policy plan on asylum. An integrated approach to the protection across the EU* [online]. Commission of the European Communities. Available from: http://eur-lex.europa.eu/LexUriServ/LexUriServ.do?uri=COM:2008:0360:FIN:EN:PDF [Accessed 1 March 2015].

EU Migration and Home Affairs. *Common European Asylum System* [online]. European Commission. Available from: http://ec.europa.eu/dgs/home-affairs/what-we-do/policies/asylum/index_en.htm [Accessed 10 January 2016].

Eurostat, 2015. *Asylum Statistics* [online]. Eurostat. Available from: http://ec.europa.eu/eurostat/statistics-explained/index.php/Asylum_statistics [Accessed 20 March 2015].

FNARS, 2014. *Garantir le droit d'asile en Méditerranée. Le travailleur social entre politiques publiques et accueil des demandeurs d'asile. Les cas de l'Italie et de la France* [online]. Asilo in Europa. Available from: http://iremam.cnrs.fr/IMG/pdf/Programme_Droit_asile_avec_PILOTAGE_octobre_2014.pdf [Accessed 15 March 2015].

Gaitanides, S., 2011. 'L'ouverture interculturelle des services sociaux. État des lieux et perspectives', in A. Schleyer-Lindenmann and T. Neuer-Miebach, eds, *Soziale Arbeit im Dialog. Le travail social en dialogue.* Frankfurt: Fachhochschulverlag, 243–45.

Guéguen, J.-Y., 2012. *Bilan des politiques sociales, perspectives de l'action sociale. L'année de l'action sociale 2012.* Paris: Dunod.

Guélamine, F., 2000. *Intervenir auprès des populations immigrées.* Paris: Dunod.

Hirliet, Ph., Meyer, J.L., Molina, Y. and Muller, B., eds, 2013. *Travail social sans frontières. Innovation et Adaptation.* Rennes: Presses de l'Ecole des Hautes Etudes en Santé Publique.

Le Pors, A., 2011. *Le droit d'asile.* Paris: Presses Universitaires de France.

Legifrance.gouv.fr, 2015. *LOI n° 2015-925 du 29 juillet 2015 relative à la réforme du droit d'asile* [online]. Available from: www.legifrance.gouv.fr/eli/loi/2015/7/29/INTX 1412525L/jo [Accessed 10 January 2016].

Legifrance.gouv.fr, 2016. *Code de l'entrée et du séjour des étrangers et du droit d'asile* [online]. Available from: www.legifrance.gouv.fr/affichCode.do?cidTexte=LEGI TEXT000006070158 [Accessed 10 January 2016].

Lochak, D., 2013. *L'Europe, terre d'asile? La revue des droits de l'homme* [online]. Available from: http://revdh.revues.org/401 [Accessed 17 February 2015].

Ministère de l'intérieur, 2015. *Les demandes d'asile* [online]. Ministère de l'intérieur. Available from: www.immigration.interieur.gouv.fr/Info-ressources/Statistiques/Tableaux-statistiques/Les-demandes-d-asile [Accessed 12 March 2015].

MIOMCTI, 2011. *Circulaire of August 19th* [online]. Ministère de l'Intérieur, de l'Outre Mer, des Collectivités territoriales et de l'Immigration. Available from: http://circulaire.legifrance.gouv.fr/pdf/2011/08/cir_33657.pdf [Accessed 1 March 2015].

OFII [online]. Office Français de l'immigration et de l'intégration. Available from: www.ofii.fr/ [Accessed 10 January 2016].

OJEC, 2000. *Charter of fundamental rights of the European Union* [online]. Official Journal of the European Communities. Available from: www.europarl.europa.eu/charter/pdf/text_en.pdf [Accessed 15 January 2015].

REM, 2013. *L'organisation des structures d'accueil pour demandeurs d'asile en France* [online]. Réseau Européen des Migrations. Available from: www.immigration.interieur. gouv.fr/Europe-et-International/Le-reseau-europeen-des-migrations-REM/Les-publications-du-REM/Les-etudes/L-organisation-des-structures-d-accueil-pour-demandeurs-d-asile-en-France [Accessed 15 January 2015].

The European Parliament and of the Council of the European Union, 2013. *Directive 2013/32/ EU of the European parliament and of the council of 26 June 2013. On common procedures for granting and withdrawing international protection* [online]. The European Parliament and of the Council of the European Union. Available from: http://eur-lex.europa.eu/legal-content/EN/TXT/PDF/?uri=CELEX:32013L0032&from=FR [Accessed 26 January 2016].

UNHCR, 2013. *Global trends 2012* [online]. United Nations High Commissioner for Refugees. Available from: www.unhcr.org/51bacb0f9.html [Accessed 5 January 2015].

UNHCR, 2014. *Global trends 2013* [online]. United Nations High Commissioner for Refugees. Available from: www.unhcr.org/5399a14f9.html [Accessed 5 January 2015].

Verbunt, G., 2009. *La question interculturelle dans le travail social*. Paris: La Découverte.

# 17  Legitimacy versus legality

## Comment on the French case study from a German perspective

*Therese Neuer-Miebach*

Germany and France have a lot of points in common concerning the treatment of asylum seekers. The European Convention on Human Rights, ECHR, 1950, the Geneva Refugees Convention, GRC, 1951, and the Dublin Covenant III, 2013, apply to both countries. As in France, the right to asylum is a constitutional human right in Germany.[1]

Similar to France, Germany has a Federal Office for Migration and Refugees (BAMF), a subordinate agency of the Federal Ministry of the Interior, with branch offices in all Federal States (*Länder*).[2] As a centre of excellence for migration and integration, it is responsible for conducting asylum procedures, granting refugees protection, supporting integration and resettlement, and additionally undertaking research on migration and integration.[3]

Since the recruitment freeze for migrant workers in 1973, German legislation on immigration for people from outside the EU has been severely restricted. Beyond the concession of family reunification and the selected recruitment of highly skilled employees since 2012 and 2013 respectively, there no longer exists any real chance of legal immigration. This means, applying for asylum seems to be the only chance for anyone seeking to escape from poverty, or racial/ethnic discrimination, or 'simply' seeking to achieve better living conditions.

### Case study: Family D in Germany

According to German law, a family would need to provide plausible proof that they feared (repeated) persecution on the grounds of membership of a certain social group (§ 3, section 1 AsylVfG) or that they had justified reasons to expect serious harm, such as torture or inhuman treatment, if they returned to their country of origin, and thus could eventually be granted asylum.

According to the latest amendments in 2015, a family would not be allowed without express permission to leave their designated place of residence (initial reception centres) during the first three months – the so-called residential obligation. A job could be taken up after three months, but only if there were no German applicants for the position in question. The family would receive an allowance below the standard rate of social benefit (HARTZ IV), plus the costs for accommodation and heating.

For family D, from Kosovo, social workers might provide psychological and social care, organise accommodation and prepare them for their first interview to explain their flight, i.e. their own personal account of the reasons for their flight including the necessary evidence/proof with the aim of obtaining the right to reside in Germany for the duration of their asylum proceedings. This could only happen if the initial reception centres were staffed with significantly more social workers than at present. The interview at the Federal Office for Migration and Refugees is the key to the subsequent course of the asylum procedure and thus of existential importance to the asylum seekers.

In addition to the initial reception centres a number of social and legal advice options exist, offering thorough preparation for this interview. Family D would, however, need to know of the existence of these and access them quickly. In addition to an interpreter, family D may name a person in their trust, such as a social worker, who can be present at the interview but has no right to intervene.

If family D were granted the right to reside in Germany, they would, as a consequence of the asylum procedure, be moved to a communal dwelling in a federal state – consideration being given to arguments for family reunification, but also for administrative reasons (so-called Königstein quota).

During this phase of continuing uncertainty, families are under constant pressure to demonstrate their willingness to be integrated. Here social workers – if employed by migration advice centres or specialist migration services – have a crucial motivating and support function to fulfil, for example through involvement in integration courses, or by helping to find schooling or vocational training for the son who is still a minor, helping to find a flat, or accompanying and supporting family members to communicate with the authorities.

Within the framework of the National Action Plan for Integration (Die Bundesregierung 2012) there are a number of accompanying and follow-up services, concerning language, education or vocational training, labour-market access and social integration into the local community.

If family D's application for asylum was approved, they would receive a residence permit for three years and a work permit. If not, they could apply for subsidiary protection in the case where they are at risk of serious injury when going back to their country of origin: a limited resident concession (one year), without the right to family reunification.[4]

Should family D be seeking asylum or subsidiary protection in Germany after September 2015, they would have very little chance of success, unless they were well prepared to justify their application,[5] to explain the reasons for their flight and to prove a fear of serious injury in an extremely shortened asylum procedure, and this despite the fact that Kosovo has been declared a safe country of origin.[6] Under these recently aggravated conditions, it would probably be very difficult to plausibly explain their need to be protected on the grounds of their belonging to a particular social group – the Roma community. Arguments concerning education and employment prospects in order to provide a better future for their children would, according to the latest guidelines, have a slight chance of success, but only if the application for asylum had been lodged in their home country and if an employment or vocational training contract already existed.

The current EU-wide debate, which pits 'political' against 'economic' refugees and asylum seekers, leaves little scope for the recognition of poverty as an existential crisis and, so far, this is not accepted as a reason for granting asylum or refugee status. Refusal of entry at the border, encouragement towards voluntary return to their country of origin, residence in an initial reception centre under discriminatory conditions, pending judgement on their application for asylum or, at the end of the day, deportation, are the options currently being discussed.

'Training and learning' on the part of asylum seekers probably increases the 'inclination' of the administrative authorities to deal favourably with their applications; they also help toward the integration of asylum seekers into German society (Bundesamt für Migration und Flüchtlinge 2015: 42ff, 58; Bundesamt für Migration und Flüchtlinge 2013).

Social work conceives its own ethical self-image and legitimacy as a Human and Civil Rights profession (Wronka and Staub-Bernasconi 2012), a vision with which German social work agrees. Being a branch of social policy, social work is not only about human interaction with those in need, nor simply about carrying out governmental measures to control migration. Social work must be involved in issues relating to the acceptance and integration of immigrants, refugees and asylum seekers into society. This requires fundamental 'intercultural awareness' (Langenohl *et al.* 2015), specific knowledge of the legal framework surrounding migration and of the social security system, and also the ability to use all possibilities when conducting advice and mediation in cooperation with other disciplines.

The social work profession is one of the players in the field of policy towards refugees and asylum seekers and, as implied in the chapter on the French situation, its clear and unequivocal involvement as an agent of change and social justice is long overdue, be it on the national or the European scene. Any moves towards a professional crossing of national borders in social work should be encouraged, insofar as they are directed towards 'an action-based and agent-centred perspective on social processes and towards the development of transnational social formations and transnational social space' (Friesenhahn and Kniephoff-Knebel 2011; Staub-Bernasconi 2007).

## Concluding remarks

Current treatment of refugees, including that of family D above, clearly shows that Germany is still not a country of immigration. On the one hand, the fundamental right to asylum is maintained, although it was strongly constrained by the asylum compromise of 1993. On the other hand, it is striking how restrictive Germany's migration policy seems when compared with the post-war situation, when in unprecedentedly difficult economic conditions a much greater number of refugees were accommodated, and in view of the clear advantages that Germany can expect from an influx of migrants in terms of demographic development, the labour market and tax revenue. This German position cannot evolve without a common, coherent – a fortiori, human rights based – migration policy in the EU.

# Notes

1   See article 16a, German Constitution, GG, 1993.
2   The current legal base in 2015, latest amendments on 24 October 2015: the Asylverfahrensgesetz (AsylVfG), named Asylgesetz (AsylG) since 24.10.2015, the Asylbewerberleistungsgesetz, AsylbLG, the Aufenthaltsgesetz, AufenthG. Gesetz zur Verbesserung der Rechtsstellung von Asyl suchenden und geduldeten Ausländern (1.1.2015), das Gesetz zur Neubestimmung des Bleiberechts (u.a. beschleunigte Abschiebung) 1.8.2015.
3   See § 75 AufenthG, as well as: Bundesamt für Migration und Flüchtlinge: Das Bundesamt und seine Aufgaben. Nürnberg 2013.
4   See: § 4 AsylG.
5   Stand der Abschiebungen in den Kosovo Ende 2014 (Deutscher Bundestag 2015: 2; 15f).
6   Reintegration and Emigration Programme for Asylum-Seekers in Germany, REAG, and Government Assisted Repatriation Programme, GARP Bundesamt für Migration und Flüchtlinge

# References

Bundesamt für Migration und Flüchtlinge. *Kosovo-Rückkehrprojekt 'URA 2'* [online]. Available from: www.bamf.de/DE/Rueckkehrfoerderung/ProjektKosovo/projektkosovo-node.html [Accessed 10 January 2016].

Bundesamt für Migration und Flüchtlinge, 2013. *Migrationsbericht des Bundesamtes für Migration und Flüchtlinge im Auftrag der Bundesregierung* [online]. Available from: www.bamf.de/SharedDocs/Anlagen/DE/Publikationen/Migrationsberichte/migrations bericht-2013.pdf?__blob=publicationFile [Accessed 10 January 2016].

Bundesamt für Migration und Flüchtlinge, 2015. *Das Bundesamt in Zahlen 2014. Asyl, Migration und Integration* [online]. Available from: www.bamf.de/SharedDocs/ Anlagen/DE/Publikationen/Broschueren/bundesamt-in-zahlen-2014.pdf?__blob= publicationFile [Accessed 10 January 2016].

Deutscher Bundestag, 2015. *Kleine Anfrage der Abgeordneten Ulla Jelpke, Jan Korte, Sevim Dağdelen, Kerstin Kassner, Martina Renner, Dr. Petra Sitte, Frank Tempel, Halina Wawzyniak, Jörn Wunderlich und der Fraktion DIE LINKE* [online]. Available from: http://dip21.bundestag.de/dip21/btd/18/041/1804142.pdf [Accessed 10 January 2016].

Die Bundesregierung, 2012. *Nationaler Aktionsplan Integration Zusammenhalt stärken. Teilhabe verwirklichen* [online]. Available from: www.bundesregierung.de/Content/DE/_ Anlagen/IB/2012-01-31-nap-gesamt-barrierefrei.pdf?__blob=publicationFile [Accessed 10 January 2016].

Friesenhahn, G.J., and Kniephoff-Knebel, A., 2011. *Europäische Dimensionen sozialer Arbeit*. Schwalbach/Ts.: Wochenschau-Verlag.

Langenohl, A., Poole, R., and Weinberg, M., eds, 2015. *Transkulturalität. Klassische Texte*. Bielefeld: transcript.

Staub-Bernasconi, S., 2007. *Soziale Arbeit als Handlungswissenschaft. Systemtheoretische Grundlagen und professionelle Praxis*. Bern, Stuttgart: UTB.

Wronka, J., and Staub-Bernasconi, S., 2012. 'Human Rights', in K.H. Lyons *et al.*, eds, *Sage handbook of international social work*. London: SAGE Publications, 70–85.

# 18 Seeking refuge in India

## Comment on the French case study from an Indian perspective

*Sohini Sengupta*

Population movement across borders in the South Asian region is a long-standing historical phenomenon. A total of 200,000 refugees and asylum seekers lived in India in 2015 (UNHCR 2015a, 2015b). These numbers are predicted to increase in coming years. The refugee situation in India is complicated by the absence of a standard legal and administrative system for refugee recognition and status determination. Like other countries in this region, the national government's political priorities shape the fortunes of refugees. Absence of uniform standards and primacy of bilateral relations in decisions about refugee status leads to differential treatment of asylum seekers in India (Weiner 1993; Chimni 2003; Bhattacharjee 2008).

Despite the heterogeneity of practice and outcomes, India is often lauded as providing a credible protection regime for millions of refugees from border countries displaced by or escaping conflict, political instability and persecution (UNHCR 2015b). According to the UNHCR, refugee human rights are protected under the Indian constitution (UNHCR 2012). The National Human Rights Commission and the Judiciary, along with non-governmental organisations, have been key institutions whose activism and intervention have contributed towards recognition and safeguarding of refugee rights in India. Not surprisingly then, work with refugees and asylum seekers constitutes a highly challenging domain of intervention at multiple levels for social work professionals in India.

The objective of this commentary is to compare the situation of refugees and asylum seekers in India with the case study from France (see Mellon-Mustafa and Schleyer-Lindenmann, Chapter 16). It begins with an introduction to the legal and other humanitarian standards guiding responses to the refugee situation in India. This is followed by a section that compares the situation in India with that of France, highlighting the similarities and differences in intervention realities. The commentary ends with a discussion about the complex context and challenges of social work among refugees in India.

### Humanitarian laws, standards and the status of refugees in India

Legal status of asylum seekers in India is based on two laws – the Foreigner's Act 1946 and the Citizenship Act 1955. These define all those who enter without visas to be illegal migrants, with no exceptions made for refugees or asylum seekers (HRLN 2007). India is neither a signatory to the 1951 United Nations Convention on the status of Refugees nor to the 1967 Protocol. Although it is one of the largest receiving countries for refugees in the region, specific national legislation to determine the status and treatment of refugees is absent (Bhattacharjee 2008). This is generally viewed as a problem and influential debates about the cause of this state of affairs and consequences for refugee experiences in India exist (Weiner 1993; Chimni 2003; Bhattacharjee 2008; Chaudhary 2004).

National governments in South Asia, newly independent with a complex mix of ethnic groups among its citizenry and lacking resources to effectively police their boundaries, have traditionally been wary of multilateral standards for refugee issues, viewing these as a compromise of national sovereignty (Weiner 1993). Instead, they have upheld the primacy of bilateral relations between national governments as the principle framework for evaluating refugee status. This perspective has led to two clear outcomes: first, differential treatment of refugees by the state and, second, contravention of the humanitarian principle of Non-Refoulement (Chimni 2003).

Lacking citizenship status or legal credentials, refugees are unable to access essential services such as schools and hospitals. Compelled to depend on informal relations with members of the local community on unequal terms, refugees face poverty and experience discrimination (Bhalla 2014). Recent news items cite the traumatic experiences of Rohingya Muslims seeking asylum in India to escape persecution in Myanmar (Bhalla 2014). Compared to the Rohingya, the Sri Lankan Tamils and Afghans have received better treatment and achieved greater local integration (Brar 2013).

While India has provided some groups of refugees and asylum seekers with social security, medical help and visas (Brar 2013), differential treatment remains a cause for concern. For instance, the state has made better provisions for Tibetan refugees compared to Chakma refugees from Bangladesh or Tamils from Sri Lanka (Chimni 2003). However, border and coast guards, unaware of the principle of '*non-refoulement*' have also turned back asylum seekers (Chimni 2003: 463).

Despite the absence of any standardised protection regime, the Indian judiciary has made significant contributions to the protection of refugee rights using the framework of the Indian constitution and interpretation of international laws (Bhattacharjee 2008). The establishment of the National Human Rights Commission in 1993 also enabled closer monitoring of refugee rights. In 1995, the NHRC filed public-interest litigation on behalf of 65,000 Chakma refugees who had been settled in the north-eastern state of Arunachal Pradesh since 1965. The Commission sought the intervention of the Supreme Court of India to safeguard the life and freedom of the refugees and enabled them to obtain citizenship rights (Chimni 2003: 457). More recently, the state government in the southern state of Tamil Nadu has extended basic social welfare benefits on a par with Indian citizens to Tamil Sri Lankan refugees residing in government camps (rediff news 2014).

## Institutions, laws and practice context: France and India

In India in 2014, the UNHCR registered 5,074 asylum seekers and 25,865 refugees (UNHCR). According to recent media reports unregistered refugees living in India numbered 30,000 (Bhalla 2014).

UNHCR is the key agency for refugees in India (UNHCR 2015b). Activities undertaken by humanitarian organisations such as the UNHCR provide some of the needs, legal frameworks and support services that are required by people seeking refuge or asylum (Brar 2013). At present the UNHCR undertakes the following activities: registering and providing documentation to asylum seekers and refugees; seeking long-term solutions, including returning to home countries once a conflict situation has stabilised; and local integration and initiatives to promote economic self-reliance (Brar 2013). The UNHCR works closely with the government and civil society organisations to ensure state services such as health and primary education for refugee families.

In the context of India, a great deal of social work and welfare activities takes place within the broader context of 'informal security regimes'. These regimes have been defined as a 'set of conditions where people rely heavily upon community and family relationships to meet their security needs' (Gough 2008: 33). The liminal position of asylum seekers limits their access to state welfare entitlements for eligible citizens. Potential asylum seekers from neighbouring countries seek out ties of kin and ethnic groups, merge into local communities and actively pursue citizenship rights by obtaining required documents. Media and human rights advocacy groups play an important role in making appeals for rights protection and against human rights violations to the Human Rights Commission and the Courts.

## Challenges for social work

Social workers need to work within a diverse set of social and institutional contexts within India to address issues pertaining to refugees and asylum seekers. Often this includes establishing identities, establishing links with state welfare services, advocating for asylum seekers' rights, initiating legal action and helping to secure required documentation. The social work professionals working on refugee issues tend to be most often located outside the sphere of the formal state administration – and form a crucial bridge between invisible asylum seekers and unresponsive government bureaucracy.

A critical requirement for social workers therefore is to be well trained with appropriate skills to work within various flexible, unstructured, low-paid and often conflict-prone community settings. They are required to possess in-depth knowledge of diverse cultural, socio-economic and political contexts that shape refugee identities, situations and strategies. The current nature of social intervention on this issue also indicates that social workers must be trained in constitutional law, international human rights law and national legal regimes and should have abilities to build coalitions and networks with other formal and informal institutions working with refugees.

## Conclusion

Social workers in India are similar to social workers in France in their broader commitment towards empowering refugees and asylum seekers. However, unlike in France, the commitment of Indian social workers goes beyond provisioning and administering of better services and creating a just and humane context of implementation. In India, social workers at the outset must work towards building a case for rights and entitlements of refugees and state responsibility for each new crisis situation as it emerges. The extent to which they are able to meet the broader goal of refugee protection and empowerment is constrained by the absence of uniform standards. However, Indian social workers also achieve remarkable successes through advocacy initiatives around human rights. Social work among refugees in India, despite its long-standing nature, remains as yet largely undocumented and defies classification and standardisation.

## References

Bhalla, N., 2014. *Myanmar's Rohingya stuck in refugee limbo in India* [online]. Thomson Reuters. Available from: www.reuters.com/article/us-foundation-stateless-india-rohingya-idUSKBN0HA07F20140915 [Accessed 12 December 2015].

Bhattacharjee, S., 2008. 'India needs a refugee law', *Economic & Political Weekly* 43(9): 71–5.

Brar, A., 2013. *India much advanced in refugee protection. UNHCR CoM* [online]. Observer Research Foundation (ORF). Available from: www.orfonline.org/research/india-much-advanced-in-refugee-protection-unhcr-com/ [Accessed 11 December 2015].

Chaudhary, O.N., 2004. 'Turning back: An assessment of non-refoulement under Indian law', *Economic & Political Weekly* 39(24): 3257.

Chimni, B.S., 2003. 'Status of refugees in India. Strategic ambiguity', in R. Samaddar, ed., *Refugees and the state. Practices of asylum and care in India, 1947-2000.* New Delhi, Thousand Oaks, Calif.: SAGE Publications, 443–71.

Gough, I., 2008. 'Welfare Regimes in Development Contexts. A Global and Regional Analysis', in I. Gough, G.D. Wood, and A. Barrientos, eds, *Insecurity and welfare regimes in Asia, Africa and Latin America. Social policy in development contexts.* Cambridge: Cambridge University Press, 15–48.

HRLN, 2007. *Report of refugee populations in India* [online]. Human Rights Law Network. Available from: www.hrln.org/admin/issue/subpdf/Refugee_populations_in_India.pdf [Accessed 10 December 2015].

rediff news, 2014. *'We have been treated well in India, this is the best model of refugee welfare'* [online]. Available from: www.rediff.com/news/special/we-have-been-treated-well-in-india-this-is-the-best-model-of-refugee-welfare/20140212.htm [Accessed 12 December 2015].

UNHCR. *What do we do in India* [online]. United Nations High Commissioner for Refugees. Available from: www.unhcr.org.in/index.php?option=com_content&view=article&id=8&Itemid=130 [Accessed 12 December 2015].

UNHCR, 2012. *Refugees in India share daily struggles with UNHCR chief* [online]. United Nations High Commissioner for Refugees. Available from: www.unhcr.org/50d47f056.html [Accessed 12 December 2015].

UNHCR, 2015a. *The refugee story in data and statistics* [online]. United Nations High Commissioner for Refugees. Available from: www.unhcr.org/pages/49c3646c4d6.html [Accessed 17 August 2015].

UNHCR, 2015b. *UNHCR subregional operations profile - South Asia* [online]. United Nations High Commissioner for Refugees. Available from: www.unhcr.org/pages/49e4876d6.html [Accessed 12 December 2015].

Weiner, M., 1993. Rejected people and unwanted migrants in South Asia. *Economic & Political Weekly* 28(34): 1737–46.

# 19 Narcotic and psychotropic drugs, transnational intersections and social work with drug users in Germany

*Irmgard Vogt*

Issues around drugs are always crossing from local to global, from national to transnational. This is also valid for concepts of how to handle drugs which were categorised as dangerous to consumers and/or societies. For more than half a century, 185 nations agreed to prohibit the trade and use of a number of so-called dangerous or narcotic drugs. As a consequence, dealers of such drugs as well as users were criminalised and – when caught by police – went to prison. This chapter tries to outline the transformation of the concept of prohibition into a concept of harm reduction which addresses the demands of users/addicts in a way which helps them survive and reintegrate into society.

The prohibition concept was established internationally by the United Nations in the 1950s, followed by conventions on the production and supply of narcotics and other psychotropic drugs.

> The 1961 convention covered drugs derived from three plants: opioids from the poppy (Papaver somniferum) and derivatives, cocaine from the coca bush (Erythroxylum coca), and cannabis from the cannabis plant (Cannabis sativa). A separate 1971 convention made the non-medical use of a wide range of synthetic drugs a punishable offence. A 1988 convention on trafficking consolidated the focus of the control system on suppression of illicit markets by including provisions to prevent money laundering and extending controls to precursor chemicals.
>
> (Room and Reuter 2012: 84)

The Commission on Narcotic Drugs and the World Health Organization were empowered to add and remove drugs from the list of controlled substances. Currently, the conventions are signed by 185 nations who agreed to fulfil the treaty obligations: prohibition of trade and use of narcotics and of psychotropic substances. However, the medical and scientific use of drugs was and is permitted under strict control (for instance in scientific studies). To enforce the prohibitive laws on narcotics, the law is armed with drastic punishments which differ to some degree between the countries.

The conventions and national laws prohibiting narcotics and psychotropic drugs have not prevented the development of illicit production, trade and markets for these substances all over the world. Narcotics have effects on the human body and mind which are unique and difficult to achieve otherwise. People who try narcotics and find the effects pleasurable often develop an urge to repeat the experience. They get hooked on the substances and develop dependency symptoms (American Psychiatric Association 2013). The symptoms are most pronounced when withdrawal sets in, which in the case of opiates, goes together with physical pain. Thus, there are always people willing to buy narcotics to alter their mental states as well as to avoid withdrawal. For those addicted to substances the need for it is much stronger than the fear of committing a crime. And the trade in narcotics is extremely profitable due to the fact that it is prohibited and has to be organised clandestinely. The drugs trade is organised transnationally and run by cartels which connect nations that produce the drugs (e.g. heroin from Afghanistan) with those with large numbers of consumers (e.g. England, Germany, France, USA).

Furthermore, addiction guarantees steady customers. On the streets illicit drugs are often sold by addicted dealers to addicted users – both are victims of the so-called war on drugs, declared by president of the USA, Richard Nixon, in 1971. Dealers and users are aware that they are committing crimes when they are selling and buying, but this does not stop them from engaging in drug dealing and drug using.

## Case study of a drug addict, part 1

Walter[1] is a man in his late forties. He finished school after nine years, got a placement in vocational training, was in an apprenticeship for three years and finished with a diploma in electro-mechanics. He then landed in a job in a medium-sized enterprise and worked there for some years. In those years his consumption of alcoholic beverages, tobacco and hashish was rather unspectacular – at least in terms of the average consumption patterns of Germans aged between 15 and 25 years (Vogt 2004; Pfeiffer-Gerschel *et al.* 2014).

When Walter met new friends who used heroin, he started using it as well. Shooting-up gave him a kick which he had never experienced before. Very quickly he became addicted. Some months after using heroin regularly he lost his job. To earn money to support his drug-use habit he engaged in drug dealing on the streets and, if necessary, pickpocketing and stealing goods from department stores.

For some years he was not motivated to change his lifestyle and give up drug use. But then he was caught by the police and was sentenced to prison for at least one year.

At the time when Walter had to go to prison, Germany was about to revise its policies regarding the treatment of drug addicts: they were no longer seen only as criminals but also as people with a chronic illness who needed support, counselling and treatment (for details see below).

Walter got in touch with an addiction treatment centre and a social worker who helped him to a place in a rehabilitation centre to undergo abstinence-based treatment for a year. Soon after he left the centre he relapsed and went back to the street drug milieu. In the following years he regularly visited a drop-in centre offering counselling, needle and syringe exchange and – some years later – a safe injection room. When necessary, he went on detoxification in hospitals. Eventually, he met a woman, fell in love with her and they moved into a flat. In the following nine years they were both off drugs, held down jobs and enjoyed life together.

However, Walter missed the feelings he once got from injecting heroin. Over the years, an urge built up to go back to using heroin again. In an interview, he said: 'When I relapsed, it was not an accident – I wanted it! And I wanted to know what happens afterwards. Do I get addicted at once or do I end up with feelings of guilt and tell myself: you are such an idiot, why did you do it?' (Vogt 2015). Unfortunately, he relapsed at once and went straight back to his habits: cocaine or crack in the morning and in the afternoon and evening heroin to calm himself down. He soon lost his job, his girlfriend and the flat.

Still, he was lucky because he did not end up on the streets but in his mother's house. His mother had always supported him emotionally and to some extent financially. Once again, he came into contact with social workers who told him to go into detox to get off cocaine/crack and go on a methadone maintenance programme to substitute prescription methadone for heroin.

## Markets for illicit drugs and consumers of heroin and cocaine

As mentioned in the case report, Walter uses heroin and cocaine – drugs which are illegal according to international conventions and to German drugs laws. Where do the drugs come from and who are the users?

The bulk of heroin which is sold in European countries is imported from Afghanistan, Myanmar, and Laos. In Germany, the percentage of those using heroin occasionally or habitually increased after 1970 with a peak of 200,000 addicts around the turn of the century. In the last 15 years, the number of heroin users has been decreasing steadily. On the other hand, cocaine is imported mainly from South American countries such as Bolivia, Peru and Colombia. In Germany, the percentage of those using cocaine occasionally or habitually has not changed much during the last 20 years. However, there are indications that the demand for synthetic uppers has increased heavily in the last ten years. Synthetic amphetamines have similar effects to cocaine but are much cheaper and can be produced anywhere. Cocaine, then, is the preferred drug of people who are affluent, and synthetic amphetamines are the drug of those who are poor.

In Germany today, the average consumer of illicit drugs such as heroin is in his/her late twenties, often poor with a low level of education and poor prospects of finding a place in the workforce. Of course there is some variation in demographic characteristics of users of illicit drugs. Often, drug use starts due to peer pressure or as a way for self-medication of physical and emotional pain. However, after starting, drug-use problems may evolve at school, at work and at home. In Germany, most long-term users of heroin and other illicit drugs do not have a job; they therefore depend on welfare subsidies or on their families for financial support (Schay *et al.* 2013).

In western and central Europe, the annual prevalence rate of the use of illicit opiates is estimated at 0.4 per cent, for cocaine at 1 per cent, and for synthetic uppers at 0.6 per cent and increasing. Overall, the percentage of people who recently used cocaine or synthetic uppers is much higher than that of those injecting illicit opiates

(UNODC 2014). In other regions of the world including eastern and south-eastern Europe, North America and China, annual prevalence rates are much higher.

## Health problems associated with illicit drug use and the introduction of harm reduction measures

Injecting illicit drugs is associated with severe health problems. On top of the list are unintended deaths by overdosing and blood-borne infections such as HIV, which if untreated progresses to AIDS, and Hepatitis B/C virus infections which may cause liver cancer. Cohort studies of injecting users of amphetamines, cocaine and heroin 'suggest that these drugs increase the risk of premature death, morbidity and disability' (Degenhardt and Hall 2012: 60). These risks can be reduced with harm-reduction measures instead of incarceration and treatment by abstinence as the only option (Schmid 2003).

Pressure to introduce harm-reduction measures came from all sorts of agents in Germany including a fraction of social workers active in the field of addiction who advocated programmes such as needle exchange in support of their clients. These social workers were aware that implementing harm-reduction measures did not go along easily with the principles of international treaties and national drugs laws. They also were aware that their actions could provoke conflicts with the police and – more generally – with the justice system as well as with politicians at the community, state and national level. However, until the 1990s the misery of drug addicts was so obvious that a change of strategy in dealing with them became necessary. The need for change was intensified when the numbers of HIV-infections of injecting drug users increased dramatically in the 1980s and politicians feared a spill-over into the general population. After years of struggling, social workers in favour of changes in dealing with drug addicts succeeded: drop-in centres opened their doors for drug addicts with counselling services and needle and syringe exchange programmes and soon after with safe injection facilities (Vogt and Schmid 1998). Shelters for homeless drug addicts were also set up with hygienic services etc. Social workers were involved in developing the programmes and are now running them, including disseminating messages to drug addicts regarding safer use (e.g. no shared use of needles and syringes or smoking equipment) and safer sex (using condoms when offering sex work or having sex with unknown people) (Pates and Riley 2012). In the 1990s, medical therapies were added to the measures which include methadone maintenance therapy (MMT) and – in a number of western European countries – heroin-assisted therapy (HAT). Social workers who in the 1980s and 1990s fought hard to establish a better drug treatment system are to be praised for their engagement and their stamina in this matter.

Data show that the introduction of harm-reduction measures was successful (Global Commission on Drug Policy 2014). First, at the community level as well as at the national level, the number of unintended deaths due to drug overdose decreased. Second, HIV infection rates in populations of injecting drug users decreased. Overall, the health of injecting drug users improved and their chances of living a long life have become better (Vogt 2011). Third, public nuisance caused by people using and injecting drugs openly on the streets decreased. Thus, everybody gained from the introduction of harm-reduction measures: addicts, social workers, politicians and the public.

Harm-reduction measures spread around the world, although not all countries implemented the whole package. Full-fledged harm-reduction measures with needle exchange programmes, safe injection rooms and MMT are implemented in a number of western European countries, Australia and Canada. The USA and China adopted needle exchange programmes and MMT but not safe injection rooms. Countries such as Thailand and Russia still oppose harm-reduction measures; they are paying a high price with ever increasing HIV infection rates and overdose death rates (Global Commission on Drug Policy 2011).

## Social work in the modern German drug treatment system: the case study of a drug addict, part 2

Since the 1990s, with the nationwide implementation of harm-reduction measures, social workers in Germany have offered a wide range of services to drug addicts. These include counselling in drop-in centres and regular counselling facilities, medically supported treatment (e.g. MMT or HAT, Strang *et al.* 2012), drug-use reduction group treatment, outpatient and inpatient abstinence treatment (including detoxification treatment, outpatient psychotherapy, inpatient rehabilitation treatment, aftercare support etc.; for more details of the German drug treatment system cf. Vogt 2009). Social workers are involved in all parts of service provision for drug addicts, in most cases as counsellors and/or case managers (Schmid *et al.* 2012). While social work counsellors in addiction work more often with groups in outpatient and inpatient settings, case managers engage more in network building and helping their clients find the support and treatment institutions which best fit their needs. However, social workers can also switch from group work to single case work and to case management and back again: it all depends on their training and the needs of the clients.

To illustrate social work in addiction, we go back to the case report. As described above, Walter became a client at drop-in centres. Social workers offered him counselling services on a regular basis[2] but Walter came to the meetings only when he was dearly in need of help. When he got caught by police and had to go to court, his contact intensified with one of the social workers, who then became his first case manager. The latter helped him to clarify his financial obligations and his health insurance protection. The case manager also arranged a deal with the judge which allowed Walter to undergo mandatory treatment (as an alternative to imprisonment) in a rehabilitation centre.

In the centre, Walter underwent a highly structured programme including skills and work trainings, therapeutic single and group sessions and spare time activities. He took lessons in relapse prevention and learnt to identify physical and psychic signals of craving, to withstand peer pressure to take drugs and to control his emotional states better (especially aggressive impulses and feelings of frustration).

After several relapses Walter was suffering from quite a lot of health problems at the age of 40 and he thought of going on MMT. To enter a programme, he once again needed a case manager/social worker to determine if he would benefit more from MMT or from HAT. Walter opted for MMT; he now takes his daily dose of methadone at his doctor's office. He attends an outpatient self-control programme to cut down his use of cocaine and crack and has plans to start a hepatitis-C treatment programme to improve his health. His case manager supports him with his plans, monitors progress and gives him feedback to encourage him to pursue his plans even in bad times when he is down and depressed.

Furthermore, Walter is looking to find a job and enter the workforce again. Since Walter worked in IT for some years, his chances of finding a job are relatively good but he may need some further training on the job. With support of his case manager he may be able to find a training course which fits his needs. Payment for the course may be taken over by the local labour agency which would very much prefer to see Walter in the workforce than on welfare payment. However, it will take quite some effort by his case manager and the liaison officer at the local labour agency and himself, to find employment and secure a living.

Research studies show that methadone maintenance programmes as well as heroin assisted treatment programmes have positive effects for heroin addicts such as improvement of their physical health and stabilisation of their everyday life. However, reintegration into the workforce is difficult, at least for those with long careers of illicit drug use.

## Conclusion

In West European countries, social work is deeply involved in shaping our understanding of addiction as a sickness or a way of life and in the support and treatment of people who abuse legal and illegal psychoactive substances or indulge in addictive behaviour (such as gambling, internet gaming, shopping addiction, sex addiction etc.). On the theoretical level, the excessive use of psychoactive substances is understood as an illness which cannot be treated by imprisonment but needs psychosocial and psychotherapeutic interventions. On the practical level, harm-reduction measures prevail and are implemented transnationally, although in variations.

To accomplish all this, social work in addiction is in a constant process of professionalisation on the national level as well as on the transnational level, resulting in relevant master's and PhD programmes being set up in institutions of higher education in Western Europe, North America and other places around the world. To further develop social work in addiction, the political involvement of social workers in the ongoing transnational dialogue on addiction is needed as well as social work involvement in inventing new treatment settings and tools for those who develop addictive behaviours.

## Notes

1  Name and details of the case have been anonymised.
2  Since the 1990s, motivational interviewing has had an ever increasing impact on the art of counselling in addiction (for more details cf. Miller and Rollnick (2013)).

# References

American Psychiatric Association, 2013. *Diagnostic and statistical manual of mental disorders*. 5th ed. Arlington: American Psychiatric Association.

Degenhardt, L., and Hall, W., 2012. 'Extent of illicit drug use and dependence, and their contribution to the global burden of disease', *The Lancet* 379(9810): 55–70.

Global Commission on Drug Policy, 2011. *War on drugs. Report of the Global Commission on Drug Policy* [online]. Global Commission on Drug Policy. Available from: www.globalcommissionondrugs.org/wp-content/themes/gcdp_v1/pdf/Global_Commission_Report_English.pdf [Accessed 14 December 2015].

Global Commission on Drug Policy, 2014. *Taking control. Pathways to drug policies that work* [online]. Global Commission on Drug Policy. Available from: www.gcdpsummary2014.com/#foreword-from-the-chair [Accessed 14 December 2015].

Miller, W.R., and Rollnick, S., 2013. *Motivational interviewing. Helping people change*. 3rd ed. New York, NY: Guilford Press.

Pates, R., and Riley, D., 2012. *Harm reduction in substance use and high-risk behaviour*. London: Wiley-Blackwell.

Pfeiffer-Gerschel, T., Jakob, L., and Stumpf, D., 2014. *2014 national report (2013 data) to the EMCDDA by the Reitox National Focal Point. Germany. Drug situation 2013/2014* [online]. European Monitoring Centre for Drugs and Drug Addiction. Available from: www.dhs.de/fileadmin/user_upload/pdf/EBDD_Jahresberichte/REITOX_Report_2014_Germany_EN.pdf [Accessed 10 January 2016].

Room, R., and Reuter, P., 2012. 'How well do international drug conventions protect public health?' *The Lancet* 379(9810): 84–91.

Schay, P., Lojewski, I., and Siegele, F., 2013. *Integrative Therapie in der Drogenhilfe. Theorie - Methoden - Praxis in der sozialen und medizinischen Rehabilitation*. 1st ed. Stuttgart, New York, Thieme.

Schmid, M., 2003. *Drogenhilfe in Deutschland. Entstehung und Entwicklung 1970-2000*. Frankfurt/Main, New York: Campus.

Schmid, M., Schu, M., and Vogt, I., 2012. *Motivational case management. Ein Manual für die Drogen- und Suchthilfe*. Heidelberg: Medhochzwei-Verlag.

Strang, J., Groshkova, T., and Metrebian, N., 2012. *New heroin-assisted treatment. EMDCCA insights*. Luxembourg: Publications Office of the European Union.

UNODC, 2014. *World drug report 2014* [online]. United Nations Office on Drugs and Crime. Available from: www.unodc.org/documents/wdr2014/World_Drug_Report_2014_web.pdf [Accessed 14 December 2015].

Vogt, I., 2004. *Beratung von süchtigen Frauen und Männern*. Weinheim: Beltz Juventa.

Vogt, I., 2009. 'Drug problems, community reactions and policy changes in Frankfurt/Main', *Drugs: Education, Prevention and Policy* 16(6): 512–26.

Vogt, I., ed., 2011. *Auch Süchtige altern. Probleme und Versorgung älterer Drogenabhängiger*. Frankfurt am Main: Fachhochschulverlag.

Vogt, I., 2015. *Ältere Drogenabhängige mit ihren Beschwerden und Wünschen an die Zukunft. Handlungsansätze der Sozialen Arbeit*. Weitramsdorf: ZKS-Verlag.

Vogt, I., and Schmid, M., 1998. 'Drugs in Germany and the emergence of the modern drug treatment system', in G. Hunt and H. Klingemann, eds, *Drugs, demons and delinquents. Drug treatment systems in an international perspective*. London: Sage, 145–57.

# 20  Drug use

## Comment on the German case study from a British perspective

*John Watson*

A British 'Walter' may in fact have a remarkably similar profile to his German peer. The drug-using career that Vogt outlines for Walter is one that many British opioid users and workers in support agencies would recognise. The neo-liberal policies of the Conservative Government of 1979–97 saw huge increases in unemployment and poverty. These social changes are often linked to the big rises in the numbers of people with heroin problems in Britain in the 1980s and 1990s (Pearson 1987; Buchanan 2004; Reuter and Stevens 2007; Watson 2013). British Walters, unemployed workers from the former heavy industries, often saw heroin as a release and a substitute for the void of poverty and the loss of identity associated with long-term unemployment (Buchanan 2004). Many of the current substance users in contact with British treatment agencies are of a similar age to Walter, having had long drug-using careers. Indeed, many of these people may have begun using in the 1980s or 1990s and have had similar periods of abstinence, controlled use and relapse. As in Germany and most of western Europe, the average age of heroin users in treatment in the UK is rising, the number of new heroin users falling, and the number of those injecting drugs is on the decline (EMCDDA 2013). However, this trend has been more gradual in the United Kingdom than many of our European partners (EMCDDA 2013; Hughes and Stevens 2010). It is also thought possible that heroin may simply have gone out of fashion, replaced to some degree by other new psychoactive substances (NPS), or legal highs. There has been evidence of an increase in people using other forms of opioids and NPS drugs (EMCDDA 2013; Power 2013). Recent surveys appear to have shown that the fall in overall drug use seen since the mid/late 1990s has levelled out, with overall drug use in Britain more or less stable in recent years (Home Office 2014). Worryingly, the latest drug-related death statistics for England and Wales have shown a sharp rise (ONS 2014). It is too early to ascertain whether this is part of a longer-term trend. It is also too soon to hypothesise whether policy changes described below will have been a factor in this sudden upsurge.

Whilst Vogt is right to point to the various international treaties that limit the scope of national drugs policies, there is perhaps more room for manoeuvre than she suggests on the issues of penalties against users and dealers and on the forms of treatment and support that are offered. Portugal is a prime example of a country that has chosen a different path, with possession becoming a civil offence (Greenwald 2009; Hughes and Stevens 2010). The UK however, in the Misuse of Drugs Act (1971), has some of the toughest criminal penalties in the western world (HoC Science and Technology Committee 2006) and calls for Portuguese-style decriminalisation were roundly rejected in the government drugs strategy of 2010 (HM Government 2010).

However, over the years differing governments have responded flexibly to the potential harms that drugs may cause users and society. In response to the revelation that injecting drug users sharing equipment could contribute to the spread of the HIV/AIDS virus, the government of the time pursued a policy of harm reduction, setting up needle exchange schemes and promoting substitute-prescribing as an alternative to street heroin and an acknowledged way to reduce harm at individual, community and societal levels (ACMD 1988; Buchanan 2010; Watson 2013). Britain has not gone as far as some of its more innovative European neighbours (including Germany) in this regard, rejecting innovations such as drug consumption rooms, for example (HoC Science and Technology Committee 2006; HoC Select Committee on Home Affairs 2002). However, in spite of this, a policy of harm reduction was the consensus view among British policy makers until the election of the Conservative-led government in 2010 heralded a change in direction.

Since the 1980s, social workers, working in predominantly voluntary sector agencies, have been pivotal in providing psychosocial support along similar lines to those described in Vogt's case study, providing initial assessment and harm-reduction advice, psychosocial support and care co-ordination (Watson 2014). However, British drugs treatment has still been criticised as lacking a holistic focus, being more focused on individual psychological interventions and with a still dominant medical profession, instead of focusing on the root structural causes of drug use such as poverty and inequality (Buchanan 2004). It has often been social workers in voluntary agencies who have been vital in shaping specialist drugs work towards a more holistic view of drug issues. This has been in spite of a rather limited focus on drug issues in the majority of British social work programmes, where direct work with drug issues has perhaps been implicitly seen as the remit of the medical profession (Watson 2014). Research by Galvani and Forrester questioned British social workers on the amount of drugs-specific training on their qualifying programmes. The findings were quite alarming, as over a third of participants reported having had no training at all and half reported having less than half a day's training (Galvani and Forrester 2011). Overall they found that newly qualified social workers reported feeling less able to work with drug users than any other client group (Galvani and Forrester 2011). There are courses which offer specialist modules in supporting drug users, but these are unfortunately in a minority. One can only assume then that those social work specialists working with British Walters have acquired their skills and training post-qualifying, or gained their knowledge at the large number of drugs support agencies that have offered practice placements to social work students over recent decades.

The last decade did see some big increases in funding for drugs services, opening new opportunities for social workers to specialise in this field and influence the direction of drugs treatment. Most of this funding however was focused on interventions for drug users within the criminal justice system who were subject to court-sanctioned treatment orders (Buchanan 2010).

As mentioned earlier, since 2010 the United Kingdom has set on the path of potentially very radical changes in the way drug users are supported, at least in England, with as yet uncertain results. Devolution has given Scotland and Wales a large degree of autonomy over the direction of drugs treatment policy (but not in the respect of challenging the criminalisation of certain types of drugs and drug users). Drug services have seen the end of ring-fenced funding for drug treatment, with responsibility devolved to local public health bodies. These bodies have seen large cuts in their overall funding since 2010 and many may be disinclined to dedicate resources to services, seeing drug addiction as less deserving than the other issues that come under their remit. It appears that there is now uneven provision across localities with some areas seeing gaps in provision and funding (Roy and Buchanan 2015).

Other major changes will potentially impact on the range of services available. The Conservative government has increasingly focused on abstinence over harm reduction in recent years (HM Government 2010; Watson 2013). The emphasis has been on pursuing abstinence-based treatment, sometimes at the expense of the harm-reduction interventions described above. This is potentially compounded by the government's imposition of 'payment by results' (PbR) regimes, whereby some funding is withheld until agencies can demonstrate they have met certain targets, often in terms of how many clients are drugs free. The danger here, one that has already been proven to happen in other areas where PbR has taken place, is that agencies will focus their energies on the clients who are most stable as those most likely to achieve abstinence, at the expense of those with more chaotic drug use who may in fact require more intensive support (Watson 2013; Mohammadi 2014).

The recent government spending plans point to further cuts in overall spending for local public health authorities. Increasingly local agencies and commissioning bodies will take different approaches to drugs support. Some may indeed shape services in an innovative manner, taking account of local populations and issues such as poverty, migration and unemployment. Others however may choose to cut services altogether, or focus only on the most stable drug-using clients to maximise their potential funding in a time of austerity (Watson 2013; Roy and Buchanan 2015). British Walters will increasingly find the sort of services and support dependent on the local area in which they live, with some receiving holistic social work and medical support and others slipping through the net, or receiving minimal intervention. Others may find their peers receiving support, whilst they are deemed a poor investment in the age of payments by results. The British drugs policy with regard to social work and medical support is increasingly fragmented compared to that of its European neighbours. The opportunities for getting involved as social workers and taking an international, or even a national perspective are becoming increasingly rare in a time of austerity, fragmentation of services and localisation.

## References

ACMD, 1988. *AIDS and drug misuse. Part one*. London: Advisory Council on the Misuse of Drugs.

Buchanan, J., 2004. 'Missing Links? Problem drug use and social exclusion', *Probation Journal* (51): 387–97.

Buchanan, J., 2010. 'Drug policy under new labour 1997–2010. Prolonging the war on drugs', *Probation Journal* (57): 250–62.

EMCDDA, 2013. *European drug report. Trends and developments.* Lisbon: European Monitoring Centre for Drugs and Drug Addiction (EMCDDA).

Galvani, S., and Forrester, D., 2011. 'How well prepared are newly qualified social workers for working with substance use issues? Findings from a national survey in England', *Social Work Education* 30(4): 422–39.

Greenwald, G., 2009. *Drug decriminalization in Portugal. Lessons for creating fair and successful drug policies.* Washington, D.C: CATO Institute.

HM Government, 2010. *Drug strategy 2010. Reducing demand, restricting supply, building recovery: Supporting people to live a drug free life.* London: Crown Publications.

HoC Science and Technology Committee, 2006. *Drug classification: Making a hash of it? Fifth report of session 2005-2006* [online]. The Stationery Office. Available from: www.publications.parliament.uk/pa/cm200506/cmselect/cmsctech/1031/1031.pdf [Accessed 10 June 2016].

HoC Select Committee on Home Affairs, 2002. *The government's drugs policy. Is it working?* [online]. Her Majesty's Stationery Office (HMSO). Available from: www. cannabislegal.de/international/uk-home.htm [Accessed 10 January 2016].

Home Office, 2014. *Drug misuse. Findings from the 2013/2014 crime survey for England and Wales (CSEW)* [online]. Her Majesty's Government (HMG). Available from: www.gov.uk/government/publications/drug-misuse-findings-from-the-2013-to-2014-csew/drug-misuse-findings-from-the-201314-crime-survey-for-england-and-wales [Accessed 30 July 2015].

Hughes, C.E., and Stevens, A., 2010. 'What can we learn from the Portuguese decriminalisation of illicit drugs?' *British Journal of Criminology* (50): 999–1022.

Mohammadi, D., 2014. 'Addiction services in England. In need of an intervention', *The Lancet* 1(6): 421–2.

ONS, 2014. *Deaths related to drug poisoning in England and Wales* [online]. Office for National Statistics. Available from: www.ons.gov.uk/ons/dcp171778_414574.pdf [Accessed 10 January 2016].

Pearson, G., 1987. 'Social deprivation, unemployment and patterns of heroin use', in N. Dorn and N. South, eds, *A land fit for heroin?* Basingstoke: Macmillan, 62–94.

Power, M., 2013. *Drugs 2.0. The web revolution that's changing how the world gets high.* London: Portobello Books.

Reuter, P., and Stevens, A., 2007. *An analysis of UK drug policy. A report by professor Peter Reuter and Alex Stevens* [online]. UK Drug Policy Commission (UKDPC). Available from: www.ukdpc.org.uk/wp-content/uploads/Policy%20report%20-%20An%20analysis%20of%20UK%20drug%20policy%20%28summary%29.pdf [Accessed 10 January 2016].

Roy, A., and Buchanan, J., 2015. 'The paradoxes of recovery policy. Exploring the impact of austerity and responsibilisation for the citizenship claims of people with drug problems', *Social Policy & Administration* 49(3): 1–16.

Watson, J., 2013. 'The good, the bad and the vague. Assessing emerging conservative drugs policy', *Critical Social Policy* 33(2): 285–304.

Watson, J., 2014. 'Alcohol and other drug treatment', in B. Teater, ed., *Contemporary social work practice. A handbook for students.* Maidenhead: Open University Press, 178–93.

# 21 Drug use and health related problems among former Soviet Union drug users in Israel

## Considerations for social work practice

## Comment on the German case study from an Israeli perspective

*Richard Isralowitz and Alexander Reznik*

The use of drugs – such as illicit drugs, alcohol and other addictive substances including those medically prescribed – is not a new phenomenon but one that takes on meaning and importance in relation to its social context that varies over time and location. In the case of Walter, Irmgard Vogt outlines the restriction and the possibilities of social workers dealing with drug users. The aims and the strategies differ throughout time, and various political decisions and perspectives strongly influence this field of social work.

The following chapter sheds light on the influence of gender and migration on social work with drug users. It will take a closer look at the meaning of country of origin and place of current residence for immigrant drug users.

In the late 1980s when exit policies were liberalised, millions of people left the former Soviet Union (FSU) to settle elsewhere (e.g. Israel, Germany and the United States). These immigrants, mostly from Russia and the Ukraine, came from an environment with extremely high rates of drug use as well as blood-borne viruses (HIV/AIDS, hepatitis B virus (HBV), hepatitis C virus (HCV) and multidrug-resistant tuberculosis) (Isralowitz *et al.* 2013).

A review of professional literature reveals scant information about transnational drug use, risk behaviours, police reports and service utilisation (Guarino *et al.* 2012; Isralowitz *et al.* 2013). Conclusions are limited due to the poor precision results from study cohorts. Presently, Russian-speaking immigrants make up 13 per cent of Israel's population and constitute about 25 per cent of the illicit drug users in the country (Isralowitz and Reznik 2013).

### Gender and drug use differences among FSU immigrants

Since 1995, the Regional Alcohol and Drug Abuse Resources (RADAR) Center, Ben Gurion University, Israel has been researching drug use among FSU immigrants, their background characteristics, attitudes and behaviour. For the most part, the RADAR Center's sampling efforts have been geared to generating 'useable knowledge' about lifetime drug users for prevention and treatment purposes. The primary data collection tools used by the RADAR Center have been the Addiction Severity Index (ASI), 5th Edition; the Substance Use Survey Institute (SUSI) developed by the RADAR Center; and the Short Acculturation Scale (SAS). More than 1,000 FSU immigrant drug users in Israel have been interviewed since 1995.

A comparison of FSU female and male drug users shows that females tend to be younger, married or living with a partner. They are less likely to have a criminal record resulting in a conviction, incarceration and/or parole and are in more danger of being sexually abused. Women report more chronic illness; however, their level of HIV/HCV/TB infection is similar to males. Patterns of heroin, alcohol and other drug use are similar among females and males; cannabis use is higher among males and cocaine use higher among females. Also, females are more likely than males to prefer short-term detoxification (only) as a treatment intervention. Table 21.1 provides a comparison of FSU immigrant drug users based on selected health, alcohol and drug-use patterns.

Generally, there is considerable progress toward understanding of drug-use patterns based on gender – men and women use drugs for different reasons. Females are more vulnerable to abuse and addiction because they become more dependent on drugs faster and suffer the consequences sooner than males. Generally, female drug users who have been studied make up about 20 per cent of the heroin-addicted population receiving treatment. Female addicts tend to sustain their addiction through illegal income-earning activities such as prostitution, and/or their partners provide them with drugs or supply the money necessary to purchase drugs. Regardless of how women support their addiction, they tend to have little interest in going through processes of detoxification and treatment. It has been reported that women who abuse drugs have problems related to co-dependency and relations with significant others (Isralowitz and Reznik 2009; Bryant *et al.* 1991; Swett *et al.* 1991; Fiorentine and Anglin 1996; Bush and Kraft 2001).

The drug treatment presented by the United Nations (O'Neil and Lucas 2013) reflects a lack of gender-specific services including individual and group counselling linked to the needs of immigrants, especially women with health problems, child-care responsibilities, under- and unemployment, absence of a familial support network, and acculturation difficulties. The world of drug addiction treatment tends to be a male domain; consequently, female addicts may feel out of place in a treatment facility and reluctant to become involved with the services provided if they are not gender-specific and attuned to their cultural needs.

Results of male and female FSU immigrants over time in Israel show that drug use appears to affect acculturation. Those who use drugs before immigration tend to be less acculturated; information shows a possible link between acculturation and the type of treatment preferred by addicts regardless of gender status.

Some experts, including social workers, believe treatment of special populations such as immigrant women may be enhanced if their particular needs are considered

*Table 21.1* Former Soviet Union drug users in Israel: a gender comparison

| | Gender | |
| --- | --- | --- |
| | *Male*<br>*(n = 454)[1]* | *Female*<br>*(n = 87)[1]* |
| Mean age (SD) | 33.8 (9.6)** | 31.0 (7.6)** |
| Married, % (n) | 24.6 (106)*** | 43.8 (35)*** |
| Jewish, % (n) | 70.8 (320)*** | 47.1 (40)*** |
| Victim of sexual abuse, % (n) | 4.0 (18)*** | 63.5 (53)*** |
| Chronic Medical Problems, % (n) | 52.6 (40)*** | 76.7 (66)*** |
| Hepatitis C, % (n) | 67.3 (304) | 58.6 (51) |
| HIV/AIDS, % (n) | 4.4 (20) | 9.3 (8) |
| Tuberculosis, % (n) | 4.0 (18) | 1.2 (1) |
| Heroin Use, % (n) | 91.6 (412) | 94.3 (82) |
| Alcohol Use, % (n) | 66.6 (299) | 60.9 (53) |
| Cannabis Use, % (n) | 84.4 (379)*** | 58.6 (51)*** |
| Sedatives Use, % (n) | 39.8 (174) | 44.0 (37) |
| Cocaine Use, % (n) | 33.1 (143)** | 48.8 (42)** |
| Amphetamine Use, % (n) | 15.5 (68) | 15.1 (13) |
| Hallucinogens Use, % (n) | 27.8 (123) | 36.0 (31) |
| Inhalants Use, % (n) | 6.6 (29) | 6.0 (5) |
| Other Opiate Use, % (n) | 49.8 (217) | 48.8 (42) |
| Poly drugs Use, % (n) | 86.3 (380) | 85.1 (72) |
| Drug treatment,[2] % (n) | *** | *** |
| Detox only | 35.5 (134) | 58.1 (43) |
| Detox and other | 36.1 (136) | 24.3 (18) |
| Never once | 28.4 (107) | 17.6 (13) |

Notes: **p<.01; ***p<.001 comparison of FSU females and males using t-test for means or chi square for percentages
1  up to 6 subjects in each group missing data on some variables.
2  significant differences in drug treatment by gender (from chi square for 3 × 2 table).

and met in a treatment environment (APA 1995; Kauffman and Woody 1995; Walton-Moss and McCaul 2006; Isralowitz and Reznik 2013; Bartholomew *et al.* 2005). However, there is not full agreement that separate programmes for female drug users based on ethnic and cultural factors are superior to mainstream efforts with respect to outcomes (Sullivan and Fleming 1997). Regardless of the treatment approach, social workers and other addiction prevention and treatment personnel need to be cognisant of ethno-specific prevention and treatment needs of immigrants through policy, programmes and services provision.

# References

APA, 1995. *Practice guide for treatment of patients with substance use disorders. Alcohol, cocaine, opioids:* American Psychiatric Association.

Bartholomew, N., Courtney, K., Rowan-Szal, G.A., and Simpson, D.D., 2005. 'Sexual abuse history and treatment outcomes among women undergoing methadone treatment', *Journal of Substance Abuse Treatment* 29(3): 231–5.

Bryant, V., Eliach, J., and Green, S., 1991. 'Adapting the traditional EAP model to effectively serve battered women in the workplace', *Employee Assistance Quarterly* 6(2): 1–10.

Bush, I.R., and Kraft, M.K., 2001. 'Self-Sufficiency and Sobriety. Substance-abusing women and welfare reform', *Journal of Social Work Practice in the Addictions* 1(1): 41–64.

Fiorentine, R., and Anglin, M., 1996. 'More is better. Counseling participation and the effectiveness of outpatient drug treatment', *Journal of Substance Abuse Treatment* 13(4): 341–8.

Guarino, H., Moore, S.K., Marsch, L.A., and Florio, S., 2012. 'The social production of substance abuse and HIV/HCV risk. An exploratory study of opioid-using immigrants from the former Soviet Union living in New York City', *Substance Abuse Treatment, Prevention, and Policy* 7(2). Available from: http://substanceabusepolicy.biomedcentral. com/articles/10.1186/1747-597X-7-2 [Accessed 30 December 2015].

Isralowitz, R., and Reznik, A., 2009. 'Problem severity profiles of substance abusing women in therapeutic treatment facilities', *International Journal of Mental Health and Addiction* 7(2): 368–75.

Isralowitz, R., and Reznik, A., 2013. 'Former Soviet Union immigrant women. Drug use profiles and special needs', in L.A. O'Neil and J. Lucas, eds, *DAWN. Drugs and alcohol women network: Promoting a gender responsive approach to addiction.* Turin: UNICRI, 275–306.

Isralowitz, R., Reznik, A., and Peleg, T., 2013. 'Former Soviet Union immigrant illicit drug use in Israel (1989-2010). Implications for prevention and treatment policy', *Journal of Addictive Behaviors Therapy & Rehabilitation* 2(1): 1–2.

Kauffman, J., and Woody, G., 1995. *Matching treatment to patient needs in opioid substitution therapy. Treatment improvement protocol (TIP) Series* [online]. Department of Health and Social Services (DHHS). Available from: www.taadas.org/publications/ prodimages/TIP%2020.pdf [Accessed 10 January 2016].

O'Neil, L.A., and Lucas, J., eds, 2013. *DAWN. Drugs and alcohol women network: Promoting a gender responsive approach to addiction.* Turin: UNICRI.

Sullivan, E., and Fleming, M., 1997. *A guide to substance abuse for primary care clinicians.* Washington, D.C: Department of Health and Social Services (DHHS).

Swett, C., Surrey, J., Compaine, A., and Chaves, R., 1991. 'High rates of alcohol use and history of physical and sexual abuse among women outpatients', *The American Journal of Drug and Alcohol Abuse* 17(1): 49–60.

Walton-Moss, B., and McCaul, M., 2006. 'Factors associated with lifetime history of drug treatment among substance dependent women', *Addictive Behaviors* 31(2): 246–53.

# 22 An exploration of issues of culture and diversity within England's statutory child protection system

*Adrian Braithwaite and Sarah Cresswell*

Headlines in the UK tell us that asylum seekers are flocking to the UK every year. However, do the facts bear this out? Not according to the Red Cross: of the 13 million refugees worldwide, it was estimated that there were only 126,000 in the UK in 2014, just 0.19 per cent of the UK population (British Red Cross 2014). When considering asylum and immigration issues within the UK it is worth considering the historical context of the Commonwealth. Following the Second World War, when most former colonies were granted independence, the majority of immigration to the UK was from former or remaining colonies. The introduction of the British Nationality Act 1948 enabled subjects of the Commonwealth to enter the UK without the need for a visa. Later legislation imposed immigration restrictions and the Immigration Acts of the 1960s, '70s and '80s significantly reduced citizenship rights for people from the Commonwealth, particularly the Caribbean, the Indian subcontinent and Africa (Hayes 2004: 14). However, Commonwealth subjects can still make claims for asylum under the 1951 Convention.

Migration is a contemporary social work issue which transcends national boundaries: there are overlapping issues of diversity, culture, lifestyle and the right to family life, as well as socio-economic factors. Transnational knowledge and strategies need to be developed to recognise and balance individual and cultural rights. This case study considers issues of statutory child protection within the context of diversity and cultural issues embedded within the state, where the right to family life is balanced against the rights of the child to be protected. This case study is an amalgamation of factual cases we worked on whilst practising as social workers in England.

The case study considers a Congolese family who obtain refugee status via the Resettlement Programme, which is also known as the Gateway Protection Programme. This is the United Kingdom's contribution to the Office of the United Nations High Commissioner for Refugees (UNHCR) global resettlement programme. The British government works in partnership with the UNHCR to identify refugees considered particularly vulnerable and eligible under the 1951 Convention relating to the status of refugees; the Resettlement Programme accepts 1,000 people a year. In 2014, the UK received a total of only 31,400 asylum applications; of these only 41 per cent were granted asylum as an initial decision, reflecting how difficult it is to secure asylum within the UK (British Red Cross 2014).

The case study family consists of the following members:

- Rose Kombo, mother, 35 years
- Reine Kombo, daughter, 12 years
- Gautier Kombo, son, 6 years
- Alban Kombo, son, 3 months

## Prior to arrival in the UK

Rose and her family fled to Rwanda from the Democratic Republic of the Congo due to unrest. They then resided in a refugee camp for several months and were subsequently identified by UNHCR field officers as being particularly vulnerable. Rose was ill and suffered from a heart problem, Reine was at an age where she could be sexually exploited and the family had to meet the care needs of Alban. The children's father died in the conflict and Reine provided care for all the family while in the camp.

Under the Resettlement Programme they were accepted as refugees and, as such, are provided *indefinite leave to remain* in the UK (Refugee Council 2015). Once *indefinite leave to remain* has been granted, refugees have similar rights to UK citizens. The Resettlement Programme is delivered by a partnership of participating local authorities and non-governmental organisations, such as the Refugee Council and Refugee Action. Refugees have access to social housing or private tenancies through the provision of housing benefit. Rose and her family were housed in a small property in an area of low-demand housing. Refugees can also claim social benefits to provide an income and they have access to health care. Under the Resettlement Programme family status, relationships and dependency are assessed (HGM 2010).

In a refugee camp Rose would have focused primarily on survival and basic necessities. Now that Rose has achieved refugee status life is still difficult but not at a survival level. Rose receives treatment for her heart problem and it emerges that she is suffering from Post-Traumatic Stress Disorder (PTSD), following being raped and witnessing her husband being tortured and murdered as they made their way to the camp. Through the Refugee Council, Rose is referred to therapeutic services for further support. However, a study (MIND 2009) identifies mental health services to refugees as being largely deficient and inaccessible to asylum seekers, which can cause them to be more marginalised (McColl and Johnson 2006). Other studies (McKenzie *et al.* 2007) found that the asylum seeking process is so stressful that it can exacerbate the symptoms of anyone with a mental health problem.

Bhugra and Jones (2001) identify that PTSD can be triggered by 'cultural bereavement', as asylum seekers will have left a way of life that is familiar to them to begin again in a new country with a way of life and customs that are very different (Collett 2004: 82). However, there is little in the way of statistics to measure the impact of conditions such as PTSD on asylum seekers. The interrogative approach of the entry interview by the UK Visas and Immigration

Agency would be a nerve-wracking experience, considering the consequences should the asylum application be turned down. Asylum seekers will be wary of state officials due to previous negative experiences. Interviews will also stir memories and emotions of unpleasant events and previous statements will be cross-examined. Asylum seekers receive little in the way of support and the few agencies which can provide support (such as the Haven Project in Hull) are stretched to capacity.

## Arrival in the UK

The children attend local schools and slowly begin the process of integration. However, the family comes to the attention of the local authority, as 12-year-old Reine is frequently late or has unauthorised absences from school. The school makes a referral to the Children and Young People's Services, which is the local authority department responsible for assessing and implementing state intervention. A multi-agency approach to working with families is a key feature of supporting children and meeting care and protection needs. Past investigations, including enquiries into the circumstances of child deaths, have consistently identified the failure of agencies to share information effectively in the safeguarding of children (HMSO 1974; Laming 2003; Department for Education 2008). Recommendations from the Laming Report (2003) led to the introduction of the Children Act 2004 which placed a duty on agencies to share information and promote multi-agency working and shared responsibilities between relevant stakeholders in the well-being of children. However, it is understandable that such interest by the state would cause Rose and her family concern. Asylum seekers will not be familiar with the assessment process. Asylum seekers' first experience of UK officials will possibly be the UK Visa and Immigration Agency, so fear and suspicion regarding the consequences of assessment would be understandable.

The principal piece of legislation relating to state intervention in meeting children's needs is the Children Act 1989. This act largely governs, and provides a baseline for the duties social workers have in regard to meeting children's care and protection needs (Brayne *et al.* 2013). The underlying philosophy of the Children Act 1989 is that the welfare of the child is the paramount consideration; this principle is applied specifically to legal proceedings, but also guides social workers when working with children and young people.

A social worker undertakes an assessment using the *National Framework for the Assessment of Children in Need and their Families* (DoH 2000). In most authorities, assessment will now include aspects of the Strengthening Families Approach which was advocated in Eileen Munro's review of Child Protection (Munro 2011). However, language is a barrier, and some knowledge of the Congolese culture is also needed. The use of interpreters can be problematic and should be approached with caution. There are issues regarding what exactly is being said and also regarding confidentiality; the family are not likely to want a third party to be privy to their situation, which may be in part due to feelings of shame. The effective use of an interpreter relies on trust, honesty and transparency.

All this impacts on the working relationship and assessment of the family's need. Rose is initially mistrustful by what she perceives as sudden interest by the state in her family life; however, she is also supported by a worker from the Refugee Council who explains why the social worker is visiting. This support is invaluable in helping Rose understand some of the concerns expressed by the social worker and the process of assessment. Furthermore, what needs to be considered in the assessment is the impact of factors which can affect any family in the UK, such as poverty, housing and health, as not all issues are related to asylum and culture.

In the UK health care and advice are universal services offered by a health visitor until the child reaches the age of five. Beyond this, health advice is given by the school nurse in the school that the child attends. The health visitor allocated to the Kombo family has also expressed concerns about Alban's care, as Reine is undertaking much of this. In the UK this would be contrary to the social mores, whereby a child of Reine's age should be concentrating on her school work, not caring for her sibling. The health visitor has also expressed concerns about different (hygienic) standards concerning the baby's nutrition and about the children's safety, as she has observed both children handling large, sharp kitchen knives and pans of boiling water while preparing food.

There follows a discussion about attempting to apply some boundaries for Gautier, who is frequently playing out unsupervised, and who has a faint mark on the back of his legs, observable by those at school. He says that Rose hit him with her open hand when he did not comply with her wishes. Via the interpreter, he discloses witnessing the brutal murder of his mother and insists that Rose is an 'aunt' but it is unclear if she is a blood relative or a friend. Rose admits to hitting Gautier and explains that this is acceptable in their culture. She struggles to understand how this can be damaging, especially given the hardships the family endured in the refugee camp. She also dismisses the concerns of the health visitor about her parenting of Alban and Reine taking on too much responsibility due to Rose's ill health. However, she agrees to work with the social worker and, via an interpreter, some progress is made. It is clear that Rose wants and needs support.

## Cultural conflicts and conflicting norms

Under the Children Act 1989 all children are protected and entitled to services that meet their needs. Section 47 of the 1989 Act places a duty on local authorities to investigate if there is reasonable cause to suspect that a child is suffering, or likely to suffer, significant harm. Social work intervention is based on a holistic assessment of the young person's situation and diversity and cultural issues would form part of this assessment. Assessment is a key feature of UK social work intervention (Parker and Bradley 2014).

Rose's experience of caring for her children is within Congolese cultural norms, and practices around parenting and providing care will be, perhaps, very different to what is considered the norm within the UK. These are value-laden issues that require social workers to have skills of cultural competence when delivering support to families. The overarching framework for professional social work development within the UK is the Professional Capabilities Framework (The British Association of Social Workers). One domain within the framework is diversity and social workers develop a professional understanding of the multi-dimensional nature of diversity and how oppression, marginalisation and alienation can impact on service user experience, as well as an understanding of how family life and social expectations have been shaped by culture. Although it is important to develop cultural competency and awareness, every child has the right to be protected. Being culturally competent promotes an understanding of childcare norms within diverse contexts. Practitioners must be able to challenge abusive behaviour without being labelled discriminatory, or conversely, must not fail to act for fear of being accused of being discriminatory. The family has complex circumstances and making use of an assessment tool such as the Culturagram would provide information concerning values in relation to family life, education and employment (Congress and Kung 2013; Parker and Bradley 2014). A Culturagram can also be used to take into account the impact of the individual's culture and would need to take into account such issues as the reasons for their seeking asylum, their language, religious beliefs and customs around health and child-rearing practices. Kohli (2006) states that some asylum seekers may find even completing a genogram a very painful process, given that many family members may be dead or missing. Therefore any assessment needs to be undertaken very sensitively and Heapy *et al.* (2007) also allude to this, advocating the use of very skilled practitioners to help families recover from the trauma of their past, as well as the loss of family and friends.

In the case of the Kombo family situation, the social worker discusses with her manager the possibility of taking the case to an Initial Child Protection Conference, which would decide whether the children should be made the subject of a Child Protection Plan. However, the social worker recognises the cultural issues, the complexity of the case and Rose's willingness to work with professionals (Department of Education 2015). Furthermore, the physical assault was viewed as minor, as there was no lasting mark or injury. A decision is made to support the family under Section 17 of the Children Act 1989, which places a general duty on the local authority to ensure a child's needs are met. This highlights, within social work support and decision making, the complex interplay of skills, knowledge and values operating within a legislative framework. The Children Act 2004 requires cooperation and a multi-agency approach to support the family including regular meetings (every 4–6 weeks), attended by Rose and by members of relevant agencies involved in the support of the family, such as the social worker, health visitor, school nurse, educational professionals, the Refugee Council support worker, mental health services and a nursery nurse. The family situation is assessed and a child-in-need plan is put together, which includes parenting advice for Rose, a full assessment of her physical and mental health and individual work for Reine and Gautier to consider their wishes and feelings. A nursery place is also funded by the local authority for Alban, two days a week, with out-of-school clubs for Reine and Gautier.

Part of the assessment is that the social worker takes into account the wishes and feelings of the children (Munro 2011), which shows that the children have an emotionally warm relationship with Rose. This includes Gautier, who is receiving support from the Child and Adolescent Mental Health Service (CAMHS) due to acting out some of the atrocities he has witnessed. However, he makes good progress and Reine, too, begins to behave more as a child rather than a young carer. Rose has also been supported in applying for a Special Guardianship Order for Gautier, as it has been impossible to establish whether his parents or other relatives are alive and in a position to take care of him. The application is supported by the local authority, with a report that confidently states that Gautier has a very good relationship with Rose and her children and wishes to remain in their care.

## Conclusion

The Kombo family's positive outcome is largely due to the fact that they were given refugee status and selected from the refugee camps under the Resettlement Programme. Asylum seekers who arrive in the UK not on the programme are likely to have a much more protracted wait whilst their claims are assessed. The regulations for entry into the UK as asylum seekers and refugees are complex and subject to constant change. Whilst support does exist, it is set at a minimal level and difficult to access. Organisations such as the Refugee Council and local charities such as the Asylum Seekers & Refugees of Kingston upon Hull (ARKH) provide invaluable aid to people already marginalised by their circumstances.

Social workers will be regarded as agents of the state and asylum seekers will be acutely aware of this power differential. Also, workers will be active participants in a society to which asylum seekers only have limited access, due to constraints placed on them by the state. Asylum seekers will likely be suspicious of state officials and will, perhaps, be reluctant to discuss sensitive or traumatic issues. It is entirely probable within the case scenario that Rose is unable to discuss fully what has happened, as what has occurred may be perceived as shameful within her culture. This concern about shame would also be a barrier to the use of interpreters, as Rose may feel unable to discuss the matter with people within her culture. Social workers need to work on cultural competence and to develop trust within the professional relationship. An ability to advocate for family rights and challenge organisational discrimination, recognising the power within the social work role, is important. These qualities are already stated within the PCF and are essential when working with asylum seekers and refugees.

## References

Bhugra, D., and Jones, P., 2001. 'Migration and mental illness', *Advances in Psychiatric Treatment* 7: 216–23. Available from: http://apt.rcpsych.org/content/aptrcpsych/7/3/216 full.pdf [Accessed 10 January 2016].

Brayne, H., Carr, H., and Goosey, D., 2013. *Law for social workers*. 13th ed. Oxford: Oxford Univ. Press.

British Red Cross, 2014. *Refugee facts and figures* [online]. British Red Cross. Available from: www.redcross.org.uk/What-we-do/Refugee-support/Refugee-facts-and-figures [Accessed 20 July 2015].

Collett, J., 2004. 'Immigration is a social work issue', in D. Hayes and B. Humphries, eds, *Social work, immigration and asylum debates. Dilemmas and ethical issues for social work and social care practice.* London: Jessica Kingsley Publishers, 77–95.

Congress, E., and Kung, W., 2013. 'Using the culturagram to assess and empower culturally diverse families', in E. Congress and M. Gonzalez, eds, *Multicultural perspectives in working with families.* New York: Springer Publishing Company, 1–17.

Department for Education, 2008. *Haringey local safeguarding children board: first serious case review - child A* [online]. Available from: www.haringeylscb.org/sites/haringeylscb/files/executive_summary_peter_final.pdf [Accessed 10 January 2016].

Department of Education, 2015. *Working together to safeguard children. A guide to inter-agency working to safeguard and promote the welfare of children* [online]. Her Majesty's Stationery Office (HMSO). Available from: www.gov.uk/government/uploads/system/uploads/attachment_data/file/419595/Working_Together_to_Safeguard_Children.pdf [Accessed 10 January 2016].

DoH, Department of Health, 2000. *Framework for the Assessment of Children in Need and their Families* [online]. Available from: http://webarchive.nationalarchives.gov.uk/20130401151715/www.education.gov.uk/publications/eOrderingDownload/Framework%20for%20the%20assessment%20of%20children%20in%20need%20and%20their%20families.pdf [Accessed 10 January 2016].

Hayes, D., 2004. 'History and context. The impact of immigration control on welfare delivery', in D. Hayes and B. Humphries, eds, *Social work, immigration and asylum debates. Dilemmas and ethical issues for social work and social care practice.* London: Jessica Kingsley Publishers, 11–28.

Heapy, G., Ehntholt, K., and Sclare, I., 2007. 'Groupwork with unaccompanied young women', in R. Kohli and F. Mitchell, eds, *Working with unaccompanied asylum seeking children. Issues for policy and practice.* Basingstoke, New York: Palgrave Macmillan, 76–94.

HGM, 2010. *Gateway protection programme* [online]. Her Majesty's Government. Available from: www.gov.uk/government/publications/gateway-protectionprogramme-information-for-organisations/gateway-protection-programme [Accessed 10 August 2015].

HMSO, 1974. *Report of the Committee of Inquiry into the Care and Supervision Provided in Relation to Maria Colwell.* London: Department of Health and Social Security.

Kohli, R., 2006. 'The comfort of strangers. Social work practice with unaccompanied asylum-seeking children and young people in the UK', *Child and Family Social Work* 11(1): 1–10.

Laming, H., 2003. *The Victoria Climbié inquiry report. Cm 5730.* London: The Stationery Office.

McColl, H., and Johnson, S., 2006. 'Characteristics and needs of refugees and asylum-seekers in contact with London community mental health teams. A descriptive investigation', *Social Psychiatry and Psychiatric Epidemiology* 41(10): 789–95.

McKenzie, K., McColl, H., and Bhui, K., 2007. *Improving services for refugees and asylum-seekers. Position statement.* Royal College of Psychiatrists.

Munro, E., 2011. *The Munro review of child protection. A child centred system.* London: HMSO.

Parker, J., and Bradley, G., 2014. *Social work practice.* Exeter: Learning Matters.

Refugee Council, 2015. Resettlement programme. Available from: www.refugeecouncil.org.uk/what_we_do/refugee_services/resettlement_programme [Accessed 10 January 2016].

The British Association of Social Workers. *Professional Capabilities Framework (PCF)* [online]. Available from: www.basw.co.uk/pcf/ [Accessed 10 January 2016].

# 23 Refugee resettlement and child protection in France

## Comment on the British case study from a French perspective

*Nathalie Durand-Le Zallic*

Since the framework agreement was signed in 2008 by the Ministry of Foreign Affairs and the Office of the United Nations High Commission for Refugees (UNHCR), France has been examining, each year, about a hundred refugee resettlement files (these numbers will increase in 2015/2016, in particular in relation to Syrian refugees).

The cases of persons under protection of UNHCR and to be resettled in France are selected by the French Ministry of the Interior. The reception of refugees to be resettled is coordinated by the French Office for Immigration and Integration (OFII). This public institution under the authority of the Ministry for Immigration is involved in the transfer and initial reception of refugees in France. It collects information on the refugees to be resettled through the Ministry of the Interior and the International Organization for Migration (IOM) and transmits them to the reception agencies.

The refugees arrive in France with an asylum visa or are admitted on humanitarian grounds. They are directed towards one of the five home institutions offering accommodation or housing. These operators are, however, present only in some parts of the country: Belfort, Les Deux Sevres, Haute Loire, the Isle of France, the Rhone, the Atlantic Pyrenees. The speed of rehousing and the support by the General Councils (elected body of the 'Département') remains variable from one department to another.

In the case study presented it is stated that Rose did not have the choice of place of residence. In France the recent Law Reform on Asylum (29 July 2015) also advocates the establishment of a policy of mandatory accommodation for those who obtain refugee status, similar to the UK.

As part of a humanitarian admission, determination of refugee status depends on the French Office for the Protection of Refugees and Stateless Persons (OFPRA). In this case, OFPRA is notified of the people concerned immediately upon their arrival at the airport. Thus Rose and her children could be directly eligible to obtain a residence permit – which is not the case for the majority of refugees resettled in France admitted outside special operations and having arrived under common law for asylum seekers for whom administrative procedures are much more tedious (see Mellon-Mustafa and Schleyer-Lindenmann, Chapter 16). The rapid reception and obtaining of a ten-year resident card would have allowed Rose and her children in France to benefit from access to universal health coverage, the active solidarity income, family benefits, access to employment etc.

Concerning child protection in France, assistance mechanisms and services to the endangered child apply to all minors regardless of their nationality or the nationality of their parents. Child protection is governed by the law of 5 March 2007. Like the Children Act 1989 in England, the 2007 law emphasises the child's interest and places him/her at the heart of the protection mechanisms through management that seeks to be adaptive and varied. The administrative protection is entrusted to the General (Departmental) Council while the judicial protection of minors falls under the State administration (Ministry of Justice). It is implemented by the public prosecutor and the juvenile judge. The establishment of administrative protection requires the agreement of the family. This is not the case in the context of judicial measures when a danger to the child is recognised (Article 375 of the Civil Code).

In this case study, the teaching staff at Reine's school address a report to the Children's and Young Persons' Services (the local authority); in France this would be the Departmental Houses of Solidarity. This report describes 'alarming information',[1] a term which points to the violation of the child's rights, and would be subject to peer review. Indeed, since the 2007 law in France, this information is processed in a specific framework: in departmental cells for the collection, processing and evaluation of such information. The evaluation is conducted by a multidisciplinary team coming from different institutions, with expertise in the social, educational, and medical fields. Associations and police services can also cooperate in this evaluation. However, assessment tools such as the 'looking after children' (LAC programme) in England have no equivalent in France and cultural characteristics are not systematically included in these evaluation procedures.

The 'Good Practice Guide', published by the Ministry of Health and Solidarity, poses the basic principles and key steps necessary for the situation assessment and aims to provide, as stated in its preamble, 'a national reference framework to the professionals responsible for evaluating individual situations involving minors' (Ministère de la Santé et des Solidarités 2007: 1), but without mentioning explicitly the interest of the intercultural approach.

Margalit Cohen-Emerique, doctor of psychology, expert in intercultural communication and relationships, highlights in her work (Cohen-Emerique 2000, 2015) that the development of the socio-educational practices concerning child protection in France was not accompanied by a specific intercultural approach evaluation of child abuse. Medical and psychosocial workers, who increasingly face challenges, especially in their work with migrants, have the opportunity to integrate an intercultural perspective, mainly through the ethno-psychiatric approach in order to refine their assessments. These intercultural consultations can be conducted in the homes of families or in a place selected by them.

The management of the family situation of Rose would probably be approached somewhat differently in France by social workers or socio-medical actors with some specificities related to different institutional logics, methodologies and means of intervention. Regarding child protection several strategies/pathways could be considered under two frameworks;

1    As part of administrative protection:
     Several monitoring and guidance actions could be implemented under condition that Rose accepts them and works with various actors in the interest of the children, e.g.
     - Educational activities at the home or place of residence of the family with social intervention teams, socio-medical and medical departmental services;
     - Reine and Gautier could receive psychological care;
     - Intervention by maternal and child health services (team of physicians, nurses, psychologists) of the General Council with medical monitoring for Gautier and Alban (medical care from 0 to 6 years);
     - Social monitoring for Rose with orientation towards medical and psychological care.

2    In the context of judicial protection (Article 375 of the Civil Code):[2]
     In view of the information gathered concerning the minors (dropping out of school for Reine, care of the baby by the adolescent girl, bruises observed on Gautier who is described as without supervision, the absence of maternal bonds with Rose) and concerning Rose (important medical problems, traumatic experiences), in France the situation would probably have produced a court report to the Prosecutor of the Republic by the General Council's services. In this case, the juvenile judge whose mission is to remedy dangerous situations involving minors, may impose judicial investigative measures (e.g. medical or psychological expert investigation of the child conducted by medical experts from courts).
     And/or put in place educational support measures to provide help and support to the family such as:
     - educational measures in the home environment;
     - children's home monitoring by social workers or medico-social workers in the framework of a judicial mandate;
     - keeping the juvenile judge regularly informed of the development of the minor's situation.

     This direction would undoubtedly have been proposed for the three children in the case study presented. Depending on the evolution of the situation and evaluation by the intervening social workers, the juvenile judge could assign (or not) Gautier to Rose as a trusted third party.
     Lastly, placement in a foster care home or an institution like an orphanage could be considered as a last resort, as the parent–child relationship should be maintained as long as possible.

Be it in the administrative or judicial framework, the systematic intervention of an interpreter for all parties implied would have been difficult due to lack of material means. A referral to ethno-psychiatric consultations and/or an ethno-clinical mediation would have been left up to the decision of the social services.

Very recently legislative and regulatory measures, and measures supporting practice[3] have been designed to further improve the organisation of child protection, which still lacks financial resources, manpower and trained staff. In a context where institutional functioning sometimes tends to dominate the field, initial and continuous training, research, and the sharing of knowledge and experience of professional practices may trigger changes, including promoting the refocusing of the intervention on the understanding of the family situation and a co-construction with families, whenever possible.

## Notes

1 Definition of alarming information (Law of 5 March 2007): 'any information, including medical, likely to raise concerns that a child is in danger or risk of danger, could need help, and must be transmitted at the departmental cell for evaluation and action'.
2 Article 375 of the Civil Code: 'If the health, safety or morals of an un-emancipated minor are in danger or if the conditions of his education or his physical, emotional, intellectual and social development are seriously compromised, educational assistance measures may be ordered by Justice at the request of the father and mother jointly, or one of them, the person or service to which the child has been trusted, or the guardian, or the minor himself or the public prosecutor.'
3 Law Proposal on Child Protection (18 November 2015) and Roadmap for child protection (2015–2017) of the Ministry of Social Affairs and Health of Women's Rights, Ministère des Affaires Sociales de la Santé et des Droits des Femmes.

## References

Cohen-Emerique, M., 2000. 'Carmel Camilleri et la recherche-action. La maltraitance de l'enfant dans les familles en situation interculturelle', in J. Costa-Lascoux, M.A. Hily, and G. Vermès, eds, *Pluralité des cultures et dynamiques identitaires. Hommage à Carmel Camilleri.* Paris: L'Harmattan, 237–52.
Cohen-Emerique, M., 2015. *Pour une approche interculturelle. Théories et pratiques.* 2nd ed. Rennes: Presses de l'EHESP.
Ministère de la Santé et des Solidarités, 2007. *Guide de la cellule départementale de recueil, de traitement et d'évaluation* [online]. Ministère de la Santé et des Solidarités. Available from: www.social-sante.gouv.fr/IMG/pdf/Guide_Cellule_depart_3_BAT-3. pdf [Accessed 27 November 2015].
Ministère des Affaires sociales de la Santé et des Droits des femmes [online]. Available from: www.social-sante.gouv.fr [Accessed 10 January 2016].

# 24 Child protection in a multicultural context

## Comment on the British case study from an Israeli perspective

*Yochay Nadan*

The body of knowledge concerned with risk, well-being and protection is founded primarily on universal developmental theories such as attachment theory (Bowlby 1988), which were formulated from empirical research and clinical experience largely conducted in Western countries (Korbin 1981; Henrich *et al.* 2010). These theories, answering such questions as 'What is proper parenting?' and 'What constitutes proper treatment of a child?' owe their primacy to Western values, worldviews and norms. They are also the source from which definitions of risk, abuse and neglect are derived.

The cross-cultural literature, however, is fraught with examples of child-rearing practices that can be classified in different ways – either as normative, abusive or neglectful – by different cultural groups. It is well known that some minority groups in multicultural societies might define certain parenting roles and practices as normative, even though they run counter to the pervasive majority views in the hegemonic culture (Korbin 1991). This gap in perception is evident within welfare agencies and child protection services, between professionals who underwent Western professional socialisation and the parents from minority groups, as demonstrated in the case study of a Congolese family in the UK (see Braithwaite and Cresswell, Chapter 22). Such differences are often a source of misunderstanding and tension that is ultimately not in the child's best interests. In many cases, solutions proposed by social workers tend to be neither acceptable nor appreciated by parents, who typically fail to implement them (Rosenthal and Roer-Strier 2001).

### Culturally competent child protection practice

'Cultural competence' is frequently defined as 'a set of congruent behaviours, attitudes, and policies that come together in a system, agency, or among professionals and enable the system, agency, or those professionals to work effectively in cross-cultural situations' (Cross *et al.* 1989: iv; NASW 2001, 2007).

Applying cultural competence when working in the field of child protection is no easy task. When we take as an example the above-mentioned case of the Congolese asylum seeker's family in the UK, many questions arise: should the social worker accept corporal punishment because it is described as a normative Congolese child-rearing practice? Or should they educate the mother regarding the laws in the UK as well as the long-term and potentially damaging psychological consequences of physical abuse? Or should the mother be given advice, for example, on the importance of mentally stimulating a child and some techniques for doing so? What should be the threshold that would make the social worker recommend an out-of-home placement? Which intervention would be considered more culturally competent?

Korbin and Spilsbury (1999) argue that culturally competent child protection practices avoid both unmoderated ethnocentrism and unmoderated cultural relativism. An unmoderated ethnocentric position imposes a single standard on child care practices. It attempts to impose the beliefs and behaviours of one group (the hegemonic group) on minority populations. Besides being morally and ethically problematic, such an approach was found to be counterproductive for effective child protection. In addition, it runs the risk of viewing normative cultural practices as abuse or neglect (a false positive). Conversely, an unmoderated relativist position suspends all standards and accepts all parental behaviours as 'culture'. Therefore, it runs the risk of misidentification of abuse or neglect as cultural practice (a false negative). A behaviour that can be identified as part of a cultural heritage does not necessarily mean that it is 'good' for children. In addition, culture cannot be used as an excuse for abuse or neglect. Exclusive reliance on either position fails to meet the objective of cultural competence (Korbin and Spilsbury 1999).

With the intention of trying to enhance their cultural competence, professionals tend to focus on gaining and applying knowledge about cultures. Such knowledge usually concerns a specific cultural or ethnic group, most often those with which their services work. It includes knowledge of that group's history, norms, traditional cultural characteristics, child-rearing practices and discipline, values, gestures, communication styles, behaviours, attitudes, help-seeking patterns and the group's explanatory models of their problems (Nadan 2014). Gaining this knowledge is indeed an important element of cultural competence. However, such an essentialist knowledge tends to ignore intra-cultural diversity, as well as the impact of other crucial contextual factors besides culture (e.g. migration, poverty, minority status). It is imperative, especially in the field of child protection, to go beyond those essentialist and homogenic cultural descriptions and to be aware of the continuum of acceptable and unacceptable parental behaviours within a particular culture. Such a perspective can be helpful in differentiating cultural practices from maltreatment (Korbin 2003).

Applying cultural competence to child protection would also mean adopting and giving priority to a strengths-based approach (Saleebey 1996) over a deficiency approach. This means that practitioners focus not only on searching for markers of deviant behaviours that can be labelled as abuse or neglect, but at the same time and equally importantly they focus on specific cultural strengths and protective factors that can mitigate risk for children (Korbin and Spilsbury 1999).

Research can be a crucial tool for developing knowledge on acceptable and unacceptable parental behaviours within a culture, as well as gaining insight into cultural risk and protective factors. For example, with my research group we are currently conducting a research project at the Hebrew University of Jerusalem that examines the Jewish Ultra-Orthodox community's perceptions of risk and protection with regard to children, and the local ways in which the concepts of 'risk', 'neglect' and 'abuse' are defined by people from the community. The study aims to develop a culturally informed definition of risk and protection as perceived by the Ultra-Orthodox community, to serve as a basis for developing a relevant assessment tool for professionals working with children and families, as well as programmes for prevention and intervention.

To grasp the complexity of culture, context and maltreatment and to avoid essentialising cultures, such research should adopt an intersectionality-driven framework (Nadan *et al.* 2015). Such an approach seeks to understand how multiple identities such as gender, race and socioeconomic status simultaneously shape human experience at the individual level, through interlocking systems of bias and inequality that exist at the macro socio-structural level. Applying insights gained from such research into practice can promote culturally competent prevention and intervention programmes and encourage practitioners and services to operate from a more ethical and anti-oppressive position when working with minority groups (Nadan 2014).

## Reflectivity: zooming out and looking inwards

The tension between ethnocentrism and relativism when aspiring to work in a more culturally competent manner and to protect children in cross-cultural situations can be bridged through critical reflectivity. One aspect of this would be 'zooming out' – looking beyond 'culture' at other, broader contextual elements, especially concerning the situation of disadvantaged minority groups in society, who live under personal, institutional, legal and structural forces that restrict, oppress, humiliate and prevent them from obtaining equal access to resources and opportunities (Sisneros *et al.* 2008). When working with families where children are at risk of abuse or neglect, such a broader view can foster deeper understanding of the complexity of their situation, as well as empathy rather than judgemental attitudes.

Another aspect of critical reflectivity is related to practitioners' exploration of their own identities and (largely privileged) social positions, and the ways in which these shape their assumptions, attitudes and images with regard to the 'other' (Kondart 1999; Nylund 2006; Abrams and Gibson 2007; Nadan 2016). Such reflection can facilitate acknowledgement of the ways in which fears, ignorance and the '-isms' (racism, sexism, ethnocentrism, heterosexism, ageism, classism, etc.) influence practitioners' attitudes, beliefs and feelings in both their personal and professional lives (NASW 2001; Latting 1990). Such exploration urges a shift in attention from the 'other' to the Self and calls for the exploration of the power relations and privileges involved in the construction of the 'other' (Kondart 1999; Jeyasingham 2012).

Exploring the Self with regard to the 'other' is extremely important in the field of child protection, because minority children are disproportionately represented in child welfare systems, as documented in many countries around the world

(Euser *et al.* 2011; Dettlaff 2014). One contributing element is racial bias and discrimination (Roberts 2002; Rivaux *et al.* 2008), either by individual child welfare staff or through institutional racism in welfare services that is evident in their policies and practices (Barn 2007). This explanation involves what has been referred to as a deficiency approach (Park 2005), in which minority status is itself used as a marker of risk and maltreatment. Examining ourselves and reflecting on our own biases is therefore crucial for trying to enhance our cultural competence in child protection.

Culturally competent work in child protection is therefore the delicate art of balancing the particular with the hegemonic, while reflecting on and taking into account the complex contexts of people's lives, in order to ensure children's safety. Cultural competence is never fully realised, achieved, or completed, but is rather a lifelong process of self-reflectivity and ongoing learning that should be integral to our professional lives.

## References

Abrams, L.S., and Gibson, P., 2007. 'Reframing multicultural education. Teaching white privilege in the social work curriculum', *Journal of Social Work Education* 43(1): 147–60.

Barn, R., 2007. '"Race", ethnicity and child welfare. A fine balancing act', *British Journal of Social Work* (37): 1425–34.

Bowlby, J., 1988. *A secure base. Clinical applications of attachment theory.* London: Routledge.

Cross, T.L., Bazron, B.J., Dennis, K.W., and Isaacs, M.R., 1989. *Towards a culturally competent system of care: A monograph on effective services for minority children who are severely emotionally disturbed.* Washington, D.C: Georgetown University Child Development Center.

Dettlaff, A.J., 2014. 'The evolving understanding of disproportionality and disparities in child welfare', in J.E. Korbin and R.D. Krugman, eds, *Handbook of child maltreatment.* Dordrecht: Springer Publishing Company, 149–68.

Euser, E.M., van Ijzendoorn, M.H., Prinzie, P. and Bakermans-Kranenburg, M.J., 2011. 'Elevated child maltreatment rates in immigrant families and the role of socioeconomic differences', *Child Maltreatment* (16): 63–73.

Henrich, J., Heine, S.J. and Norenzayan, A., 2010. 'The weirdest people in the world?' *Behavioral and Brain Sciences* 33(2–3): 61–83.

Jeyasingham, D., 2012. 'A clarification of "white noise" and some observations about Paul Michael Garrett's response', *British Journal of Social Work* 42: 1416–20.

Kondart, M.E., 1999. 'Who is the "self" in self-aware. Professional self-awareness from a critical theory perspective', *The Social Service Review* 73(4): 451–77.

Korbin, J.E., 1981. *Child abuse and neglect. Cross-cultural perspectives.* Berkeley, Los Angeles: University of California Press.

Korbin, J.E., 1991. 'Cross-cultural perspectives and research directions for the 21st century', *Child Abuse and Neglect* (15): 67–77.

Korbin, J.E., 2003. 'Children, childhoods, and violence', *Annual Review of Anthropology* (32): 431–46.

Korbin, J.E., and Spilsbury, J., 1999. 'Cultural competence and child neglect', in H. Dubowitz, ed., *Neglected children. Research, practice and policy.* Newbury Park: SAGE Publications, 69–88.

Latting, J.K., 1990. 'Identifying the "isms". Enabling social work students to confront their biases', *Journal of Social Work Education* 26(1): 36–44.

Nadan, Y., 2014. 'Rethinking "cultural competence" in international social work', *International Social Work* 57(5): 1–10.

Nadan, Y., 2016. 'Teaching note – Revisiting stereotypes: Enhancing cultural awareness through a web-based tool', *Journal of Social Work Education* 52(1): 50–56.

Nadan, Y., Spilsbury, J., and Korbin, J., 2015. 'Culture and context in understanding child maltreatment. Contributions of intersectionality and neighborhood-based research', *Child Abuse and Neglect* (41): 40–48.

NASW, 2001. *NASW standards for cultural competence in social work practice* [online]. National Association of Social Workers (NASW). Available from: www.socialworkers. org/practice/standards/NASWCulturalStandards.pdf [Accessed 1 October 2015].

NASW, 2007. *Indicators for the achievement of the NASW standards for cultural competence in social work practice* [online]. National Association of Social Workers. Available from: www.socialworkers.org/practice/standards/naswculturalstandardsindicators2006.pdf [Accessed 10 January 2016].

Nylund, D., 2006. 'Critical multiculturalism, whiteness, and social work. Towards a more radical view of cultural competence', *Journal of Progressive Human Services* 17(2): 27–42.

Park, Y., 2005. 'Culture as deficit. A critical discourse analysis of the concept of culture in contemporary social work discourse', *Journal of Sociology and Social Welfare* 32(3): 11–33.

Rivaux, S.L., James, J., Wittenstrom, K., Baumann, D., Sheets, J., Henry, J. and Jeffries, V., 2008. 'The intersection of race, poverty, and risk. Understanding the decision to provide services to clients and to remove children', *Child Welfare* 87: 151–68.

Roberts, D., 2002. 'Shattered bonds. The color of child welfare', *Children and Youth Services Review* 24: 877–80.

Rosenthal, M.K., and Roer-Strier, D., 2001. 'Cultural differences in mothers' developmental goals and ethnotheories', *International Journal of Psychology* 36(1): 20–31.

Saleebey, D., 1996. 'The strengths perspective in social work practice. Extensions and cautions', *Social Work* 41(3): 296–305.

Sisneros, J., Stakeman, C., Joyner, M.C. and Schmitz, C.L., 2008. *Critical multicultural social work*. Chicago: Lyceum Books.

# 25 Jyoti's case – a study on transnational advocacy

*Abha Bhaiya*

## The case

The Delhi gang rape case on 16 December 2012 involved a rape and a fatal assault. The incident happened when a 23-year-old girl, a physiotherapy intern, Jyoti Singh Pandey, boarded a bus at 8:30 p.m. with a male friend, after watching a movie. This was an off-duty private bus, with six men on board – five adults and a juvenile. The men beat the friend and each one raped the woman in turn, before assaulting her viciously with an iron instrument which damaged all her internal organs. By the time the police picked her up and took her to hospital she had bled profusely. After being hospitalised for 13 days, she was transferred to a hospital in Singapore for emergency treatment, but died from her injuries two days later.

One of the accused adults died in police custody; it is not clear whether it was suicide or murder (after he had been taunted by fellow prisoners). The four surviving adult defendants denied the charges. They went on trial in a fast-track court and, three days later, were sentenced to death by hanging. In March 2014, the Delhi High Court upheld the guilty verdict and the death sentences. The minor defendant was tried as a juvenile (not as an adult), and therefore, even though convicted for rape and murder, only sentenced to the maximum of three years' imprisonment in a reform institution.

The brutality and ruthlessness of the crime shook the conscience of the people and ignited protests by activist groups, cutting across caste/class divide. The protests that followed included an enormous mobilisation of ordinary citizens including the unprecedented involvement of women's groups, activists and large-scale turnout of young students. The ensuing protests moved beyond the incident – within days the case was in the media; this was most prevalent within India, but a study found one-third of articles in the Anglo-American press (Phillips *et al.* 2015) with more than 1,500 articles being published in the US in the two months following the incident (Roychowdhury 2013). The questions have to be asked: Why this case (Kaur 2013), and why did it become an international cause (Roychowdhury 2013)?

This then pressurised the Indian government to set up an independent commission led by a former Chief Justice of the Supreme Court, J.S. Verma. Nearly 80,000 people sent in recommendations, including women's organisations, who also met with the committee. In record time a 600-plus page report was tabled to the Parliament with extensive recommendations to address sexual violence (Justice J.S. Verma).

## Transnational advocacy networks

Violence against women is a global, and especially in cases of trafficking, a transnational phenomenon. The issue of violence against women has been taken up and pursued by what Keck and Sikkink (1999) describe as transnational advocacy networks: non-state actors who interact with each other, with states and with international organisations. They are bound together by shared values, a common discourse, and a dense exchange of information and services. This case study looks at these advocacy networks (considering the Indian perspective) – of which Social Work Professionals could and should be part. We will look at the major areas: research, the legal framework and feminist activism.

### Transnational research

All societies consider some form of non-consensual sex as against social norms and punishable. A number of studies have demonstrated that those communities in which there are higher levels of sexist beliefs and norms, also have higher rates of violence against women (McMahon and Banyard 2012: 6). Still there seem to be other factors contributing to this violence, including the use of sexually degrading language, high levels of harassment, combined with violent media images or pornography. A conceptual framework distinguishes six categories of 'accepted rape' in non-industrialised societies: marital rape, exchange rape, punitive rape, theft rape, ceremonial rape and status rape (Da Silva 2013: 13). Punitive rape might target women for not respecting a man's authority, for rejecting a man, for behaving 'like a man' or as punishment for her husband's (or brother's) wrongdoing.

'Gang rapes' occur around the world. Names differ (Da Silva 2013: 10), but they all point to disregard towards women: gang-bang (US/Germany), line-up (UK), streamlining (South Africa) or tournante (France). In academic terms 'gang rape' has been defined as any sexual assault committed by a 'group of individuals who operate together on the basis of a covenant, a certain shared identity and shared norms' (Bijleveld and Hendriks 2003: 237).

Many authors make a distinction between assaults committed by two perpetrators only, and those with three and more perpetrators – as in the Delhi case. Numbers seem to matter (Lambine 2013). Multi-perpetrator rapes account – across nations – approximately for one in ten rape cases (Da Silva 2013: 12). A national report on violence against women in the US found that 13 per cent of the reported rapes were committed by two or more perpetrators, and 8 per cent of cases registered more than two perpetrators. Similar figures exist for South Africa, and when it comes to hospital treatment, 27 per cent of the cases suggest multiple perpetrators. This might indicate that injuries inflicted on the victims are more severe in these cases (Lambine 2013: 70), and probably suggests significant underreporting to the police.

International research on multiple-perpetrator rape, including as part of transnational, often feminist, advocacy networks, can help in understanding what happens: studies suggest that key characteristics of rape crimes vary as the number of perpetrators increase. Multiple perpetrator rapes are offences mostly perpetrated by men in their early twenties, also the younger the offenders the bigger the group size. Mackenzie Lambine (2013) suggests that for young offenders, group relationships might outweigh the importance of the sexual act itself. 'Rape gangs' have leaders, but their leadership model might also differ by the size of the group: duo rapes often present as an older perpetrator giving orders to a younger one, whilst three-plus perpetrator gangs seem to be 'led' by example and direct action, sometimes with two perpetrators competing, making the situation more complex and chaotic, and they take longer and turn out to be much more violent (Lambine 2013). Research findings (Lambine 2013: 72) suggest that multiple perpetrator rapes are mostly committed outdoors, and many involve vehicles at different stages, and as in the Delhi rape, perpetrators are many and they increase the vulnerability of their victims through the ability to block possible exit routes. Lone perpetrators on the other hand commit their crimes indoors by using elements of surprise rather than cornering their victim. Victim and perpetrators of multiple perpetrator rape are more often strangers.

Some researchers (Lambine 2013: 74f) try to classify 'typical' interactions between perpetrators and victims of rape – interactions where 'choices' are offered to the victim, situations where the perpetrators build up a 'pseudo-relationship', others where the perpetrator is in complete control of the situation, and interactions that are defined by their hostility through aggressive and violent behaviour. Clearly, in the Delhi rape case, attention is caught by the hostility of the interactions, and the control of the situation in a driving, off-duty bus with tinted windows. The violence that is used in the situation, the demonstration of sexual prowess, and the excitement of deviant behaviour (Lambine 2013: 15) adds to it.

## Human rights activism

The International Federation of the Social Work Profession (IFSW) defines social work as a practice-based profession and an academic discipline that promotes social change and development, social cohesion, as well as empowerment and liberation of people based on principles of social justice, human rights, collective responsibility and respect for diversities. IFSW and IASSW entrust social workers with a responsibility to promote social justice. They published a Global Agenda to ensure the dignity and worth of the person (see IFSW, IASSW and ICSW). This is why social work is named a 'human rights profession'.

One important human rights issue is the abolition of the death penalty (Amnesty International). In the Jyoti case many in the streets and in the government called for the death penalty, whereas the Indian women's movement issued a strong statement opposing it. They recognised that every human being has a right to life, and added: 'Our rage cannot give way to what are, in no uncertain terms, new cycles of violence … A huge set of changes are required in the system to end the widespread and daily culture of rape' (Menon 2012). Evidence does not suggest that the death penalty acts as a deterrent to rape. A review of crimes that warrant capital punishment in India had revealed the discriminatory ways in which such laws are selectively and arbitrarily applied to disadvantaged communities, as well as religious and ethnic minorities (as in the United States and other places). The statement also pointed to the problem of the psychological and social trauma that women in India would have to face if they had to report against their own relatives – as an overwhelming number of women are sexually assaulted by people known to them (like everywhere else on the globe). The Indian women's movement also feared that in countries where conviction of sexual assault is notoriously difficult, the death penalty would make conviction next to impossible.

### Women's rights as human rights

The Concept of Women's Human Rights, developed during the United Nations Decade for Women, (1976–1985) results from women's voices from many geographical, ethnic, religious, cultural, and class backgrounds who have been actively engaged in challenging structural discrimination against women and transforming their status (Bunch 2000) as well as possibilities of exchange facilitated at the United Nations-sponsored women's conferences in Mexico City (1975), Copenhagen (1980), Nairobi (1985), and Beijing (1995).

When, in 1993, the World Conference on Human Rights took place in Vienna, the agenda initially did not mention women or any gender aspects. Then a petition to recognise gender violence as a universal phenomenon and a violation of human rights gathered half a million signatures from 124 countries; a whole chapter on 'the equal status and human rights of women' was integrated into the final document. The Vienna Declaration and Programme of Action called upon the General Assembly to adopt the draft declaration on violence against women and urged states to combat violence. Taking up the human rights framework entailed examining this framework through a gender lens and describing women's lives through a human rights framework. Eventually, experiences of violence were evaluated against formulations enshrined in other conventions such as 'no one shall be subjected to torture or to cruel, inhuman or degrading treatment or punishment' from the Convention against Torture and Other Cruel, Inhuman or Degrading Treatment or Punishment (UNHCR 1984).[1]

Subsequently, the Declaration on the Elimination of Violence against Women was accepted by the General Assembly in 1993. It defined violence against women as 'any act of gender-based violence that results in, or is likely to result in, physical, sexual or psychological harm or suffering to women …, whether occurring in public or in private life' (Article 1). It urged states to exercise due diligence to prevent, investigate and, in accordance with national legislation, punish acts of violence against women, whether those acts are perpetrated by the state or by private persons, and recognise the important role of women's movements and non-governmental organisations worldwide (Article 4). In addition, it demanded from the United Nations system, to contribute to the recognition and realisation of rights and principles in the Declaration (Article 5). This made fighting violence against women a priority of international policies.

The Verma Report, after Jyoti's death, explicitly referred to 'Gender Justice and India's Obligations under International Conventions', i.e. under the Declaration on Elimination of Violence against Women (UN 1993) and the Convention on the Elimination of All Forms of Discrimination against Women (Justice J.S. Verma: 62). The report saw the failure to frame a domestic law, which was considered requisite for dealing with violence against women, as a breach of the international Convention. It demanded implementation of the Convention on the Elimination of All Forms of Discrimination against Women (CEDAW) in a manner that satisfies the criteria of impartial administration of justice.

On 1 April 2014, the Special Rapporteur on violence against women also submitted her report on her mission to India following the 'Jyoti case' (A/HRC/26/38/Add.1). She concluded:

> The Government of India has recognized the need to address violence against women as a human rights violation. It has taken legislative measures in that regard, including measures to address rape and sexual violence. However, significant gaps remain in the legislative framework as regards the failure to recognize all forms of violence against women and to adopt a holistic approach that addresses the root and structural causes of violence against women … The persistence of harmful practices, pervasive gender stereotypes and deeply entrenched patriarchal social and cultural norms is of serious concern. Based on the idea of superiority of men over women, those manifestations exacerbate women's position of dependence and subordination and significantly obstruct effective implementation of relevant legislative and policy measures.
>
> (A/HRC/26/38/Add.1)

Her recommendations to the government cover law and policy reforms, accountability, societal transformation, and statistics and data collection.

In 2014 the CEDAW Committee issued its concluding observations to India's fourth and fifth reports. Based on the report of the special rapporteur, the committee addressed the issue of violence against women, especially 'the stark increase in violent crimes against women, especially rape and abduction, and the high number of cases of rape reported by the National Crime Records Bureau in 2012, indicating an increase by 902.1 per cent since 1971, and continuing impunity for such acts' (CEDAW Committee – 58th Session 2014: 16). It urged India (as other states before) to define gang rape as constituting an aggravating factor meriting a more severe punishment; to establish one-stop crisis centres; to provide systematic training on women's rights to all law enforcement personnel, medical staff and judicial officials, and to ensure that police officers fulfil their duty to protect women and girls against violence; and to put in place an effective system to monitor and evaluate the implementation, effectiveness and impact of legislation to combat sexual violence (CEDAW Committee – 58th Session 2014).

India ratified CEDAW into law in 1993 – after having been amongst the first signatories in 1980. One year earlier the CEDAW Committee had issued 'General Recommendations' on (the reporting on) violence against women. The recommendations were based on the assumption that 'gender-based violence is a form of discrimination that seriously inhibits women's ability to enjoy rights and freedoms on a basis of equality with men' (CEDAW: 1). State parties were asked to take appropriate and effective measures to overcome all forms of gender-based violence, whether by public or private act, and report on them. The proposed measures included laws against rape; statistics and research; ensuring media reporting of women; identifying and addressing the nature and extent of patriarchal attitudes, customs and practices that perpetuate violence against women; and establishing support services for victims.

CEDAW was also instrumental in one of India's landmark cases: *Vishaka vs State of Rajasthan*, where Chief Justice Verma issued guidelines and norms: 'TAKING NOTE of the fact that the present civil and penal laws in India do not adequately provide for specific protection of women from sexual harassment at work place and that enactment of such legislation will take considerable time' (Justice J.S. Verma 1997). The Protection of Women against Sexual Harassment Bill followed in September 2012 (PRS Blog 2013).

Gull and Shafi (2014: 53) found that activists were always sceptical regarding any transformative capacity of law, but also aware that there may not be viable alternatives. The women's movement in India was and is involved in campaigns and agitations, actively involved in running shelters for women who are victims of violence, providing counselling, legal aid and medical support. Activists formed alternative justice systems, and projects to make women economically self-reliant, and they conducted training workshops on various issues. Some of these activities are deeply embedded transnational advocacy networks (Keck and Sikkink 1999), for example, women's tribunals and public hearings, campaigns to end violence, and the creation of regional networks for peace and security.

The first International Tribunal on Crimes against Women took place in March 1976 in Brussels. Many more followed, each addressing issues of violence against women. Some of the more significant events include the Women's International War Crimes Tribunal on Japan's Military Sexual Slavery held from 2000 to 2002 in The Hague (Sakamoto 2001). One of the early women's courts was the Asian Court of Women on Crimes against Women and the Violence of Development (Albert 1996). National Tribunals on Violence against Dalit Women in India were conducted in 1994, and again in October 2013 (NCDHR). Nepal saw tribunals on trafficking and tourism (1994) and heard from survivors of sexual violence in armed conflict in 2014 (APWLD 2014; Human Rights Watch 1995). One should not forget the International Criminal Tribunals for Rwanda or Yugoslavia that have been monumental in exposing the extent and form of sexual violence against women in these wars. All the tribunals covered areas including economic, political, and cultural violence against women. Hearings and interventions also take place on local levels: e.g. the Women's Courts (Nari Adalats) managed by barefoot village-level legal activists (International Center for Research on Women 2002).

India's women's movements also take part in international campaigns to end violence: on 25 November (International Day for the Elimination of Violence against Women) the campaign for '16 days of activism against gender-based violence' starts to raise awareness building up to International Human Rights Day, 10 December. Similarly, as a response to the UN data stating that one billion girls and women are subjected to violence globally, a large-scale campaign was launched in 2013. The call of the campaign is simple – One Billion Rising (people and not only women) must rise to stop violence against women. The campaign chose Valentine's Day as the symbolic day to launch the campaign every year. Today nearly 172 countries are actively participating and the circle is ever enlarging (One Billion Rising 2016).

Similarly, a Women's Regional Network was formed in 2011 in Nepal, with the objective of documenting women's voices from the conflict zones of Afghanistan, India and Pakistan – a sub-region, torn by conflicts and counter-conflict where the voices of women are missing in the local and regional peace processes. Based on six key risk areas – sexual violence, non-sexual violence, cultural or religious factors; discrimination and lack of access to resources and trafficking – gender experts ranked Afghanistan, Pakistan and India – together with Congo and Somalia – as the worst places in the world to be a woman (Women's Regional Network 2013: 5). The ultimate goal of the network therefore is to work towards sustainable peace in this sub-region of South Asia, especially for women.

## Conclusion

Transnational solidarity alliances and networks are a legacy of global women's movements acting through a transformative political agenda to make states accountable, amplify women's voices and concerns in national and international fora, thus providing a critical perspective and innumerable strategic actions. The mounting pressure created by such alliances has led to the formation of international instruments such as CEDAW, the establishment of a UN commission on violence against women, national-level women's commissions, and the inclusion of human rights and multiple identity frameworks to inform the policies and actions of various states.

## Note

1  This resulted in an evolving jurisprudence of the crime of rape in international criminal law (Weiner 1993).

## References

Albert, O., 1996. *Women's Courts in Asia* [online]. Available from: http://base.d-p-h.info/en/fiches/premierdph/fiche-premierdph-5563.html [Accessed 10 January 2016].

Amnesty International. *Death Penalty* [online]. Available from: www.amnesty.org/en/what-we-do/death-penalty/ [Accessed 10 January 2016].

APWLD, 2014. *Women's Tribunal in Nepal hears from survivors of sexual violence in armed conflict* [online]. Asia Pacific Forum on Women, Law and Development. Available from: http://apwld.org/womens-tribunal-in-nepal-hears-from-survivors-of-sexual-violence-in-armed-conflict/ [Accessed 10 January 2016].

Bijleveld, C., and Hendriks, J., 2003. 'Juvenile Sex Offenders. Differences between Group and Solo Offenders', *Psychology, Crime and Law* 9(3): 237–45.

CEDAW. *Statement of the Committee on the Elimination of Discrimination against Women on the Need for a Gender Perspective in the Text of the Arms Trade Treaty* [online]. Available from: www.ohchr.org/Documents/HRBodies/CEDAW/Statements/StatementGenderPerspective. pdf [Accessed 10 January 2016].

CEDAW Committee – 58th Session, 2014. *Concluding observations on the combined fourth and fifth periodic reports of India* [online]. Available from: http://docstore. ohchr.org/SelfServices/FilesHandler.ashx?enc=6QkG1d%2FPPRiCAqhKb7yhsgA84 bcFRy75ulvS2cmS%2F%2BhR1fgqxKiywURS0aVJOk6sBezpV1AKQkt7wGc58af2o KanQAXf3ZokcF4lLNQW3aowezgzPbWNFk6DxKOdgBL3jR4b3T%2FI4Sd708k Jzmcxvg%3D%3D [Accessed 10 January 2016].

Da Silva, T., 2013. 'Multiple perpetrator rape. An international phenomenon', in M. Horvath and J. Woodhams, eds, *Handbook on the study of multiple perpetrator rape. A multidisciplinary response to an international problem.* London, New York: Routledge, 10–38.

Gull, R., and Shafi, A., 2014. 'Indian women's movement after independence', *International Research Journal of Social Sciences* 3(5): 46–54. Available from: www.isca.in/IJSS/ Archive/v3/i5/10.ISCA-IRJSS-2014-66.pdf [Accessed 24 August 2015].

Human Rights Watch, 1995. *Rape for Profit. Trafficking of Nepali Girls and Women to India's Brothels* [online]. Available from: www.hrw.org/reports/1995/India.htm [Accessed 10 January 2016].

IASSW [online]. International Association of Schools of Social Work. Available from: www.iassw-aiets.org/ [Accessed 25 November 2015].

ICSW [online]. International Council on Social Welfare. Available from: www.icsw.org/ [Accessed 10 January 2016].

IFSW. *Global Agenda for Social Work and Social Development* [online]. International Federation of Social Workers. Available from: http://ifsw.org/the-global-agenda-observatory/ [Accessed 25 November 2015].

International Center for Research on Women, 2002. *Women-Initiated Community Level Responses to Domestic Violence* [online]. Available from: www.icrw.org/sites/default/ files/publications/Domestic-Violence-in-India-5-Women-initiated-Community-Level-Responses-to-Domestic-Violence.pdf [Accessed 10 January 2016].

Justice J.S. Verma. *Report of the Committee on Amendments to Criminal Law* [online]. Available from: www.prsindia.org/uploads/media/Justice%20verma%20committee/ js%20verma%20committe%20report.pdf [Accessed 10 January 2016].

Justice J.S. Verma, 1997. *Supreme Court of India. Vishaka & Ors vs State of Rajasthan & Ors* [online]. Available from: http://indiankanoon.org/doc/1031794/ [Accessed 10 January 2016].

Kaur, R., 2013. 'Representation of crime against women in print media. A case study of Delhi gang rape', *Anthropol* 2(1): 1–3.

Keck, M.E., and Sikkink, K., 1999. *Transnational advocacy networks in international and regional politics* [online]. UNESCO. Available from: http://isites.harvard.edu/fs/docs/icb. topic446176.files/Week_7/Keck and_Sikkink_Transnational_Advocacy.pdf [Accessed 10 January 2016].

Lambine, M., 2013. 'Numbers matter. Characteristic differences between, lone, duo and 3+ group rapes', in M. Horvath and J. Woodhams, eds, *Handbook on the study of multiple perpetrator rape. A multidisciplinary response to an international problem.* London, New York: Routledge, 67–81.

McMahon, S., and Banyard, V.L., 2012. 'When can I help? A conceptual framework for the prevention of sexual violence through bystander intervention', *Trauma, Violence & Abuse* 13(1): 3–14. Available from: http://tva.sagepub.com/content/13/1/3 [Accessed 28 November 2015].

Menon, N., 2012. *Statement by women's and progressive groups and individuals condemning sexual violence and opposing death penalty* [online]. Available from: http://kafila.org/2012/12/24/statement-by-womens-and-progressive-groups-and-individuals-condemning-sexual-violence-and-opposing-death-penalty/ [Accessed 24 August 2015].

NCDHR. *Violence against Dalit Women in India* [online]. National Campaign on Dalit Human Rights. Available from: www.ncdhr.org.in/others/Report-on-National-Tribuna-%28Final%29.pdf [Accessed 10 January 2016].

One Billion Rising, 2016. *The Revolution Escalates! Rise for Revolution: Sign up to Disrupt!* [online]. Available from: www.onebillionrising.org [Accessed 10 January 2016].

Phillips, M., *et al.*, 2015. 'Media coverage of violence against women in India: A systematic study of a high profile rape case', *BMC women's health* 15:3. Available from: www.biomedcentral.com/1472-6874/15/3 [Accessed 24 August 2015].

PRS Blog, 2013. *Verma Committee on the Sexual Harassment Bill* [online]. Available from: www.prsindia.org/theprsblog/?p=2542 [Accessed 10 January 2016].

Roychowdhury, P., 2013. 'The Delhi gang rape. The making of international causes', *Feminist Studies* 39(1): 282–92. Available from: www.jstor.org/stable/23719317

Sakamoto, R., 2001. 'The women's international war crimes tribunal on Japan's military sexual slavery. A legal and feminist approach to the "Comfort Women" issue', *New Zealand Journal of Asian Studies* 3(1): 49–58. Available from: www.nzasia.org.nz/downloads/NZJAS-June01/Comfortwomen.pdf [Accessed 13 May 2016].

UN, 1993. *Declaration on Elimination of Violence against Women* [online]. United Nations. Available from: www.un.org/documents/ga/res/48/a48r104.htm [Accessed 10 January 2016].

UNHCR, 1984. *Convention against Torture and Other Cruel, Inhuman or Degrading Treatment or Punishment* [online]. United Nations High Commissioner for Refugees. Available from: www.ohchr.org/EN/ProfessionalInterest/Pages/CAT.aspx [Accessed 10 January 2016].

Weiner, M., 1993. 'Rejected people and unwanted migrants in South Asia', *Economic & Political Weekly* 28(34): 1737–46.

Women's Regional Network [online]. Available from: www.womensregionalnetwork.org/ [Accessed 10 January 2016].

Women's Regional Network, 2013. *The Women's Regional Network Community Conversations* [online]. Available from: www.womensregionalnetwork.org/images/uploads/OverviewNov2013.pdf [Accessed 10 January 2016].

# 26 Combating violence against women

## Transnational perspectives on social work in Germany

## Comment on the Indian case study from a German perspective

*Ute Zillig*

A representative study found that 13 per cent of German women above the age of sixteen have experienced a criminal form of sexual violence. In only 14 per cent of the cases were the perpetrators unknown to the women (Müller and Schröttle 2004: 65, 78). German criminal law imposes a sentence of ten years up to life for a convicted rape resulting in death.

The following article covers transnational aspects in German social work regarding violence against women, and key layers of European advocacy.

### German social work addressing violence against women

Since the 1970s the women's movement in Germany has brought the issue of violence against women into public debate. For its current population of around 82 million people, about 350 women's shelters now exist, and around 17,000 women and a similar number of children find support in these shelters each year. There are about 750 rape crisis/counselling centres with different specialisms such as intimate partner violence, sexual violence, sexual abuse, forced marriage, female genital mutilation, trafficking, and stalking (BMFSFJ: 13). As well as providing shelter and counselling, preventative interventions including school outreach, training of professionals and campaigning are an integral part of the work of German support services for women.

### Transnational perspectives – legal implications, racism and cultural competencies

A transnational aspect might enter social work practice when a woman, who was born and/or raised in another country, accesses a German shelter or rape crisis centre. The woman, particularly if she has no permanent residency and therefore lacks insurance/health coverage, might not be able to have all her needs met (e.g. seeing a specialised gynaecologist, having translation support). Other issues such as immigration status intrude and the social worker's time is likely to be taken up more with talking to the lawyer, writing reports and dealing with bureaucracy, than focusing on personal support and counselling. This changes the focus from personal support and counselling to handling bureaucratic procedures that might allow her to leave her violent partner or an abusive environment.

Racism and everyday discrimination might be another transnational aspect of social work in the field of gender-based violence. Experiences of sexual violence are often strongly connected to experiences in the context of racist stereotypes and discrimination (Crenshaw 1996; Dovidio *et al.* 2010).

Finally, gender-based violence is always – as any other social situation – experienced in culturally specific ways. Social work, in its aspiration to be a diversity-embracing profession, encourages an awareness of the interplay that ethnicity, culture and religion might have within its different settings.[1] Gender-based violence is experienced and articulated in culturally specific ways and experiences of sexual violence have been shown to be strongly connected to experiences of racist discrimination (Crenshaw 1996; Dovidio *et al.* 2010). If a social work professional wants to establish equal communication, which is crucial for survivors of sexual violence (Herman 1997), she cannot ignore the woman's personal biography and the norms and values she is subject to or has grown up with. In turn, becoming aware of one's own cultural assumptions can help in the appropriate appreciation of each woman's individual story, and be supportive of the framework of human rights and social justice (Rosenstreich 2007; Ife 2012; Oberlies 2015). However, among German women's shelters and rape and counselling centres, there are only a few[2] which explicitly address multiple discriminations when counselling women victims of violence.

## Transnational perspectives – advocating across borders

Since the late 1990s national networks on violence against women have been established in Germany, and shelters and counselling centres have coalesced into four umbrella organisations.[3] Campaigns aiming for changes within German laws on sexual offences or on practical aspects in terms of court procedures or health care are often initiated and organised at this overarching level, and carried out by local and regional institutions. These umbrella organisations are active parts of transnational networks, especially at the European level.

Germany ratified the Convention on the Elimination of All Forms of Discrimination against Women (CEDAW) in 1985. German umbrella organisations contribute to alternative reports to the CEDAW committee which provide a basis for the committee's recommendations to the German government. In 2009, for example, the committee raised concerns about the lack of sustained funding for women's shelters, and pointed out the need for improving the German Protection against Violence Act. It also highlighted parts of German migration law with particularly negative impacts on migrant women experiencing violence from their husbands (CEDAW 2009). Obviously, these kinds of recommendation provide an important background for lobbying for women's rights at a national level – sometimes in sync with international partners in Europe and elsewhere advocating similarly.

The European Union, and the European Parliament in particular, has adopted various legal measures and guidelines to combat violence against women in recent years (EUR-Lex 2008; European Parliament 2010). The European Commission passed a directive on minimum standards on the rights, support and protection of victims of crime in 2012. Through this directive, each European state is required to provide specialist support services for victims of gender-based violence including trauma support and counselling, accessible and understandable information and support for family members of victims (European Commission). It implies more concrete rights for victims and clearer obligations for member states than previous legal frameworks.

In 1997, the European Commission started a broad funding programme 'DAPHNE' to support victims of violence and to combat violence against women, children and young people. This is now in its fourth phase, from 2014 to 2020. DAPHNE entails support for a huge number of projects related to social work, research and advocacy: the European NGO 'Women Against Violence Europe' (WAVE) under which many German shelters, rape and counselling centres are organised, was initially funded under the EU-DAPHNE programme. WAVE specifically aims to promote European measures for combating violence against women. In this regard, an observatory evaluates the impacts of developments in member states. Among others, WAVE is working on issues such as European standards of support services and development of training materials. It initiates, and is part of international campaigns, and successfully brought a case to the European Court of Human Rights in 2012 (WAVE).

In 2005, the Council of Europe, a European institution advocating human rights through international conventions and recommendations for its 47 member states, adopted an Action Plan to Combat Violence against Women and established a task force consisting of international experts. One outcome of this task force was a study on minimum standards for support services that has become an important reference advocating adequate funding at national and local levels (Kelly 2008). In 2011, the Council of Europe adopted the Convention of the European Council on preventing and combating violence against women and domestic violence ('the Istanbul Convention'). This came into force in August 2014. It outlines each state's obligation to implement all necessary measures in order to prevent and combat violence against women (Art. 7, sec. 1) (Council of Europe 2011). It is a crucial document for negotiating improved policy and funding for social services on a national basis. The Istanbul Convention was the result of a long process of advocacy, in which NGOs, the European Union and UN agencies were involved. As a direct impact of this Convention, Germany established a nationwide helpline for women (Bundesministerium für Familie und zivilgesellschaftliche Aufgaben). It is also a crucial document for national umbrella organisations when negotiating for sufficient funding for social services on a national legal basis.

As has been pointed out by Abha Bhaiya and argued in the minimum standards of support services mentioned above, a sufficient transnational strategy in prevention and combating violence against women needs to incorporate not only helplines, safe shelters, support and advocacy services which are accessible for all women but also training for professionals, work with perpetrators and prevention programmes that address gender relations as well.

> By concentrating solely on the individual survival of abused women and children, whether through our own projects or campaigning for changes in law and professional practice, we run the danger of losing sight of our ultimate aim: ending sexual violence.

(Kelly 1988: 238)

## Notes

1  The National Association of Social Workers standards on cultural competence NASW (2001).
2  For example: kargah, IKB, Frauenberatung TARA, LesMigraS.
3  bff, FHK, KOK, ZIF.

## References

bff. *Empowering women and standing firm against violence* [online]. Frauen gegen Gewalt e.V. Available from: www.frauen-gegen-gewalt.de/home.html [Accessed 7 December 2015].

BMFSFJ. *Bericht der Bundesregierung zur Situation der Frauenhäuser, Fachberatungsstellen und anderer Unterstützungsangebote für gewaltbetroffene Frauen und deren Kinder* [online]. Bundesministeriums für Familie, Senioren, Frauen und Jugend. Available from: www.bmfsfj.de/RedaktionBMFSFJ/Broschuerenstelle/ Pdf-Anlagen/Bericht-der-Bundesregierung-zur-Situation-der-Frauenh_C3_A4user,prop erty=pdf,bereich=bmfsfj,sprache=de,rwb=true.pdf [Accessed 5 October 2015].

Bundesministerium für Familie und zivilgesellschaftliche Aufgaben. *Support for women in need. The Violence against women support hotline* [online]. Available from: www. hilfetelefon.de/en/about-us.html [Accessed 9 October 2015].

CEDAW, 2009. *Concluding observations of the Committee on the Elimination of Discrimination against Women. Germany* [online]. Available from: www2.ohchr.org/ english/bodies/cedaw/docs/co/CEDAW-C-DEU-CO6.pdf [Accessed 7 October 2015].

Council of Europe, 2011. *Übereinkommen des Europarats zur Verhütung und Bekämpfung von Gewalt gegen Frauen und häuslicher Gewalt* [online]. Available from: http:// conventions.coe.int/Treaty/EN/Treaties/Html/210.htm [Accessed 10 October 2015].

Crenshaw, K., 1996. 'Mapping the Margins. Intersectionality, Identity Politics, and Violence Against Women of Color', in K. Crenshaw, G. Peller, and K. Thomas, eds, *Critical race theory. The key writings that formed the movement.* New York: Norton, 357–83.

Dovidio, J.F., Hewstone, M., Glick, P. and Esses, V.M., 2010. 'Prejudice, stereotyping and discrimination. Theoretical and empirical overview', in J.F. Dovidio, M. Hewstone, P. Glick and V.M. Esses, eds, *The SAGE Handbook of prejudice, stereotyping and discrimination.* London: SAGE Publications, 3–28.

EUR-Lex, 2008. *EU guidelines on violence against women and girls* [online]. Available from: http://eur-lex.europa.eu/legal-content/EN/TXT/?uri=uriserv:dh0003 [Accessed 10 October 2015].

European Commission. *Rights of the victim* [online]. Available from: http://ec.europa.eu/ justice/criminal/victims/rights/index_en.htm [Accessed 9 October 2015].

European Parliament, 2010. *The issue of violence against women in the European Union* [online]. Available from: www.europarl.europa.eu/RegData/etudes/note/join/2010/419623/IPOL-FEMM_NT%282010%29419623_EN.pdf [Accessed 10 October 2015].

FHK [online]. Frauenhauskoordinierung.V. Available from: www.frauenhauskoordinierung.de/english-summary.html [Accessed 7 December 2015].

Frauenberatung TARA [online]. Fachberatungs-und Interventionsstelle bei häuslicher Gewalt. Available from: www.frauenberatung-tara.de/spr/eng.html [Accessed 7 December 2015].

Herman, J.L., 1997. *Trauma and recovery. The aftermath of violence - From domestic abuse to political terror.* New York: BasicBooks.

Ife, J., 2012. *Human Rights and Social Work. Towards rights-based practice.* Cambridge: Cambridge University Press.

IKB [online]. Interkulturelle Begegnungsstätte. Available from: www.ikb-frauen.de/index.php?id=2&L=2 [Accessed 7 December 2015].

kargah. *SUANA* [online]. Verein für interkulturelle Kommunikation, Migrations- und Flüchtlingsarbeit. Available from: www.kargah.de/index.php?lang=de&Itemid=682 [Accessed 7 December 2015].

Kelly, L., 2008. *Combating violence against women. Minimum standards for support services* [online]. Available from: www.coe.int/t/dg2/equality/domesticviolencecampaign/Source/EG-VAW-CONF%282007%29Study%20rev.en.pdf [Accessed 9 October 2015].

Kelly, L., 1988. *Surviving sexual violence.* Cambridge: Polity Press.

KOK. *German NGO network against trafficking in human beings* [online]. Available from: www.kok-gegen-menschenhandel.de/en/home.html [Accessed 7 December 2015].

LesMigraS [online]. Lesbenberatung Berlin e.V. Available from: www.lesmigras.de/english.html [Accessed 7 December 2015].

Müller, U., and Schröttle, M., 2004. *Lebenssituation, Sicherheit und Gesundheit von Frauen in Deutschland. Eine repräsentative Untersuchung zu Gewalt gegen Frauen in Deutschland. Im Auftrag des Bundesministeriums für Familie, Senioren, Frauen und Jugend* [online]. Bundesministeriums für Familie, Senioren, Frauen und Jugend (BMFSFJ). Available from: www.bmfsfj.de/RedaktionBMFSFJ/Abteilung4/Pdf-Anlagen/langfassung-studie-frauen-teil-eins,property=pdf,bereich=bmfsfj,sprache=de,rwb=true.pdf [Accessed 5 October 2015].

NASW, 2001. *NASW standards for cultural competence in social work practice* [online]. National Association of Social Workers (NASW). Available from: www.socialworkers.org/practice/standards/NASWCulturalStandards.pdf [Accessed 1 October 2015].

Oberlies, D., 2015. 'Soziale Arbeit als Menschenrechtsprofession', *Sozial Extra* 39(2): 6–9.

Rosenstreich, G.D., 2007. 'The mathematics of diversity training. Multiplying identities, adding categories and intersecting discrimination', in A. Broden and P. Mecheril, eds, *Re-Präsentationen. Dynamiken der Migrationsgesellschaft.* Düsseldorf: IDA-NRW, 131–59.

WAVE. *Current Projects & Activities* [online]. Women Against Violence Europe. Available from: http://wave-network.org/content/current-projects-activities [Accessed 9 October 2015].

ZIF [online]. Zentrale Informationsstelle Autonomer Frauenhäuser. Available from: www.autonome-frauenhaeuser-zif.de/ [Accessed 7 December 2015].

# 27 Transnational advocacy networks

## The examples of APWLD and NCWO

## Comment on the Indian case study from a Malayan perspective

*Rashila Ramli*

Jyoti's case in India is an extreme example of gender violence. However, the way it became a cause of many different groups and coalitions, some of which are based outside of India, is not so unusual: transnational advocacy relating to domestic violence has been happening and continues to take place at multiple levels and in varying spaces. At the international level, the Convention on the Elimination of Discrimination against Women (CEDAW) and the United Nations Security Council Resolution 1325 (UNSCR 1325) on women, peace and security, are two pivotal international instruments dealing with violence against women and are used at the international level. Article 1 of the Declaration on the Elimination of Violence against Women (DEVAW) accepted by the General Assembly in 1993 defines violence against women as 'any act of gender-based violence that results in, or is likely to result in, physical, sexual or psychological harm or suffering to women, whether occurring in public or in private life' (Article 1).

The UN also recognises the prevalence of intimate partner violence (both physical and sexual) as well as the prevalence of other forms of violence against women and girls, such as female genital mutilation/cutting and child marriage. It is accepted that 'gendered divisions of violence are the hierarchical dichotomies of self–other, us–them, aggressive–passive, soldier–victim, and protector–protected that divide the world into masculinised offenders and defenders and feminized populations over which they fight and seek to conquer or defend' (Peterson and Runyan 2010: 143f).

CEDAW, UNSCR 1325 and DEVAW are explicit instruments for UN governments and civil society organisations to use in their advocacy work. How civil society organisations advocate transnationally including to the UN bodies themselves, is the focus of this chapter. As a commentary on transnational advocacy, I focus on the role of civil society at the regional and national levels, i.e. the Asia Pacific Forum for Women, Law and Development (APWLD) based in Chiang Mai and the National Council of Women's Organisations (NCWO 2013) in Malaysia. Both organisations work at the regional and national level respectively to promote gender justice, especially in the eradication of violence against women including people being in an irregular situation[1] (UN Women 2011).

## Regional advocacy: knowing APWLD

The Asia Pacific Forum for Women, Law and Development (APWLD) is a grassroots-based organisation formed in 1987 when lawyers, activists and scholars gathered in Manila for a conference focusing on the role of law. The organisation has members from 25 countries. The grassroots members operate within organising committees answerable to the regional council. The regional council is the elected body, representing six sub-regions in Asia Pacific, providing directions for the programme and management committee members who work with the Secretariat of APWLD. The 28-year-old organisation has developed extensive networks in its member countries with the main aim of enabling legislations to ensure the protection and empowerment of women.

In 2008, there were four major programmes organised by APWLD (APWLD 2016): Beyond Marginalization, Women in Power, Feminist Legal Theory, and Grounding the Global. By 2015, there were two additional programmes – Feminist Development Justice and Climate Change. One of the common threads that binds the programmes together is the desire to eradicate all forms of violence against women. APWLD members see violence against women as a cross-cutting issue that must be addressed by all programmes.

Through the years, many cases of violence against women have been documented by APWLD occurring in rural areas, the workplace, public spaces as well as within the home. Thus, each programme developed approaches to confront violence against women in a targeted manner. For example, the Feminist Legal Theory programme explicitly highlights laws, regulations, and support systems relating to women and violence. Comparative analyses were undertaken to compare and contrast actions taken by state enforcement agencies, as well as support given by NGOs to victims of violence.

APWLD believes in the concept of Women's Human Rights developed during the UN decade for Women (1975–1985). This is the second common thread running across all APWLD programmes. In at least three cases when women human rights defenders were arrested by their governments' law enforcement agencies, APWLD would send out Urgent Appeals to state its position and to galvanise support for their release (APWLD). In these cases (see Table 27.1), violence was committed by the states.

APWLD works closely with UN Women and International Women's Rights Action Watch-Asia Pacific (IWRAW-AP) to monitor the progress made by states in implementing CEDAW. APWLD has pressured governments to be accountable for their actions. Different countries address violence against women in different ways – in Malaysia, the government has instituted the following measures: collection of statistics; reform of the laws regarding rape (1989); establishment of a Domestic Violence Act (1994); launching of a Code of Practice on the Elimination of Sexual Harassment in the Workplace (1999); launching a Code of Practice on the Elimination of Sexual Harassment in the public sector (2005).

*Table 27.1* Cases of violence fought by APWLD

|  | Name of WHRD, country, violence against women issue in brief | Date of statement | Expected outcome/ outcome |
|---|---|---|---|
| Case 1 | Imrana Jalal, Fiji, Prominent lawyer criticising the Fijian military regime | 30/10/2010 | Court dropped all charges |
| Case 2 | Women Human Rights Defender Statement (adopted by UN) | 26/9/2013 | Creation of awareness |
| Case 3 | Ain O Salish Kendra (ASK), Bangladesh, attempted abduction of Nur Khan, Director of ASK | 16/5/2014 | Getting the attention of law enforcement on the matter |
| Case 4 | Mary Jane Veloso, a Filipino woman accused of drug trafficking in Indonesia | 27/6/ 2015 | The death penalty is practised in Indonesia. Her execution was stopped |
| Case 5 | Teesta Setalvad and Javed Anand, India. Harassment due to their work supporting victims of violence, predominantly women | 5/8/2015 | Decreased harassment |

Source: APWLD (2016)

## National advocacy: knowing NCWO

The National Council of Women's Organisations (NCWO) is one of the leading civil society organisations advocating for the eradication of Violence against Women in Malaysia (NCWO 2013). The efforts made by NCWO coincide with NCWO's participation as member of the national delegation to the UN Conference on Women in Nairobi, Kenya in 1985. As a follow-up to the conference, NCWO presented a memorandum to the government, where substantive recommendations for legal reform on major legislation were made resulting in the following actions by the government (see Table 27.2).

NCWO partnered with other civil society organisations such as the Joint Action for Group for Gender Equality (JAG) and Women's Aid Organisation to lobby the Malaysian government in passing the Domestic Violence Act. Both organisations realised that there is strength in partnership. By combining multiple strategies based on each organisation's strength, NCWO and JAG were able to get the Domestic Violence Act 1994 passed by Parliament.

When NCWO was established in 1963, transnational advocacy was in its infancy. Almost 25 years later, when APWLD was formed in 1987, transnational advocacy gained a foothold in regional women's movements which can then be linked to national organisations. Current issues involving violence against women, such as human trafficking, climate change, armed conflicts and drug mules, are addressed through joint efforts of Civil Society Organisations (CSOs). Many of

*Table 27.2* Milestones in claiming rights

| Year | Action |
|------|--------|
| 1986 | The Royal Malaysian Police set up a special unit of women police officers to investigate cases of rape |
| | A rape investigation kit is produced by the Ministry of Health |
| 1987 | A memorandum on the draft Domestic Violence Bill is presented to the government culminating in Parliament passing the Domestic Violence Act in 1994 |
| 1994 | The Domestic Violence Act is adopted |
| 1994 | A One-Stop Rape Crisis Centre is set up in Kuala Lumpur Hospital. This is further extended to other public hospitals to also cover women victims of domestic violence, and rape of men (sodomy cases). |
| | The NCWO-YWCA Shelter is established in Klang |
| | The Penal Code is amended to include mandatory five-year jail sentences |
| 1996 | The Domestic Violence Act 1994 comes into force |
| 1999 | The Sexual Harassment Law is adopted |
| 2006 | NCWO launches the Coalition of Citizens Against Crime (CCAC) |
| 2011 | NCWO, in collaboration with the LPPKN's SEKTA programme to promote safety of the family, conducted 40 workshops nationwide for parents, youth, kindergarten teachers, child care providers and NCWO affiliates |

Source: NCWO (2013)

these co-organise programmes such as capacity building workshops, rallies, flash mobs and forums to publicise their stance on violence against women. An example is the One Billion Rising Campaign which started in 2013. The 2016 campaign with the theme 'Rise for Revolution! Listen! Act! Rise!' was launched on 20 October 2015 (One Billion Rising 2016).

## Conclusion

This commentary offers complementary material on ideas of combating violence against women at the regional and national levels. Based on examples given at the regional and national levels, one can emulate actions taken in one's own environment. Moreover, with increasing recognition given to rules and regulations pertaining to violence against women, it will be interesting to see the convergence of CSOs to achieve a common goal. For Malaysia, the cooperation between NCWO and JAG is a good example: the Domestic Violence Act of 1994 provides the foundation for law enforcement agencies and the Ministry of Women, Family and Community Development of Malaysia to curb violence against women. At the regional level, APWLD monitors compliance with CEDAW. APWLD views violence against women as a cross-cutting issue existing in all of its programmes. However, despite laws in many countries, violence against women and girls still persists. One then has to study the cultural, socioeconomic aspects of a community to determine the possible causes and most appropriate solutions to the problem.

## Note

1 Person in an 'irregular situation': 'A person who, owing to unauthorized entry, breach of a condition of entry, or the expiry of his or her visa, lacks legal status in a transit or host country. The definition covers inter alia those persons who have entered a transit or host country lawfully but have stayed for a longer period than authorized or subsequently taken up unauthorized employment (also called clandestine/undocumented migrant or migrant in an irregular situation). The term "irregular" is preferable to "illegal" because the latter carries a criminal connotation and is seen as denying migrants' humanity' (IOM 2011).

## References

APWLD. *Women Human Rights Defenders* [online]. Asia Pacific Forum on Women, Law and Development. Available from: http://apwld.org/category/women-human-rights-defenders/ [Accessed 10 January 2016].

APWLD, 2016. *Empowering women to use law as an instrument of change and promoting women's human rights in the Asia Pacific region* [online]. Asia Pacific Forum on Women, Law and Development (APWLD). Available from: www.apwld.org [Accessed 20 January 2016].

IOM, 2011. *Key Migration Terms* [online]. International Organization for Migration. Available from: www.iom.int/key-migration-terms [Accessed 10 January 2016].

NCWO, 2013. *NCWO golden jubilee. Milestones in our journey* [online]. National Council of Women's Organisations. Available from: www.ncwomalaysia.com/ [Accessed 10 January 2016].

One Billion Rising, 2016. *The Revolution Escalates! Rise for Revolution: Sign up to Disrupt!* [online]. Available from: www.onebillionrising.org [Accessed 10 January 2016].

Peterson, V.S., and Runyan, A.S., 2010. *Global gender issues in the new millennium.* Colorado: Westview Press.

UN Women, 2011. *In pursuit of justice. Progress of the world's women (2011-2012)* [online]. United Nations. Available from: www.unwomen.org/~/media/headquarters/attachments/sections/library/publications/2011/progressoftheworldswomen-2011-en.pdf [Accessed 25 January 2016].

# 28 Elderly people in a war zone in Israel

## The impact of community resources on psychological well-being and life review intervention in a resilience centre

*Irit Regev*

In the spring of 2001, missiles were fired toward the southern part of Israel, and the barrage was ongoing, subordinating everyday routine to the physical, psychological, and social realities of life in a war zone, and threatening personal well-being. The stress affects one's sense of physical and emotional security and causes difficulties in adjustment. Elderly people, who have relatively few economic and social resources, are especially vulnerable (Carballo *et al.* 2004).

Although this study was conducted in Israel, the plight of elderly people who live in war zones worldwide is similar, and aside from their age-related developmental losses they live under extreme stress brought about by the belligerence around them.

The cases presented in this chapter highlight the importance of an environment (in this case: community resilience centres) that is able to provide resources to people in situations of tension and threat. The role played by social workers in these centres is crucial to the well-being of the elderly population experiencing a situation of threat and stress that accompany war.

In response to this reality, resilience centres have been established in Israeli regions bordering Gaza, creating an innovative psychological model for providing clinical treatment and counselling.

### Elderly people in Israel: demographic trends and background characteristics

Elderly people (age 65 and over) constitute 10 per cent of Israel's Jewish population and 8 per cent of its Arab population (Muslims, Christian Arabs, and Druze) (Brodsky *et al.* 2013). Life expectancy in Israel is relatively high – in 2012 it was 82.8 years for women and 78.5 years for men. According to Central Bureau of Statistics (CBS) projections, in 2020 elderly people will constitute 12 per cent of the population, reaching 14 per cent by 2030 (Brodsky *et al.* 2013; MASHAV 2011).

On the whole, elderly people in Israel are less educated and poorer than the general population (Brodsky *et al.* 2013). Furthermore, most of the elderly people in Israel are immigrants – about 8 per cent of all those who have immigrated to

Israel since 1948 are aged 65 and older upon arrival. The majority of the elderly population, even those 85 and older, continue to live in their own homes. This fact weighs heavily on the formal community service system, and even more so on informal support systems, which comprise the mainstay of assistance for the aged, especially when they are ill and dependent (Clarfield *et al.* 2006).

Social services for the elderly in Israel are divided into community services, provided in the home of the elderly person or in day-care facilities, and institutional long-term care services, provided in residential facilities for the elderly. Since the 1980s, a system of services designed to preserve the quality of life for the elderly has been added to long-term care services (Brodsky *et al.* 2013).

## Elderly people in a war zone in Israel – stress and coping

Comparative studies conducted among different age groups have revealed conflicting findings regarding the responses of the elderly population to traumatic situations (Carballo *et al.* 2004; Knight *et al.* 2000; Norris *et al.* 2000). Some researchers (Carballo *et al.* 2004) have indicated that elderly people, who have relatively few financial and social resources, are more vulnerable. As such, they may have difficulties coping with a continuous stress situation, which may be a serious risk for developing symptoms of mental illness such as post-traumatic reactions and depression. Other researchers have argued that elderly people are more resilient to symptoms of illness following traumatic events and that they are less afraid, desperate, or worried than younger people (Knight *et al.* 2000; Norris *et al.* 2000).

Since 2001, Israel's western border with the Palestinian Authority has been the target of more than 10,000 missile and mortar attacks. This situation calls for dealing not only with the physical and emotional damage in the immediate aftermath of the attack, but also with the long-term stress caused by the ongoing threat (Braun-Lewensohn *et al.* 2009; Nuttman-Shwartz 2015).

Seeking a response to this reality, five Resilience Centres have been established in the localities along the border with Gaza, serving some 60,000 people. Four are in regional authorities and the fifth in the town of Sderot. The programmes in these centres were designed to increase the social resilience of the local population, and enhance their ability to cope with the ongoing security threat. The centres, which were established in collaboration with government ministries, local authorities, and third sector organisations (the Israel Trauma Coalition), are an innovative psychological model for providing clinical treatment and counselling to residents of the war zone in all age groups at the individual, community, and municipal levels. Since 2007, approximately 15,000 individuals (one-quarter of the population) have turned to the centres where they received treatment or participated in coping seminars (ITC).

## Gerontological social work and social work with trauma victims

The main goal of gerontological social workers is to enhance the psychological well-being of adults who are experiencing aging-related changes such as deteriorating health, decreased mobility, or increased need for social support and service delivery systems. These social workers provide psychosocial treatments, while also serving as educators.

Social workers in war zones deal with situations in which stress (such as caused by missile attacks) is a threat to the psychological well-being and the sense of physical and emotional security of the population. Social work interventions are based on several psychological methods: behavioural and cognitive methods, trauma and stress management, and narrative therapy (Breckenridge and James 2010; Nuttman-Shwartz 2015).

One unique and efficient method of promoting well-being among elderly persons is narrative therapy, specifically life review. Life review entails remembering one's life events, and relating them as a narrative that has its own significance. During the process, memories of the past, present feelings, and perception of the future combine to create harmony among the various parts of the life stories. Coming closer to the end of one's life can increase the need for life review, as can life-threatening events, in this case, ongoing exposure to missile attacks (Butler 1963; Whitbourne and Whitbourne 2011).

## Life review as a gerontological intervention

Erikson (1963, 1978, 1982) highlighted the importance of looking back at earlier life stages in old age, in an attempt to integrate the past into the present and future and gain a meaningful conception of life as a whole. Guided life review activities help people come to terms with unresolved conflicts from the past in their present life when they face vulnerability, dependency, and death (Blando 2011; Butler 1963; Kenyon *et al.* 2011).

Social workers who work with life review must be trained in the principles and techniques of the method, and be able to use it appropriately for each age group, in our case, the elderly person (Butler 1963; Greene 2008; Steunenberg and Bohlmeijer 2011). Using this method, the practitioner views the memories that elderly persons share during the structured intervention – whether in an individual setting or in a group session – as a reflection of the self which serves interpersonal and intrapersonal functions that help the narrators connect with themselves and with others, especially with the social worker. In this process, they develop awareness of the journey they have undergone, and gain insights into their own strengths as well as their weaknesses (Haight and Haight 2007).

During the structured sessions, the social worker uses the stories of the older persons to help them form a positive self-identity and facilitate the acquisition of better coping skills that will empower them in their current life struggle and improve their mood disturbance (Steunenberg and Bohlmeijer 2011; Zanjani *et al.* 2015). Structured interventions with older adults can be based on several methods, including looking at family albums, sculpting, drawing, reading letters from the past, and writing the older person's life story (Haight *et al.* 1998).

Janoff-Bulman (1992) worked with victims of trauma, and suggested three dimensions that should be covered in the process of life review intervention (Tromp 2011):

- Meaningful order of the world: elderly clients have to tell their story in a way that makes sense to them as a whole, and enables them to see the world they live in as just and understandable.
- Benevolence in the world: the assumption that there are positive intentions in the social context.
- Self-worth: elderly clients have to tell their story in a way that highlights the positive value of their actions and sense of self.

## The person in environment model: two types of communities in one war zone

As personal and social resources enable people to cope with the aftermath of traumatic events (Ben-Sira 1991; Lazarus and Folkman 1984), the impact of exposure to war may depend on the wider social context in which it occurs. The social context of this exposure can be defined by the capacity of individuals and communities to navigate their way to resources that sustain well-being (Ungar 2008).

Research findings have revealed that communities with high levels of social cohesion, organised social networks, and strong social institutions demonstrate remarkable resilience when exposed to traumatic conditions (Ungar 2008; Wicke and Silver 2009). Kawachi and Berkman (2001) have highlighted the importance of the availability of social connections as a buffer against the impact of disasters. Accordingly, it has been claimed that residents of poor communities and residents of communities with limited economic resources (Cutter *et al.* 2006) are more vulnerable to stressful conditions.

The population discussed here lives in rural and urban communities. The urban community is the town of Sderot, and the rural communities, for the most part, are kibbutzim (communal settlements), which emphasise socioeconomic equality and cooperation, and have relatively abundant social and economic resources (Dekel and Nuttman-Shwartz 2009).

Following are two cases of working with elderly women living under constant threat to their personal safety. At first glance, these cases seem very specific to the Israeli situation of a civilian population being under missile bombardment, a situation which is not replicated worldwide. However, the personality traits and life histories revealed in the two cases described here are generalisable to other situations involving elderly people.

### Case 1: Monika

Monika, 79 years old, was born in Argentina, emigrated as a young woman to Israel, and settled in a kibbutz. She was referred to the social worker at the resilience centre because the welfare staff members at the kibbutz were concerned that her emotional condition had deteriorated. She had sleeping problems, and she described anxiety and fears concerning missile attacks. She cared for her husband, who had Parkinson's disease and was disabled. Monika felt responsible for her husband, and the sound of the alarms as well as the short notice between the alarms and the missile explosions aroused distress and anxiety.

In the first meeting, the social worker asked Monika to tell her about her life. She said that she did not go out of the house much because of her husband's illness, and because she was afraid of the constant shooting. At the next meeting, Monika told how she met her husband in a youth group in Buenos Aires, Argentina. This was before the establishment of the State of Israel, and the youth group prepared them for their emigration. She had been selected for the group because, as she put it, she was 'friendly and dominant in the group'. When she talked about that period, she suddenly looked more energetic and she smiled at the social worker.

In the next two meetings she told the story of her emigration to Israel and her first impressions and experiences. When the social worker asked what helped her in the present, with the ongoing missile attacks, she responded that they were all together and coped as a group: 'We had made a revolution. That's what helped me. I think I had the strength to cope despite the difficulties. Even during the war last month, our war room functioned remarkably well. What really helped was that our community was involved, and we helped each other.'

### Case 2: Annette

Annette is 76 years old. She and her husband were born in Morocco and live in Sderot. Extremely distressed, she arrived at the resilience centre after a day of several air-raid sirens, and asked the social worker to make a home visit to her and her husband, because they are both sick, hardly go out of the house and have no one to talk to.

The social worker asked Annette about family, neighbours, or friends, without using the structured method of life review. Annette said that she has two sons living in the central region of Israel and no family nearby. Her two friends are sick and cannot help her. In the past, she had visited the community club, but today she's afraid to go out of the house. The social worker referred a volunteer organisation to her, and a volunteer came to her home. These visits eased her burden, alleviated some of the loneliness she and her husband felt, and allowed her the time to go out of the house for shopping and on errands.

### Analysis of Monika's and Annette's stories: the person in environment model

Both stories exemplify the relationship between individuals and their social environment in situations of stress resulting from continuous combat. Monika, who lives on a kibbutz, talked about her sense of belonging and about the ideological framework that protected her in the threatening situations that she experienced. In contrast, Annette shared feelings of distance and alienation, and her urban community failed to provide her with the sense of security that could alleviate her anxieties. While Monika described the social support she received, the sense of caring, and the feeling that someone is looking out for her, Annette lacked this support and felt lonely and isolated. The difference in resilience between the two women has much to do with their living environment – collective living for Monika (rural community), and urban living for Annette. Whereas Monika easily availed herself of the help around her, Annette, due to personal age-related difficulties, failed to do so, although the service was available.

This is consistent with previous findings regarding the protective force of the rural kibbutz community (Nuttman-Shwartz 2014), and is indicative of the importance of the sensitivity and skills that social workers must have when approaching diverse populations. The establishment of formal and informal social support networks, as well as the provision of daily services such as counselling services to vulnerable populations poses a challenge for social workers involved in formulating policies at the social, communal, and individual levels.

When people feel that they are part of a social fabric that is characterised by mutual responsibility, social support, and appropriate organisation of services, the stress experienced in situations of continuous military tension is mitigated. An organised communal environment can inhibit stress situations and alleviate the sense of helplessness, loneliness and anxiety.

The experience gained in the resilience centres in working with elderly people is not limited to Israel. There are many conflict areas in the world, and though the details vary, the human experience of stress is a common denominator. Social workers, working alongside other mental health professionals, could use the life review method to assist younger and elderly people in areas of war and conflict.

## Summary

This chapter dealt with how elderly persons living in a war zone in the southern part of Israel cope with the threat of missile attacks as well as with changes that accompany the aging process. The evidence suggests that communities characterised by a social environment that provides a sense of protection and social support in which the residents feel a sense of belonging to the community can alleviate the feelings of stress that accompany the ongoing security threat and the losses of old age. It is the role of social workers, in such extreme situations, to strengthen community resources and intra-community ties. The resilience centres act as a place to which individuals turn for building their coping abilities and are used by the authorities to help prepare the population for emergency situations. The social worker's close ties with the population, and the use of life review methods of treatment, are significant in maintaining community cohesion, and strengthen individuals of all ages within it under ongoing, life-threatening situations.

## References

Ben-Sira, Z., 1991. *Regression, stress and readjustment in aging. A structured, biopsychosocial perspective on coping and professional support*. New York: Praeger.

Blando, J., 2011. 'Approaches to counseling older adults', in J. Blando, ed., *Counseling older adults.* New York: Routledge, 131–57.

Braun-Lewensohn, O., Celestin-Westreich, S., Celestin, L.P., Verleye, G., Verte, D. and Ponjaert-Kristoffersen, I., 2009. 'Adolescents' mental health outcomes according to different types of exposure to ongoing terror attacks'. *Journal Youth and Adolescence* (36): 850–62.

Breckenridge, J., and James, K., 2010. 'Educating social work students in multifaceted interventions for trauma', *Social Work Education* (29), 259–75.

Brodsky, J., Shnoor, Y., and Be'er, S., 2013. *The elderly in Israel. The 2011 statistical abstract*. Jerusalem: Myers-JDC-Brookdale Institute.

Butler, R.N., 1963. 'The life review. An interpretation of reminiscence in the aged', *Psychiatry* (26): 65–76.

Carballo, M., Smajkic, A., and Zeric, D., 2004. 'Mental health and coping in a war situation. The case of Bosnia and Herzegovina', *Journal of Biosocial Science* 36(4): 463–77.

Clarfield, A.M., Brodsky, J., and Leibovitz, A., 2006. 'Care of the elderly in Israel. Old age in a young land', in M.S.J. Pathy, A. Sinclair, and J.E. Morely, eds, *Principles and practice of geriatric medicine*. Chichester, Hoboken, NJ: Wiley, 1947–52.

Cutter, S.L., Emrich, C.T., Mitchell, J.T., Boruff, B.J., Gall, M., Schmidtlein, M.C., Burton, C.G. and Melton, G., 2006. 'The long road home. Race, class, and recovery from hurricane Katrina', *Environment: Science and Policy for Sustainable Development* 48(2): 8–20.

Dekel, R., and Nuttman-Shwartz, O., 2009. 'Posttraumatic stress and growth. The contribution of cognitive appraisal and sense of belonging to the country', *Journal of Health and Social Work* 34(2): 87–96.

Erikson, E.H., 1963. *Childhood and society*. 2nd ed. New York: Norton.

Erikson, E.H., 1978. *Adulthood*. New York: Norton.

Erikson, E.H., 1982. *The life cycle completed. A review*. New York: Norton.

Greene, R.R., 2008. *Social work with the aged and their families*. 3rd ed. New Brunswick: Aldine Transaction.

Haight, B., Michel, Y., and Hendrix, S., 1998. 'Life review: Preventing despair in newly relocated nursing home residents. Short and long-term effects', *International Journal of Aging and Human Development* (47): 119–42.

Haight, B.K., and Haight, B.S., 2007. *The handbook of structured life review*. Baltimore: Health Professions Press.

ITC. *Resilience Centers* [online]. Israel Trauma Coalition. Available from: www. israeltraumacoalition.org/?CategoryID=211 [Accessed 10 January 2016].

Janoff-Bulman, R., 1992. 'Understanding people in terms of their assumptive worlds', in D. Ozer, J. Healy, and A. Stewart, eds, *Self and emotion*. London: Jessica Kingsley Publishers, 99–116.

Kawachi, I., and Berkman, L.F., 2001. 'Social ties and mental health', *Journal of Urban Health* (78): 458–67.

Kenyon, G.M., Bohlmeijer, E., and Randall, W.L., eds, 2011. *Storying later life. Issues, investigations, and interventions in narrative gerontology*. New York: Oxford University Press.

Knight, B.G., Gatz, M., Heller, K. and Bengston, V.L., 2000. 'Age and emotional response to the Northridge earthquake. A longitudinal analysis', *Psychological Aging* (15): 627–34.

Lazarus, R.S., and Folkman, S., 1984. *Stress, appraisal, and coping*. New York: Springer Publishing Company.

MASHAV, 2011. *Israel's elderly. Facts and figures 2011* [online]. MASHAV Planning for the Elderly – A National Data Base. Available from: http://brookdale.jdc.org.il/_Uploads/ dbsAttachedFiles/FactsFiguresElderly-ENGLISH-2011.pdf [Accessed 30 November 2015].

Norris, F.H., Friedman, M.J., Watson, P.J., Byrne, C.M., Diaz, E. and Kaniasty, K., 2000. '60,000 disaster victims speak. An empirical review of the empirical literature, 1981-2001', *Psychiatry* (65): 207–39.

Nuttman-Shwartz, O., 2014. 'Fear, functioning and coping during exposure to a continuous security threat', *Journal of Loss and Trauma* 19(3): 262–77.

Nuttman-Shwartz, O., 2015. 'Post-traumatic stress in social work', in J.D. Wright, ed., *International encyclopedia of the social and behavioral sciences*. Amsterdam: Elsevier, 707–13.

Steunenberg, B., and Bohlmeijer, E., 2011. 'Life review using autobiographical retrieval. A protocol for training depressed residential home inhabitants in recalling specific personal memories', in G.M. Kenyon, E. Bohlmeijer, and W.L. Randall, eds, *Storying later life. Issues, investigations, and interventions in narrative gerontology*. New York: Oxford University Press, 290–306.

Tromp, T., 2011. 'Older adults in search of new stories. Measuring the effects of life review on coherence and integration in autobiographical narratives', in G.M. Kenyon, E. Bohlmeijer, and W.L. Randall, eds, *Storying later life. Issues, investigations, and interventions in narrative gerontology*. New York: Oxford University Press, 252–72.

Ungar, M., 2008. 'Resilience across cultures', *British Journal of Social Work* (38): 218–35.

Whitbourne, S.K., and Whitbourne, S.B., 2011. *Adult development and aging. Biopsychosocial perspectives*. 4th ed. Hoboken, NJ: Wiley.

Wicke, T., and Silver, R.C., 2009. 'A community responds to collective trauma. An ecological analysis of the James Byrd murder in Jasper, Texas', *American Journal of Community Psychology* (44): 233–48.

Zanjani, F., Downer, B.G., Hosier, A.F. and Watkins, J.D., 2015. 'Memory banking. A life story intervention for aging preparation and mental health promotion', *Journal of Aging and Health* (27): 355–76.

## 29 Elderly people with cancer in hospital in Shanghai, China

Social group work intervention

Comment on the Israeli case study
from a Chinese perspective

*Fang Yang and Ziqian Xu*

Dr Irit Regev introduced the situation of elderly people in a war zone and the interventions conducted by social workers to help the elderly in Israel. One method she used is the life review method and such an approach is also useful in other stress contexts, such as elderly people living with cancer. In this chapter, we will introduce the stress experienced by elderly patients with cancer and the social work interventions we have conducted among cancer patients in Longhua Hospital, in Shanghai, China. In particular, we focused on strengthening patients' self-efficacy via the life review method and building up their social support; the latter is different from the community-based intervention in Regev's chapter.

According to the World Cancer Report 2014, cancer is a leading cause of morbidity and mortality worldwide and cancer cases are expected to increase annually from 14 million in 2012 to 22 million by 2032 (Stewart 2014). The elderly with cancer, referred to in this chapter, experience stress and uncertainty due to cancer and the aging process, which is similar for patients in other countries. Research shows that social work interventions would greatly benefit the disease prognosis and patients' quality of life. The case of the elderly with cancer in China might shed light on similar situations in other countries.

### Elderly patients with cancer and social work intervention

In China, the prevalence of cancer is 235 per 100,000 with an increasing trend upwards, and cancer is the second top cause of mortality among chronic diseases. Shanghai, one of the most developed Chinese cities, has a large older population with 18.8 per cent of the population aged 65 years and above (Gerontological Society of Shanghai 2015). Half of these elderly people suffer from chronic illness, and more and more elderly people are diagnosed with cancer in Shanghai.

Elderly people with cancer experience high levels of stress – physical, psychological and social (Ridder *et al.* 2008). For instance, cancer causes psychological distress and threatens patients' belief in their ability to influence outcomes (self-efficacy). Meanwhile, cancer requires long-term treatment and care, during which patients' psychological health usually deteriorates due to constant efforts at disease management and lack of improvement in health status. Nevertheless, psychosocial factors play a significant role in the disease prognosis in addition to biomedical factors. Thus it is equally important to target patients' psychological status and provide psychosocial intervention as well as addressing their physical needs.

In this social group intervention, the methods we used were aimed at building social support and creating a life review. Research has shown that social support is critical to adjustment when people face stress (Nausheen *et al.* 2009). Social support is important for cancer patients to deal with the emotional stress and uncertainties of the disease. Patients' self-efficacy is also beneficial to their adjustment (Kreitler *et al.* 2007). Life review, a process of recalling one's life experience or retelling critical events and presenting interpretations, can be an important source of self-efficacy and can motivate patients to adopt adaptive coping strategies (Haber 2006).

Drawing on these theories, we designed three social group work sessions, with the aim of making patients aware of social support availability, encouraging them to seek social support, re-building or strengthening their confidence to cope with the disease, and improving their coping capabilities. We recruited participants via a flyer in the ward. Given that patients usually stay in the hospital only for around ten days for a course of treatment, it is difficult to keep the group closed. Instead, the group was open to the patients who were interested in the group. Ten to twelve patients participated in the social work group which lasted about an hour and a half every time.

The first session: this session aimed to make the patients aware that their family, fellow patients, health care professionals, and social workers are there for them. In the sharing session followed by one team task, one female patient said 'I was so desperate upon the diagnosis, but my family didn't give up on me, and they encouraged me to take part in the activities in the cancer club. Then I went to the club and met many fellow patients. As we have similar experiences, we support each other. We chat about the food, the daily activities, and other things that are good for cancer recovery. Now I am not that scared any more. For me, family and fellow patients are really important.'

The second session: patients were asked to reflect on critical life events they had experienced in the previous five years and how they had dealt with those events. By doing so, we hoped to strengthen patients' confidence in their own abilities to cope with the disease. The majority of the patients talked about their experience of living with cancer. One patient, with stage 4 breast cancer, was in a very good state. After she shared her struggle with the disease, she said 'I am grateful, I am still alive. Cancer hit me and made me realise that my lifestyle is not healthy, I used to take my health for granted. I feel lucky that I still have the chance to make a change. I now slow my life pace down, and maintain a positive mind'. This patient continued to say, 'Cancer is not a completely bad experience. It can make people rethink and take action to make the change now'.

The third session: patients shared their experiences with the disease and how they went through them. This session aimed to boost patients' faith in recovery by listening to and learning from fellow patients' experiences. One male patient used to be the Commissioner of Public Safety in a western city, and was very proud of his job. Unfortunately, the diagnosis of cancer had beaten him. He felt desperate and hopeless because of the lack of effectiveness of the treatment, physical suffering and not being able to work. His wife accompanied him all the way from his hometown to Shanghai, and tried to comfort him, but it did not work. In this group, he learnt of others' experiences in coping with the disease and became positive and confident in himself, and he said, 'If others can make it, I can also make it'.

## Discussion: the cases in Israel and China

Although the elderly in China face different stressors from their counterparts in Israel, they may experience similar physical suffering and psychological distress. Considering the importance of social support in adjusting to stress, social workers can help construct a supportive environment to empower the elderly and instil in them a sense of confidence to deal with the stress. For the elderly in Israel, social workers eased the elderly's physical and emotional burden using community-based interventions, whereas the social group work in this chapter made patients recognise that social support is available and encouraged them to seek social support. A supportive family and community will further benefit patients' recovery when they are discharged from hospital. The importance of community support and resources have been well demonstrated by Regev's work. Unfortunately, such interventions are very rare in China. Along with the department of social work in Longhua Hospital we attempted to establish an alliance between the hospital and the community and to extend the interventions to the community. We believe that such an alliance could consolidate the treatment effect and improve patients' quality of life. So far, what we have done is to conduct education on healthy lifestyle promotion and cancer prevention for the general public in the community. We are still exploring conducting group work for the discharged patients and their family members in the community when we have a better understanding of the needs of patients and their family members.

Furthermore, social workers could use the life review method to assist the elderly who are facing stressors, such as missile attacks or life-threatening cancer. In Israel's case, social workers used life review to help the elderly find their strength and construct a positive attitude. In China's case, we used life review to help cancer patients re-build and fortify their confidence and coping abilities by reflecting their own experience. Patients in the group may also benefit from others' life stories, especially when they face the same adversity. However, there are several factors that limited the effectiveness of the life review method in our group work. First, one session of life review is far from enough, especially for patients with cancer, who experience tremendous stress. These would benefit from a series of life-review sessions. Second, patients in the group mostly talked about their experience of cancer possibly due to the time limit, the group dynamic, or the culture. Such sharing by patients may not fully re-build their self-efficacy in the group work because of the narrow focus (i.e. experience with cancer), although patients could learn from others' experiences. Nevertheless, the life review in Regev's case work might better motivate the elderly to reflect on their past life experience and explore their selves more deeply. It might be better to use the life review method in both case work and group work jointly.

Taken together, as aging is universal and the older population may experience certain forms of stress, social workers could use different methods, such as social support provision and the life review method, to help them cope better with the stress and achieve optimal adjustment. However, more research is needed on how to maximise the effects of the interventions.

## References

Gerontological Society of Shanghai, 2015. *Monitor of aging population and aging services in Shanghai in 2014* [online]. Gerontological Society of Shanghai. Available from: www.shanghaigss.org.cn/news_view.asp?newsid=9687 [Accessed 14 December 2015].

Haber, D., 2006. 'Life review. Implementation, theory, research and therapy', *International Journal of Aging and Human Development* 63(2): 153–71.

Kreitler, S., Peleg, D., and Ehrenfeld, M., 2007. 'Stress, self-efficacy, and quality of life in cancer patients', *Psycho-Oncology* 16(4): 329–41.

Nausheen, B., Gidron, Y., Peveler, R. and Moss-Morris, R., 2009. 'Social support and cancer progression. A systematic review', *Journal of Psychosomatic Research* 67(5): 403–15.

Ridder, D. de, *et al.*, 2008. 'Psychological adjustment to chronic disease', *The Lancet* 372(9634): 246–55.

Stewart, B.W., 2014. *World cancer report*. Lyon: IARC Press.

# 30 Aging and conflict outside and behind your front door

## Comment on the Israeli case study from a British perspective

*Charlotte L. Clarke*

There are three phrases in Irit Regev's chapter which stand out for me as being of immense significance and which thread through this response:

1 'the relationship between individuals and their social environment',
2 'sense of belonging … feelings of distance and alienation',
3 'when people feel that they are part of a social fabric that is characterised by mutual responsibility, social support, and appropriate organisation of services, the stress experienced in situations of continuous [military] tension is mitigated'.

The opportunity to respond to Regev's chapter on elderly people in a war zone from the perspective of Britain is a fascinating challenge! Britain has not been an active war zone since the 1940s and the end of the Second World War. However, that does not mean that older people living in the Britain have not experienced living in war zones. There are, arguably, three ways in which British citizens experience sustained conflict and tension which impacts on being an older person: living through war earlier in life; migration into Britain away from conflict; and the introduction of conflict and oppression into everyday life as a result of socially experienced ill-health such as dementia.

### Experiencing past conflict and life course

First, very many of the oldest old in Britain today lived through the Second World War. They may have experienced direct conflict. They may have lost close friends and family. They may have lost their homes to bombing or been forced to relocate away from centres of bombing, often separated from parents and wider families. Second, people may be immigrants into Britain, fleeing from conflict areas – very much in our consciousness at the moment are those fleeing conflict in Syria, but the British population includes many who have fled earlier conflicts such as in Cyprus. For these older people, they may have a complex sense of what and where 'home' is and may have experienced considerable separation from family members (Botsford *et al.* 2011).

The life-course approach to understanding the experiences of older people is critical, as emphasised by Regev. Britain has developed a range of interventions that focus on life-story work and which seek to support people to re-tell, or re-narrate, their lives as a way of integrating their past and present experiences (Keyes *et al.* 2014). Often this has focused on those whose identity is threatened through the development of dementia. However, to date, we have a relatively poor understanding of how childhood and early adult experiences impact on later life – for example, in what ways does post-traumatic stress disorder developed during times in a conflict zone impact on well-being in later life; in what ways does conflict-related separation from family result in attachment disorder and how does this influence social relationships and help-seeking abilities in older age? For those older people who have relocated to Britain from conflict areas earlier in life, how are they to reconcile the sense of belonging to somewhere that they are unable to return to, with a sense of distance and even perhaps alienation from their immediate social and physical environment (Botsford *et al.* 2011). These social connections, developed over a lifetime, are critical to an older person's resilience – in a multinational study of people over the age of 65 years, Moyle *et al.* (2010) found that maintaining community connections, particularly across the generations, was critical to engendering positive mental health for older people – and experiences of being in a conflict area may compromise this.

## Experiencing current conflict and exclusion

If we ask ourselves whether any of Britain's older population are living in situations of conflict in the present day, the answer has to be 'yes' if we draw on micro-sociological concepts such as domestic abuse and the psychological undermining experienced by people with cognitive loss such as dementia (Clarke *et al.* 2010). What characterises these experiences that individuals may have, is a loss of power and influence within their own lives and exclusion from participation from decision-making together with threats to their sense of identity, safety and security. It results in living with a sense of oppression. Beard and Fox (2008) argue that a diagnosis of dementia can lead to 'social disenfranchisement', in which the person with dementia is viewed as having a rupture in their biography, with habitual ways of living being compromised.

The social and psychological changes that are a consequence of a diagnosis of dementia mean that the 'everyday relationships and attachments to, with and between people and place', which are significant aspects of how a person may or may not continue to affirm their identity, are compromised (Bailey *et al.* 2013). Indeed, a proportion of people with dementia feel that there are shortfalls in their inclusion in their community – the Alzheimer Society (Alzheimer's Research UK 2012) reported that 22 per cent of people with dementia did not feel part of their community and 38 per cent only sometimes felt part of their community. Similarly, members of the general public recognised a lack of inclusion in their community for people with dementia, with 60 per cent indicating that inclusion was fairly, or very, bad (Alzheimer's Research UK 2012).

# Conclusion

The examples above of the ways in which older people in Britain may experience conflict, illustrate the importance of the social fabric and everyday relationship between the individual and their social environment and the tensions, for some, between a sense of belonging and a sense of alienation – some of the key issues highlighted in Regev's chapter.

As well as social networks, in situations of conflict, people draw on their inner resources and resilience, defined by Windle (2010) as 'the process of effectively negotiating, adapting to, or managing significant sources of stress or trauma' (Windle 2010: 152). Collins and Smyer (2005) argue that older people use a range of cognitive strategies to protect their self-esteem and well-being and deploy different sources of strength to adapt constructively to stressful life events (Janssen *et al.* 2011). The mental health of older people can be protected through social support, informal help and resources, and access to social networks (Dowrick *et al.* 2008; Mehta *et al.* 2008) and the reduction of loneliness in old age (Victor *et al.* 2005) – the challenge lies in better understanding the role of past and present conflict when accessing such support.

To understand the complexity of the issues highlighted here requires novel ways of understanding physical and mental health aging which are grounded in an exploration of the contribution of life course, society and culture to conferring risk, resilience and rights in the experience of ill-health and well-being. Critical research questions which need to be addressed are:

1 How do life time accumulated risks and resiliencies, shaped by society and culture, influence later life?
2 How can societies and care services engage with a life-course perspective to optimise well-being?
3 How do older people interact with their social and physical environment to assert their citizenship?

# References

Alzheimer's Research UK, 2012. *The power to defeat dementia* [online]. Alzheimer's Research UK. Available from: www.alzheimersresearchuk.org [Accessed 29 November 2012].

Bailey, C., Clarke, C.L., Gibb, C., Haining, S., Wilkinson, H. and Tiplady, S., 2013. 'Risky and resilient life with dementia. Review of and reflections on the literature', *Health, Risk & Society* 15(5): 390–401.

Beard, R., and Fox, P., 2008. 'Resisting social disenfranchisement. Negotiating collective identities and everyday life with memory loss', *Social Science and Medicine* (66): 1509–20.

Botsford, J., Clarke, C.L., and Gibb, C.E., 2011. 'Research and dementia, caring and ethnicity. A review of the literature', *Journal of Research in Nursing* 16(5), 437–49.

Clarke, C.L. *et al.*, 2010. 'Dementia and risk. Contested territories of everyday life', *Journal of Nursing and Healthcare in Chronic Illness* 2(2): 102–12.

Collins, A., and Smyer, M.A., 2005. 'The resilience of self-esteem in late adulthood', *Journal of Aging and Health* 17(4): 471–89.

Dowrick, C., Kokanovic, R., Hegarty, K., Griffiths, F. and Gunn, J., 2008. 'Resilience and depression. Perspectives from primary care', *Health* 12(4): 439–52.

Janssen, B., van Regenmortel, T., and Abma, T., 2011. 'Identifying sources of strength. Resilience from the perspective of older people receiving long-term community care', *European Journal of Ageing* 8(3): 145–56.

Keyes, S.E., Clarke, C.L., and Wilkinson, H., 2014. ' "We're all thrown in the same boat…". A qualitative analysis of peer support in dementia care', *Dementia*. Available online at: http://dem.sagepub.com/content/early/2014/04/04/1471301214529575 [Accessed 10 January 2016].

Mehta, M., Whyte, E., Lenze, E., Hardy, S., Roumani, Y., Subashan, P., *et al.*, 2008. 'Depressive symptoms in late life. Associations with apathy, resilience and disability vary between young-old and old-old', *International Journal of Geriatric Psychiatry* (23): 238–43.

Moyle, W., Clarke, C.L., Gracia, N., Reed, J., Cook, G., Klein, B., Marais, S. and Richardson, E., 2010. 'Older people maintaining mental health well-being through resilience. An appreciative inquiry study in four countries', *Journal of Nursing and Healthcare in Chronic Illness* 2(2): 113–21.

Victor, C.R., Scambler, S.J., Bowling, A. and Bond, J., 2005. 'The prevalence of, and risk factors for, loneliness in old age. A survey of older people in Great Britain', *Ageing & Society* (25): 357–75.

Windle, G., 2010. 'What is resilience? A review and concept analysis', *Reviews in Clinical Gerontology* 21(2): 152–69.

# 31 Migrant workers

## Statute limitation and the missing social work

*Kartini Aboo Talib*

This chapter examines the conditions of domestic migrant workers in Malaysia due to legal limitations and the absence of a qualified social work service which leads to intolerable abuse. The cases of abuse of migrant workers and the violation of human rights has affected Malaysia's world ranking in the Trafficking in Persons Report of 2014 (U.S. State Department). This chapter delineates the limitations and shares a few feasible suggestions for overcoming the issues.

Migration has been defined as a change of residence which might include states and provinces at the national level or from one country to another at the international level (Voss *et al.* 2001; Roseman 1971). Migrant workers in Malaysia mainly come from Indonesia, Bangladesh, Myanmar, Vietnam, Cambodia, and the Philippines. The majority of migrant workers in Malaysia are labourers, who may have low levels of education in their country of origin. In fact, new surroundings, rules, cultures, and values make adaptation a difficult process for migrants. New migrant workers take long periods of time to accommodate into their new society and successful integration requires active participation on the part of local authorities (Jennissen 2007; Schoeni 1998; Pettigrew 1998). Suàrez-Orozco (1991) points out that minority groups – which he refers to as a foreign-born generation in the host society – are often left behind in education and cross-cultural integration. Immigrants in Malaysia are workers migrating from other countries carrying with them hopes of starting a new life and prospering economically in the host country. However, often they are poor and uneducated, which limits their opportunity to find suitable jobs.

Slack and Jensen (2007), and Chandra (1985) propose that local authorities should consider creating an information system for immigrants. The success of integrating immigrants into local society could be increased by the provision by local authorities of a learning centre to help new inhabitants learn the language of the country and to further assist them entering into the labour market. Social work can always add value to this form of assistance to migrant workers, for example by facilitating and assisting in a learning centre for immigrants.

### Missing social work

The well-being of migrant workers in Malaysia can be questioned based on the insufficient protection in the present legal system, for example the Employment

Act of 1995. In Malaysia social work agencies do not deal with migrants. This situation is due to a few reasons: first, social welfare services are provided for citizens only, thus the rules automatically deny access to non-citizens. Second, social work has the focus of helping only those people in need as defined by the social welfare services including elderly people, people with disabilities, people who live below the poverty line, etc. This list does not include migrant workers – although their manner of entrance is legal, their rights are limited. Third, social work in Malaysia is concentrated in the medical and patient context only. It is clear that the need for professional social work in other areas is vital. Social workers could, for example, assist victims by integrating all sources of assistantship and enhancing social justice in a credible manner.

## Cases of abused migrants

From 2000 to 2007, more than 1,000 abuse cases of legal migrants were reported to the authorities (Yuspilman Asli *et al.* 2007). In the physical abuse cases most victims were maids from Indonesia. Some victims suffered tremendous injury and were treated in Intensive Care Units (ICU) or died (Ibrahim 2010). The abused victims commonly seek shelter and assistance from the Indonesian embassy. The media highlighted several forms of abuse including physical and mental abuse, rape and assault, non-payment for work performed, discrimination, ending of contracts without prior notice, contract renewal by force, insufficient compensation, strenuous workloads in several different places that deviate from the actual contract, the holding of passport and entry paperwork without consent, and life without medical insurance and sick leave (Talib *et al.* 2012). Highly publicised maid-abuse cases have triggered anger among segments of Indonesian society. Although both states are able to handle such issues separately so as not to let it develop into a serious conflict, relations are strained, and procedures clearly need to be established to curb massive protest[1] by the masses.

Case 1: Ceriyati Daplin,[2] 37 years old, a mother with a handicapped son, had no choice but to work as a migrant domestic worker in order to support her family and to assist her husband Ridwan, who worked as an Ojek (motorcycle taxi) driver in Central Java. She came to Malaysia in 2006 after being recruited as a domestic worker with a working contract of MYR450[3] a month. Problems developed at work when she was frequently assigned to complete administrative office tasks for her employer's wife which were not suited to her skills level. Due to her frequent mistakes, she was regularly slapped, kicked and beaten on the head. She was given only one meal a day with tap water. Ceriyati's weight dropped drastically due to starvation. She ran away after she could no longer stand the continuous physical abuse from her employer. She filed a formal legal complaint with the Malaysian police assisted by the Indonesian embassy.

Case 2: *Nirmala Bonat vs. Yim Pek Ha*: The Kuala Lumpur Session Court sentenced housewife Yim Pek Ha to 18 years in jail after she was found guilty of three charges: four counts of voluntarily causing injury to 19-year-old Nirmala Bonat, incidents with a hot iron, hot water and a metal cup at her house. Each offence under Section 326 of the Penal Code carries a maximum of 20 years in jail, a fine or whipping. The Court of Appeals has turned down her appeal.

Case 3: In another case in October 2009, the court sentenced a night trader to death for the murder of an Indonesian maid, Mantik Hani. The Muntik case in 2009 was alarming and heartbreaking to most Malaysians. Muntik, also known as Mantik, was a 36-year-old maid from Indonesia. She was physically abused by her employer, Mr. A Murugan from Klang. The victim was pronounced dead after all efforts to save her failed. She suffered extreme physical injury and was found by a janitor on a bathroom floor with her head half-shaved, unable to breathe, and too weak to respond to any medication (Ibrahim 2010).

Different approaches are utilised to resolve these issues through courts, tribunals, mediation, and negotiation. Cases involving rape, assault and battery are processed in the courts, while cases such as insufficient wages, contract breaches, and discrimination are resolved through internal mechanisms including tribunals, mediation, and negotiation. Such cases take years to settle. If a settlement is reached, compensation is often insufficient to cover the physical and emotional damages caused by an abusive employer.

If a legal migrant faces any type of discrimination at work, or unpaid salary, he or she can lodge a report to the labour office. An investigation will be conducted and action will be taken under the employment act. However, this action is impossible for illegal migrant workers. Looking at the processes that took place before the court, none involves a social work agency or unit as a platform for abused legal migrants to channel their complaints and grievances, or to seek temporary shelter.

## Law: the master–servant element

The root of this problem is that the Malaysian legal system does not have the capability to protect legal migrants and especially domestic workers. The law is viewed as a possible way to regulate and discipline the labour force (Snyder and Hay 1987: 7), but regarding coercive enforcement it most often favours a master-and-servant model. Although ironically effective in this regard, on a wider scale it has many times been detrimental to workers (Snyder and Hay 1987: 14ff).

A glaring weakness in the Employment Act of 1955 is that there is no specific definition of domestic work in the Act itself, and this exposes migrant workers such as maids to exploitation. Such absence excludes domestic workers from enjoying rest days, having clear working hours, and employment benefits. As a result they are on call for work 24 hours a day and seven days a week without a break in a year. It is time for the law to grant labour rights and protection to domestic legal migrant workers (Hassan 2007).

Section 2 of the 1955 Act defines a foreign employee as an employee who is not a citizen. Part XIIB of the Act is the only part dealing specifically with migrant workers. Under this provision, the Director General is empowered to inquire into any complaints made by the foreign worker regarding discrimination pertaining to his/her work condition or contract. However, the statutory language was designed to give the Director General the power to make inquiries rather than to provide the victim with the opportunity to speak for himself or herself in securing his or her claims. In a situation where competing interests might occur, the actual incident could be redefined by the Director General's interpretations, leading to various forms of penalty. Additionally, even if a complaint by a worker is upheld, the employer or state might face a reduced or light sentence with no compensation reserved for the employee or victim of abuse.

The Malaysian Industrial Relations Act of 1967 Section 17(1) and the Trade Unions Act of 1959 both contain provisions that do not prohibit legal migrant workers from participating in trade unions (Hassan 1996; Hassan and Rahman 2009). However, some limitations apply in Section 28 of the Trade Unions Act of 1959 where members of unions must be citizens of the federation. As a result, migrant workers are denied membership on the basis of citizenship although they could be legal alien residents of the state for a number of years.

## Strengthening the legal tool and social work involvement

There are possible strategies to overcome these issues, and prevent future abuse of migrant workers, aside from attention to the legal deficiencies. First, the Malaysian government can enforce license suspensions to agencies that have been identified as failing to conform to the government's rules for supplying maids for household assistance. Violations include recruiting and supplying under-age house maids; failing to declare the proper documents for workers, including real names and health records; failing to provide household training prior to job appointments; overcharging clients; committing fraud by registering a non-existent company that cannot be reached when complaints of unanticipated domestic problems arise (UNODC 2015). A new procedure allows the government to suspend identified licenses and the agency may then appeal to review their suspension within a week after the suspension is in effect.

Second, the government has the authority to black-list identified employers with previous or present records of abuse and to ban them from hiring maids. This black-listed employer list should be updated frequently as and when agencies that face legal charges for abusing their maids are heard in the local courts. In fact, Malaysia and Indonesia signed a Letter of Intent (LOI) in May 2010, to amend the Memorandum of Understanding (MoU) on the recruitment and placement of maids from Indonesia and the agreement granted maids one day off a week and ensured that they can keep their passport while in service.[4] Another effort by the Malaysian government to curb maid abuse and to reduce wrongdoing by maids is to make compulsory a requirement for foreign maids and employers to attend a half-day course on their respective responsibilities (Izatun 2010).

Rationally, access to justice must be provided to all employees. However, obstacles preventing migrant workers from accessing and filing their grievances are numerous, such as ignorance of the legal system, lack of education, and lack of representation at the trade union level, depriving them of receiving legal advice or representation. Article 60(1) of the Employment Act of 1955 provides access to legal migrant workers to file a complaint against an employer with the Director-General of Labor, but terms and conditions are applied to qualify such complaints. Illegal migrants, on the other hand, lack locus standi and do not qualify for such access.

Third, introducing mandatory unannounced house visits in any month of a calendar year would help the government keep track of migrant workers' safety and security. Insofar as the Employment Act of 1955 stipulates penalties for failure or non-compliance in relation to rest days, overtime, holidays, annual leave and sick leave, it could be used as a channel to observe the well-being of migrant workers.

Fourth, an interactive telephone hotline was introduced in 2007 following the case of Ceriyati Daplin, the 34-year-old Indonesian maid mentioned above, who attempted to run away after she could no longer stand the continuous physical abuse from her employer. This hotline is responsible to the Ministry of State Affairs and allows both employer and employee to file complaints and grievances.

Fifth, the government must establish a social service and welfare unit that is able to serve the needs and cope with issues of migrant workers. The existing social services are concentrated in the hospital, shelter home, prison, and juvenile departments dealing with citizens within the said contexts (see Talib, Chapter 11). The absence of a unit that focuses on migrant workers will further the agony of this deprived minority. Setting up a team for cross-cultural social work will help the government address practical matters dealing with migrants' cultural competence. This could address issues of social justice including migrants' basic rights to health care provisions, education for migrants' children, and their social security rights as employees.

## Conclusion

The government has to acknowledge that over three million legal migrants presently work in Malaysia and this significant growing force of migrant workers must be viewed seriously. The government must be able to show that a world-class standard of employment conditions exists through the provision of a legal system that will guarantee labour rights to these workers. The government should consider setting up a team for transnational social work to ensure that the health and human rights of the burgeoning number of migrants are protected. If their predicaments continue, then their experience of being part of society will be harsh.

## Notes

1  Street protests were held at the Malaysian embassy in Jakarta. The Indonesian embassy stated that there were more than 1,500 maids seeking help in their offices across Malaysia complaining of unpaid wages and physical abuse. See details at Aljazeera (2008).
2  With the help of Migrant Care, Ceriyati eventually received five months' salary from her former employer, Rp. 40 million in compensation from the government-appointed insurance agency that provides cover for migrant domestic workers, another Rp 11.5 million from the Indonesian embassy and Rp 5 million from the Central Java provincial administration. See details at ILO (2011).
3  Appr. 105 USD in October 2015.
4  Indonesia is expected to lift the maid ban. See details at asiaone news (2010).

# References

Aljazeera, 2008. *Maid abuse draws 18-year sentence. Malaysian mother of four found guilty of vicious attacks on Indonesian domestic worker* [online]. Available from: www.aljazeera.com/news/asia-pacific/2008/11/200811281524738743.html [Accessed 15 June 2015].

asiaone news, 2010. *Indonesia expected to lift maid ban in two months* [online]. Available from: http://news.asiaone.com/News/Latest%2BNews/Asia/Story/A1Story20100519-217068.html [Accessed 15 June 2015].

Chandra, A., 1985. *The family migration process in peninsular Malaysia.* Chapel Hill: The University of North Carolina at Chapel Hill.

Hassan, K.H., 1996. 'Principles of international labor standards and Malaysia law on anti union discrimination', *Industrial Law Reports*, xxvii–xxx.

Hassan, K.H., 2007. 'Sejarah, polisi dan perundangan pekerja asing di Malaysia', in Ngah, Anisah Che *et al.*, eds, *Undang-undang Malaysia. 50 tahun merentasi zaman.* Bangi, 395–435.

Hassan, K.H., and Rahman, R.A., 2009. *Hubungan Undang-undang Majikan dan Pekerja.* 2nd ed. Kuala Lumpur: Dewan Bahasa dan Pustaka.

Ibrahim, N.A., 2010. *Peniaga di hukum gantung* [online]. Available from: http://ww1.utusan.com.my/utusan/info.asp?y=2010&dt=0720&pub=Utusan_Malaysia&sec=Mahkamah&pg=ma_01.htm [Accessed 8 January 2011].

ILO, 2011. *The story of Ceriyati. Escaping abuse in Malaysia* [online]. International Labour Organization. Available from: www.ilo.org/jakarta/info/public/WCMS_184984/lang--en/index.htm [Accessed 15 June 2015].

Izatun, S., 2010. *Foreign maids, employers must attend course from end of march* [online]. The Star online. Available from: www.thestar.com.my/story/?file=%2F2010%2F2%2F21%2Fnation%2F20100221193954 [Accessed 30 November 2015].

Jennissen, R., 2007. 'Causality chains in the international migration systems approach', *Population Research and Policy Review* 26(4): 411–36.

Pettigrew, T.F., 1998. 'Reactions toward the new minorities of Western Europe', *Annual Review of Sociology* (24): 77–103.

Roseman, C.C., 1971. 'Migration as a spatial and temporal process', *Annals of the American Geographers* 6(3): 589–98.

Schoeni, R.F., 1998. 'Labor market outcomes of immigrant women in the United States. 1970 to 1990', *Migration Review* 32(1): 57–77.

Slack, T., and Jensen, L., 2007. 'Underemployment Across Immigrant Generations', *Social Science Research* 36(4): 1415–30.

Snyder, F.G., and Hay, D., 1987. 'Comparison in the Social History of Law. Labour and Crime', in F.G. Snyder and D. Hay, eds, *Labour, law, and crime. A historical perspective.* London, New York: Tavistock Publications, 1–41.

Suàrez-Orozco, M.M., 1991. 'Migration, minority status, and education. European dilemmas and responses in the 1990s', *Anthropology & Education Quarterly* 22(2): 99–120.

Talib, K.A., Hassan, K.H., Isa, S.M., Yusoff, A., Shaikh, S. and Mustafa, C.N. 2012. Labor law and immigrants. Legal impact to minority. *Asian Social Science,* 8(6), 52–62.

U.S. State Department. *Malaysia. 2014 Trafficking in Persons Report* [online]. Available from: www.state.gov/j/tip/rls/tiprpt/countries/2014/226770.htm [Accessed 10 January 2016].

UNODC, 2015. *The role of recruitment fees and abusive and fraudulent practices of recruitment agencies in trafficking in persons* [online]. United Nations Office of Drugs and Crime. Available from: www.unodc.org/documents/human-trafficking/2015/Recruitment_Fees_Report-Final-22_June_2015_AG_Final.pdf [Accessed 8 July 2015].

Voss, P.R., Hammer, R.B., and Meier, A.M., 2001. 'Migration analysis. A case study for local public policy', *Population Research and Policy Review* 20(6): 587–603.

Yuspilman Asli, O., Yatim, N., and Kumar, A., 2007. *Adakah kita kejam? Berikutan kes terbaru penderaan pembantu rumah Indonesia* [online]. Available from: http://ww1.utusan. com.my/utusan/special.asp?pr=PR11&y=2007&dt=0618&pub=Utusan_Malaysia&sec= Muka_Hadapan&pg=mh_01.htm [Accessed 7 January 2015].

# 32 Domestic migrant workers in China

## Silent victims and social work interventions

## Comment on the Malayan case study from a Chinese perspective

*Diqing Jiang*

In 2015 a piece of news from Shenzhen drew wide public attention across China; a migrant worker in domestic service suffered serious abuse from her employer, she was unlawfully detained and had been beaten and intimidated for more than two months. Fortunately, she received aid from a social service agency. Social workers from the agency made arrangements for support and therapy, helped her to obtain compensation, and ensured her abusive employer went to prison in the end (Wang 2015). This event not only exposes serious abuses experienced by domestic migrant workers (DMW) but also shows how social work can help in a professional way.

Abuse is far from unusual for DMWs. However, as a form of social violence and injustice it has long been neglected. Why have so many DMWs become silent victims? Why are they unable or unwilling to resort to law or collective action to protect their interest? How can social workers help them? This chapter attempts to address those issues.

## DMWs: gender-based labour division and rapid development

Before 1978 domestic workers in China were only available to members of the most privileged classes like high-ranking officials or celebrities.[1] After China embraced economic reforms the field of domestic service boomed. Since the first of its kind was set up in 1983 (Su 2011), domestic service agencies reached 500,000 in number all over the country by 2008, with about 20 million people engaged in domestic service (XINHUANET 2007).

A variety of economic, social and political factors have contributed to the striking rise of domestic service in China. Within just one generation, the average annual income per capita increased from $195.6 in 1981 to $1,047.5 in 2001 (The World Bank). China's urban middle class has become increasingly able and willing to pay for domestic service. Furthermore, under the one-child policy, the structure of urban Chinese families has transformed as the size of the average nuclear family has decreased to less than 3.1 persons (Family division of the National Health and Family Planning Commission 2015). The country has entered the aging society and by 2014, the population aged over 60 reached 200 million (Zhang 2015). Ironically, the women's equality movement launched in part by Mao's revolution has greatly increased demand for household services – women, in cities and villages, are called 'half the sky', a phrase propagated by revolutionary slogans. Since the 1950s many of them no longer stay at home and instead become professionals in offices or factories. They often have to purchase domestic services to take care of the young and aged. Estimates put the demand for domestic services at 40 per cent of China's urban families in large cities (Li 2007).

On the other hand, the 'Household Contract Responsibility System' in the countryside has raised agricultural productivity dramatically and generated a huge number of surplus labourers (Zhou 1996). Millions of women in rural areas lacking professional skills have flocked into cities to seek jobs. Since domestic service is often regarded as a profession requiring no special training, it becomes a vehicle for absorption of those rural migrant female workers.

Short of accurate nationwide surveys, we have to rely on regional information to describe the basic characteristics of the social group of DMWs. The first thing to notice is the gender imbalance among DMWs – domestic work is a highly gender-based job (Ma 2011) and, in many large cities, primarily performed by women who are migrant workers. It appears their educational backgrounds are limited: 36.9 per cent have graduated from primary school, 37.4 per cent have dropped out of middle school, and only 15 per cent have obtained a high school diploma. DMWs get jobs either through domestic service agencies or via acquaintances. One-third of them receive pre-job training organised by those agencies.[2] Typical training programmes cover cleaning, shopping, cooking, care of children, elderly people or nursing home patients. Furthermore, many DMWs are exposed to one or several of the following six common problems:

- Discrimination – DMWs are often treated as being inferior in employers' families, e.g. some of them are not even allowed to take food at the same table with employers.
- No social benefits – the majority of DMWs have no social insurance under current social insurance law (Wang 2005). With the exception of Shanghai, local governments tend to regard domestic services as an informal sector and are reluctant to extend social benefits to the workers.
- Long working hours without overtime compensation – as many DMWs live with their employers and do not have a fixed work schedule, they often have to endure long hours. For example, in Beijing, about 40 per cent of domestic workers work about 10 hours per day and 20–35 per cent of domestic workers have no weekend breaks (Ma 2011).
- Isolation and lack of social life – most 'live-in workers' are on constant duty to serve their employers. Their social networks are highly limited. Often, the only opportunity to meet other DMWs is when they take employers' children to play in community parks.
- Lack of privacy – most 'live-in workers' do not have a private bedroom. They frequently live in the same bedroom as the children or the sick or elderly they

attend to. Thus, it is hard to demarcate the boundary between work and life for DMWs (Feng 2004).

- Sexual harassment or physical abuse – because DMWs mostly work in private and isolated environments, the public tend to seriously underestimate the problem, assuming for example that about 10 per cent of DMWs experience sexual harassment (Ma 2011). Since many victims consider sexual harassment as shame the real percentage is likely to be much higher.

## DMWs: why silent victims?

It is common for migrant workers to suffer discrimination and even abuse. Unlike workers in other fields, most DMWs choose to keep silent about their experiences and rarely seek legal advice. Several factors lead to their silence.

First, in China as in many other countries, legal protection for DMWs is needed. The current Chinese Labour Law defines the relationship between employers and DMWs as based on informal service agreements rather than official labour contracts. This makes it difficult for DMWs to obtain legal support – and when there is an open dispute between DMWs and employers, they normally lose the battle on legal grounds (Hu 2011).

Second, since domestic labour is widely regarded as being part of the informal sector, there are few government agencies devoted to the regulation and well-being of DMWs (Sun and Guo 2013). The Ministry of Human Resources and Social Security only provides guidelines on their professional skills' training. Many cities establish Domestic Service Associations to provide job information and offer training to DMWs, but, on the whole, these semi-governmental associations are unable to implement regulations protecting DMWs without legislative support.

Third, due to low educational levels, most DMWs lack awareness of their rights. For example, when their employers refuse to give them holidays, DMWs usually do not know their rights and therefore do not push for time off or claim compensation.

Finally, DMWs often have limited time or means with which to communicate with one another or share their experiences (Su 2011). Therefore, it is difficult for them to generate agreements or a sense of common identity, which are preconditions for collective struggles for justice.

## How social work can help

As the abuse case in Shenzhen illustrates, the role of social workers is important – they can act as case managers, counsellors or therapists to protect DMWs or act as resource brokers to connect communities and lawyers to promote DMWs' well-being. On the one hand, the professional skills of social workers enable DMWs to realise and defend their rights and interests; on the other hand, social workers' professional reputation and social status can bring pressure on the government and local communities to offer effective support. The testimony of social work professionals can influence judges' decisions to punish abusive employers.

In sum, social work can help DMWs at different levels; on a micro level, social workers can provide counselling and therapy; on a meso level, social workers can cooperate with domestic service agencies and local communities to implement training programmes for DMWs; on a macro level, social work can influence social policy in favour of the disadvantaged (Adams 2002).Though it is hard to reform policies in the short term, it is possible for social workers to cooperate with NGOs to achieve this goal. For instance, non-governmental organisations such as the Cultural Development Centre for Rural Women, which is affiliated to the All-China Women's Federation, has spent years drafting a legal proposal for the household service sector in Beijing (Shen 2011).

China's economic and social reforms require effective social support for those in need, including children, families and elderly people. The increasing demand for domestic work in urban society requires more legal protection for migrant workers in domestic service. This situation makes it imperative for social workers to contribute to support and protect DMWs.

## Notes

1 Under Mao's centrally planned economy, the government hired domestic workers for officials of rank (Yan 2006).
2 Survey conducted by an NGO named Dagongmei zhijia (Home of female rural workers) in 2005. See Zhao *et al.* (2011).

## References

Adams, R., 2002. *Social policy for social work*. Basingstoke: Palgrave.

Family division of the National Health and Family Planning Commission, 2015. *China Family Development Report. Zhongguo Jiating Fazhan Baogao*. Beijing: China Population Press.

Feng, X., 2004. 'zhuanxing shehui zhong de baomu yu guzhu guanxi', in X. Meng, ed., *Zhuan xing she hui zhong de Zhongguo fu nü*. Beijing: Zhongguo she hui ke xue chu ban she, 25–46.

Hu, D., 2011. 'Woguo Fada Diqu Jiazheng Fuwuyuan Laodongquanyi Baozhang de Falü Sikao—Jiyu Shenzhen shi de shizheng fenxi', *Henansheng zhengfa guanli ganbu xueyuan xuebao* 26(5): 135–41.

Li, J., 2007. 'Woguo jiazheng fuwuye de zhengguihua celue. The Formalization strategy of Chinese domestic services', *Exploitation of Chinese Human Resources* (3): 22–5.

Ma, D., 2011. 'Beijingshi jiazhenggong yanjiu. Study of Beijing domestic workers', *Beijing Journal of Social Science* 26(2): 64–68.

Shen, G., 2011. 'Funü minjian zuzhi de fazhan jiqi zhiduhuanjing fenxi', *Xuzhou gongcheng xueyuan xuebao (shehuikexueban)* 26(4): 18–23.

Su, Y., 2011. 'Kongzhi yu dikang: guzhu yu jiazhenggong zai jiawu laodong guochengzhong de boyi', 'Labor Control and Resistance: the Dynamics between Employers and Home Workers in the Labor Process of Domestic Work', *Chinese Journal of Sociology* (31): 178–205.

Sun, W., and Guo, Y., 2013. *Unequal China. The political economy and cultural politics of inequality*. New York: Routledge.

The World Bank. *GDP per capita (current US$)* [online]. Available from: http://data.worldbank.org/indicator/NY.GDP.PCAP.CD [Accessed 10 January 2016].

Wang, H., 2005. 'Some considerations over social insurance for domestic workers', *Journal of Insurance professional college* (3): 55–6.

Wang, Y., 2015. *Baomu beinue jiugeyue, jingshen huanghu shanghen leilei, Shenzhen Wanbao* [online]. Available from: http://wb.sznews.com/html/2015-05/07/content_3216252.htm [Accessed 5 July 2015].

XINHUANET, 2007 [online]. Available from: http://news.xinhuanet.com/newscenter/2007-11/17/content_7093196.htm [Accessed 10 January 2016].

Yan, H., 2006. 'Rurality and Labor Process Autonomy. The Question of Subsumption in the Waged Labor of Domestic Service', *Cultural Dynamics* (18): 5–31.

Zhang, C., 2015. 'Yanglao zhidu gaige yingzhan yinfa langchao. Pension System Reform in Response to Ageing Process', *Watch* 10: 34.

Zhao, S., Wang, X., and Xing, L., 2011. 'Beijingshi jiazheng fuwuye congye renyuan zhuangkuang de yanjiu fenxi', *Beijing Xingzheng Xueyuan Xuebao* (1): 107–10.

Zhou, K.X., 1996. *How the farmers changed China. Power of the people*. Boulder, Colorado: Westview Press.

# 33 Feminisation of migration – migration in a changing world

## Comment on the Malayan case study from a Turkish perspective

*Uğur Tekin*

Since the late 1980s and early 1990s, with the regime changes in neighbouring socialist countries, Turkey has become a target destination for new waves of immigrants from countries in Central Asia and the Black Sea region and countries of the former Soviet Union. With the end of the Cold War, citizens of the former Eastern Bloc countries who had difficulties getting out of their countries can now do so more easily. However, they now face visa regulations adopted as restrictive policies by the Western European countries in order to regulate migration. Thus migration not only affects the member states of the EU but also candidate states and third countries. With its geographic location, flexible visa regulations and candidacy of the EU, Turkey serves both as a bridge for many asylum seekers heading to Europe and as an alternative to those who cannot reach Europe (Kirişci 2003).

Labour migration into Turkey has two characteristic features which are also observed in international labour migration in different parts of the world; one feature is the increase in women's participation in international migration (the feminisation of migration) (Akis 2012: 379ff), while the other is that immigrant workers hold a semi-legal status under precarious conditions and with low wages (irregular migration) (Atasü-Topçuoğlu 2012: 501ff). With the globalisation of production (e.g. trade of goods, international fragmentation of production to countries with cheap labour) comes also the globalisation of social care work. In particular, the demand for highly educated workers opens up windows for well-educated women. At the same time the load of social care work is still seen as women's work. Thus immigrant women become major elements in an irregular transnational market. The labour that provides reproduction (domestic labour) constitutes an international hierarchical structure; at the top of this hierarchy there are the native women in immigration-receiving countries who are liberalising themselves from unpaid domestic labour. Immigrant women are at the second level and female relatives in emigration countries who cannot find the means or opportunities to migrate and provide domestic and caretaking services – at home – are at the bottom of the hierarchy (Parrenas 2000). Thus, migration of women supports the inclusion of women from different regions into the labour market.

After the dissolution of the Soviet Union, Turkey adopted flexible visa regulations in order to develop free trade with the countries of the Black Sea Basin, Central Asia and the Middle East. In 1992, with the founding of the

Organization of the Black Sea Economic Cooperation, the practice of entry through border visas was adopted in order to provide easy movement to people coming from these countries.[1] As a result, throughout the 1990s, there were rising export and import activities called the 'suitcase trade' between Turkey and Russia, Ukraine, Georgia, Azerbaijan, Romania, Moldova, Armenia and the Central Asian Republics (Kirişçi 2011).

Flexible visa regulations not only supported border trade but also motivated many people to work abroad, earn money and then return to their countries. These immigrants enter Turkey with a tourist visa, return to their countries when the visa expires and then come back to work when they need it (circular migration). On one hand, immigrants can cross borders to enter the labour market easily in Turkey, where the informal economy is strong and informal employment is commonplace. On the other hand, promoting factors such as unemployment, low income, commodification of education and healthcare and the search for a better life have surely been determinant in people's decisions to migrate (İçduygu 2007).

## Female labour migration to Turkey

In Turkey, the sector with the strongest demand for immigrant labour is domestic and caretaking services, which constitute a gendered sector, open mainly to female labour. A significant proportion of women who come to Turkey to work in domestic and caretaking services enter Turkey as tourists for a limited period of time, work without a work permit and usually extend their stay and continue to live in Turkey illegally (Erder 2007). Because the current welfare state regime in Turkey offers extremely insufficient institutional social care e.g. for children, or especially the elderly and sick, informal care is often provided by the family. When the family cannot provide care, it must be acquired from the labour market. Since local women do not prefer to offer live-in services, there is a strong demand for immigrant women in the domestic care sector. Immigrant women prefer to stay with a family and provide 24-hour care services for the following reasons: solving their accommodation issues, providing monetary advantages like reduced food expenses, the opportunity of hiding from the police by living in a secluded and safe home environment (Erder 2007). Beside the expectation of 24-hour care the employment of a migrant domestic worker has other advantages – education levels are higher and work discipline is stronger among immigrant female caregivers when compared to their Turkish counterparts (Erder 2006). Moreover, their lack of legal rights with no support from any organisation makes them more vulnerable and in greater demand than locals. The main reason behind the vulnerability of immigrant women is their illegal status and lack of a work permit. Immigrant women's wages might not be lower than what locals earn simply because they are staying in Turkey with a tourist visa (Erder 2007). However, they work without any insurance, they do not get paid for overtime despite the long hours, and they work without annual paid leave and similar social rights. They are cheaper to employ and preferred over local women. From one perspective these working conditions within a family look safe, but from another, they may also create a situation open to all kinds of abuse. Relevant studies revealed the forms of violence and abuse suffered, such as not receiving their well-earned wages on some occasions, humiliation, physical and sexual harassment, denial of their weekend leave, getting locked inside the house, not receiving meals, and being forced to hand wash clothes and dishes (Kalfa 2008; Atatimur 2008; Ozinian 2009). A significant proportion of immigrant women continue to work under these adverse conditions due to the lack of any mechanisms to protect them.

## Legal domain

Changes have been brought by Law no 4817 (Law on the Work Permit for Foreigners) which was enacted in 2003, and Law no 6458 (Law on Foreigners and International Protection) which was enacted in 2013. These laws opened the door for the adoption of modern and universal legal norms on granting work permits. With these legal changes, for the first time in Turkey, the integration of foreign immigrants was defined as a responsibility of the state. With the 2013 Law, an institution named the Directorate General of Migration Management was founded with the expectation to specialise in foreign migrants and to provide solutions to their issues. However, despite these legal and institutional changes, in practice, not much improvement has yet been achieved to solve the problems of immigrant workers, e.g. there has been no change in the policies that restrict immigrant workers in a series of fields. Failing to address immigrants' problems, these new regulations are in fact pushing them out of the legal domain and failing to provide effective protection against human rights violations faced by the immigrants (Özçelik 2013: 255).

Apart from several non-governmental organisations working for human rights advocacy with very limited resources, there are no organisations in Turkey for the protection of immigrant women's rights employed in domestic and caretaking services. In order for the irregularly migrating women from former Eastern Bloc countries to Turkey to live and work with human dignity, the visa and employment policies must be regulated by international standards. This would include the participation of public institutions and of non-governmental organisations, trade unions and immigrant-run organisations. The isolation these immigrants working in the domestic area experience prevents them from forming protective organisations or raising political demands. Therefore, the problems surrounding international migration should be discussed and approaches need to be developed on local, national and international levels for global migration management. Platforms for debate and political decision-making should bring together actors of international migration including public institutions, non-governmental organisations and immigrants' organisations. In addition to the steps to be taken by national and international mechanisms to regulate (immigrant) women's rights, it is also important for the media, human rights organisations and women's organisations to make efforts in preventing violations of rights, discrimination, stigmatisation, and abuse towards immigrant women.

# Note

1 Turkey's liberal visa regime was a main point of criticism by the EU during the membership negotiations between the EU and Turkey. The EU wants Turkey to adopt the restrictive Schengen visa regime as soon as possible.

# References

Akis, Y., 2012. 'Uluslararası Zorunlu Göç Literatüründe Toplumsal Cinsiyet. Başlıca Yaklaşimlar ve Eleştiriler', in S.G. Ihlamur-Öner and N.A. Şirin Öner, eds, *Küreselleşme Çağında Göç.* İstanbul: İletişim Yayıncılık, 379–98.

Atasü-Topçuoğlu, R., 2012. 'Düzensiz Göç. Küreselleşmede Kısıtlanan İnsan Hareketliliği', in S.G. Ihlamur-Öner and N.A. Şirin Öner, eds, *Küreselleşme Çağında Göç.* İstanbul: İletişim Yayıncılık, 501–18.

Atatimur, N., 2008. *Reasons and consequences of international labor migration of women into Turkey. Ankara case.* Master's thesis: Middle East Technical University.

Erder, S., 2006. 'Yabancısız Kurgulanan Ülkenin Yabancıları', in A. Arı, ed., *Uluslararası Göç, İşgücü ve Nüfus Hareketleri.* İstanbul: Derin Yayınları, 1–74.

Erder, S., 2007. '"Yabancısız" Kurgulanan Ülkenin "Yabancıları"', in A. Arı, ed., *Türkiye'de Yabancı İşçiler. Uluslararası Göç, İşgücü ve Nüfus Hareketleri.* İstanbul: Derin Yayınları, 1–82.

İçduygu, A., 2007. *Türkiye-Avrupa Birliği İlişkileri Bağlamında Uluslararası Göç Tartışmaları.* İstanbul: TÜSİAD.

Kalfa, A., 2008. *Eski Doğu Bloku Ülkeleri Kaynaklı İnsan Ticareti ve Fuhuş Sektöründe Çalışan Kadınlar.* Master's thesis: Ankara University.

Kirişci, K., 2003. *Turkey. A transformation from emigration to immigration* [online]. Migration Policy Institute (MPI). Available from: www.migrationpolicy.org/article/turkey-transformation-emigration-immigration [Accessed 30 December 2015].

Kirişçi, K., 2011. 'Turkey's "demonstrative effect" and transformation in the Middle East', *Insight Turkey* 13(2): 33–5.

Özçelik, G.B., 2013. 'Yabancılar ve Uluslararası Koruma Kanunu Hükümleri Uyarınca Yabancıların Türkiye'den Sınır Dışı Edilmesi', *Türkiye Barolar Birliği Dergisi* (108): 211–58.

Ozinian, A., 2009. *Identifying the state of Armenian migrants in Turkey* [online]. Eurasia Partnership Foundation (EPF). Available from: http://epfarmenia.am/wp-content/uploads/2014/06/epf_migration_report_feb_2010_final_march_5_1.pdf [Accessed 10 January 2016].

Parrenas, R.S., 2000. 'Migrant and domestic workers and the international division of reproductive labour', *Gender & Society* 14(4): 560–80.

# 34 Returnees

## Neither there nor here, at Araf[1]

*Filiz Demiröz*

Migration is defined in various contexts depending on where the focus is – the destinations, the causes or occasionally the consequences. Turkey is both an immigrant-receiving and an emigrant-sending country within and beyond her territory. This study focuses on the people returning after migrating abroad.

Although migration often starts individually, its processes continue with families and open a period of change involving both immigrant-receiving and emigrant-sending countries. One of the dimensions experienced during the migration processes is repatriation. Therefore I especially wanted to focus on a family who lives between two countries, the Yilmaz family. As understood in transnational social work there are many families like the Yilmaz family and these need trans-boundary services because of their complex life across borders (Furman *et al.* 2010).

## Case study

Fatma Yilmaz applied to a social service centre. The social worker there asked about her motives. Fatma had had an arranged marriage with Ali, who was a worker in a car factory in Germany. She said she liked her husband and they had a happy marriage. When they emigrated to Germany she was scared at first but after attending language courses and starting to speak German she felt more comfortable. They have three children; the elder daughter Zeynep works at a bank, is divorced and has one child, the middle son Ahmet is married and has one child. The younger daughter Ayşe is attending high school. Fatma mentioned that after living in Germany for 56 years, being a returnee in 2012 was difficult and she enumerated the difficulties. Their son and younger daughter returned to Turkey as well. Their elder daughter stayed in Germany and being apart from this daughter made the parents sad.

### *First phase: migration from Turkey to Western Europe*

Emigration from Turkey for working purposes began at the signing of a Labour Recruitment Agreement with the Federal Republic of Germany in 1961 and continued with other bilateral labour recruitment agreements signed with various European countries. During this period objectives and expectations have changed dramatically for emigrants and for the residents of immigrant-receiving countries. There are different periods defined for this migration process: the period between 1961 and 1973 is defined as the early period of migration. Initially, urbanite and well-educated male emigrants chose to emigrate (Abadan Unat 2015). At first men left their wives and children behind for the purpose of earning money to afford a house, land and/or arable fields. During this time there have been changes in intra-familial relationships and family role distribution. While the role and responsibilities undertaken by women increased, empowerment of women and their participation in decision-making processes did not take place at the same rate (Yenisey 1976; Sayıl 1977; Gitmez 1983; Kağıtcıbaşı 1985). There are children living with single parents while other children need to stay with relatives. Changes in the family structure caused by migration processes brought about a loss of familiarity within families, including estrangement and alienation (Gitmez 1983; Dilsiz 1977; Hisli 1985).

Men that emigrated alone in that early period were stressed due to not knowing the language of their new country. Also, there were difficulties in meeting basic needs, including accommodation, nutrition and health. Homesickness, loneliness and uncertainties derived from living in an unknown environment led to psychological disorders. For these reasons, those who achieved their goals in the first stage and those who could not orientate themselves returned home in the first three years of emigration (Abadan Unat 1977; Toksöz 2006; Gitmez 1983; Gökdere 1978; Tufan 1987; Küçükkaraca 1998). Those who could orientate themselves to working life wanted their family nearby. Women's participation in this process began with the need for a female labour force in Germany at the beginning of the 1970s and continued with family reunifications (Abadan Unat 1977; Abadan Unat 2006; Toksöz 2006).

Families mostly started to live abroad after the oil crisis in 1973. During this period European countries stopped importing labourers and started to fulfil their needs from the existing labour force, including from children of immigrants. When family unifications started to occur, services were increased in many European countries in order to assist labourers and their families. Although language problems were somewhat resolved, housing and health services continued to be major problems. Emigration of children created new challenges, including child-care and education (Abadan Unat 1977). The children often failed educationally because they emigrated at an older age, had insufficient language knowledge as well as lack of knowledge of the new education system, high expectations of their families, and prejudice regarding German society (Abadan Unat 1977; Demiröz and Diğerleri 1985; Tezcan 1987; Tufan and Yıldız 1993). Although families conform with the dominant societies' work-life they preserve their original norms and values through their family lives. Fearing losing their children to a foreign environment results in an increase in oppressive cultural attitudes. This sometimes causes children to be sent back to Turkey to live with relatives (Tufan 1987; Demiröz and Diğerleri 1985; Tufan and Yıldız 1993; Yörükoğlu 1985).

Coming back to the Yilmaz family: Fatma told the social worker that her son Ahmet was working as a stonemason in a German firm, was married and was the father of a child with a German woman. As one of the neighbours made negative comments regarding Turks, the family decided that Fatma, with her younger daughter, her son Ahmet and his wife Helga and their son Deniz should all return to Turkey. The social worker talked about how difficult it is to repatriate and start a new life back in Turkey. Fatma told of her son's failure in his new business venture. This process caused disputes between husband and wife. The social worker advised that he could send his CV to German-owned companies operating in Turkey. The social worker also advised Fatma to support her daughter-in-law and gave her information about language centres. They planned to talk about her daughter, Zeynep, who was in Germany, at the next meeting. Zeynep was born in Germany when Fatma started to work, but was initially left in Turkey with her grandmother. She came back to Germany to start school, but she had problems with the language and adapting to her parents. With support from the Consulate's Education Attaché and associations like Türk-Danis, Zeynep worked hard and became literate.

### Second phase: migration from Western Europe to Turkey

Starting from 1980, west European countries started to impose visas on Turkish citizens. Some other measures also preventing family unifications were as well on the agenda, for example, during 1983–1984 the German government applied some incentives for people going back to their home country. Besides these incentives decisions to return were made due to reasons such as insufficient health care, fear of losing children, education of the children, unemployment, xenophobia, retirement (Abadan-Unat 2015; Toksöz 2006; Erdoğan *et al.* 2013). Neither the home country nor their relatives were as they had been when they left. As one worker stated: they were foreigners abroad and 'Germans' at home. In research caried out by Demiröz (1989a) difficulties faced by the families were as follows:

1  Difficulties finding a job or setting up a business were determined as the most important problems. Most of the families returned home unprepared and could not find secure investments or made bad investments (Abadan-Unat 2015; Gitmez 1983; Küçükkaraca 1998; Güven 1977; Yasa 1979; Köksal 1986).

2  The second largest difficulty faced by returned families were relations with their relatives (Köksal 1986: 154f).

3  Difficulties regarding relations with the neighbours come in third place of importance: most of the neighbours criticise their family life and the behaviour of their children, most families stated that they were generally establishing relationships with families who had also been abroad as they face the same difficulties (Yenisey 1976; Yasa 1979; Gürel and Kudat 1978).

4  The fourth difficulty regards housing and residence: most of the families complained about not having the same facilities at their houses and the residing area as they had had abroad (Demiröz 1989b).

5  The fifth difficulty concerns the education of their children; this difficulty stems from differences in the education systems between the two countries

and from insufficient knowledge of the native language (Tufan 1987; Demiröz and Diğerleri 1985; Tezcan 1987).

6   Intra-family relationship difficulties rank last: as most of the difficulties are derived from external factors, intra-family relationships are required to be stronger in the process of reorientation (Abadan Unat 1977; Yenisey 1976; Kağıtcıbaşı 1985; Tufan 1987; Demiröz 1998; Demiröz 2000; Demiröz 2003).

During these years it was determined that repatriations were less than expected (Abadan-Unat 2015; Toksöz 2006; Tufan 1987; Demiröz 1989a). Each stage – the refugee movements in the 1980s, asylum seekers in the 1990s, irregular migration movements such as education and illegal employment in the 2000s – has brought a different dimension to the migration process, especially for Germany (Abadan-Unat 2015; Toksöz 2006; Sırkeci *et al.* 2012). Therefore, repatriations are no longer the same as those experienced in the early 1980s. It is evident that even those who intend to return to the country of origin frequently fail to turn their thoughts into action, and that these are not definite returns as they prefer to live in both countries (Abadan-Unat 2015; Diehl and Liebau 2015).

Coming back to the case study: at the beginning of the third meeting Fatma reported that she had achieved successful results after speaking to her son and daughter-in-law. The social worker reminded Fatma that the interview was arranged for the issues related to Zeynep. Fatma said that her daughter had had a difficult childhood, the university education had been good for her but she was unhappy in her marriage, which had been an arranged one, and neither party knew each other in advance. After the wedding feast their son-in-law came to Germany but had orientation problems. Her daughter became pregnant and after childbirth suffered postpartum depression which was compounded by violence from her husband. Her husband asked Zeynep to return to Turkey, but upon her refusal he returned alone. He accepted divorce as a condition to obtaining custody of the child. The social worker pointed out that restoring the broken relationship with their former son-in-law and his family would be feasible, for example by requesting support from elders.

In the fourth interview the social worker asked about Ayşe – Ayşe's education level in Germany corresponded to vocational high schools in Turkey and she was thinking whether to quit school or go back to Germany. The social worker informed Fatma about educational projects through the Ministry of Education, Ministry of Youth and Sports, NGOs, and EU programmes. In the next interview Fatma said that she had missed her husband and the neighbours in Germany, she did not want to give up the rights she had in Germany and she did not know how to live in two countries simultaneously.

Towards the end of the interview sessions with Fatma the social worker realised that she also benefited from the interviews – she herself experienced the conflict of values between two countries and how to address diversity issues. She realised the importance of experiencing different cultures, educational systems and study systems for social services in different countries, as well as on-site observation and evaluation of problems. She realised that previous experience gained from working with refugees and domestic migrants at a social centre supported this case study. During the consultancy she recognised the usefulness of interpersonal relationships, social services and the framework of a strengthening approach which is linked to services and resources, as well as ensuring their sustainability using mediators, counsellors and educators within a social justice approach.

Migration is a process. The generations following migrated parents do not have the same difficulties of orientation but, instead, have challenges such as protection of rights, education and xenophobia. According to research undertaken by HUGO (Erdoğan, 2013), 91 per cent of people of Turkish origin in Europe were either born in Europe or had been living in Europe for more than 11 years. Approximately half of them, meaning around 2.5 million, have the citizenship of the country that they live in. According to the latest data, nearly 3 million people of Turkish origin are living in Germany (Statistisches Bundesamt 2014: 82). Half of them preserve Turkish citizenship. In spite of increases in permanency the feeling of belonging to Turkey and of Turkishness is getting stronger. People of Turkish origin residing in Europe have the perception of not having a problem with integration (Erdoğan, 2013). Therefore, living in both countries is more pronounced than the idea of returning to their homeland.

Young people, particularly those belonging to the third generation, have different characteristics compared to their families, as they were born and fully grew up abroad. However, families want to raise them according to their own rules. This generates particular difficulties for women. Another difficulty concerns ghettoes or districts formed solely by people of Turkish origin which increases discrimination and negative reactions by other people towards them (Abadan-Unat 2015; Moosa-Mitha and Ross-Sheriff 2010).

Returning to a home country is no longer viewed as it was in the 1980s – families now have simultaneous lives in both countries. An ecosystem perspective tells us that the living place and transitions between systems are important (Kirst-Ashman and Hull 1999) – if people live in both societies simultaneously, the services for them should be developed accordingly. Rights-based services such as permission to work, insurance, and equivalence of education need to be adapted. According to the Immigration Law of Germany, those who come to Germany through marriage are expected to demonstrate a basic knowledge of the German language. Knowledge about the country of destination is also required.

In relation to this case, we see that Fatma told the social worker that improvements in solving the problems of her children had been made; she had spoken to her husband and children and decided that she could live in both countries, she thought about the gains and the losses and realised that applying to the social service centre had opened the way for her.

Happy endings are rare in social work practice. For a start, availability of legal processes and statutory services are necessary. Bringing these services together with knowledge and skills, correct and efficient use of resources, and fair distribution of these resources should follow. Of course, the most important thing is to manage these processes with human dignity and a rights-based approach. Some important issues were not discussed, such as preparations required for repatriation, and what and for whom the gains and losses in the family would be. Investment in counselling services to provide information about services in Turkey is also needed. Help to get support when required and ensure coordination is important. Social services organisations, social workers to deliver services, and the appropriate structures through which to provide services are necessary. As emphasised before, staff working in this area should receive training and be aware of the importance of an intercultural approach.

## Conclusion

Studies on migration in Turkey have been developing in recent years. However, it is hard to say if they can keep up with developments in migration in this area. Discrete services specific for those returning home are few. Private organisations contribute to migrant studies by developing projects and allocating funds. In ministries, local governments, NGOs, and universities there are education and exchange programmes being developed. Services, as seen in this case, are provided by different units and through different forms (Furman *et al.* 2010; Moosa-Mitha and Ross-Sheriff 2010). Accessing these services is hard, therefore they have to be spread out. Social workers who have the knowledge of services should be authorised for coordination and be supported in such work. Social service specialists who are working in this field are few in number. There is a need to develop sensitivity, cooperation of countries and databases on a bigger scale. The goal should be to the substantial benefit of applicants.

## Note

1  ARAF: 'Somewhere in between'

## References

Abadan Unat, N., 1977. 'Dış göç akımının türk kadının özgürleşme ve sözde özgürleşme sürecine etkisi', *Amme İdaresi Dergisi* 10(1): 107–37.
Abadan Unat, N., 2006. *Bitmeyen göç-konuk işçilikten ulus – ötesi yurttaşlığa*. İstanbul: İstanbul Bilgi Üniversitesi Yayınları.
Abadan-Unat, N., 2015. 'Türkiye'nin Son Elli Yıllık Emek Göçü. Yorum, Eleştiri, Öngörü', in M.M. Erdoğan and A. Kaya, eds, *Türkiye'nin göç tarihi. 14. yüzyıldan 21. yüzyıla Türkiye'ye göçler*. İstanbul: İstanbul Bilgi Üniversitesi Yayınları, 259–76.
Demiröz, F., 1989a. *Yurtdışından dönen ailelerin Türkiye'de karşılaştıkları güçlükler*. Ankara: Hacettepe Üniversitesi Sosyal Bilimler Enstitüsü.
Demiröz, F., 1989b. *The difficulties of remigrant families in Turkey*. Basel.
Demiröz, F., 1998. 'Schwierigkeiten bei der Remigration und Lösungsvorschläge', in E. Koch *et al.*, eds, *Chancen und Risiken von Migration. Deutsch-türkische Perspektiven*. Freiburg im Breisgau: Lambertus, 83–96.
Demiröz, F., 2000. 'Yurtdışına göç sürecinin aile üzerindeki etkileri', in G. Erkan and V. Emiroğlu, eds, *Antropoloji ve yaşlılık. Prof. Dr. Vedia Emiroğlu'na armağan*. Ankara: Hacettepe Üniversitesi, Sosyal Hizmetler Yüksekokulu, 194–204.

Demiröz, F., 2003. *Die Rückkehr und die damit verbundenen Schwierigkeiten. Türkische Migrantinnen im Ausland. Probleme und Lösungsansätze.* Ankara: Internationales Symposium.

Demiröz, F., and Diğerleri, Z., 1985. *Yurtdışından dönen ve şu anda ankara'daki üniversitelerde okuyan gençlerimizin türkiye'de karşılaştıkları uyum güçlükleri.* Ankara: Hacettepe Üniversitesi, Sosyal Hizmetler Yüksekokulu.

Diehl, C., and Liebau, E., 2015. 'Turning back to Turkey – or turning the back to Germany? Remigration intentions and behavior of Turkish immigrants in Germany between 1984 and 2011', *Zeitschrift für Soziologie* 44(1): 22–41. Available from: www.zfs-online.org/index.php/zfs/article/viewFile/3194/2731 [Accessed 10 January 2016].

Dilsiz, B., 1977. *Göçmen işçi çocuklarının ruh sağlığı ve göçmen işçide tutum değişiklikleri ile ilgili bir araştırma.* Ankara: Hacettepe Üniversitesi Tıp Fakültesi Psikiyatri Bölümü Uzmanlık Tezi.

Erdoğan, M., Kaya, A., and Ünver, C., 2013. *Euro-Turks-Barometre* [online]. Hacettepe Üniversitesi Göç ve Siyaset Ara (HUGO). Available from: www.hugo.hacettepe.edu.tr/ETB_rapor.pdf [Accessed 10 January 2016].

Furman, R., Negi, N.J., and Salvador, R., 2010. 'An introduction to transnational social work', in N.J. Negi and R. Furman, eds, *Transnational social work practice.* New York: Columbia University Press, 3–19.

Gitmez, A., 1983. *Yurtdışına İşçi Göçü ve Geri Dönüşler.* Istanbul: Alan Yayıncılık.

Gökdere, A.Y., 1978. *Yabancı ülkelere işgücü akımı ve Türk ekonomisi üzerine etkileri.* Ankara: Türkiye İş Bankası Kültür Yayınları.

Gürel, S., and Kudat, A., 1978. 'Türk kadınının Avrupa'ya göçünün kişilik, aile ve topluma yansıyan sonuçları', *SBF Dergisi,* 33(314): 105–34. Available from: http://dergiler.ankara.edu.tr/dergiler/42/442/4950.pdf [Accessed 10 January 2016].

Güven, S., 1977. *Dışgöç ve İşçi Yatırım Ortakları.* Ankara: TODAİE Yayınları.

Hisli, N., 1985. *Yurda Dönen İşçi Çocuklarının Uyum Sorunları.* Izmir: Ege Üniversites Edebiyat Fakültesi Psikoloji Bölümü.

Kağıtçıbaşı, Ç., 1985. 'Immigrant Populations in Europe. Problem Viewed from Sending Country', in İ. Başgöz and N. Furniss, eds, *Turkish workers in Europe. An interdisciplinary study.* Bloomington: Indiana University Turkish Studies, 103–23.

Kirst-Ashman, K.K., and Hull, G.H., 1999. *Understanding generalist practice.* 2nd ed. Chicago: Nelson-Hall.

Köksal, S., 1986. *Refah Toplumunda "Getto" ve Türkler.* Istanbul: Teknografik Matbaacılık A. Ş.

Küçükkaraca, N., 1998. *Yurt Dışından Geri Dönüş Çalören Örneği.* Ankara: Sosyal Hizmet Uzmanları Derneği.

Moosa-Mitha, M., and Ross-Sheriff, F., 2010. 'Transnational Social Work and Lessons Learned From Transnational Feminism', *Journal of Women and Social Work* 25(2): 105–09.

Sayıl, I., 1977. *Hollanda'daki Türk İşçilerinin Psikiyatrik ve Sosyal Sorunları.* Ankara: SSK Yay.

Sırkecı, I., Cohen, J.H., and Yazgan, P., 2012. 'Turkish culture of migration. Flows between Turkey and Germany, socio-economic development and conflict', *Migration Letters* 9(1): 33–46. Available from: www.tplondon.com/journal/index.php/ml/article/viewFile/105/92 [Accessed 10 January 2016].

Statistisches Bundesamt, 2014. 'Bevölkerung mit Migrationshintergrund - Ergebnisse des Mikrozensus - Fachserie 1 Reihe 2.2 – 2014'. Available online at www.destatis.de/DE/Publikationen/Thematisch/Bevoelkerung/MigrationIntegration/Migrationshintergrund2010220147004.pdf?__blob=publicationFile [Accessed 10 January 2016].

Tezcan, M., 1987. *Yurt Dışından Dönen Gençlerin Uyum Sorunları.* Ankara: Engin Yayınevi.

Toksöz, G., 2006. *Uluslararası emek göçü.* İstanbul: İstanbul Bilgi Üniversitesi.

Tufan, B., 1987. *Türkiye'ye dönen ikinci kuşak işçi çocuklarının psiko-sosyal durumları.* Ankara: Sosyal Planlama Başkanlığı.

Tufan, B., and Yıldız, S., 1993. *Geri dönüş sürecinde ikinci kuşak. Almanya'dan dönen öğrencilerin benlik saygıları ve ruhsal belirtileri.* Ankara: Hacettepe Üniversitesi.

Yasa, İ., 1979. *Yurda dönen işçiler ve toplumsal değişme.* Ankara: TODAİE Yayınları.

Yenisey, L., 1976. 'Yurtdışına işçi göndermenin boğazlayan ilçesi üzerindeki sosyal etkileri. Boğazlıyan'ın iki köyünde gözlemler', in N. Abadan-Unat *et al.*, eds. *Göç ve gelişme. Uluslararası işgücü göçünün Boğazlıyan İlçesi üzerindeki etkilerine ilişkin bir araştırma:* Ajans-Türk Matbaacılık Sanayii, 351–96.

Yörükoğlu, A., 1985. *Gençlik çağı. Ruh sağlığı, eğitimi, ruhsal sorunları.* Ankara: Turkiye İş Bankası Kültür Yayınları.

# 35 Here and there

## Transnational lives of migrant workers and their families

## Comment on the Turkish case study from a German perspective

*Lena Inowlocki*

'Araf' refers to an in-between state of being, suspended by indecision, possibly holding potential for the future. Filiz Demiröz uses the metaphor to refer to the situation of Turkish economic migrants and their family members when they return to Turkey after many years in Germany. I would like to start with a closer look at the title by asking if it is the case that they are really 'neither there nor here'? They might, instead, actually be living 'there and here', as appears to be the situation in the case Filiz Demiröz describes. It could thus be more accurate to speak of transnationals rather than 'returnees', as I propose in the following.

In her article, Filiz Demiröz describes the constructive counselling process with her client, Fatma Yilmaz. After living in Germany for many years with her husband and three children, Fatma Yilmaz returned to Turkey, together with her son, his wife and child and her younger daughter who is of school age. Her husband and the older daughter remained in Germany. An incident of discrimination against her son had apparently initiated the move to Turkey. There, the son encountered difficulties when he attempted to make a living through self-employment. His wife, a native German, had problems with the Turkish language. The daughter was unhappy in her new school and considered returning to Germany. As it turned out during the series of counselling sessions, Fatma Yilmaz found it difficult to be living in both places but also did not want to give up her life in Germany. Filiz Demiröz addressed these problems with her client and also the divorce of her older daughter who had remained in Germany; she had been married to a distant relative whom she had not known well who then came to live with her in Germany.

As Filiz Demiröz notes, policies regulate the access of economic migrants and their family members to Germany, and affect many areas of their lives (Kofman 2004). One area concerns family reunion, with entry and residence permits for so-called 'imported' brides and husbands (Beck-Gernsheim 2011; Kreckel 2013). What is especially difficult and causes much strain on newly married couples is that after migrating, the spouse does not obtain a work permit for one year. This can make it very difficult to get used to a new place and instead can lead to social isolation, economic dependency, language learning difficulties and problems in partnership. We might assume that this may have been an aspect of why the daughter's husband did not want to stay in Germany and why the marriage failed.

Another important aspect the Yilmaz case highlights is the decision-making in moving to Turkey – many among the younger generation in Turkish migrant families who opt for this improve their job or self-employment opportunities because their educational and language capacities are appreciated in a globalised economy in general and in Turkey in particular. But for many who decide to return, this is also motivated by their experience of discrimination in Germany (MIGazin 2013; Spiegel Online 2014). Experiencing resentment and disrespect can thus be understood as a significant motive among the younger generation in Turkish migrant families to leave Germany and try to find a better life in Turkey.

It seems that Fatma Yilmaz chose to accompany her son's family to support them. Migration strategies are gendered and with regard to women connected to taking care of the family. In fact, this was also the case during the original move from Turkey to Germany – in some years of recruitment women constituted one-third to one-half of the workers who went as the first of their families, to send back financial support (for a biographical case analysis see Gültekin *et al.* 2006).

It is possible that living in Turkey represented something Fatma Yilmaz had been thinking about for a while and meant to try. In the process of settling in the new place, she then realised that she did not want to give up her life in Germany and would be looking instead for ways to combine living in both places: as her counsellor notes, Fatma Yilmaz 'missed her husband and the neighbours in Germany, she did not want to give up the living rights she had in Germany and she did not know how to live in two countries simultaneously' (see Demiröz, Chapter 34: 240).

Transnational space is created biographically, through lives lived in different nation states (Apitzsch and Siouti 2013; Apitzsch and Siouti 2014). Time spent in different locations establishes one's connections between them, also in terms of a 'mental space', or a biographical 'space of potentiality' (Inowlocki and Gerhard 2012). Most forms of migration no longer entail a complete break with the country of origin but rather consist of finding ways to combine family relations and care obligations, work and income, friendships and love relations, education, property, citizenship rights, etc., in both places. However, notions of 'neither there nor here' continue to reproduce a discourse of 'being uprooted' and consequently having identity problems. This is disproven by the experience of very many migrants who successfully develop transnational lives. But stereotype and prejudice against 'foreigners' and 'strangers' prevail in many nation states, as well as the claim that national belongings should be exclusive and cannot be multiple. Obtaining German citizenship is still difficult for Turkish citizens and holding two passports is nearly impossible. This does not do justice to the needs of individuals and families and their strategies for a good life.

The German school system is highly selective in terms of socioeconomic background and (non-Western) migrant status. Institutional discrimination against children from working-class families intersecting with migrant background as well as many instances of direct discrimination have been documented and discussed in regular governmental reports since 2006 (Jennessen *et al.* 2013). The older daughter encountered discrimination in the German school system when she came to join her parents as a small child. Being multilingual is discouraged in most pre-schools and schools, particularly in the case of non-Western languages such as Turkish (Gogolin 1994). So far Turkish is not taught in German schools (with few exceptions), thus children have reduced chances of acquiring fluency and literacy in Turkish except in their families or in private lessons. There are other discriminatory policies, for example, Turkish and German-speaking families can be denied an au pair from Turkey, whom they specifically want so their children would have more practice speaking Turkish (Inowlocki 2013).

The counselling sessions show that a process perspective is important in reconstructing the biographies of family members. Over a relatively short counselling period, the family members, supported by the social worker, orient themselves quite quickly, with the school difficulties the younger daughter initially experienced possibly becoming advantageous due to her experience of education in two educational systems (Siouti 2013).

I thus fully share Filiz Demiröz's conclusion, 'If people live in both societies simultaneously the services for them should be developed accordingly' (p. 242) and I would add that understanding transnational biographies is very important for social work. Similarly, as in biographical research, a reconstructive approach in social work needs to take into account one's own reflexivity as counsellor and researcher (Ruokonen-Engler *et al.* 2013).

## References

Apitzsch, U., and Siouti, I., 2013. 'Die Entstehung transnationaler Familienbiographien in Europa. Transnationales biographisches Wissen als zentrales Schlüsselkonzept zum Verständnis von transnationalen mehrgenerationalen Migrationsprozessen', in D. Bender *et al.*, eds, *Transnationales Wissen und Soziale Arbeit.* Weinheim: Beltz Juventa, 144–57.

Apitzsch, U., and Siouti, I., 2014. 'Transnational Biographies', *Zeitschrift für Qualitative Forschung (ZQF)* 15(1–2): 11–24.

Beck-Gernsheim, E., 2011. 'The marriage route to migration: Of border artistes, transnational matchmaking and imported spouses', *Nordic Journal of Migration Research* 1(2): 60–68.

Gogolin, I., 1994. *Der monolinguale Habitus der multilingualen Schule*. Münster, New York: Waxmann.

Gültekin, N., Lutz, H., and Inowlocki, L., 2006. 'Quest and query. Interpreting a biographical interview with a Turkish woman laborer in Germany', *Historical Social Research* 31(3): 50–71.

Inowlocki, L., 2013. 'Narrationsanalyse eines Interviews mit einem Ehepaar', in M. Bereswill and K. Liebsch, eds, *Geschlecht (re)konstruieren. Zur methodologischen und methodischen Produktivität der Frauen- und Geschlechterforschung*. Münster: Westfälisches Dampfboot, 98–114.

Inowlocki, L., and Gerhard, R., 2012. 'Exploring European "potential space". A study of the biographies of former foreign exchange students', in R. Miller, ed. *The evolution of European identities. Biographical approaches*. Basingstoke: Palgrave Macmillan, 129–49.

Jennessen, S., Kastirke, N., and Kotthaus, J., 2013. *Diskriminierung im vorschulischen und schulischen Bereich. Eine sozial- und erziehungswissenschaftliche Bestandsaufnahme* [online].

Antidiskriminierungsstelle des Bundes. Available from: www.antidiskriminierungsstelle.de/
SharedDocs/Downloads/DE/publikationen/Expertisen/Expertise_Diskriminierung_im_
vorschulischen_und_schulischen_Bereich.pdf;jsessionid=87DC223FB9534DD2DBA7D094
39880EDB.2_cid332?__blob=publicationFile&v=1 [Accessed 28 December 2015].

Kofman, E., 2004. 'Family-related migration. A critical review of European Studies',
*Journal of Ethnic and Migration Studies* 30(2): 243–62.

Kreckel, J., 2013. *Heiratsmigration. Geschlecht und Ethnizität.* Marburg: Tectum.

MIGazin, 2013. *Je gebildeter, desto häufiger von Diskriminierung betroffen* [online].
Available from: www.migazin.de/2013/10/23/tuerken-deutschland-je-diskriminierung/
[Accessed 10 January 2016].

Ruokonen-Engler, M., and Siouti, I., 2013. '"Doing biographical reflexivity" as a
methodological tool in transnational research settings', *Transnational Social Review* 3(2):
247–61.

Siouti, I., 2013. *Transnationale Biographien. Eine biographieanalytische Studie über
Transmigrationsprozesse bei der Nachfolgegeneration griechischer Arbeitsmigranten.*
Bielefeld: transcript.

Spiegel Online, 2014. *Drei Viertel der Türken in Deutschland fühlen sich hier zu Hause*
[online]. Available from: www.spiegel.de/politik/deutschland/tuerken-in-deutschland-
mehrheit-fuehlt-sich-hier-zu-hause-a-994191.html [Accessed 10 January 2016].

# 36 Comparative experiences of migrants in Asia

## Comment on the Turkish case study from a Malayan perspective

*Rashila Ramli*

As a 17-year-old girl, I was sent off by my family on a flight to the USA to pursue my Bachelor's Degree. Little did I realise that it was going to be a 14-year stay in a foreign land before I was to return home to continue my vocation, teaching at the National University of Malaysia. I am one of the thousands of students sent abroad by the Malaysian government in the early 1980s (Abd Aziz and Abdullah 2014: 102). The migration was devised because there were not enough universities in Malaysia at that time to accommodate the number of students (Ismail *et al.* 2014: 6). Moreover, the exposure abroad was seen as a positive experience where young impressionable Malaysians were to be infused with values and new perspectives.

Returning home 14 years later proved to be challenging since one has to adjust to one's own family, rediscover local cultures and find a job. Since there were no re-entry programmes for overseas returning students, one had to adapt to one's own culture as best as one could. While in the USA we were encouraged to speak our minds, returning home meant one had to think twice before speaking, because thinking out loud was not regarded as highly appropriate for women. Dressing was another issue – the t-shirt and jeans were replaced by *bajukurung* and shawls. More formal attire was necessary at the workplace or in public spaces. At the workplace, in this case the university, I had to rediscover and sometimes learn the academic vocabulary to teach Research Methodology in the Malay language. My American twang had to be restrained to conversation among friends who were few at that time.

Migration processes are complex. Leaving a country and living in a different environment influences the people who migrate but also the sending as well as receiving country (Ismail *et al.* 2014: 10). This could lead to a brain drain (Abd Aziz and Abdullah 2014: 117) and might result in the need to look at how to reverse it. One step in this direction is the formulation of returning experts' programmes and talent acceleration in public services (NEAC 2010). Another is substantial growth in public and private higher education (Abd Aziz and Abdullah 2014: 103). The experience of living abroad could encourage returnees to leave again and might produce a deeper culture of migration (Koh 2015).

Although from a different experience, the above example depicts several issues discussed by Filiz Demiröz in her chapter 'Returnees: Neither there nor here, at Araf'. The case of the Yilmaz family, whose readjustment into the Turkish culture after living in Germany for 56 years was assisted by social workers through the provision of cross-boundary services. Despite the hardship of resettling in Turkey, Fatma Yilmaz and her family managed to come to terms with their new living environment. They were lucky because they were able to tackle their personal problems and found possible solutions to overcome the problems.

Within Asia, migration has been prevalent throughout the centuries. The sea passage from the Indian Ocean, passing through the Straits of Melaka into the South China Sea brought traders, merchants, job seekers and colonisers. This early migration saw the growth of multicultural societies and spread of religions, especially Hinduism, Islam and Christianity, and the legacy of Occidental colonisers.

The lasting impact of this early migration and the divide and rule policy of the British left a strong ethnic cleavage in Malaya. Specifically, the Malays continued their traditional role as padi planters and fishermen while some managed to secure employment with the Malay Civil Service. The Chinese came to control the economy of the country while the Indians tended to trees in rubber plantations. Most migrants did not return to their countries of origin and therefore reshaped Malaysian society. Multiculturalism is one of the basic principles feeding into identity constructions like Malaysian Indians (Jain 2011) or Malaysian Chinese (Wang 2011). However, at the end of the twentieth century, migrants constituted domestic workers, construction and plantation workers as well as skilled workers in technology-based industries. Malaysia as a host country has to cope with the presence of over 2 million migrants, especially from Indonesia, the Philippines and more recently from Bangladesh, Nepal and Vietnam (Kassim and Zin 2011).

On the other hand, in July 2015, the Southeast Asia region, especially Thailand and Malaysia, were faced with an influx of migrants from Myanmar and Bangladesh. The informal economy accommodates refugees, whilst they are grouped under the blanket category of 'irregular' migrants. While the UNHCR (United Nations High Commissioner for Refugees) runs a resettlement programme in Kuala Lumpur, the over 100,000 refugees from Myanmar (with an estimated 45,000-plus Rohingya) remain vulnerable to arrest and harassment while spending years awaiting resettlement decisions (UNHCR 2015).

The remittances transferred by migrants back to their home countries are considered as important revenue for countries such as the Philippines and Indonesia. If one were to drive by a village in Indonesia, and one were to see a number of well-built brick houses, chances are those houses were constructed using the hard-earned salaries of migrants working in Malaysia or Saudi Arabia. Salaries are also used to finance the education of children and household maintenance. The higher purchasing power in the home country justifies the choice of some migrant workers to leave their families and countries in order to earn more compared to working in their own country.

While some people are forced to migrate, there are others who migrate by choice. In studies done by Djajic (1987) and Dustmann (2000), migration behaviour can be explained by consumption and labour supply (or lack of it) in the host countries, migration duration or a life cycle model. According to Djajic (1987), if there is a higher purchasing power in the home country of assets accumulated in the host country, then there will be a higher number of returnees to the host countries. Another reason for migrants to return home centres on the development of human capital. If there is a higher return in home economy on human capital acquired in the host country, then one will also see returnees. The duration of a stay will vary based on the needs, availability of jobs and the management of migrants through policies in the host countries.

In addition to the above-mentioned are cultural factors influencing the decision to return. In Malaysia, the family plays an important role in the feeling of belonging, which results in close transnational connections (Koh 2015). Decisions for or against migration are therefore often not taken by just one family member but by the family as a whole.

In the case of the Yilmaz family, they returned to Turkey after staying in Germany for 56 years. While there has been human capital development within the family, the work situation in Turkey was not so accommodating for Fatma's son, Ahmet. The family had to adjust their lifestyle. It was also a learning process for the social worker. When members of the family are unable to adjust, the option is to return to the host country. In other cases, returnees such as students who went abroad to study gained tremendously as their qualifications are recognised as necessary for the development of the home country. Many returnees hold high positions in their home country. On the other side, however, there are migrants who are forcefully returned to their country of origin.

Migration is a living process where humans are the units of analysis. Since migration is an ongoing process that will not diminish, there have to be better policies to cater for the needs of emigrants and immigrants. For returnees, both host and home countries must have support structures such as a social services centre with properly trained social workers to provide strategies and solutions for families in trouble due to displacement and adjustment in a 'foreign' local environment. For countries such as Malaysia and Thailand where irregular migrants are present in large numbers, sound management practice is necessary in order to ensure that migrants or refugees are treated with dignity. The training of social workers must include new techniques to cater for different categories of migrants. Finally, as migration is a complex phenomenon, one has to be constantly aware of the relations between state agencies, recruitment agencies, employers and workers. Management of migration can only be enhanced when there is a strong political will to ensure that the rights of workers /migrants are protected by both home and host countries.

## References

Abd Aziz, M.I., and Abdullah, D., 2014. 'Malaysia: Becoming an education hub to serve national development', in J. Knight, ed., *International education hubs. Student, talent, knowledge-innovation models.* Dordrecht: Springer, 101–19.

Djajic, S., 1987. 'Illegal aliens, unemployment and immigration policy', *Journal of Development Economics* (25): 235–49.

Dustmann, C., 2000. *Why go back? Return motives of migrant workers* [online]. University College London (UCL). Available from: www.ucl.ac.uk/~uctpb21/pdf/Return.pdf [Accessed 20 January 2016].

Ismail, M., Kamaruddin, N.A.Y., Baki, N.U., and Rasdi, R.M., 2014. *Predictors of Career Aspiration of Malaysian Returnees from European and Non-European Countries* [online]. Available from: www.ufhrd.co.uk/wordpress/wp-content/uploads/2014/11/Maimunah-Ismail.pdf [Accessed 10 January 2016].

Jain, R.K., 2011. *Indian transmigrants. Malaysian and comparative essays*. Petaling Jaya, Selangor: Strategic Information and Research Development Centre.

Kassim, A., and Zin, R.H.M., 2011. *Policy on irregular migrants in Malaysia. An analysis of its implementation and effectiveness*. Manila: Philippine Institute for Development Studies (PIDS).

Koh, S.Y., 2015. 'Temporalities of citizenship. Malaysian-Chinese skilled migrants in Singapore and returnees to Malaysia', *Asian and Pacific Migration Journal* 24(1): 3–27.

NEAC, 2010. *New economic model for Malaysia – Part 1* [online]. National Economic Advisory Council. Available from: www.epu.gov.my/epu-theme/pdf/nem.pdf [Accessed 10 January 2016].

UNHCR, 2015. *UNHCR subregional operations profile - South Asia* [online]. United Nations High Commissioner for Refugees. Available from: www.unhcr.org/pages/49e4876d6.html [Accessed 12 December 2015].

Wang, G., 2011. 'Malaysian Chinese and regional developments', in Centre for Malaysian Chinese Studies, ed., *Malaysian Chinese. An inclusive society*. Kuala Lumpur, 1–16.

# Part IV

# Last thoughts – and yet another perspective!

*Ursula Kämmerer-Rütten, Alexandra Schleyer-Lindenmann, Beatrix Schwarzer and Yafang Wang*

Transnational social work offers us a lens to show the normative and often unmarked foundations of social work as a discipline and as a profession. Social work often acts as if it was only played out on a local or national level whilst ignoring international and global interdependencies. In this book we have shown that transnational social work is a topic which is multilayered.

We started the book by looking at professional and disciplinary concepts and developments from different national backgrounds with the aim to stimulate mutual interest and understanding. We appreciate discussion on the international level, e.g. the debates in international (social work) organisations, but also see the need for a fundamental questioning from the peripheries of the debate from indigenous social work and social movements.

We see this book as a contribution to enhancing the dialogue between academics, professionals and students concerning the positive and negative influence of the nation state on our everyday practice as social workers, students and lecturers. To enter this dialogue we must mark the unmarked. We must make the nation visible in our thinking and doing. We must know the limits but also the opportunities a nation state can offer social work as a profession. It is the existence of social security systems that offer opportunities for social work; it is the nationality binding the individual to one nation state that limits social work; it is a national culture that results in questions like assimilation, integration or cultural positioning in general. We need to know about differences and similarities in the framework which is so important for social work practice. Therefore, we need to enter a dialogue about cases, strategies and theoretical thinking by knowing about the national framework. The exchange of ideas and knowledge from our practical and academic experience is useful for the debate on possible restrictions and can visualise and uncover boundaries or even transcend them. Professional practices and strategies on the international level (from global to regional) can inform and influence the national and local levels and vice versa. This is what we hope to achieve with the case studies and comments provided in this book: using live stories, social work cases and global challenges to shed light on common issues from different national angles.

We do not claim that these questions and perspectives are new, nor are the issues such as refuge, migration, poverty, women's rights, and children's rights.

Providing a space for dialogue and exchange is also not new. Social movements always have and will continue to have an influence on social work by voicing criticism, seeking change and functioning as a watchdog for clients concerning political developments, legal changes and institutional support. Social movements have also provided local, national, regional as well as international platforms for exchange. In common with social work, social movements are concerned with topics such as equality and inclusion.

A layer we have not addressed throughout the book is the position of the social worker from a biographical point of view. What are the stages in the professional career of a social worker seeking to develop a transnational profile? We would like to think that both scientific knowledge and a critical attitude are important for the development of this profile. Therefore, we want to end the book with a social worker's point of view.

Abha Bhaiya is one example of many working for decades in the field of social work. She is an activist and often crosses national and cultural borders engaging in politics on local, national, regional and international levels. She was educated in social work in different parts of the world and experienced the opportunities as well as difficulties that exchanges with others and living in different environments brings. She also reflects on the limitation of social work education which is shaped by textbooks mainly based on Western knowledge. She has been confronted with the limits of a social work profession which claims not to get involved in political confrontation because of the fear of losing financial support. In her description – which may be seen as an example for transcultural and transnational engagement – she strongly argues for a positioning in issues such as women's and sexual rights, which are cross-border issues and need to be addressed around the world.

# 37  Crossing boundaries within and without …

## The journey of a feminist activist

*Abha Bhaiya*

> 'Sister friends and fellow travellers – we will make a difference if we are able to learn and appreciate history and memory and wisdom and yet have the courage to take our own risk in new contexts with new issues.'
>
> *(Wilson* et al. *2005: 6)*

## The personal

This article describes my personal journey[1] as an academic social worker and as a transnational as well as community-based feminist activist. As a woman I am a product of the feminist movement of the last 45 years. The starting point is the quiet struggle with my own confined world in a traditional middle-class Indian family. A significant turning point was my decision to leave the country after I completed my Master's degree in Philosophy. I arrived in Germany in 1969 with a small stipend provided by a priest to study a social work course in Dortmund. I was greatly influenced by this external environment and encountered the welfare approach of social work practice of the 1960s in Germany, where I worked with homeless communities, and the children of the 'Gastarbeiter'.[2] I returned to India and completed a Master's course in the school of social work, at the University of Delhi, India in 1973. However, once again, to my utter disappointment, I was educated through textbooks that were primarily American or British. This social work education defeated my purpose to return to India, study in a socio-culturally contextual environment and seek some real transformations.

As I began working as a social worker under an Indo-Dutch project in the slums, my academic education did not come to my rescue. As a social worker, I was faced with the most deprived, discriminated and excluded communities, a nomadic criminal tribe and 'Dalits' (as categorised by the British in their gazettes). A process of de-learning rather than using the social work approaches of case work, group work and community organisation, began here. There were subjective realities fuelled by the power politics of different interest groups with varied hierarchies of oppressions. The case work approach was irrelevant as an individual does not exist in isolation of economic and social formations and of the external powerful political forces supported by various institutions of the state and non-state actors. The community organisation had to be replaced by community mobilisation strategies and multi-layered dialogues within the divided communities inside a slum. When violence broke out in the community, I finally decided to choose to act on behalf of the most powerless women and men. I was reprimanded by the NGO for taking sides and was gently asked to resign. That in such situations a social worker needs to remain 'objective' and 'neutral', was glaringly obvious, and yet it did not convince me, as I was too close to the conflictual reality.

In 1981, as a response to rising dowry murders and the earlier cases of custodial rapes of a dalit and a tribal minor girl, the crisis centre SAHELI (meaning a female friend) was set up in Delhi (Saheli). In 1984, seven of us set up a feminist documentation, communication and training centre, JAGORI (meaning wake up women), to work in the rural belt of North India (Jagori). In these centres and platforms in many parts of the country, there was a very vibrant search for theory and practice in alternative ways of using and applying power, new, non-hierarchical organisational forms, and thus, new ways of leading. As mentioned by Srilatha Batliwala (2010), feminists of that time engaged in experiments with alternative structures and processes, and with deep analyses of the gendered nature of power in the social, economic, and political realm.

What I am trying to show here is my fundamental belief that academic social work education and practice needs to interact with peoples' movements in order to take forward the transformative potential of social work and to become an inclusive perspective and practice.

## The political

A transnational feminist network began crystallising in the 1980s and continued to engage with global politics and the way the women's question has been (or not been) addressed by nation states and international institutions (Moghadam 2005).

### Crossing barbed wires

I want, therefore, to lay out three areas of transnational networks that I have been part of for the last 30 years, and which have created a comprehensive learning and enriching personal and political territory for me. First I will look at the transnational networks that aim to create the quintessential security without which a conflict-ridden region such as Asia (India, Pakistan, Afghanistan, Bangladesh, Sri Lanka), cannot guarantee any rights to its own population. Second, I will look into the linkages between international and local campaigns to end violence against women (see also the case study on Jyoti, Chapter 25 of this volume). And third, I will use the examples of sexual minorities, and sexual rights, as examples to create a space of (global) solidarity which is so important for discriminated persons and groups.

### Peace and security

It has been a long and difficult struggle within South Asia, especially between Pakistan and India, to demand peace and cooperation. Regional peace is an essential prerequisite for bringing peace to an individual country, and that always means to its women and children. Therefore many women's movement activities in South Asia have always been transregional by nature and necessity.

In 1983 we[3] founded SANGAT (Sangat): the South Asian Network of Activists and Trainers. Our objectives were outlined in the South Asian Feminist Declaration:

> We come from different countries in South Asia – Bangladesh, India, Nepal, Pakistan, and Sri Lanka, Maldives, Bhutan and Afghanistan and share a common regional identity. Though divided by geopolitical boundaries, the peoples of the South Asian region are bound together by shared histories and cultures, and by our collective experiences of patriarchies, globalization and militarization in the 21st century. As feminists and as activists for equality for women, we are inextricably linked through our struggles and involvement in women's movements and social movements in our countries. These links strengthen us individually and create a continued transnational network of regional solidarity.
>
> (Sangat 2006: 1)

So far, nearly 800 young activists – scholars, young women from different South Asian countries – have participated in the month-long residential training course, which is still conducted every year. In 2015 it was the twentieth such annual event. The course has even expanded to other countries and continents with women coming from Sudan, Iran, and Turkey. SANGAT has also organised a number of conferences and seminars and has been instrumental in taking the 'One Billion Rising' campaign to all nine countries of South Asia and beyond.

In 2011 we founded another Women's Regional Network for Afghanistan, Pakistan, and India (Women's Regional Network). It aims to connect communities of women leaders to learn from each other and construct common agendas across borders on the linkages between security and extremisms, corruption and militarisation. We conducted regional research and documentation (Women's Regional Network 2013) which focused on women's commentary, perception and experience of displacement, security, military and police access and corruption. We strongly believe that women's voices need to be heard. The documentation has helped in revealing that in almost all the sites of conflict, women are always on the frontline and have displayed amazing staying power, while in a number of sites, the recognised leadership continues to be in the hands of men.

### *Violence against women as a global concern*

Violence against women is another common site of struggle that emerges within transnational and national feminist struggles. In my life I can trace how I always worked on all levels – local, national and international – to fight violence against women. Violence is faced by every Indian woman.

In 1993, when I attended the Vienna conference and tribunal (Bunch and Reilly 1994), it became a focus of my transnational activism. The women's tribunal included stories of comfort women from Korea, dowry burning from Pakistan, rape of daughters by their fathers in the USA, mutilation of lesbian women in one of the South American countries, rape of sex workers and many more. This entire year of preparation and also the conference participation gave me new insights into the power of feminist movements; I met well-known feminists, pioneering women from the world over, and also witnessed the working of the UN system from close quarters. The other significant transnational action that took place in Vienna demanded that women's rights be included in the official agenda of the UN conference.

In 2013 we brought campaigning to yet another level when we started the 'One Billion Rising Campaign' (One Billion Rising 2016) that has its impetus in a UN statement that in the world one billion girls and women are subject to violence. To this day, people from 176 countries have joined this struggle. As an outcome of the mobilisation, a number of training workshops have also been organised to train lawyers, judges and protection officers as well as police personnel on the gendered nature of violence, building a more complex awareness of violence against women and its negative impacts on the economy and politics of nations.

As early as the 1990s we started the 'Nari Adalats', the 'women's courts', a community-based informal initiative to provide justice for women and men living with domestic conflict, and often in violent situations in the home. The model has been amazingly successful on the local level and has provided relief for a large number of women. Within Jagori Rural, the organisation I founded in 2003 and still work with as a senior advisor and director, there are now seven Nari adalats with nearly 25 so-called 'barefoot lawyers', who sit with women, share their pain and experiences of violence and reflect on their situation to seek a solution. With the passage of time, men have also begun to approach the courts as the community is convinced that women's courts are a place for justice where there is no bias against men.

Similarly, based on experiences of attending some of the national and international tribunals, a number of public hearings were organised as advocacy. These hearings were attended by institutional enforcement representatives. The hearings have not only worked as exposing the inefficiency of the law enforcement machinery but have helped in expediting court procedures and also made the police and others more aware of the kinds of violence faced by women. Their sharing of the tales of harassment, the alienating court systems and often delayed or no conviction, is candidly shared at times with a mix of tears and anger, thus moving the audience, especially the state representatives, to act more responsibly. This is not to say that the system has become women friendly, but shows how the employment of multiple strategies creates an environment that can progress towards seeking justice for women and other marginalised groups, as a fundamental right of all citizens.

### *Sex, sexuality and sexual rights*

My early experience with transregional and transnational advocacy made me engage with another important global clause: the sexual rights of women and minority rights.

The International Association for the Study of Sexuality, Culture and Society (IASSCS), of which I became a member in 2003, was founded in 1997 in Amsterdam, with the commitment to build equity in research capacity worldwide and to develop a broad range of multidisciplinary research activities in the social and cultural study of sexuality. IASSCS has, since its inception, held ten international conferences attended by a large number of researchers, activists and academics. In addition, the network has held a number of courses on research training, provided research support, brought out regular publications and has advanced policy and advocacy work. I have been the coordinator of the advocacy committee for the last four years, which has added to my understanding of specific country situations and emerging debates in particular regions. It has deepened my understanding of the issues surrounding sexual rights, multiple sexual identities and sexual expression. The feminist qualitative research and participatory learner-centred training methodology has resulted in two significant publications; the *Manual on Sexual Rights and Sexual Empowerment* (Bhaiya and Wierenga 2007) and *Heteronormativity, Passionate Aesthetics and Symbolic Subversion in Asia* (Wieringa *et al.* 2015), which examines life trajectories among three categories of women living beyond the bounds of heteronormativity in Jakarta and Delhi: women who have lost their husbands; sex workers; and young, urban lesbians.

The research and training has strengthened activities within our programme in Jagori Rural. Sexuality and sexual rights is an integral module within the month-long SANGAT course. It has been an amazing experience to see how a majority of participants have such inadequate knowledge around issues of sexuality and their own body. Based on these experiences and learning, over the last seven years we have initiated sessions in various schools and within the 60 village collectives for adolescent girls – sessions on what we call 'body literacy', primarily to get acceptance of the school authorities to talk about body knowledge, desires, attractions – as sex education is still not allowed in the schools. It has been our experience that a majority of cases of violence are also related to sex as one of the core issues that creates discord and a sense of lack of fulfilment, especially for women. Our work experience has made the team confident of talking about these issues in an open and non-judgmental environment.

## Concluding observations

In July 2001, both the IASSW and the IFSW reached agreement on adopting the following international definition of social work:

> It needs to be reiterated that there is a strong relationship between the social work practice and various movements working for social transformation. The social work profession has the main objective of promoting social change, problem solving in human relationships and the empowerment and liberation of people to enhance well-being ... Principles of human rights and social justice are fundamental to social work.
>
> (IFSW 2012)

However, the fact that social work is operationalised differently both within nation states and regional boundaries, and across the world, with its control and status quo maintaining functions being dominant in some contexts, cannot be disputed.

My own relationship to the words 'social work' and for many in the feminist movements in the countries of the south has been rather contentious. First, a majority of the social work schools have had as their major focus welfare programmes, not to deny that there is a gradual shift towards a more developmental approach. The approach of the various movements has been to challenge the status quo as well as confront the anti-people policies of states. Movement-oriented activism has grown weary of the term as it carries a history of seeing the individual as a problem and then fixing the individual to the societal norms. Feminist and other people's movements have been more focused on transformatory *politics*. In the initial phase all of us were more in the streets rather than in classrooms and offices. It is my experience that during the studies whenever we challenged our faculty on an issue of concern such as the reasons why a boy ends up in a juvenile/correctional home or why women are not given choice and space to make decisions about their lives, the answers were never satisfying. A majority of male students opted for industrial social worker as their selective subject and thus became managers for management systems rather than fighting for the rights of the workers.

While my education has provided me with a degree in social work, my Master's in philosophy and reading of radical literature reinforced my rebellious position and radical thoughts and practices. To be an activist working for political action is for me more than being in a comfort zone.

## Notes

1 This journey would not have been possible without the editing support of Prof Dagmar Oberlies.
2 Migrant Workers.
3 Throughout the text, the term 'we' refers to different groups of activists.

## References

Batliwala, S., 2010. *Feminist leadership for social transformation. Clearing the conceptual cloud* [online]. Creating Resources for Empowerment in Action (CREA). Available from: www.justassociates.org/sites/justassociates.org/files/feminist-leadership-clearing-conceptual-cloud-srilatha-batliwala.pdf [Accessed 10 January 2016].

Bhaiya, A., and Wierenga, S., 2007. *Manual on Sexual Rights and Sexual Empowerment* [online]. Available from: http://iiav.nl/epublications/2007/manual_on_sexual_rights_and_sexual_empowerment.pdf [Accessed 10 January 2016].

Bunch, C., and Reilly, N., 1994. *Demanding accountability. The Global Campaign and Vienna Tribunal for Women's Human Rights.* New Brunswick, NJ, New York: Center for Women's Global Leadership, Rutgers University; United Nations Development Fund for Women.

IASSCS [online]. International Association for the Study of Sexuality, Culture and Society. Available from: www.iasscs.org [Accessed 10 January 2016].

IFSW, 2012. *Statement of Ethical Principles* [online]. International Federation of Social Workers. Available from: http://ifsw.org/policies/statement-of-ethical-principles/ [Accessed 10 January 2016].

Jagori [online]. Available from: www.jagori.org/ [Accessed 10 January 2016].

Moghadam, V.M., 2005. *Globalizing women. Transnational feminist networks*. Baltimore: Johns Hopkins University Press.

One Billion Rising, 2016. *The Revolution Escalates! Rise for Revolution: Sign up to Disrupt!* [online]. Available from: www.onebillionrising.org [Accessed 10 January 2016].

Saheli [online]. Women's Resource Centre. Available from: https://sites.google.com/site/saheliorgsite/ [Accessed 10 January 2016].

Sangat [online]. Available from: www.sangatnetwork.org/ [Accessed 10 January 2016].

Sangat, 2006. *South Asian Feminist Declaration* [online]. Available from: www.sangatnetwork.org/sites/default/files/SAFM%20Declaration%202007.pdf [Accessed 10 January 2016].

Wieringa, S., Bhaiya, A., and Katjasungkana, N., 2015. *Heteronormativity, passionate aesthetics and symbolic subversion in Asia*. Brighton, Chicago, Toronto: Sussex Academic Press.

Wilson, S., Sengupta, A., and Evans, K., 2005. *Defending our dreams. Global feminist voices for a new generation*. London, New York, Toronto, Ont., New York: Zed Books; in association with the Association for Women's Rights in Development; Distributed in the USA exclusively by Palgrave Macmillan.

Women's Regional Network [online]. Available from: www.womensregionalnetwork.org/ [Accessed 10 January 2016].

Women's Regional Network, 2013. *The Women's Regional Network Community Conversations* [online]. Available from: www.womensregionalnetwork.org/images/uploads/Overview Nov2013.pdf [Accessed 10 January 2016].

# Index